CONTENTS

INTRODUCTION

Cook your favorite dishes in Cuisinart air fryer toaster oven. The oven compartment uses convection technology to deliver even heat to bake, broil and toast, and the integrated air fryer prepares classic fried foods without the need for oil.

What is an air fryer oven?

So what is an air frying oven? Air frying is a method of cooking that circulates hot air inside your oven at a high speed through the use of convection fans. This cooks food faster and creates a crispy, fried layer and even-browning on all sides using little to no oil compared to traditional deep frying.

Which is better air fryer or air fryer oven?

An air frying oven has more capacity, saving you time and allowing you to cook more food at once so that there's always enough for the whole family. Cuisinart Air Fryer Oven Cookbook 2021: 800 Quick, Vibrant and Oil-Free Recipes to Enjoy Your Favorite Crispy Meals. All the recipes are carefully selected from thousands of recipes. Different from regular air fryer, Cuisinart smart oven is a more versatile kitchen appliance and can feed an entire family because of its large capability. The book is aimed at offering fresh ideas to inspire you to cook high quality dishes and make you enjoy the fun of cooking.

APPETIZERS AND SIDE DISHES

1. Cheesy Broccoli Bites

Servings: 5   Cooking Time: 12 Minutes

Ingredients:

1 cup broccoli florets
¾ cup cheddar cheese, grated
2 tablespoons Parmesan cheese, grated
1 egg, beaten
¾ cup panko breadcrumbs
Salt and freshly ground black pepper, as needed

Directions:
In a food processor, add the broccoli and pulse until finely crumbled.   In a large bowl, mix together the broccoli, and remaining ingredients.   Make small equal-sized balls from the mixture.   Press "Power Button" of Air Fry Oven and turn the dial to select the "Air Fry" mode.   Press the Time button and again turn the dial to set the cooking time to 12 minutes.   Now push the Temp button and rotate the dial to set the temperature at 350 degrees F. Press "Start/Pause" button to start.   When the unit beeps to show that it is preheated, open the lid. Arrange the broccoli balls in "Air Fry Basket" and insert in the oven.   Serve warm.

Nutrition Info: Calories 153 Total Fat 8.2 g Saturated Fat 4.5g Cholesterol 52 mg Sodium 172 mg Total Carbs 4 g Fiber 0.5 g Sugar 0.5 g Protein 7.1 g

2. Rosemary Roasted Potatoes

Servings: 4   Cooking Time: 20 Minutes

Ingredients:

2 tablespoons olive oil
2 tablespoons minced fresh rosemary
1 tablespoon minced garlic
1 teaspoon salt, plus additional as needed
1½ pounds (680 g) small red potatoes, cut into 1-inch cubes
½ teaspoon freshly ground black pepper, plus additional as needed

Directions:
Toss the potato cubes with the olive oil, rosemary, garlic, salt, and pepper in a large bowl until thoroughly coated.   Arrange the potato cubes in the air fryer basket in a single layer.   Put the air fryer basket on the baking pan and slide into Rack Position 2, select Roast, set temperature to 400°F (205°C), and set time to 20 minutes.   Stir the potatoes a few times during cooking for even cooking.   When cooking is complete, the potatoes should be tender. Remove from the oven to a plate. Taste and add additional salt and pepper as needed.

3. Herbed Polenta

Servings: 6   Cooking Time: 6 Minutes

Ingredients:

2 tablespoons extra virgin olive oil
2 teaspoons garlic, minced
4 cups vegetable
Salt, to taste
1 bay leaf
2 tablespoons fresh parsley, diced
2 teaspoons fresh
stock
½ cup yellow onion, peeled and chopped
1 cup polenta
⅓ cup sundried tomatoes, chopped
oregano, diced
3 tablespoons fresh basil, diced
1 teaspoon fresh rosemary, diced

Directions:
Put the Instant Pot in the sauté mode, add the oil and heat. Add the onion, mix and cook for 1 minute. Add the garlic, mix again and cook for 1 minute. Add the broth, salt, tomato, bay leaf, rosemary, oregano, half the basil, half the parsley and polenta. Without stirring, cover the Instant Pot and cook for 5 minutes and release the pressure naturally for 10 minutes.   Uncover the instant pot, discard the bay leaf, gently mix the polenta, add the rest of the parsley, basil and other salts, mix, divide between the dishes and serve.

Nutrition Info: Calories: 150, Fat: 1.6, Fiber: 3.6, Carbohydrate: 35, Proteins: 3.7

4. Tasty Butternut Squash

Servings: 4   Cooking Time: 15 Minutes

Ingredients:

4 cups butternut squash, cut into 1-inch pieces
1 tbsp brown sugar
2 tbsp olive oil
1 tsp Chinese 5 spice powder

Directions:
Fit the Cuisinart oven with the rack in position 2. Toss squash into the bowl with remaining ingredients.   Transfer squash in the air fryer basket then places the air fryer basket in the baking pan.   Place a baking pan on the oven rack. Set to air fry at 400 F for 15 minutes.   Serve and enjoy.

Nutrition Info: Calories 132 Fat 7.1 g Carbohydrates 18.6 g Sugar 5.3 g Protein 1.4 g Cholesterol 0 mg

5. French Beans With Shallots & Almonds

Servings: 4   Cooking Time: 25 Minutes

Ingredients:

1 ½ pounds French beans
2 shallots, chopped
2 tbsp olive oil
½ cup almonds, toasted

Directions:
Preheat Cuisinart on AirFry function to 400 F. Blanch the beans in boiling water for 5-6 minutes. Drain and mix with oil and shallots in a baking sheet. Cook for 10 minutes. Serve with almonds.

6. Parmesan Cabbage Wedges

Servings: 4   Cooking Time: 30 Minutes

Ingredients:

½ head cabbage, cut into wedges
2 cup Parmesan cheese, grated
4 tbsp butter, melted
Salt and black pepper to taste
1 tsp smoked paprika

Directions:

Preheat Cuisinart on AirFry function to 330 F. Line a baking sheet with parchment paper. Brush the cabbage wedges with butter and season with salt and pepper. Coat the cabbage with the Parmesan cheese and arrange on the baking sheet; sprinkle with paprika. Press Start and cook for 15 minutes. Flip the wedges over and cook for an additional 10 minutes. Serve with yogurt dip.

7. Lemon Garlic Brussels Sprouts

Servings: 2   Cooking Time: 12 Minutes

Ingredients:

1/2 lb Brussels sprouts, rinse and pat dry with a paper towel	1 tbsp lemon juice
	1/4 tsp black pepper
	1 tbsp olive oil
	1/2 tsp salt
1/2 tsp garlic powder	

Directions:
Fit the Cuisinart oven with the rack in position 2. Cut the stem of Brussels sprouts and cut each Brussels sprouts in half. Transfer Brussels sprouts in a bowl and toss with garlic powder, olive oil, pepper, and salt. Transfer Brussels sprouts in air fryer basket then place air fryer basket in baking pan. Place baking pan on the oven rack. Set to air fry at 360 F for 12 minutes. Drizzle with lemon juice and serve.
Nutrition Info: Calories 114 Fat 7.5 g Carbohydrates 11.2 g Sugar 2.8 g Protein 4.1 g Cholesterol 0 mg

8. Cheesy Crisps

Servings: 3   Cooking Time: 25 Minutes

Ingredients:

4 tbsp grated cheddar cheese + extra for rolling	1/4 tsp chili powder
	1/2 tsp baking powder
1 cup flour + extra for kneading	3 tsp butter
	A pinch of salt

Directions:
In a bowl, add the cheddar cheese, flour, baking powder, chili powder, butter, and salt and mix until the mixture becomes crusty. Add some drops of water and mix well to get a dough. Remove the dough on a flat surface. Rub some extra flour in your palms and on the surface and knead the dough for a while. Using a rolling pin, roll the dough out into a thin sheet. With a pastry cutter, cut the dough into your desired lings' shape. Add the cheese lings to the greased baking tray and cook for 8 minutes at 350 F on Air Fry function, flipping once halfway through. Serve.

9. Spicy Pumpkin-ham Fritters

Servings: 4   Cooking Time: 10 Minutes

Ingredients:

1 oz ham, chopped	1 egg
1 cup dry pancake mix	1/2 tsp chili powder
2 tbsp canned puree pumpkin	3 tbsp of flour
	1 oz beer
1 oz cheddar, shredded	2 tbsp scallions, chopped

Directions:

Preheat Cuisinart on Air Fry function to 370 F. In a bowl, combine the pancake mix and chili powder. Mix in the egg, puree pumpkin, beer, shredded cheddar, ham and scallions. Form balls and roll them in the flour. Arrange the balls into the basket and fit in the baking tray. Cook for 8 minutes. Drain on paper towel before serving.

10. Air Fry Broccoli Florets

Servings: 2   Cooking Time: 10 Minutes

Ingredients:

1 lb broccoli florets	2 tbsp plain yogurt
1/2 tsp chili powder	1 tbsp chickpea flour
1/4 tsp turmeric	1/2 tsp salt

Directions:
Fit the Cuisinart oven with the rack in position 2. Add all ingredients to the bowl and toss well. Place marinated broccoli in a refrigerator for 15 minutes. Place marinated broccoli in an air fryer basket then places an air fryer basket in a baking pan. Place a baking pan on the oven rack. Set to air fry at 390 F for 10 minutes. Serve and enjoy.
Nutrition Info: Calories 114 Fat 1.5 g Carbohydrates 20.5 g Sugar 5.7 g Protein 8.5 g Cholesterol 1 mg

11. Tasty Hassel Back Potatoes

Servings: 4   Cooking Time: 30 Minutes

Ingredients:

4 potatoes, peel & cut potato across the potato to make 1/8-inch slices	1/4 cup parmesan cheese, shredded
	1 tbsp olive oil

Directions:
Fit the Cuisinart oven with the rack in position 2. Brush potatoes with olive oil. Place potatoes in the air fryer basket then place an air fryer basket in the baking pan. Place a baking pan on the oven rack. Set to air fry at 350 F for 30 minutes. Sprinkle cheese on top of potatoes and serve.
Nutrition Info: Calories 195 Fat 4.9 g Carbohydrates 33.7 g Sugar 2.5 g Protein 5.4 g Cholesterol 4 mg

12. Cheddar & Prosciutto Strips

Servings: 6   Cooking Time: 50 Minutes

Ingredients:

1 lb cheddar cheese	2 eggs, beaten
12 prosciutto slices	4 tbsp olive oil
1 cup flour	1 cup breadcrumbs

Directions:
Cut the cheese into 6 equal pieces. Wrap each piece with 2 prosciutto slices. Place them in the freezer just enough to set, about 5 minutes; note that they mustn't be frozen. Preheat Cuisinart on AirFry function to 390 F. Dip the Strips into flour first, then in eggs, and coat with breadcrumbs. Place in the frying basket and drizzle with olive oil. Press Start and cook for 10 minutes or until golden brown. Serve with tomato dip.

13. Party Pull Apart

Servings: 10   Cooking Time: 20 Minutes

Ingredients:

5 cloves garlic
1/3 cup fresh parsley
2 tbsp. olive oil
4 oz. mozzarella
cheese, sliced
3 tbsp. butter
1/8 tsp salt
1 loaf sour dough
bread

Directions:
Place the rack in position 1 of the oven.   In a food processor, add garlic, parsley, and oil and pulse until garlic is chopped fine.   Stack the mozzarella cheese and cut into 1-inch squares.   Heat the butter in a small saucepan over medium heat. Add the garlic mixture and salt and cook 2 minutes, stirring occasionally. Remove from heat.   Use a sharp, serrated knife to make 1-inch diagonal cuts across the bread being careful not to cut all the way through.   With a spoon, drizzle garlic butter into the cuts in the bread. Stack 3-4 cheese squares and place in each of the cuts.   Place the bread on a sheet of foil and fold up the sides. Cut a second piece of foil just big enough to cover the top.   Set oven to convection bake on 350°F for 25 minutes. After 5 minutes, place the bread in the oven and bake 10 minutes.   Remove the top piece of foil and bake 10 minutes more until the cheese has completely melted. Serve immediately.
Nutrition Info: Calories 173, Total Fat 7g, Saturated Fat 3g, Total Carbs 18g, Net Carbs 17g, Protein 7g, Sugar 2g, Fiber 1g, Sodium 337mg, Potassium 68mg, Phosphorus 112mg

14. Salty Baked Almonds

Servings: 4   Cooking Time: 25 Minutes
Ingredients:
1 cup raw almonds
1 egg white, beaten
½ teaspoon coarse sea salt

Directions:
Spread the almonds in the baking pan in an even layer.   Slide the baking pan into Rack Position 1, select Convection Bake, set temperature to 350°F (180°C) and set time to 20 minutes.   When cooking is complete, the almonds should be lightly browned and fragrant. Remove from the oven. Coat the almonds with the egg white and sprinkle with the salt. Return the pan to the oven.   Slide the baking pan into Rack Position 1, select Convection Bake, set temperature to 350°F (180°C) and set time to 5 minutes.   When cooking is complete, the almonds should be dried. Cool completely before serving.

15. Savory Chicken Nuggets With Parmesan Cheese

Servings: 4   Cooking Time: 25 Minutes
Ingredients:
1 lb chicken breasts, cubed
Salt and black pepper to taste
5 tbsp plain breadcrumbs
2 tbsp olive oil
2 tbsp panko breadcrumbs
2 tbsp grated Parmesan cheese

Directions:
Preheat Cuisinart on Air Fry function to 380 F. Season the chicken with salt and pepper; set aside. In a bowl, mix the breadcrumbs with the Parmesan cheese.   Brush the chicken pieces with the olive oil, then dip into breadcrumb mixture, and transfer to the Air Fryer basket. Fit in the baking tray and lightly spray chicken with cooking spray. Cook for 10 minutes, flipping once halfway through until golden brown on the outside and no more pink on the inside. Serve warm.

16. Baked Paprika Sweet Potatoes

Servings: 4   Cooking Time: 20 Minutes
Ingredients:
3 sweet potatoes, peel and cut into 1/2-inch pieces
2 tbsp olive oil
1/2 tsp pepper
2 tsp smoked paprika
1 tsp garlic salt

Directions:
Fit the Cuisinart oven with the rack in position Add sweet potatoes, paprika, oil, pepper, and salt into the mixing bowl and toss well.   Spread sweet potatoes in baking pan.   Set to bake at 425 F for 25 minutes. After 5 minutes place the baking pan in the preheated oven.   Serve and enjoy.
Nutrition Info: Calories 155 Fat 7.3 g Carbohydrates 22.2 g Sugar 0.7 g Protein 1.5 g Cholesterol 0 mg

17. Eggplant Cakes With Yogurt

Servings: 4   Cooking Time: 20 Minutes
Ingredients:
1 ½ cups flour
1 tsp cinnamon
3 eggs
2 tsp baking powder
2 tbsp sugar
1 cup milk
2 tbsp butter, melted
1 tbsp yogurt
1 eggplant, chopped
Pinch of salt
2 tbsp cream cheese

Directions:
Preheat Cuisinart on AirFry function to 350 F. In a bowl, whisk the eggs along with the sugar, salt, cinnamon, cream cheese, flour, and baking powder. In another bowl, combine all of the liquid ingredients. Gently combine the dry and liquid mixtures; stir in eggplant.   Line muffin tins and pour the batter in. Press Start and AirFry for 12 minutes. Check with a toothpick: if it doesn't come up clean, cook them for an additional 2 to 3 minutes. Serve chilled.

18. Air Fryer Chicken Breasts

Servings: 4   Cooking Time: 30 Minutes
Ingredients:
4 chicken breasts
Salt and black pepper to taste
1 tbsp olive oil
1 tsp garlic powder

Directions:
Brush the breasts with olive oil and season with salt, garlic powder, and black pepper. Arrange the breasts on the frying basket. Select AirFry function, adjust the temperature to 380 F, and press Start. Cook for 20 minutes until nice and crispy. Serve warm.

19. Vegetable & Walnut Stuffed Ham Rolls

Servings: 4   Cooking Time: 15 Minutes

Ingredients:

1 carrot, chopped	2 tbsp olive oil
4 large ham slices	1 tbsp ginger powder
¼ cup walnuts, finely chopped	2 tbsp fresh basil leaves, chopped
1 zucchini, chopped	Salt and black pepper to taste
1 garlic clove, minced	

Directions:

Heat olive oil in a pan over medium heat and sauté zucchini, carrot, garlic, and ginger for 5-6 minutes until tender. Stir in basil, walnuts, and salt. Divide the mixture between ham slices and then fold one side above the filling and roll in. Transfer to a baking tray. Select Bake function, adjust the temperature to 360 F, and press Start. Bake the rolls for 8 minutes.

20. Spicy And Sweet Nuts

Servings: 4 Cups   Cooking Time: 15 Minutes

Ingredients:

1 pound (454 g) walnut halves and pieces	3 tablespoons vegetable oil
½ cup granulated sugar	1 teaspoon cayenne pepper
	½ teaspoon fine salt

Directions:

Soak the walnuts in a large bowl with boiling water for a minute or two. Drain the walnuts. Stir in the sugar, oil and cayenne pepper to coat well. Spread the walnuts in a single layer in the baking pan. Slide the baking pan into Rack Position 1, select Convection Bake, set temperature to 325°F (163°C) and set time to 15 minutes.   After 7 or 8 minutes, remove from the oven. Stir the nuts. Return the pan to the oven and continue cooking, check frequently. When cooking is complete, the walnuts should be dark golden brown. Remove from the oven. Sprinkle the nuts with the salt and let cool. Serve warm.

21. Garlic Potato Chips

Servings: 3   Cooking Time: 30 Minutes + Marinating Time

Ingredients:

3 whole potatoes, cut into thin slices	1 tbsp garlic
¼ cup olive oil	½ cup cream
	2 tbsp rosemary

Directions:

Preheat Cuisinart on Air Fry function to 390 F. In a bowl, add oil, garlic, and salt to form a marinade. Stir in the potatoes. Allow sitting for 30 minutes. Lay the potato slices onto the Air Fryer basket and fit in the baking tray. Cook for 20 minutes. After 10 minutes, give the chips a turn. When readt, sprinkle with rosemary and serve.

22. Parmesan Zucchini Rounds

Servings: 4   Cooking Time: 20 Minutes

Ingredients:

4 zucchinis; sliced	1 egg; whisked
1 ½ cups parmesan; grated	1 egg white; whisked
¼ cup parsley; chopped.	½ tsp. garlic powder
	Cooking spray

Directions:

Take a bowl and mix the egg with egg whites, parmesan, parsley and garlic powder and whisk. Dredge each zucchini slice in this mix, place them all in your air fryer's basket, grease them with cooking spray and cook at 370°F for 20 minutes   Divide between plates and serve as a side dish.

Nutrition Info: Calories: 183; Fat: 6g; Fiber: 2g; Carbs: 3g; Protein: 8g

23. Mom's Tarragon Chicken Breast Packets

Servings: 2   Cooking Time: 15 Minutes

Ingredients:

2 chicken breasts	1 tbsp butter
Salt and black pepper to taste	¼ tsp dried tarragon

Directions:

Preheat Cuisinart on Bake function to 380 F. Place each chicken breast on a 12x12 inches foil wrap. Top the chicken with tarragon and butter; season with salt and pepper. Wrap the foil around the chicken breast in a loose way to create a flow of air. Cook the in your Cuisinart oven for 15 minutes. Carefully unwrap and serve.

24. Crispy Onion Rings With Buttermilk

Servings: 4   Cooking Time: 30 Minutes

Ingredients:

2 sweet onions	1 package cornbread mix
2 cups buttermilk	
2 cups pancake mix	1 tsp salt
2 cups water	

Directions:

Preheat Cuisinart on Air Fry function to 370 F. Slice the onions into rings. Combine the pancake mix with water. Line a baking sheet with parchment paper. Dip the rings in the cornbread mixture first, and then in the pancake batter.   Place the onion rings onto the greased basket and then into the baking tray. Cook for 8-12 minutes, flipping once until crispy. Serve with salsa rosa.

25. Ham And Cheese Grilled Sandwich

Servings: 2   Cooking Time: 15 Minutes

Ingredients:

4 slices bread	2 slices ham
¼ cup butter	2 slices cheese

Directions:

Preheat Cuisinart on Air Fry function to 360 F. Place 2 bread slices on a flat surface. Spread butter on the exposed surfaces. Lay cheese and ham on two of the slices. Cover with the other 2 slices to form sandwiches. Place the sandwiches in the cooking basket and cook for 5 minutes on Bake function. For additional crispiness, set on Toast function for 2 minutes.

26. Paprika Curly Potatoes

Servings: 2   Cooking Time: 20 Minutes

Ingredients:

2 whole potatoes, spiralized	Salt and black pepper to taste
1 tbsp olive oil	1 tsp paprika

Directions:
Preheat Cuisinart on AirFry function to 390 F. Place the potatoes in a bowl and coat with oil. Transfer them to the frying basket and place in the oven. Press Start and cook for 15 minutes. Sprinkle with salt and paprika and serve.

27. Chili Beef Sticks

Servings: 3   Cooking Time: 10 Minutes
Ingredients:

1 lb ground beef	A pinch chili powder
3 tbsp sugar	Salt to taste
A pinch garlic powder	1 tsp liquid smoke

Directions:
Place the meat, sugar, garlic powder, chili powder, salt, and liquid smoke in a bowl. Mix well. Mold out 4 sticks with your hands, place them on a plate, and refrigerate for 2 hours.   Select Bake function, adjust the temperature to 360 F, and press Start. Cook for 15 minutes.

28. Honey Corn Muffins

Servings: 8   Cooking Time: 20 Minutes
Ingredients:

2 eggs	1/2 cup sugar
1 1/4 cups self-rising flour	1/2 cup butter, melted
3/4 cup yellow cornmeal	3/4 cup buttermilk
	1 tbsp honey

Directions:
Fit the Cuisinart oven with the rack in position Spray 8-cups muffin tin with cooking spray and set aside.   In a large bowl, mix together cornmeal, sugar, and flour.   In a separate bowl, whisk the eggs with buttermilk and honey until well combined. Slowly add egg mixture and melted butter to the cornmeal mixture and stir until just mixed. Spoon batter into the prepared muffin tin.   Set to bake at 350 F for 25 minutes. After 5 minutes place muffin tin in the preheated oven.   Serve and enjoy.
Nutrition Info: Calories 294 Fat 13.4 g Carbohydrates 39.6 g Sugar 16 g Protein 5.2 g Cholesterol 72 mg

29. Buttered Corn

Servings: 2   Cooking Time: 20 Minutes
Ingredients:

Salt and freshly ground black pepper, as needed	2 corn on the cob
	2 tablespoons butter, softened and divided

Directions:
Sprinkle the cobs evenly with salt and black pepper. Then, rub with 1 tablespoon of butter.   With 1 piece of foil, wrap each cob.   Press "Power Button" of Air Fry Oven and turn the dial to select the "Air Fry" mode.   Press the Time button and again turn the dial to set the cooking time to 20 minutes. Now push the Temp button and rotate the dial to set the temperature at 320 degrees F.   Press "Start/Pause" button to start.   When the unit beeps to show that it is preheated, open the lid.

Arrange the cobs in "Air Fry Basket" and insert in the oven.   Serve warm.
Nutrition Info: Calories 186 Total Fat 12.2 g Saturated Fat 7.4 g Cholesterol 31 mg Sodium 163 mg Total Carbs 20.1 g Fiber 2.5 g Sugar 3.2g Protein 2.9 g

30. Herby Carrot Cookies

Servings: 6   Cooking Time: 30 Minutes
Ingredients:

6 carrots, sliced	½ cup oats
Salt and black pepper to taste	1 whole egg, beaten
1 tbsp parsley	1 tbsp thyme

Directions:
Preheat Cuisinart on Air Fryer function to 360 F. In a saucepan over medium heat, add carrots and cover with water. Cook for 10 minutes until tender. Remove to a plate. Season with salt, pepper, and parsley and mash using a fork.   Add in egg, oats, and thyme as you continue mashing to mix well. Form the batter into cookie shapes. Place in the frying basket and press Start. Cook for 15 minutes until edges are browned.

31. Easy Broccoli Bread

Servings: 6   Cooking Time: 30 Minutes
Ingredients:

5 eggs, lightly beaten	3 1/1 tbsp coconut flour
3/4 cup broccoli florets, chopped	1 cup cheddar cheese, shredded
2 tsp baking powder	

Directions:
Fit the Cuisinart oven with the rack in position Add all ingredients into the bowl and mix well. Pour egg mixture into the greased loaf pan.   Set to bake at 350 F for 35 minutes. After 5 minutes place the loaf pan in the preheated oven.   Cut the loaf into the slices and serve.
Nutrition Info: Calories 174 Fat 11.3 g Carbohydrates 7.4 g Sugar 1.2 g Protein 11 g Cholesterol 156 mg

32. Garlicky Mushroom Spaghetti

Servings: 4   Cooking Time: 20 Minutes
Ingredients:

½ lb white button mushrooms, sliced	12 oz spaghetti, cooked
1 tsp butter, softened	14 oz mushroom sauce
2 garlic cloves, chopped	Salt and black pepper to taste

Directions:
Preheat Cuisinart on AirFry function to 400 F. In a round baking dish, mix the mushrooms, butter, garlic, salt, and pepper. Press Start and cook for 10-12 minutes. Heat the mushroom sauce a pan over medium heat and stir in the mushrooms Pour over cooked spaghetti and serve.

33. Green Beans And Mushrooms

Servings: 4   Cooking Time: 6 Minutes
Ingredients:

1 small yellow onion, peeled and chopped
6 ounces bacon, chopped
Salt and ground black pepper, to taste
Balsamic vinegar

1-pound fresh green beans, trimmed
1 garlic clove, peeled and minced
8 ounces mushrooms, sliced

Directions:
Place the beans in the Instant Pot, add water to cover them, cover the Instant Pot and cook for 3 minutes in manual configuration.   Release the pressure naturally, drain the beans and set aside. Place the Instant Pot in the sauté mode, add the bacon and sauté for 1 to 2 minutes, stirring constantly.   Add garlic and onion, mix and cook 2 minutes. Add the mushrooms, mix and cook until tender. Add the drain beans, salt, pepper and a pinch of vinegar, mix, remove from heat, divide between plates and serve.
Nutrition Info: Calories: 120, Fat: 3.7, Fiber: 3.3, Carbohydrate: 7.5, Proteins: 2.4

34. Simple Roasted Asparagus

Servings: 4   Cooking Time: 10 Minutes
Ingredients:

1 bunch asparagus
4 tablespoons olive oil

Salt and pepper to taste

Directions:
Start by preheating toaster oven to 425°F.   Wash the asparagus and cut off the bottom inch.   Toss the asparagus in olive oil and lay flat on a baking sheet.   Sprinkle salt and pepper over asparagus. Roast in the oven for 10 minutes.
Nutrition Info: Calories: 127, Sodium: 1 mg, Dietary Fiber: 0.7 g, Total Fat: 14.0 g, Total Carbs: 1.3 g, Protein: 0.7 g.

35. Chicken Nuggets

Servings: 6   Cooking Time: 10 Minutes
Ingredients:

2 large chicken breasts, cut into 1-inch cubes
1 cup breadcrumbs
1/3 tablespoon Parmesan cheese, shredded

1 teaspoon onion powder
¼ teaspoon smoked paprika
Salt and ground black pepper, as required

Directions:
In a large resealable bag, add all the ingredients. Seal the bag and shake well to coat completely. Press "Power Button" of Air Fry Oven and turn the dial to select the "Air Fry" mode.   Press the Time button and again turn the dial to set the cooking time to 10 minutes.   Now push the Temp button and rotate the dial to set the temperature at 400 degrees F.   Press "Start/Pause" button to start. When the unit beeps to show that it is preheated, open the lid.   Arrange the nuggets in "Air Fry Basket" and insert in the oven.   Serve warm.
Nutrition Info: Calories 218 Total Fat 6.6 g Saturated Fat 1.8 g Cholesterol 67 mg Sodium 229 mg Total Carbs 13.3 g Fiber 0.9 g Sugar 1.3 g Protein 24.4 g

36. Cinnamon Sweet Potatoes

Servings: 4   Cooking Time: 30 Minutes
Ingredients:

2 large sweet potatoes, peel and cut into cubes
2 tbsp brown sugar

1/4 cup maple syrup
2 tbsp olive oil
1/4 tsp cinnamon
Salt

Directions:
Fit the Cuisinart oven with the rack in position Add sweet potatoes, oil, cinnamon, brown sugar, maple syrup, and salt into the large mixing bowl and toss well.   Spread sweet potatoes in a parchment-lined baking pan.   Set to bake at 400 F for 35 minutes. After 5 minutes place the baking pan in the preheated oven.   Serve and enjoy.
Nutrition Info: Calories 188 Fat 7.1 g Carbohydrates 31.7 g Sugar 16.3 g Protein 0.8 g Cholesterol 0 mg

37. Garlic Herb Tomatoes

Servings: 4   Cooking Time: 45 Minutes
Ingredients:

10 medium-sized tomatoes
10 garlic cloves
Bread crumbs

Thyme
Sage
Oregano

Directions:
Start by finely chopping garlic and herbs.   Cut tomatoes in half and place cut-side up on a baking sheet lined with parchment paper.   Pour garlic and herb mixture over tomatoes.   Roast at 350°F for 30 minutes in toaster oven.   Top with bread crumbs and roast another 15 minutes.
Nutrition Info: Calories: 103, Sodium: 68 mg, Dietary Fiber: 5.4 g, Total Fat: 1.3 g, Total Carbs: 21.4 g, Protein: 4.4 g.

38. Savory Parsley Crab Cakes

Servings: 6   Cooking Time: 20 Minutes
Ingredients:

1 lb crab meat, shredded
2 eggs, beaten
⅓ cup finely chopped green onion
¼ cup parsley, chopped

½ cup breadcrumbs
1 tbsp mayonnaise
1 tsp sweet chili sauce
½ tsp paprika
Salt and black pepper to taste

Directions:
In a bowl, add crab meat, eggs, crumbs, green onion, parsley, mayo, chili sauce, paprika, salt and black pepper; mix well with your hands.   Shape into 6 cakes and grease them lightly with oil. Arrange them in the fryer basket without overcrowding. Fit in the baking tray and cook for 8 minutes at 400 F on Air Fry function, turning once halfway through.

39. Ham & Pineapple Tortilla Pizzas

Servings: 2   Cooking Time: 15 Minutes
Ingredients:

2 tortillas
8 ham slices
8 mozzarella cheese slices

8 thin pineapple slices
2 tbsp tomato sauce
1 tsp dried parsley

Directions:

Preheat Cuisinart on Pizza function to 330 F. Spread the tomato sauce onto the tortillas. Arrange 4 ham slices on each tortilla. Top with pineapple and mozzarella slices and sprinkle with parsley. Place in the oven and press Start. Cook for 10 minutes and serve.

40. Butternut Squash Croquettes

Servings: 4   Cooking Time: 17 Minutes

Ingredients:

⅓ butternut squash, peeled and grated
⅓ cup all-purpose flour
2 eggs, whisked
4 cloves garlic, minced
1½ tablespoons olive oil

1 teaspoon fine sea salt
⅓ teaspoon freshly ground black pepper, or more to taste
⅓ teaspoon dried sage
A pinch of ground allspice

Directions:

Line the air fryer basket with parchment paper. Set aside.   In a mixing bowl, stir together all the ingredients until well combined.   Make the squash croquettes: Use a small cookie scoop to drop tablespoonfuls of the squash mixture onto a lightly floured surface and shape into balls with your hands. Transfer them to the basket.   Put the air fryer basket on the baking pan and slide into Rack Position 2, select Air Fry, set temperature to 345°F (174°C), and set time to 17 minutes.   When cooking is complete, the squash croquettes should be golden brown. Remove from the oven to a plate and serve warm.

41. Mac & Cheese Quiche With Greek Yogurt

Servings: 4   Cooking Time: 30 Minutes

Ingredients:

8 tbsp leftover macaroni with cheese
Extra cheddar cheese for serving
Pastry as much needed for forming 4 shells

Salt and black pepper to taste
1 tsp garlic puree
2 tbsp Greek yogurt
2 whole eggs
1 cup milk

Directions:

Preheat Cuisinart on AirFry function to 360 F. Roll the pastry to form 4 shells. Place them in a greased baking pan. In a bowl, mix leftover macaroni with cheese, yogurt, eggs, milk, and garlic.   Divide the mixture between the pastry shells. Top with the cheese evenly. Press Start and cook for 20 minutes. Serve chilled.

42. Parmesan Zucchini Chips

Servings: 4   Cooking Time: 20 Minutes

Ingredients:

1 oz. pork rinds.
½ cup grated Parmesan cheese.

2 medium zucchini
1 large egg.

Directions:

Slice zucchini in ¼-inch-thick slices. Place between two layers of paper towels or a clean kitchen towel for 30 minutes to remove excess moisture   Place pork rinds into food processor and pulse until finely ground. Pour into medium bowl and mix with Parmesan   Beat egg in a small bowl.   Dip zucchini slices in egg and then in pork rind mixture, coating as completely as possible. Carefully place each slice into the air fryer basket in a single layer, working in batches as necessary.   Adjust temperature to 320 Degrees F and set the timer for 10 minutes. Flip chips halfway through the cooking time. Serve warm.

Nutrition Info: Calories: 121; Protein: 9.9g; Fiber: 0.6g; Fat: 6.7g; Carbs: 3.8g

43. Easy Parsnip Fries

Servings: 3   Cooking Time: 15 Minutes

Ingredients:

4 parsnips, sliced
¼ cup flour
¼ cup olive oil

¼ cup water
A pinch of salt

Directions:

Preheat Cuisinart on Air Fry function to 390 F. In a bowl, add the flour, olive oil, water, and parsnips; mix to coat. Line the fries in the greased Air Fryer basket and fit in the baking tray. Cook for 15 minutes. Serve with yogurt and garlic dip.

44. Roasted Tomatoes

Servings: 4   Cooking Time: 20 Minutes

Ingredients:

4 tomatoes; halved
½ cup parmesan; grated
1 tbsp. basil; chopped.

½ tsp. onion powder
½ tsp. oregano; dried
½ tsp. smoked paprika
½ tsp. garlic powder
Cooking spray

Directions:

Take a bowl and mix all the ingredients except the cooking spray and the parmesan.   Arrange the tomatoes in your air fryer's pan, sprinkle the parmesan on top and grease with cooking spray Cook at 370°F for 15 minutes, divide between plates and serve.

Nutrition Info: Calories: 200; Fat: 7g; Fiber: 2g; Carbs: 4g; Protein: 6g

45. Mustard Cheddar Twists

Servings: 4   Cooking Time: 45 Minutes

Ingredients:

2 cups cauliflower florets, steamed
1 egg
3 ½ oz oats
1 red onion, diced

1 tsp mustard
5 oz cheddar cheese
Salt and black pepper to taste

Directions:

Place the oats in a food processor and pulse until they resemble breadcrumbs. Place the steamed florets in a cheesecloth and squeeze out the excess liquid.   Transfer to a large bowl. Add in the rest of the ingredients. Mix well. Take a little bit of the mixture and twist it into a straw.   Place on a lined baking tray and repeat with the rest of the mixture. Select AirFry function, adjust the temperature to 360 F, and press Start. Cook for 10 minutes, turn over and cook for an additional 10 minutes.

46. Baked Root Vegetables

Servings: 6   Cooking Time: 30 Minutes
Ingredients:

1 lb beetroot, cubed	1 lb sweet potato,
3 tsp paprika	cubed
1/2 lb carrots, cut	2 tsp olive oil
into chunks	

Directions:
Fit the Cuisinart oven with the rack in position Add all ingredients in a large mixing bowl and toss well.   Transfer root mixture onto a baking pan. Set to bake at 350 F for 35 minutes. After 5 minutes place the baking pan in the preheated oven.   Serve and enjoy.
Nutrition Info: Calories 133 Fat 2 g Carbohydrates 27.5 g Sugar 12.9 g Protein 3.3 g Cholesterol 0 mg

47. Salty Carrot Chips

Servings: 2   Cooking Time: 20 Minutes
Ingredients:

3 large carrots,	Salt to taste
washed and peeled	

Directions:
Using a mandolin slicer, cut the carrots very thinly heightwise. Season with salt to taste. Place in the frying basket and spray them lightly with cooking spray.   Select   AirFry   function,   adjust   the temperature to 380 F, and press Start. Cook for 14-16 minutes until crispy.

48. Ham & Mozzarella Eggplant Boats

Servings: 2   Cooking Time: 20 Minutes
Ingredients:

1 eggplant	4 ham slices, chopped
1 cup shredded	1 tsp dried parsley
mozzarella cheese,	Salt and black pepper
divided	to taste

Directions:
Preheat Cuisinart on AirFry function to 330 F. Peel the eggplant and cut it in half, lengthwise; scoop some of the flesh out. Season with salt and pepper. Divide half of mozzarella cheese between the eggplant halves and top with the ham. Sprinkle with the remaining mozzarella cheese and cook for 12 minutes until nice and golden on top. Serve topped with parsley.

49. Stuffed Mushrooms With Rice & Cheese

Servings: 10   Cooking Time: 30 Minutes
Ingredients:

10 Swiss brown	2 tbsp olive oil
mushrooms	1 tsp dried mixed
1 cup cooked brown	herbs
rice	Salt and black pepper
1 cup grated Grana	to taste
Padano cheese	

Directions:

Brush mushrooms with oil and arrange onto the Cuisinart Air Fryer baking tray. In a bowl, mix rice, Grana Padano cheese, herbs, salt, and pepper. Stuff the mushrooms with the mixture. Cook in the oven for 14 minutes at 360 F on Bake function until the cheese has melted. Serve.

50. Baked Cauliflower & Pepper

Servings: 4   Cooking Time: 30 Minutes
Ingredients:

1 cauliflower head,	2 tsp olive oil
cut into florets	2 tbsp white wine
1/2 cup fresh dill,	vinegar
chopped	3 tbsp balsamic
12/ onion, sliced	vinegar
1 red bell pepper, cut	Pepper
into 1-inch pieces	Salt

Directions:
Fit the Cuisinart oven with the rack in position Add all ingredients into the zip-lock bag. Seal the bag and shake well and place in the fridge for 1 hour. Pour marinated cauliflower mixture in the baking dish.   Set to bake at 450 F for 35 minutes. After 5 minutes place the baking dish in the preheated oven. Serve and enjoy.
Nutrition Info: Calories 86 Fat 2.7 g Carbohydrates 15.3 g Sugar 6.2 g Protein 2.8 g Cholesterol 0 mg

51. Spicy Brussels Sprouts(1)

Servings: 2   Cooking Time: 15 Minutes
Ingredients:

1/2 lb Brussels	1/4 tsp cayenne
sprouts, trimmed and	1/2 tsp chili powder
halved	1/2 tbsp olive oil
1 tbsp chives,	Pepper
chopped	Salt

Directions:
Fit the Cuisinart oven with the rack in position Add all ingredients into the large bowl and toss well. Spread Brussels sprouts in baking pan.   Set to bake at 370 F for 20 minutes. After 5 minutes place the baking pan in the preheated oven.   Serve and enjoy.
Nutrition Info: Calories 82 Fat 4.1 g Carbohydrates 10.9 g Sugar 2.6 g Protein 4 g Cholesterol 0 mg

52. Sausage Balls With Cheese

Servings: 8   Cooking Time: 10 Minutes
Ingredients:

12 ounces (340 g)	3 ounces (85 g) cream
mild ground sausage	cheese, at room
1½ cups baking mix	temperature
1 cup shredded mild	1 to 2 tablespoons
Cheddar cheese	olive oil

Directions:
Line the air fryer basket with parchment paper. Set aside.   Mix together the ground sausage, baking mix, Cheddar cheese, and cream cheese in a large bowl and stir to incorporate.   Divide the sausage mixture into 16 equal portions and roll them into 1-inch balls with your hands. Arrange the sausage balls on the parchment, leaving space between each

ball. Brush the sausage balls with the olive oil. Put the air fryer basket on the baking pan and slide into Rack Position 2, select Air Fry, set temperature to 325ºF (163ºC), and set time to 10 minutes. Flip the balls halfway through the cooking time. When cooking is complete, the balls should be firm and lightly browned on both sides. Remove from the oven to a plate and serve warm.

53. Lime Pumpkin Wedges

Servings: 4   Cooking Time: 30 Minutes
Ingredients:

1 lb pumpkin, cut into wedges	1 tbsp balsamic vinegar
1 tbsp paprika	Salt and black pepper to taste
1 whole lime, squeezed	1 tsp turmeric
1 cup paleo dressing	

Directions:
Preheat Cuisinart on AirFry function to 360 F. Add the pumpkin wedges in a baking tray and press Start. Cook for 20 minutes. In a bowl, mix lime juice, vinegar, turmeric, salt, pepper, and paprika. Pour the mixture over pumpkin and cook for 5 more minutes. Serve.

54. Lime Corn With Feta Cheese

Servings: 2   Cooking Time: 20 Minutes
Ingredients:

2 ears of corn	½ cup feta cheese, grated
Juice of 1 lime	
1 tsp paprika	

Directions:
Preheat Cuisinart on AirFry function to 370 F. Peel the corn and remove the silk. Place the corn in a baking pan and place in the oven. Press Start and cook for 15 minutes. When ready, remove, and drizzle the lime juice on top of each corn ear. Top with feta cheese and serve.

55. Baked Turnip & Sweet Potato

Servings: 4   Cooking Time: 30 Minutes
Ingredients:

1 1/2 lbs sweet potato, sliced 1/4-inch thick	2 tbsp olive oil
1 lb turnips, sliced 1/4-inch thick	1 tbsp thyme, chopped
	1 tsp paprika
	1/4 tsp pepper
	1/2 tsp sea salt

Directions:
Fit the Cuisinart oven with the rack in position Add sliced sweet potatoes and turnips in a bowl and toss with seasoning and olive oil. Arrange sliced sweet potatoes and turnips in baking dish. Set to bake at 425 F for 35 minutes. After 5 minutes place the baking dish in the preheated oven. Garnish with thyme and serve.
Nutrition Info: Calories 250 Fat 7.4 g Carbohydrates 43.5 g Sugar 15.8 g Protein 4.5 g Cholesterol 0 mg

56. Air Fried Green Tomatoes(1)

Servings: 4   Cooking Time: 20 Minutes
Ingredients:

2 medium green tomatoes	¼ cup blanched finely ground almond flour.
⅓ cup grated Parmesan cheese.	1 large egg.

Directions:
Slice tomatoes into ½-inch-thick slices. Take a medium bowl, whisk the egg. Take a large bowl, mix the almond flour and Parmesan. Dip each tomato slice into the egg, then dredge in the almond flour mixture. Place the slices into the air fryer basket Adjust the temperature to 400 Degrees F and set the timer for 7 minutes. Flip the slices halfway through the cooking time. Serve immediately
Nutrition Info: Calories: 106; Protein: 6.2g; Fiber: 1.4g; Fat: 6.7g; Carbs: 5.9g

57. Cajun Shrimp

Servings: 3   Cooking Time: 15 Minutes
Ingredients:

½ pound shrimp, deveined	Salt and black pepper to taste
½ tsp Cajun seasoning	1 tbsp olive oil

Directions:
Preheat Cuisinart on AirFry function to 390 F. In a bowl, make the marinade by mixing salt, pepper, olive oil, and seasoning. Add in the shrimp and toss to coat. Transfer the prepared shrimp to the frying basket and place in the oven. Press Start and cook for 10-12 minutes.

58. Herb Cheese Sweet Potatoes

Servings: 6   Cooking Time: 30 Minutes
Ingredients:

2 lbs sweet potatoes, peeled and cut into 1-inch cubes	2 tbsp olive oil
	1 tsp dried rosemary
1/4 cup parmesan cheese, grated	1/2 tsp garlic powder
	Pepper
	Salt

Directions:
Fit the Cuisinart oven with the rack in position Add sweet potatoes into the mixing bowl along with oil, rosemary, garlic powder, pepper, and salt and toss well. Spread sweet potatoes in baking pan. Set to bake at 425 F for 35 minutes. After 5 minutes place the baking pan in the preheated oven. Toss sweet potatoes with parmesan cheese and serve.
Nutrition Info: Calories 232 Fat 5.8 g Carbohydrates 42.6 g Sugar 0.8 g Protein 3.6 g Cholesterol 3 mg

59. Preparation Time: 20 Minutes

Servings: 2   Cooking Time: 20 Minutes
Ingredients:

2 bell peppers, tops and seeds removed	2 tablespoons mayonnaise
Salt and pepper, to taste	1 tablespoon fresh celery stalks, chopped
2/3 cup cream cheese	

Directions:
Arrange the peppers in the lightly greased cooking basket. Cook in the preheated Air Fryer at 400 degrees F for 15 minutes, turning them over halfway through the cooking time. Season with salt and

pepper. Then, in a mixing bowl, combine the cream cheese with the mayonnaise and chopped celery. Stuff the pepper with the cream cheese mixture and serve.

Nutrition Info:378 Calories; 38g Fat; 6g Carbs; 5g Protein; 1g Sugars; 6g Fiber

60. Apple & Cinnamon Chips

Servings: 2   Cooking Time: 25 Minutes
Ingredients:

1 tsp sugar	½ tsp cinnamon
1 tsp salt	
1 whole apple, sliced	Confectioners' sugar for serving

Directions:
Preheat your Cuisinart oven to 400 F on Bake function. In a bowl, mix cinnamon, salt, and sugar. Add in the apple slices and toss to coat. Transfer to a greased baking tray. Press Start and set the time to 10 minutes. When ready, dust with sugar and serve chilled.

61. Parmesan Cauliflower

Servings: 5 Cups   Cooking Time: 15 Minutes
Ingredients:

8 cups small cauliflower florets (about 1¼ pounds / 567 g)	1 teaspoon garlic powder
3 tablespoons olive oil	½ teaspoon salt
	½ teaspoon turmeric
	¼ cup shredded Parmesan cheese

Directions:
In a bowl, combine the cauliflower florets, olive oil, garlic powder, salt, and turmeric and toss to coat. Transfer to the air fryer basket.   Put the air fryer basket on the baking pan and slide into Rack Position 2, select Air Fry, set temperature to 390°F (199°C), and set time to 15 minutes.   After 5 minutes, remove from the oven and stir the cauliflower florets. Return to the oven and continue cooking.   After 6 minutes, remove from the oven and stir the cauliflower. Return to the oven and continue cooking for 4 minutes. The cauliflower florets should be crisp-tender.   When cooking is complete, remove from the oven to a plate. Sprinkle with the shredded Parmesan cheese and toss well. Serve warm.

62. Green Bean Casserole(1)

Servings: 4   Cooking Time: 20 Minutes
Ingredients:

1 lb. fresh green beans, edges trimmed	¼ cup diced yellow onion
½ oz. pork rinds, finely ground	½ cup chopped white mushrooms
1 oz. full-fat cream cheese	½ cup chicken broth
½ cup heavy whipping cream.	4 tbsp. unsalted butter.
	¼ tsp. xanthan gum

Directions:

In a medium skillet over medium heat, melt the butter. Sauté the onion and mushrooms until they become soft and fragrant, about 3–5 minutes. Add the heavy whipping cream, cream cheese and broth to the pan. Whisk until smooth. Bring to a boil and then reduce to a simmer. Sprinkle the xanthan gum into the pan and remove from heat   Chop the green beans into 2-inch pieces and place into a 4-cup round baking dish. Pour the sauce mixture over them and stir until coated. Top the dish with ground pork rinds. Place into the air fryer basket   Adjust the temperature to 320 Degrees F and set the timer for 15 minutes. Top will be golden and green beans fork tender when fully cooked. Serve warm.

Nutrition Info: Calories: 267; Protein: 3.6g; Fiber: 3.2g; Fat: 23.4g; Carbs: 9.7g

63. Cheese Scones With Chives

Servings: 6   Cooking Time: 25 Minutes
Ingredients:

1 cup flour	3 tbsp butter
Salt and black pepper to taste	1 whole egg
	1 tbsp milk
1 tsp fresh chives, chopped	1 cup cheddar cheese, shredded

Directions:
Preheat Cuisinart on AirFry function to 340 F. In a bowl, mix butter, flour, cheddar cheese, chives, milk, and egg to get a sticky dough. Dust a flat surface with flour. Roll the dough into small balls. Place the balls in the frying basket and place in the oven. Press Start and cook for 20 minutes.

64. Delicious Baked Potatoes

Servings: 6   Cooking Time: 50 Minutes
Ingredients:

3 lbs potatoes, peeled	3 tbsp coconut oil, melted
1 tsp pepper	
3 tbsp olive oil	2 tsp salt

Directions:
Fit the Cuisinart oven with the rack in position Slice potatoes 1/4-inch thick using a slicer. Transfer sliced potatoes to the bowl and toss with olive oil and coconut oil.   Arrange potato slices in a baking dish in a circular pattern. Season with pepper and salt.   Set to bake at 450 F for 55 minutes. After 5 minutes place the baking dish in the preheated oven.   Serve and enjoy.

Nutrition Info: Calories 276 Fat 14 g Carbohydrates 35.9 g Sugar 2.6 g Protein 3.9 g Cholesterol 0 mg

65. Coriander Artichokes(1)

Servings: 4   Cooking Time: 20 Minutes
Ingredients:

12 oz. artichoke hearts	½ tsp. cumin seeds
1 tbsp. lemon juice	½ tsp. olive oil
1 tsp. coriander, ground	Salt and black pepper to taste.

Directions:
In a pan that fits your air fryer, mix all the ingredients, toss, introduce the pan in the fryer and

cook at 370°F for 15 minutes   Divide the mix between plates and serve as a side dish.
Nutrition Info: Calories: 200; Fat: 7g; Fiber: 2g; Carbs: 5g; Protein: 8g

66. Artichoke Hearts And Tarragon

Servings: 4   Cooking Time: 20 Minutes
Ingredients:

12 oz. artichoke hearts
2 tbsp. tarragon; chopped.
Juice of ½ lemon
4 tbsp. butter; melted
Salt and black pepper to taste.

Directions:
Take a bowl and mix all the ingredients, toss, transfer the artichokes to your air fryer's basket and cook at 370°F for 15 minutes   Divide between plates and serve as a side dish.
Nutrition Info: Calories: 200; Fat: 7g; Fiber: 2g; Carbs: 3g; Protein: 7g

67. Beef Enchilada Dip

Servings: 8   Cooking Time: 10 Minutes
Ingredients:

2 lbs. ground beef
2 cloves garlic, chopped fine
2 cups enchilada sauce
½ onion, chopped fine
2 cups Monterrey Jack cheese, grated
2 tbsp. sour cream

Directions:
Place rack in position   Heat a large skillet over med-high heat. Add beef and cook until it starts to brown. Drain off fat.   Stir in onion and garlic and cook until tender, about 3 minutes. Stir in enchilada sauce and transfer mixture to a small casserole dish and top with cheese.   Set oven to convection bake on 325°F for 10 minutes. After 5 minutes, add casserole to the oven and bake 3-5 minutes until cheese is melted and mixture is heated through. Serve warm topped with sour cream.
Nutrition Info: Calories 414, Total Fat 22g, Saturated Fat 10g, Total Carbs 15g, Net Carbs 11g, Protein 39g, Sugar 8g, Fiber 4g, Sodium 1155mg, Potassium 635mg, Phosphorus 385mg

68. Spicy Tortilla Chips

Servings: 4   Cooking Time: 5 Minutes
Ingredients:

½ teaspoon ground cumin
½ teaspoon paprika
½ teaspoon chili powder
½ teaspoon salt
Pinch cayenne pepper
8 (6-inch) corn tortillas, each cut into 6 wedges
Cooking spray

Directions:
Lightly spritz the air fryer basket with cooking spray. Stir together the cumin, paprika, chili powder, salt, and pepper in a small bowl.   Place the tortilla wedges in the basket in a single layer. Lightly mist them with cooking spray. Sprinkle the seasoning mixture on top of the tortilla wedges.   Put the air fryer basket on the baking pan and slide into Rack Position 2, select Air Fry, set temperature to 375°F (190°C), and set time to 5 minutes.   Stir the tortilla wedges halfway through the cooking time. When cooking is complete, the chips should be lightly browned and crunchy. Remove from the oven. Let the tortilla chips cool for 5 minutes and serve.

69. Crispy Cinnamon Apple Chips

Servings: 4   Cooking Time: 10 Minutes
Ingredients:

2 apples, cored and cut into thin slices
Cooking spray
2 heaped teaspoons ground cinnamon

Directions:
Spritz the air fryer basket with cooking spray.   In a medium bowl, sprinkle the apple slices with the cinnamon. Toss until evenly coated. Spread the coated apple slices on the pan in a single layer. Put the air fryer basket on the baking pan and slide into Rack Position 2, select Air Fry, set temperature to 350°F (180°C) and set time to 10 minutes. After 5 minutes, remove from the oven. Stir the apple slices and return to the oven to continue cooking.   When cooking is complete, the slices should be until crispy. Remove from the oven and let rest for 5 minutes before serving.

70. Parmesan Baked Asparagus

Servings: 4   Cooking Time: 12 Minutes
Ingredients:

1 lb asparagus, wash, trimmed, and cut the ends
1 tbsp dried parsley
2 garlic cloves, minced
2 tbsp olive oil
3 oz parmesan cheese, shaved
1 tsp dried oregano
Pepper
Salt

Directions:
Fit the Cuisinart oven with the rack in position Arrange asparagus in baking pan. Drizzle with olive oil and season with pepper and salt.   Spread cheese, oregano, parsley, and garlic over the asparagus   Set to bake at 425 F for 17 minutes. After 5 minutes place the baking pan in the preheated oven.   Serve and enjoy.
Nutrition Info: Calories 155 Fat 11.8 g Carbohydrates 6 g Sugar 2.2 g Protein 9.5 g Cholesterol 15 mg

71. Baked Eggplant Pepper & Mushrooms

Servings: 4   Cooking Time: 20 Minutes
Ingredients:

2 eggplants
2 cups mushrooms
1/4 tsp black pepper
4 bell peppers
2 tbsp olive oil
1 tsp salt

Directions:
Fit the Cuisinart oven with the rack in position Cut all vegetables into the small bite-sized pieces and place in a baking dish.   Drizzle vegetables with olive oil and season with pepper and salt.   Set to bake at 390 F for 25 minutes. After 5 minutes place the baking dish in the preheated oven. Serve and enjoy.
Nutrition Info: Calories 87 Fat 4 g Carbohydrates 13.2 g Sugar 7.4 g Protein 2.5 g Cholesterol 0 mg

72. Holiday Pumpkin Wedges

Servings: 3   Cooking Time: 30 Minutes
Ingredients:

½ pumpkin, washed and cut into wedges

1 tbsp paprika

1 whole lime, squeezed

1 cup paleo dressing

1 tbsp balsamic vinegar

Salt and black pepper to taste

1 tsp turmeric

Directions:
Preheat Cuisinart on Air Fry function to 360 F. Place the pumpkin wedges in your Air Fryer baking tray and cook for 20 minutes. In a bowl, mix lime juice, vinegar, turmeric, salt, pepper and paprika to form a marinade. Pour the marinade over pumpkin and cook for 5 more minutes.

73. Homemade Cod Fingers

Servings: 3   Cooking Time: 25 Minutes
Ingredients:

2 cups flour

Salt and black pepper to taste

1 tsp seafood seasoning

2 whole eggs, beaten

1 cup cornmeal

1 pound cod fillets, cut into fingers

2 tbsp milk

2 eggs, beaten

1 cup breadcrumbs

1 lemon, cut into wedges

Directions:
Preheat Cuisinart on Air Fryer function to 400 F. In a bowl, mix beaten eggs with milk. In a separate bowl, combine flour, cornmeal, and seafood seasoning. In another mixing bowl, mix spices with the eggs. In a third bowl, pour the breadcrumbs. Dip cod fingers in the seasoned flour mixture, followed by a dip in the egg mixture, and finally coat with breadcrumbs. Place the fingers in your Air Fryer basket and fit in the baking tray. Cook for 10 minutes until golden brown. Serve with lemon wedges.

74. Cabbage & Carrot Canapes With Amul Cheese

Servings: 2   Cooking Time: 15 Minutes
Ingredients:

1 whole cabbage, cut in rounds

1 cube Amul cheese

½ carrot, cubed

¼ onion, cubed

¼ bell pepper, cubed

1 tbsp fresh basil, chopped

Directions:
Preheat Cuisinart on AirFry function to 360 F. In a bowl, mix onion, carrot, bell pepper, and cheese. Toss to coat everything evenly. Add cabbage to the frying basket. Top with the veggie mixture and place in the oven. Press Start and cook for 8 minutes. Serve topped with basil.

75. Potatoes Au Gratin

Servings: 6   Cooking Time: 17 Minutes
Ingredients:

½ cup yellow onion, chopped

2 tablespoons butter

½ cup sour cream

1 cup Monterey jack cheese, shredded

1 cup chicken stock

6 potatoes, peeled and sliced

Salt and ground black pepper, to taste

For the topping:

3 tablespoons melted butter

1 cup breadcrumbs

Directions:
Put the Instant Pot in Saute mode, add the butter and melt. Add the onion, mix and cook for 5 minutes. Add the stock, salt and pepper and put the steamer basket in the Instant Pot also.   Add the potatoes, cover the Instant Pot and cook for 5 minutes in the Manual setting. In a bowl, mix 3 tablespoons of butter with breadcrumbs and mix well. Relieve the pressure of the Instant Pot, remove the steam basket and transfer the potatoes to a pan.   Pour the cream and cheese into the instant pot and mix. Add the potatoes and mix gently.   Spread breadcrumbs, mix everywhere, place on a preheated grill and cook for 7 minutes. Let cool for a few minutes and serve.
Nutrition Info: Calories: 340, Fat: 22, Fiber: 2, Carbohydrate: 32, Proteins: 11

76. Mac & Cheese

Servings: 10   Cooking Time: 20 Minutes
Ingredients:

1 lb cooked macaroni

4 1/2 cups almond milk

1/2 cup flour

1/2 cup breadcrumbs

12 oz cheddar cheese, shredded

1/2 cup butter

Pepper

Salt

Directions:
Fit the Cuisinart oven with the rack in position Melt butter in a pan over medium heat.   Remove pan from heat and slowly mix flour salt and pepper in melted butter.   Add 1/2 cup milk and stir until well blended.   Return to heat and slowly add remaining milk.   Add cheese and stir until cheese is melted.   Pour over cooked macaroni and mix well.   Transfer macaroni in a casserole dish and sprinkle with breadcrumbs.   Set to bake at 350 F for 25 minutes. After 5 minutes place the casserole dish in the preheated oven.   Serve and enjoy.
Nutrition Info: Calories 679 Fat 47.3 g Carbohydrates 49 g Sugar 5.4 g Protein 18.3 g Cholesterol 60 mg

77. Crispy Cauliflower Poppers

Servings: 4   Cooking Time: 20 Minutes
Ingredients:

1 egg white

1½ tablespoons ketchup

1 tablespoon hot sauce

1/3 cup panko breadcrumbs

2 cups cauliflower florets

Directions:
In a shallow bowl, mix together the egg white, ketchup and hot sauce.   In another bowl, place the breadcrumbs.   Dip the cauliflower florets in ketchup mixture and then coat with the breadcrumbs.   Press "Power Button" of Air Fry Oven and turn the dial to select the "Air Fry" mode. Press the Time button and again turn the dial to set the cooking time to 20 minutes.   Now push the Temp button and rotate the dial to set the

temperature at 320 degrees F.　Press "Start/Pause" button to start.　When the unit beeps to show that it is preheated, open the lid.　Arrange the cauliflower florets in "Air Fry Basket" and insert in the oven.　Toss the cauliflower florets once halfway through.　Serve warm.

Nutrition Info: Calories 55 Total Fat 0.7 g Saturated Fat 0.3g Cholesterol 0 mg Sodium 181 mg Total Carbs 5.6 g Fiber 1.3 g Sugar 2.6 g Protein 2.3 g

78. Garlicky Potatoes

Servings: 4　Cooking Time: 6 Minutes

Ingredients:

1 pound new potatoes, peeled and sliced thin	Salt and ground black pepper, to taste
1 cup water	2 garlic cloves, peeled and minced
1 tablespoon extra-virgin olive oil	¼ teaspoon dried rosemary

Directions:

Place the potatoes and water in the Instant Pot steamer basket, cover and cook for 4 minutes in manual mode. In a heat-resistant dish, mix the rosemary with olive oil and garlic, cover and microwave for 1 minute.　Release the pressure from the Instant Pot, drain the potatoes and spread them over an upholstered pan. Add the oil, salt and pepper mixture, mix to cover, divide between the plates and serve.

Nutrition Info: Calories: 94, Fat: 1, Fiber: 2.2, Carbohydrate: 21, Proteins: 2.5

79. Baked Ratatouille

Servings: 6　Cooking Time: 55 Minutes

Ingredients:

1 large eggplant, steamed and sliced	2 tbsp olive oil
1/4 tsp dried thyme	4 medium zucchini, sliced
2 bell pepper, sliced	1 tsp dried basil
4 tomatoes, sliced	1/2 tsp dried oregano

Directions:

Fit the Cuisinart oven with the rack in position Add all vegetable slices to a large bowl and season with salt and drizzle with oil.　Layer vegetable slices into the greased baking dish.　Set to bake at 400 F for 60 minutes. After 5 minutes place the baking dish in the preheated oven.　Sprinkle with dried herbs.　Serve and enjoy.

Nutrition Info: Calories 108 Fat 5.3 g Carbohydrates 15.2 g Sugar 8.7 g Protein 3.5 g Cholesterol 0 mg

80. Cheesy Stuffed Sliders

Servings: 10　Cooking Time: 50 Minutes

Ingredients:

2 tbsp. garlic powder	2 tsp pepper
1 ½ tsp salt	2 lbs. ground beef
8 oz. mozzarella slices, cut in 20 small pieces	20 potato slider rolls

Directions:

Place baking pan in position 2.　In a small bowl, combine garlic powder, salt, and pepper.　Use 1 ½ tablespoons ground beef per patty. Roll it into a ball and press an indentation in the ball with your thumb. Place a piece of cheese into beef and fold over sides to cover it completely. Flatten to ½-inch thick by 3-inches wide. Season both sides with garlic mixture. Place patties in fryer basket in a single layer and place on the baking pan. Set oven to air fry on 350°F for 10 minutes. Turn patties over halfway through cooking time. Repeat with any remaining patties. Place patties on bottoms of rolls and top with your favorite toppings. Serve immediately.

Nutrition Info: Calories 402, Total Fat 14g, Saturated Fat 5g, Total Carbs 31g, Net Carbs 29g, Protein 38g, Sugar 3g, Fiber 2g, Sodium 835mg, Potassium 397mg, Phosphorus 400mg

81. Spicy Broccoli With Hot Sauce

Servings: 6　Cooking Time: 14 Minutes

Ingredients:

1 medium-sized head broccoli, cut into florets	Broccoli:
1½ tablespoons olive oil	½ teaspoon granulated garlic
1 teaspoon shallot powder	⅓ teaspoon fine sea salt
1 teaspoon porcini powder	⅓ teaspoon celery seeds
½ teaspoon freshly grated lemon zest	Hot Sauce:
½ teaspoon hot paprika	½ cup tomato sauce
	1 tablespoon balsamic vinegar
	½ teaspoon ground allspice

Directions:

In a mixing bowl, combine all the ingredients for the broccoli and toss to coat. Transfer the broccoli to the air fryer basket.　Put the air fryer basket on the baking pan and slide into Rack Position 2, select Air Fry, set temperature to 360°F (182°C), and set time to 14 minutes.　Meanwhile, make the hot sauce by whisking together the tomato sauce, balsamic vinegar, and allspice in a small bowl.　When cooking is complete, remove the broccoli from the oven and serve with the hot sauce.

82. Blistered Shishito Peppers With Lime Juice

Servings: 3　Cooking Time: 9 Minutes

Ingredients:

½ pound (227 g) shishito peppers, rinsed	Sauce:
Cooking spray	2 teaspoons fresh lime juice
1 tablespoon tamari or shoyu	2 large garlic cloves, minced

Directions:

Spritz the air fryer basket with cooking spray. Place the shishito peppers in the basket and spritz them with cooking spray.　Put the air fryer basket on the baking pan and slide into Rack Position 2, select Roast, set temperature to 392°F (200°C), and set time to 9 minutes.　Meanwhile, whisk together all the ingredients for the sauce in a large bowl. Set aside. After 3 minutes, remove from the oven. Flip the peppers and spritz them with cooking spray. Return to the oven and continue cooking. After another 3 minutes, remove from the oven. Flip the peppers and spray with cooking spray. Return to the oven and continue roasting for 3 minutes more, or until the peppers are blistered and nicely browned. When cooking is complete, remove the peppers from the oven to the bowl of sauce. Toss to coat well and serve immediately.

83. Mini Salmon Quiches

Servings: 15   Cooking Time: 20 Minutes
Ingredients:

15 mini tart cases	Salt and black pepper
4 eggs, lightly beaten	6 oz feta cheese,
½ cup heavy cream	crumbled
3 oz smoked salmon,	2 tsp fresh dill,
chopped	chopped

Directions:
Mix together eggs and heavy cream in a bowl. Arrange the tarts on a greased baking tray. Fill them with the egg mixture, about halfway up the side and top with salmon and feta cheese. Cook for 10 minutes at 360 F on Bake function, regularly checking to avoid overcooking. Sprinkle with dill and serve chilled.

84. Garlicky Roasted Chicken With Lemon

Servings: 4   Cooking Time: 60 Minutes
Ingredients:

1 whole chicken	1 tbsp olive oil
(around 3.5 lb)	1 lemon, cut into
Salt and black pepper	quarters
to taste	5 garlic cloves

Directions:
Rub the chicken with olive oil and season with salt and pepper. Stuff the cavity with lemon and garlic. Place chicken, breast-side down on a baking tray. Tuck the legs and wings tips under. Select Bake function, adjust the temperature to 360 F, and press Start. Bake for 30 minutes, turn breast-side up, and bake it for another 15 minutes. Let rest for 5-6 minutes then carve.

85. Yogurt Masala Cashew

Servings: 2   Cooking Time: 25 Minutes
Ingredients:

8 oz Greek yogurt	1 tsp coriander
2 tbsp mango powder	powder
8¾ oz cashew nuts	½ tsp masala powder
Salt and black pepper	
to taste	½ tsp black pepper
	powder

Directions:
Preheat Cuisinart on Air Fry function to 350 F. In a bowl, mix all powders, salt, and pepper. Add in cashews and toss to coat thoroughly. Place the cashews in your Air Fryer baking pan and cook for 15 minutes, shaking every 5 minutes. Serve.

86. French Fries

Servings: 4   Cooking Time: 10 Minutes

Ingredients:

8 medium potatoes,	¼ teaspoon baking
peeled, cut into	soda Oil for frying
medium matchsticks,	Salt, to taste
and patted dry	1 cup water

Directions:
Put the water in the Instant Pot, add the salt and baking soda and mix. Place the potatoes in the steam basket and place them in the Instant Pot, cover and cook with manual adjustment for 3 minutes. Release the pressure naturally, remove the chips from the Instant Pot and place them in a bowl. Heat a pan with enough oil over medium-high heat, add the potatoes, spread and cook until they are golden brown. Transfer the potatoes to the paper towels to drain the excess fat and place them in a bowl. Salt, mix well and serve.
Nutrition Info: Calories: 300, Fat: 10, Fiber: 3.7, Carbohydrate: 41, Proteins: 3.4

87. Broccoli Poppers

Servings: 4   Cooking Time: 10 Minutes
Ingredients:

2 tablespoons plain	¼ teaspoon ground
yogurt	turmeric
½ teaspoon red chili	1 lb. broccoli, cut into
powder	small florets
¼ teaspoon ground	2 tablespoons
cumin	chickpea flour
Salt, to taste	

Directions:
In a bowl, mix together the yogurt, and spices. Add the broccoli and coat with marinade generously. Refrigerate for about 20 minutes. Press "Power Button" of Air Fry Oven and turn the dial to select the "Air Fry" mode. Press the Time button and again turn the dial to set the cooking time to 10 minutes. Now push the Temp button and rotate the dial to set the temperature at 400 degrees F. Press "Start/Pause" button to start. When the unit beeps to show that it is preheated, open the lid. Arrange the broccoli florets in "Air Fry Basket" and insert in the oven. Toss the broccoli florets once halfway through. Serve warm.
Nutrition Info: Calories 69 Total Fat 0.9 g Saturated Fat 0.1 g Cholesterol 0 mg Sodium 87 mg Total Carbs 12.2 g Fiber 4.2 g Sugar 3.2 g Protein 4.9 g

88. Garlic Brussels Sprouts

Servings: 4   Cooking Time: 25 Minutes
Ingredients:

1 pound Brussels	2 tbsp olive oil
sprouts	Salt and black pepper
1 garlic clove, minced	to taste

Directions:
Wash the Brussels sprouts thoroughly under cold water and trim off the outer leaves, keeping only the head of the sprouts. In a bowl, mix olive oil and garlic. Season with salt and pepper. Add in the prepared sprouts let rest for 5 minutes. Place the coated sprouts in the frying basket. Select AirFry function, adjust the temperature to 380 F, and press Start. Cook for 15 minutes.

89. Paprika Potatoes

Servings: 4   Cooking Time: 30 Minutes
Ingredients:

1 lb baby potatoes, quartered
1/4 tsp rosemary, crushed
1/2 tsp thyme
2 tbsp paprika
2 tbsp coconut oil, melted
1 tbsp olive oil
Pepper
Salt

Directions:
Fit the Cuisinart oven with the rack in position Place potatoes in a baking dish and sprinkle with paprika, rosemary, thyme, pepper, and salt. Drizzle with oil and melted coconut oil.   Set to bake at 425 F for 35 minutes. After 5 minutes place the baking dish in the preheated oven.   Serve and enjoy.

Nutrition Info: Calories 165 Fat 10.9 g Carbohydrates 16.2 g Sugar 0.4 g Protein 3.4 g Cholesterol 0 mg

90. Goat Cheese & Pancetta Bombs

Servings: 10   Cooking Time: 25 Minutes
Ingredients:

2 tbsp fresh rosemary, finely chopped
1 cup almonds, chopped into small pieces
16 oz soft goat cheese
Salt and black pepper
15 dried plums, chopped
15 pancetta slices

Directions:
Line the Cuisinart Air Fryer tray with parchment paper. In a bowl, add goat cheese, rosemary, almonds, salt, pepper, and plums; stir well. Roll into balls and wrap with pancetta slices. Arrange the bombs on the tray and cook for 10 minutes at 400 F. Let cool before serving.

91. Cauliflower And Barley Risotto

Servings: 4   Cooking Time: 1 Hour
Ingredients:

1 cauliflower head, separated into florets
4 tablespoons extra virgin olive oil
Salt and ground black pepper, to taste
½ cup Parmesan cheese, grated
1 cup pearled barley
2 garlic cloves, peeled and minced
2 tablespoons fresh parsley, chopped
1 tablespoon butter
1 yellow onion, peeled and chopped
3 cups chicken stock
2 thyme sprigs

Directions:
Spread the cauliflower florets in an upholstered pan, add 3 tablespoons of oil, salt and pepper, mix to coat, place in the oven at 425 degrees Fahrenheit and bake for 20 minutes, turning every 10 minutes. Remove the cauliflower from the oven, sprinkle with ¼ cup of cheese and cook for 5 minutes. Put the Instant Pot in the sauté mode, add 1 tablespoon of oil and heat.   Add the onion, mix and cook for 5 minutes. Add the garlic, mix and cook for 1 minute. Add the broth, thyme and barley, mix, cover the Instant Pot and cook for 25 minutes in the Manual setting.   Release the pressure, uncover the Instant Pot, mix the barley, throw away the thyme, add the butter, the rest of the cheese, the cauliflower, salt, pepper and parsley. Mix the risotto, divide it between the plates and serve.

Nutrition Info: Calories: 350, Fat: 16, Fiber: 10, Carbohydrate: 25, Proteins: 14.6

92. Rice Broccoli Casserole

Servings: 8   Cooking Time: 40 Minutes
Ingredients:

2 cups brown rice, cooked
3 cups broccoli florets
1 tbsp olive oil
2 garlic cloves, minced
1 onion, chopped
For sauce:
1 tbsp onion, chopped
1/4 cup nutritional yeast flakes
1 cup of water
1 garlic clove, minced
1 tbsp tapioca starch
1 cup cashews
1 1/2 tsp salt

Directions:
Fit the Cuisinart oven with the rack in position For the sauce: add all sauce ingredients into the blender and blend until smooth.   Heat oil in a pan over medium-high heat.   Add garlic and onion and sauté until onion is softened.   Add broccoli and cook for a minute.   Add rice and sauce and stir to combine.   Transfer broccoli rice mixture into the greased casserole dish.   Set to bake at 400 F for 45 minutes. After 5 minutes place the casserole dish in the preheated oven.   Serve and enjoy.

Nutrition Info: Calories 327 Fat 11.4 g Carbohydrates 49.2 g Sugar 2.1 g Protein 9.7 g Cholesterol 0 mg

93. Thyme & Carrot Cookies

Servings: 8   Cooking Time: 30 Minutes
Ingredients:

6 carrots, sliced
Salt and black pepper to taste
1 tbsp parsley
1 ¼ oz oats
1 whole egg, beaten
1 tbsp thyme

Directions:
Preheat Cuisinart on Air Fryer function to 360 F. In a saucepan, add carrots and cover with hot water. Cook over medium heat for 10 minutes until tender. Remove to a plate. Season with salt, pepper, and parsley and mash using a fork. Add the beaten egg, oats, and thyme as you continue mashing to mix well. Form the batter into cookie shapes. Place in your Air Fryer baking tray and cook for 15 minutes until edges are browned. Serve chilled.

94. Rice Flour Bites

Servings: 4   Cooking Time: 12 Minutes
Ingredients:

6 tablespoons milk
½ teaspoon vegetable oil
¾ cup rice flour
1 oz. Parmesan cheese, shredded

Directions:
In a bowl, add milk, flour, oil and cheese and mix until a smooth dough forms.   Make small equal-sized balls from the dough.   Press "Power Button" of Air Fry Oven and turn the dial to select the "Air Fry" mode.   Press the Time button and again turn the dial to set the cooking time to 12 minutes. Now push the Temp button and rotate the dial to set

the temperature at 300 degrees F. Press "Start/Pause" button to start. When the unit beeps to show that it is preheated, open the lid. Arrange the balls in "Air Fry Basket" and insert in the oven. Serve warm.

Nutrition Info: Calories 148 Total Fat 3 g Saturated Fat 1.5 g Cholesterol 7 mg Sodium 77 mg Total Carbs 25.1 g Fiber 0.7 g Sugar 1.1 g Protein 4.8 g

95. Cheesy Chicken Breasts With Marinara Sauce

Servings: 2   Cooking Time: 25 Minutes
Ingredients:

2 chicken breasts, beaten into ½ inch thick	½ cup breadcrumbs
1 egg, beaten	2 tbsp marinara sauce
Salt and black pepper to taste	2 tbsp Grana Padano cheese, grated
	2 mozzarella cheese slices

Directions:
Dip the breasts into the egg, then into the crumbs and arrange on the fryer basket. Select AirFry function, adjust the temperature to 400 F, and press Start. Cook for 5 minutes, turn over, and drizzle with marinara sauce, Grana Padano and mozzarella cheeses. Cook for 5 more minutes.

96. Mini Salmon & Cheese Quiches

Servings: 15   Cooking Time: 20 Minutes
Ingredients:

15 mini tart cases	3 oz smoked salmon
4 eggs, lightly beaten	6 oz cream cheese, divided into 15 pieces
½ cup heavy cream	6 fresh dill
Salt and black pepper	

Directions:
Mix together eggs and heavy cream in a pourable measuring container. Arrange the tarts on the basket. Fill them with the mixture, halfway up the side and top with salmon and cream cheese. Bake for 10 minutes at 340 F on Bake function, regularly checking to avoid overcooking. Sprinkle with dill and serve chilled.

97. Sausage Mushroom Caps(1)

Servings: 2   Cooking Time: 20 Minutes
Ingredients:

½ lb. Italian sausage	2 tbsp. blanched finely ground almond flour
6 large Portobello mushroom caps	
¼ cup grated Parmesan cheese.	1 tsp. minced fresh garlic
¼ cup chopped onion	

Directions:
Use a spoon to hollow out each mushroom cap, reserving scrapings.   In a medium skillet over medium heat, brown the sausage about 10 minutes or until fully cooked and no pink remains. Drain and then add reserved mushroom scrapings, onion, almond flour, Parmesan and garlic.   Gently fold ingredients together and continue cooking an additional minute, then remove from heat   Evenly spoon the mixture into mushroom caps and place

the caps into a 6-inch round pan. Place pan into the air fryer basket   Adjust the temperature to 375 Degrees F and set the timer for 8 minutes. When finished cooking, the tops will be browned and bubbling. Serve warm.

Nutrition Info: Calories: 404; Protein: 23g; Fiber: 5g; Fat: 28g; Carbs: 12g

98. Shrimp With Spices

Servings: 3   Cooking Time: 15 Minutes
Ingredients:

½ pound shrimp, deveined	½ tsp Cajun seasoning
Salt and black pepper to taste	1 tbsp olive oil
	¼ tsp paprika

Directions:
Preheat Cuisinart on Air Fry function to 390 F. In a bowl, mix paprika, salt, pepper, olive oil, and Cajun seasoning. Add in the shrimp and toss to coat. Transfer the prepared shrimp to the AirFryer basket and fit in the baking tray. Cook for 10-12 minutes, flipping halfway through.

99. Savory Curly Potatoes

Servings: 2   Cooking Time: 20 Minutes
Ingredients:

2 potatoes, spiralized	Salt and black pepper to taste
1 tbsp extra-virgin olive oil	1 tsp paprika

Directions:
Preheat Cuisinart on Air Fry function to 350 F. Place the potatoes in a bowl and coat with oil. Transfer them to the cooking basket and fit in the baking tray. Cook for 15 minutes, shaking once. Sprinkle with salt, pepper, and paprika and to serve.

100. Cheese & Zucchini Cake With Yogurt

Servings: 4   Cooking Time: 20 Minutes
Ingredients:

1 ½ cups flour	1 tbsp yogurt
1 tsp cinnamon	½ cup zucchini, shredded
3 eggs	
1 tsp baking powder	A pinch of salt
2 tbsp sugar	2 tbsp cream cheese, softened
1 cup milk	
2 tbsp butter, melted	

Directions:
In a bowl, whisk eggs with sugar, salt, cinnamon, cream cheese, flour, and baking powder. In another bowl, combine all of the liquid ingredients. Gently combine the dry and liquid mixtures.   Stir in zucchini. Line the muffin tins with baking paper and pour in the batter. Arrange on a baking tray and place in the oven. Press Start and cook for 15 minutes. Serve chilled.

101. Sunday Calamari Rings

Servings: 4   Cooking Time: 20 Minutes
Ingredients:

1 lb calamari (squid), cut in rings	2 large beaten eggs
¼ cup flour	1 cup breadcrumbs

Directions:
Coat the calamari rings with the flour and dip them in the eggs. Then, roll in the breadcrumbs. Refrigerate for 2 hours. Line them in the frying basket and spray with cooking spray. Select AirFry function, adjust the temperature to 380 F, and press Start. Cook for 14 minutes. Serve with garlic mayo and lemon wedges.

---

102.   Air Fryer Corn

Servings: 2   Cooking Time: 10 Minutes
Ingredients:

2 fresh ears of corn, remove husks, wash, and pat dry	1 tbsp fresh lemon juice
2 tsp oil	Pepper
	Salt

Directions:
Fit the Cuisinart oven with the rack in position 2. Cut the corn to fit in the air fryer basket. Drizzle oil over the corn. Season with pepper and salt. Place corn in the air fryer basket then places an air fryer basket in the baking pan. Place a baking pan on the oven rack. Set to air fry at 400 F for 10 minutes.   Serve and enjoy.   Drizzle lemon juice over corn and serve.

Nutrition Info: Calories 122 Fat 5.6 g Carbohydrates 18.2 g Sugar 4.2 g Protein 3.1 g Cholesterol 0 mg

---

103.   Jicama Fries(3)

Servings: 4   Cooking Time: 20 Minutes
Ingredients:

1 small jicama; peeled.	¼ tsp. ground black pepper
¼ tsp. onion powder.	¼ tsp. garlic powder.
¾tsp. chili powder	

Directions:
Cut jicama into matchstick-sized pieces. Place pieces into a small bowl and sprinkle with remaining ingredients. Place the fries into the air fryer basket Adjust the temperature to 350 Degrees F and set the timer for 20 minutes. Toss the basket two or three times during cooking. Serve warm.

Nutrition Info: Calories: 37; Protein: 8g; Fiber: 7g; Fat: 1g; Carbs: 7g

104.   Yummy Savory French Toasts

Servings: 2   Cooking Time: 4 Minutes

Ingredients:

¼ cup chickpea flour
3 tablespoons onion, chopped finely
2 teaspoons green chili, seeded and chopped finely
Water, as required
4 bread slices
½ teaspoon red chili powder
¼ teaspoon ground turmeric
¼ teaspoon ground cumin
Salt, to taste

Directions:

Preheat the Air fryer to 375F and line an Air fryer pan with a foil paper.   Mix together all the ingredients in a large bowl except the bread slices. Spread the mixture over both sides of the bread slices and transfer into the Air fryer pan.   Cook for about 4 minutes and remove from the Air fryer to serve.

Nutrition Info: Calories: 151 Cal Total Fat: 2.2 g Saturated Fat: 0 g   Cholesterol: 0 mg   Sodium: 234 mg   Total Carbs: 26.7 g   Fiber: 0 g   Sugar: 4.3 g   Protein: 6.5 g

105.   Bacon Ranch Breakfast Bake

Servings: 6   Cooking Time: 35 Minutes

Ingredients:

Nonstick cooking spray
1 can refrigerated crescent rolls
1 ½ lbs. bacon, chop & cook crisp
6 eggs
1 ½ cups cheddar cheese, grated
½ cup milk
1 ½ tbsp. dry Ranch dressing mix
½ tsp pepper

Directions:

Place the rack in the oven in position one. Lightly spray an 8x11-inch baking pan with cooking spray. Unroll crescents and press on the bottom and sides of prepared pan, pressing the seams together. Sprinkle bacon over the bottom then top with cheese. In a medium bowl, whisk together eggs, milk, dressing mix, and pepper until combined. Pour over bacon and cheese.   Set to bake at 350°F for 35 minutes. After 5 minutes, place the pan in the oven and bake until the center is set.   Let cool slightly before cutting and serving.

Nutrition Info: Calories 706, Total Fat 48g, Saturated Fat 17g, Total Carbs 17g, Net Carbs 16g, Protein 24g, Sugar 4g, Fiber 1g, Sodium 915mg, Potassium 300mg, Phosphorus 349mg

106.   Simply Bacon

Servings: 1 Person   Cooking Time: 10 Minutes

Ingredients:

4 pieces of bacon

Directions:

Place the bacon strips on the instant vortex air fryer. Cook for 10 minutes   at 200 degrees Celsius. Check when it browns and shows to be ready. Serve.

Nutrition Info: Calories 165, Fat 13g, Proteins 12 g, Carbs 0g

107.   Sweet Potato Chickpeas Hash

Servings: 4   Cooking Time: 30 Minutes

Ingredients:

14.5 oz can chickpeas, drained
1 tsp paprika
1 tsp garlic powder
1 sweet potato, peeled and cubed
1 tbsp olive oil
1 bell pepper, chopped
1 onion, diced
1/2 tsp ground black pepper
1 tsp salt

Directions:

Fit the Cuisinart oven with the rack in position Spread sweet potato, chickpeas, bell pepper, and onion in a baking pan.   Drizzle with oil and season with paprika, garlic powder, pepper, and salt. Stir well.   Set to bake at 390 F for 35 minutes, after 5 minutes, place the baking pan in the oven.

Nutrition Info: Calories 203 Fat 4.9 g Carbohydrates 34.9 g Sugar 4.7 g Protein 6.5 g Cholesterol 0 mg

108.   Savory Cheddar & Cauliflower Tater Tots

Servings: 4   Cooking Time: 35 Minutes

Ingredients:

2 lb cauliflower florets, steamed
5 oz cheddar cheese, shredded
1 onion, diced
1 cup breadcrumbs
1 tsp fresh parsley, chopped
1 egg, beaten
1 tsp fresh oregano, chopped
1 tsp fresh chives, chopped
1 tsp garlic powder
Salt and black pepper to taste

Directions:

Mash the cauliflower and place it in a large bowl. Add in the onion, parsley, oregano, chives, garlic powder, salt, pepper, and cheddar cheese. Mix with your hands until thoroughly combined and form 12 balls out of the mixture.   Line a baking sheet with parchment paper. Dip half of the tater tots into the egg and then coat with breadcrumbs. Arrange them on the AirFryer Basket and spray with cooking spray. Fit in the baking sheet and cook in the fryer oven at 390 minutes for 10-12 minutes on Air Fry function. Serve.

109.   Buttery Orange Toasts

Servings: 6   Cooking Time: 15 Minutes

Ingredients:

12 bread slices
½ cup sugar
1 ½ tbsp vanilla extract
1 stick butter
1 ½ tbsp cinnamon
2 oranges, zested

Directions:

Mix butter, sugar, and vanilla extract and microwave the mixture for 30 seconds until it melts. Add in orange zest. Spread the mixture onto bread slices. Lay the bread slices on the cooking basket and cook in the Cuisinart oven for 5 minutes at 400 F on Toast function. Serve warm.

110.   Strawberry Cheesecake Pastries

Servings: 6   Cooking Time: 20 Minutes

Ingredients:

1 sheet puff pastry, thawed	1 ½ cups strawberries, sliced
¼ cup cream cheese, soft	1 egg
1 tbsp. strawberry jam	1 tbsp. water
	6 tsp powdered sugar, sifted

Directions:

Line the baking pan with parchment paper.   Lay the puff pastry on a cutting board and cut into 6 rectangles. Transfer to prepared pan, placing them 1-inch apart.   Lightly score the pastry, creating a ½-inch border, do not cut all the way through. Use a fork to prick the center.   In a small bowl, combine cream cheese and jam until thoroughly combined. Spoon mixture evenly into centers of the pastry and spread it within the scored area.   Top pastries with sliced berries.   In a small bowl, whisk together egg and water. Brush edges of pastry with the egg wash.   Set to bake at 350°F for 20 minutes. After 5 minutes, place the baking pan in position 1 and bake pastries until golden brown and puffed.   Remove from oven and let cool. Dust with powdered sugar before serving.

Nutrition Info: Calories 205, Total Fat 13g, Saturated Fat 4g, Total Carbs 19g, Net Carbs 18g, Protein 3g, Sugar 6g, Fiber 1g, Sodium 107mg, Potassium 97mg, Phosphorus 50mg

111. Healthy Breakfast Cookies

Servings: 12   Cooking Time: 15 Minutes

Ingredients:

2 cups quick oats	1/2 cup mashed banana
1/4 cup chocolate chips	1/4 cup applesauce
1 1/2 tbsp chia seeds	1/4 cup honey
1/4 cup shredded coconut	1/2 tsp cinnamon
	3/4 cup almond butter

Directions:

Fit the Cuisinart oven with the rack in position Line baking pan with parchment paper and set aside. Add all ingredients into the mixing bowl and mix until well combined.   Using a cookie scoop drop 12 scoops of oat mixture onto a prepared baking pan and lightly flatten the cookie.   Set to bake at 325 F for 20 minutes. After 5 minutes place the baking pan in the preheated oven.   Serve and enjoy.

Nutrition Info: Calories 117 Fat 3.4 g Carbohydrates 20.1 g Sugar 9.2 g Protein 2.6 g Cholesterol 1 mg

112. Hearty Sweet Potato Baked Oatmeal

Servings: 6   Cooking Time: 30 Minutes

Ingredients:

1 egg, lightly beaten	1 tsp baking powder
1 tsp vanilla	1/4 tsp nutmeg

1 1/2 cups milk	2 tsp cinnamon
2 tbsp ground flax seed	1/3 cup maple syrup
1 cup sweet potato puree	2 cups old fashioned oats
	1/4 tsp salt

Directions:

Fit the Cuisinart oven with the rack in position Spray an 8-inch square baking pan with cooking spray and set aside.   Add all ingredients except oats into the mixing bowl and mix until well combined.   Add oats and stir until just combined. Pour mixture into the prepared baking pan.   Set to bake at 350 F for 35 minutes. After 5 minutes place the baking pan in the preheated oven.   Serve and enjoy.

Nutrition Info: Calories 355 Fat 6.3 g Carbohydrates 62.3 g Sugar 17.1 g Protein 10.9 g Cholesterol 32 mg

113. Crispy Tilapia Tacos

Servings: 4   Cooking Time: 5 Minutes

Ingredients:

2 tablespoons milk	1 pound (454 g) skinless tilapia fillets, cut into 3-inch-long and 1-inch-wide strips
1/3 cup mayonnaise	
¼ teaspoon garlic powder	
1 teaspoon chili powder	4 small flour tortillas
1½ cups panko bread crumbs	Lemon wedges, for topping
½ teaspoon salt	Cooking spray
4 teaspoons canola oil	

Directions:

Spritz the air fryer basket with cooking spray. Combine the milk, mayo, garlic powder, and chili powder in a bowl. Stir to mix well. Combine the panko with salt and canola oil in a separate bowl. Stir to mix well.   Dredge the tilapia strips in the milk mixture first, then dunk the strips in the panko mixture to coat well. Shake the excess off. Arrange the tilapia strips in the pan.   Put the air fryer basket on the baking pan and slide into Rack Position 2, select Air Fry, set temperature to 400°F (205°C) and set time to 5 minutes.   Flip the strips halfway through the cooking time.   When cooking is complete, the strips will be opaque on all sides and the panko will be golden brown.   Unfold the tortillas on a large plate, then divide the tilapia strips over the tortillas. Squeeze the lemon wedges on top before serving.

114. Easy Zucchini Frittata

Servings: 4   Cooking Time: 30 Minutes

Ingredients:

2 zucchinis, chopped and cooked	8 eggs
1 tbsp fresh parsley, chopped	1/2 tsp Italian seasoning
3 tbsp cheddar cheese, grated	Pepper
	Salt

Directions:

Fit the Cuisinart oven with the rack in position   In a bowl, whisk eggs with Italian seasoning, pepper, and salt.   Add parsley, cheese, and zucchini and stir well.   Pour egg mixture into the greased baking dish.   Set to bake at 350 F for 35 minutes. After 5 minutes place the baking dish in the preheated oven.   Serve and enjoy.

Nutrition Info: Calories 165 Fat 10.9 g Carbohydrates 4.2 g Sugar 2.5 g Protein 13.6 g Cholesterol 333 mg

115. Lemon Vanilla Cupcakes With Yogurt Frost

Servings: 4   Cooking Time: 25 Minutes

Ingredients:

Lemon Frosting:	½ cup flour + extra
1 cup natural yogurt	for basing
2 tbsp sugar	¼ tsp salt
1 orange, juiced	2 tbsp sugar
1 tbsp orange zest	1 tsp baking powder
7 oz cream cheese, softened	1 tsp vanilla extract
Cupcake:	2 eggs
2 lemons, seeded and quartered	½ cup butter, softened
	2 tbsp milk

Directions:

In a bowl, add the yogurt and cream cheese. Mix until smooth. Add in the orange juice and zest; mix well. Gradually add the sugar while stirring until smooth. Make sure the frost is not runny. Set aside. Place the lemon quarters in a food processor and process it until pureed. Add the flour, baking powder, butter, milk, eggs, vanilla extract, sugar, and salt. Process again until smooth.   Preheat Cuisinart on Bake function to 360 F. Flour the bottom of 8 cupcake cases and spoon the batter into the cases ¾ way up. Place them in the Air Fryer tray and bake for 8-12 minutes. Once ready, remove and let cool. Design the cupcakes with the frosting and serve.

116. Easy Cheese Egg Casserole

Servings: 10   Cooking Time: 40 Minutes

Ingredients:

12 eggs	1/3 cup milk
8 oz cheddar cheese, shredded	1/4 tsp pepper
	1 tsp salt

Directions:

Fit the Cuisinart oven with the rack in position Spray 9*13-inch casserole dish with cooking spray and set aside.   In a bowl, whisk eggs with milk, pepper, and salt.   Add shredded cheese and stir well.   Pour egg mixture into the prepared casserole dish.   Set to bake at 350 F for 45 minutes. After 5 minutes place the casserole dish in the preheated oven.   Serve and enjoy.

Nutrition Info: Calories 171 Fat 12.9 g Carbohydrates 1.1 g Sugar 0.9 g Protein 12.6 g Cholesterol 221 mg

117. Wheat &seed Bread

Servings: 4   Cooking Time: 18 Minutes

Ingredients:

3 1/2 ounces of flour	3 &1/2 ounces of
1 tsp. of yeast	wheat flour ¼ cup of
1 tsp. of salt	pumpkin seeds

Directions:

Mix the wheat flour, yeast, salt, seeds and the plain flour together in a large bowl. Stir in ¾ cup of lukewarm water and keep stirring until dough becomes soft.   Knead for another 5 minutes until the dough becomes elastic and smooth. Mold into a ball and cover with a plastic bag. Set aside for 30 minutes for it to rise.   Heat your air fryer to 392°F. Transfer the dough into a small pizza pan and place in the air fryer. Bake for 18 minutes until golden. Remove and place on a wire rack to cool.

Nutrition Info: Calories 116   Fat 9.4 g Carbohydrates 0.3 g   Sugar 0.2 g   Protein 6 g Cholesterol 21 mg

118. Eggs In A Hole

Servings: 1   Cooking Time: 7 Minutes

Ingredients:

2 eggs	Pepper and salt to
2 slices of bread	taste
2 tsp butter	

Directions:

Using a jar punch two holes in the middle of your bread slices. This is the area where you will place your eggs.   Preheat your fryer to 330-degree Fahrenheit for about 5 minutes. Spread a tablespoon of butter into the pan and then add bread from the slices.   Crack the eggs and place them at the center of the bread slices and lightly season them with salt and pepper.   Take out your slices and rebutter the pan with the remaining butter and fry the other part for 3 minutes.   Serve while hot.

Nutrition Info: Calories 787 Fat 51g, Carbohydrates 60g, Proteins 22g.

119. Spinach Egg Breakfast

Servings: 4   Cooking Time: 20 Minutes

Ingredients:

1/4 cup parmesan cheese, grated 4 oz	3 eggs
spinach, chopped	1/4 cup coconut milk
	3 oz cottage cheese

Directions:

Preheat the air fryer to 350 F.   Add eggs, milk, half parmesan cheese, and cottage cheese in a bowl and whisk well. Add spinach and stir well.   Pour mixture into the air fryer baking dish.   Sprinkle remaining half parmesan cheese on top.   Place dish in the air fryer and cook for 20 minutes. Serve and enjoy.

Nutrition Info: Calories 144   Fat 8.5 g Carbohydrates 2.5 g   Sugar 1.1 g   Protein 14 g Cholesterol 135 mg

120.   Spiced Squash Mix

Servings: 4   Cooking Time: 15 Minutes

Ingredients:

1 cup almond milk	¼ teaspoon allspice,
1 butternut squash, peeled and roughly cubed	ground
	¼ teaspoon
½ teaspoon cinnamon powder	cardamom, ground
	2 tablespoons brown
¼ teaspoon nutmeg, ground	sugar
	Cooking spray

Directions:
Spray your air fryer with cooking spray, add the squash, milk and the other ingredients, toss, cover and cook at 360 degrees F for 15 minutes. Divide into bowls and serve for breakfast.
Nutrition Info: calories 212, fat 5, fiber 7, carbs 14, protein 5

121. Banana Coconut Muffins

Servings: 12   Cooking Time: 15 Minutes
Ingredients:

1 egg	2 tsp baking powder
3 ripe bananas, mashed	1/2 tsp baking soda
1/2 cup shredded coconut	1 cup of sugar
	1 tsp vanilla
2 cups all-purpose flour	1/2 cup milk
	1/2 cup applesauce
	1/2 tsp salt

Directions:
Fit the Cuisinart oven with the rack in position Line a 12-cup muffin tray with cupcake liners and set aside. In a mixing bowl, whisk the egg with vanilla, milk, applesauce, and salt until well combined. Add baking powder, baking soda, and sugar and mix well. Add flour and mix until just combined. Add shredded coconut and stir well. Pour mixture into the prepared muffin tray. Set to bake at 350 F for 20 minutes. After 5 minutes place the muffin tray in the preheated oven. Serve and enjoy.
Nutrition Info: Calories 193 Fat 2 g Carbohydrates 41.9 g Sugar 22.1 g Protein 3.4 g Cholesterol 14 mg

122. Flavorful Pumpkin Bread

Servings: 12   Cooking Time: 55 Minutes
Ingredients:

2 eggs	1/4 tsp ground cloves
8 oz pumpkin puree	1/2 tsp ground nutmeg
1 3/4 cups flour	1/2 tsp ground cinnamon
1 1/2 cups sugar	
1/3 cup water	
1/2 cup vegetable oil	1 tsp baking soda
1/8 tsp ground ginger	3/4 tsp salt

Directions:
Fit the Cuisinart oven with the rack in position In a bowl, whisk eggs, sugar, water, oil, and pumpkin puree until combined. In a separate bowl, mix dry ingredients. Add dry ingredient mixture into the egg mixture and mix until well combined. Pour batter into the greased loaf pan. Set to bake at 350 F for 60 minutes, after 5 minutes, place the loaf pan in the oven. Slice and serve.
Nutrition Info: Calories 258 Fat 10.1 g Carbohydrates 40.7 g Sugar 25.8 g Protein 3 g Cholesterol 27 mg

123. Cheesy Potato & Spinach Frittata

Servings: 4   Cooking Time: 35 Minutes
Ingredients:

3 cups potato cubes, boiled	1 cup grated mozzarella cheese
2 cups spinach,	1/2 cup parsley,

chopped
5 eggs, lightly beaten
1/4 cup heavy cream

chopped
Fresh thyme, chopped
Salt and black pepper to taste

Directions:
Spray the Cuisinart Air Fryer tray with oil. Arrange the potatoes inside. In a bowl, whisk eggs, cream, spinach, mozzarella, parsley, thyme, salt and pepper, and pour over the potatoes. Cook in your Cuisinart for 16 minutes at 360 F on Bake function until nice and golden. Serve sliced.

124. Vanilla Brownies With White Chocolate & Walnuts

Servings: 4   Cooking Time: 35 Minutes
Ingredients:

6 oz dark chocolate, chopped	3/4 cup flour
6 oz butter	1/4 cup cocoa powder
3/4 cup white sugar	1 cup chopped walnuts
3 eggs, beaten	1 cup white chocolate chips
2 tsp vanilla extract	

Directions:
Line a baking pan with parchment paper. In a saucepan, melt chocolate and butter over low heat. Do not stop stirring until you obtain a smooth mixture. Let cool slightly and whisk in eggs and vanilla. Sift flour and cocoa and stir to mix well. Sprinkle the walnuts over and add the white chocolate into the batter. Pour the batter into the pan and cook for 20 minutes in the Cuisinart oven at 350 F on Bake function. Serve chilled with raspberry syrup and ice cream.

125. Crispy Cauliflowers With Alfredo Sauce

Servings: 4   Cooking Time: 20 Minutes
Ingredients:

4 cups cauliflower florets	1/4 cup alfredo sauce
1 tbsp butter, melted	1 cup breadcrumbs
	1 tsp salt

Directions:
Whisk alfredo sauce with butter. In a bowl, combine breadcrumbs with salt. Dip cauliflower into the alfredo mixture and then coat in the crumbs. Drop the prepared florets into the frying basket. Set the temperature to 350 F and press Start. Cook for 15 minutes on AirFry function.

126. Delicious Pumpkin Bread

Servings: 12   Cooking Time: 55 Minutes
Ingredients:

2 eggs	1 tsp cinnamon
1/4 cup olive oil	1/2 tsp baking soda
1/2 cup milk	2 tsp baking powder
1 cup of sugar	2 cups flour
1 cup pumpkin puree	1/2 tsp salt

Directions:
Fit the Cuisinart oven with the rack in position In a bowl, mix flour, baking soda, salt, and baking powder. In a separate bowl, whisk eggs with oil,

milk, sugar, and pumpkin puree. Add flour mixture into the egg mixture and mix until well combined. Pour mixture into the greased loaf pan. Set to bake at 350 F for 60 minutes. After 5 minutes place the loaf pan in the preheated oven. Slice and serve.

Nutrition Info: Calories 198 Fat 5.4 g Carbohydrates 35.3 g Sugar 17.9 g Protein 3.6 g Cholesterol 28 mg

127.Spicy Apple Turnovers

Servings: 4   Cooking Time: 20 Minutes
Ingredients:

1 cup diced apple	¼ teaspoon cinnamon
1 tablespoon brown sugar	
1 teaspoon freshly squeezed lemon juice	⅛ teaspoon allspice
1 teaspoon all-purpose flour, plus more for dusting	½ package frozen puff pastry, thawed
	1 large egg, beaten
	2 teaspoons granulated sugar

Directions:
Whisk together the apple, brown sugar, lemon juice, flour, cinnamon and allspice in a medium bowl. On a clean work surface, lightly dust with the flour and lay the puff pastry sheet. Using a rolling pin, gently roll the dough to smooth out the folds, seal any tears and form it into a square. Cut the dough into four squares. Spoon a quarter of the apple mixture into the center of each puff pastry square and spread it evenly in a triangle shape over half the pastry, leaving a border of about ½ inch around the edges of the pastry. Fold the pastry diagonally over the filling to form triangles. With a fork, crimp the edges to seal them. Place the turnovers in the baking pan, spacing them evenly. Cut two or three small slits in the top of each turnover. Brush with the egg. Sprinkle evenly with the granulated sugar. Slide the baking pan into Rack Position 1, select Convection Bake, set temperature to 350°F (180°C) and set time to 20 minutes. When cooking is complete, remove the pan from the oven. The turnovers should be golden brown and the filling bubbling. Let cool for about 10 minutes before serving.

128.   Spinach Egg Bites

Servings: 12   Cooking Time: 20 Minutes
Ingredients:

8 eggs	1/4 cup almond milk
1/4 cup green onion, chopped	1 cup roasted red peppers, chopped
1 cup spinach, chopped	1/2 tsp salt

Directions:
Fit the Cuisinart oven with the rack in position Spray 12-cups muffin tin with cooking spray and set aside. In a bowl, whisk eggs with milk and salt. Add spinach, green onion, and red peppers to the egg mixture and stir to combine. Pour egg mixture into the greased muffin tin. Set to bake at 350 F for 25 minutes, after 5 minutes, place muffin tin in the oven. Serve and enjoy.

Nutrition Info: Calories 59 Fat 4.2 g Carbohydrates 1.7 g Sugar 1.1 g Protein 4.1 g Cholesterol 109 mg

129.   Basil Prosciutto Crostini With Mozzarella

Servings: 1   Cooking Time: 7 Minutes
Ingredients:

½ cup tomatoes, chopped	3 prosciutto slices, chopped
3 oz mozzarella cheese, chopped	1 tsp dried basil
1 tbsp olive oil	6 small slices of French bread

Directions:
Preheat Cuisinart on Toast function to 350 F. Place in the bread slices and toast them for 5 minutes. Top the bread with tomatoes, prosciutto, and mozzarella. Sprinkle with basil. Drizzle with olive oil. Return to oven and cook for 1 more minute, enough to become melty and warm.

130.   Walnuts And Mango Oatmeal

Servings: 4   Cooking Time: 20 Minutes
Ingredients:

2 cups almond milk	1 cup mango, peeled and cubed
½ cup walnuts, chopped	3 tablespoons sugar
1 teaspoon vanilla extract	½ cup steel cut oats

Directions:
In your air fryer, combine the almond milk with the oats and the other ingredients, toss and cook at 360 degrees F for 20 minutes. Divide the mix into bowls and serve for breakfast.

Nutrition Info:calories 141, fat 4, fiber 7, carbs 8, protein 5

131.Zucchini Omelet

Servings: 2   Cooking Time: 14 Minutes
Ingredients:

1 teaspoon butter	¼ teaspoon red pepper flakes, crushed
1 zucchini, julienned	
4 eggs	
¼ teaspoon fresh basil, chopped	Salt and ground black pepper, as required

Directions:
In a skillet, melt the butter over medium heat and cook the zucchini for about 3-4 minutes. Remove from the heat and set aside to cool slightly. Meanwhile, in a bowl, mix together the eggs, basil, red pepper flakes, salt, and black pepper. Add the cooked zucchini and gently, stir to combine. Place the zucchini mixture into a small baking pan. Press "Power Button" of Air Fry Oven and turn the dial to select the "Air Fry" mode. Press the Time button and again turn the dial to set the cooking time to 10 minutes. Now push the Temp button and rotate the dial to set the temperature at 355 degrees F. Press "Start/Pause" button to start. When the unit beeps to show that it is preheated, open the lid. Arrange pan over the "Wire Rack" and insert in the oven. Cut the omelet into 2 portions and serve hot.

Nutrition Info: Calories 159 Total Fat 10.9 g Saturated Fat 4 g Cholesterol 332 mg Sodium 224 mg Total Carbs 4.1 g Fiber 1.1 g Sugar 2.4 g Protein 12.3 g

132.   Asparagus And Cheese Strata

Servings: 4   Cooking Time: 17 Minutes

Ingredients:

- 6 asparagus spears, cut into 2-inch pieces
- 1 tablespoon water
- 2 slices whole-wheat bread, cut into ½-inch cubes
- 3 tablespoons whole milk
- 4 eggs
- 2 tablespoons chopped flat-leaf parsley
- ½ cup grated Havarti or Swiss cheese
- Pinch salt
- Freshly ground black pepper, to taste
- Cooking spray

Directions:

Add the asparagus spears and 1 tablespoon of water in the baking pan.   Slide the baking pan into Rack Position 1, select Convection Bake, set temperature to 330°F (166°C) and set time to 4 minutes. When cooking is complete, the asparagus spears will be crisp-tender.   Remove the asparagus from the pan and drain on paper towels.   Spritz the pan with cooking spray. Place the bread and asparagus in the pan.   Whisk together the eggs and milk in a medium mixing bowl until creamy. Fold in the parsley, cheese, salt, and pepper and stir to combine. Pour this mixture into the baking pan.   Select Bake and set time to 13 minutes. Put the pan back to the oven. When done, the eggs will be set and the top will be lightly browned.   Let cool for 5 minutes before slicing and serving.

133.   Thai Pork Sliders

Servings: 6 Sliders   Cooking Time: 14 Minutes

Ingredients:

- 1 pound (454 g) ground pork
- 1 tablespoon Thai curry paste
- 1½ tablespoons fish sauce
- 2 tablespoons minced peeled fresh ginger
- 1 tablespoon light brown sugar
- ¼ cup thinly sliced scallions, white and green parts
- 1 teaspoon ground black pepper
- 6 slider buns, split open lengthwise, warmed
- Cooking spray

Directions:

Spritz the air fryer basket with cooking spray. Combine all the ingredients, except for the buns in a large bowl. Stir to mix well.   Divide and shape the mixture into six balls, then bash the balls into six 3-inch-diameter patties.   Arrange the patties in the basket and spritz with cooking spray.   Put the air fryer basket on the baking pan and slide into Rack Position 2, select Air Fry, set temperature to 375°F (190°C) and set time to 14 minutes.   Flip the patties halfway through the cooking time.   When cooked, the patties should be well browned. Assemble the buns with patties to make the sliders and serve immediately.

134.   Creamy Vanilla Berry Mini Pies

Servings: 4   Cooking Time: 20 Minutes

Ingredients:

- 4 pastry dough sheets
- 2 tbsp mashed strawberries
- 2 tbsp mashed raspberries
- ¼ tsp vanilla extract
- 2 cups cream cheese, softened
- 1 tbsp honey

Directions:

Preheat fryer on Bake function to 375 F. Divide the cream cheese between the dough sheets and spread it evenly. In a small bowl, combine the berries, honey, and vanilla. Spoon the mixture into the pastry sheets. Pinch the ends of the sheets to form puff. Place the puffs in a lined baking dish. Place the dish in the toaster oven and cook for 15 minutes. Serve chilled.

135.   Sweet Breakfast Casserole

Servings: 4   Cooking Time: 30 Minutes

Ingredients:

- 3 tablespoons brown sugar
- 4 tablespoons margarine
- 2 tablespoons white sugar
- 1/2 tsp. cinnamon powder
- 1/2 cup flour
- For the casserole:
- 2 eggs
- 2 tablespoons white sugar
- 2 and 1/2 cups white flour
- 1 tsp. baking soda
- 1 tsp. baking powder
- 2 eggs
- 1/2 cup milk
- 2 cups margarine milk
- 4 tablespoons margarine
- Zest from 1 lemon, grated
- 1 and 2/3 cup blueberries

Directions:

In a bowl, mix eggs with 2 tablespoons white sugar, 2 and 1/2 cups white flour, baking powder, baking soda, 2 eggs, milk, margarine milk, 4 tablespoons margarine, lemon zest and blueberries, stir and pour into a pan that fits your air fryer.   In another bowls, mix 3 tablespoons brown sugar with 2 tablespoons white sugar, 4 tablespoons margarine, 1/2 cup flour and cinnamon, stir until you obtain a crumble and spread over blueberries mix.   Place in preheated air fryer and bake at 300 °F for 30 minutes.   Divide among plates and serve for breakfast.

Nutrition Info: Calories 101   Fat 9.4 g Carbohydrates 0.3 g   Sugar 0.2 g   Protein 7 g Cholesterol 21 mg

136.   Apple Butter Pancake

Ingredients:

- 1 tsp cinnamon
- ½ tsp ginger
- 3 large eggs, room temperature
- ¾ cup whole milk
- ¾ cup all-purpose flour
- 1 tsp almond extract
- ¼ tsp salt
- 2 Granny Smith apples, peeled, cored and sliced
- 1 Tbsp sugar
- 4 Tbsp butter, divided
- 2 tsp light brown sugar

Directions:

Preheat oven to 400°F. Whisk together eggs, milk, flour, extract and salt. Place sliced apples in a bowl with sugar, cinnamon and ginger. Melt 2 Tbsp butter in heated Cuisinart oven. Sprinkle brown sugar inside pot. Add apples and cook until apples have softened. Transfer to plate. Wipe out Cuisinart oven and melt remaining 2 Tbsp butter. When pot is very hot, add apples and pour batter. Bake for about 13-15 minutes.

137. Apple Fritter Loaf

Servings: 10   Cooking Time: 1 Hour

Ingredients:

Butter flavored cooking spray	½ cup + ½ tbsp. butter, soft, divided
1/3 cup brown sugar, packed	2 ¼ tsp. vanilla, divided
1 tsp. cinnamon, divided	1 ½ cups flour
1 ½ cups apples, chopped	2 tsp baking powder
2/3 cup + 1 tsp. sugar, divided	¼ tsp salt
2 eggs	½ cup + 2 tbsp. milk
	1/2 cup powdered sugar

Directions:

Place rack in position 1 of the oven. Spray an 8-inch loaf pan with cooking spray. In a small bowl, combine brown sugar and ½ teaspoon cinnamon. Place apples in a medium bowl and sprinkle with remaining cinnamon and 1 teaspoon sugar, toss to coat. In a large bowl, beat remaining sugar and butter until smooth. Beat in eggs and 2 teaspoons vanilla until combined. Stir in flour, baking powder, and salt until combined. Add ½ cup milk and beat until smooth. Pour half the batter in the prepared pan. Add half the apples then remaining batter. Add the remaining apples over the top, pressing lightly. Sprinkle brown sugar mixture over the apples. Set oven to convection bake at 325°F for 5 minutes. Once timer goes, off place bread on the rack and set timer to 1 hour. Bread is done when it passes the toothpick test. Let cool in pan 10 minutes, then invert onto wire rack to cool. In a small bowl, whisk together powdered sugar and butter until smooth. Whisk in remaining milk and vanilla and drizzle over cooled bread.

Nutrition Info: Calories 418, Total Fat 14g, Saturated Fat 8g, Total Carbs 44g, Net Carbs 43g, Protein 4g, Sugar 28g, Fiber 1g, Sodium 85mg, Potassium 190mg, Phosphorus 128mg

138.   Cinnamon-orange Toast

Servings: 6   Cooking Time: 15 Minutes

Ingredients:

12 slices bread	1 stick butter
½ cup sugar	1½ tbsp cinnamon
1½ tbsp vanilla extract	2 oranges, zested

Directions:

Mix butter, sugar, and vanilla extract and microwave for 30 seconds until everything melts. Add in orange zest. Pour the mixture over bread slices. Lay the bread slices in your Cuisinart Air Fryer pan and cook for 5 minutes at 400 F on Toast function. Serve with berry sauce.

139.   Bacon And Hot Dogs Omelet

Servings: 2   Cooking Time: 10 Minutes

Ingredients:

4 eggs	2 hot dogs, chopped
1 bacon slice, chopped	2 tablespoons milk
2 small onions, chopped	Salt and black pepper, to taste

Directions:

Preheat the Air fryer to 325F and grease an Air Fryer pan. Whisk together eggs and stir in the remaining ingredients. Stir well to combine and place in the Air fryer. Cook for about 10 minutes and serve hot.

Nutrition Info: Calories: 418 Cal Total Fat: 31.5 g Saturated Fat: 0 g Cholesterol: 0 mg Sodium: 1000 mg Total Carbs: 9.7 g Fiber: 0 g Sugar: 5.6 g Protein: 23.4 g

140.   Caprese Sandwich With Sourdough Bread

Servings: 2   Cooking Time: 15 Minutes

Ingredients:

4 slices sourdough bread	1 tomato, sliced
2 tbsp mayonnaise	2 slices mozzarella cheese
2 slices ham	Salt and black pepper to taste
2 lettuce leaves	

Directions:

On a clean board, lay the sourdough slices and spread with mayonnaise. Top 2 of the slices with ham, lettuce, tomato, and mozzarella cheese. Season with salt and pepper. Top with the remaining two slices to form two sandwiches. Spray with oil and transfer to the Cuisinart Air Fryer basket. Fit in the baking tray and cook for 10 minutes at 350 F on Bake function, flipping once halfway through cooking. Serve hot.

141. Raspberries Maple Pancakes

Servings: 4   Cooking Time: 15 Minutes

Ingredients:

2 cups all-purpose flour	1 ½ tsp vanilla extract
1 cup milk	½ cup frozen raspberries, thawed
3 eggs, beaten	
1 tsp baking powder	2 tbsp maple syrup
1 cup brown sugar	A pinch of salt

Directions:

Preheat Cuisinart on Bake function to 400 F. In a bowl, mix the flour, baking powder, salt, milk, eggs, vanilla extract, and sugar until smooth. Stir in the raspberries. Do it gently to avoid coloring the batter. Grease a pie pan with cooking spray. Drop the batter onto the pan. Make sure to leave some space between the pancakes. Cook for 10-15 minutes. Drizzle with maple syrup and serve.

142. Egg And Avocado Burrito

Servings: 4   Cooking Time: 4 Minutes

Ingredients:

4 low-sodium whole-wheat flour tortillas
Filling:
1 hard-boiled egg, chopped
1 ripe avocado, peeled, pitted, and chopped
1 (1.2-ounce / 34-g) slice low-sodium, low-fat American cheese, torn into pieces

2 hard-boiled egg whites, chopped
1 red bell pepper, chopped
3 tablespoons low-sodium salsa, plus additional for serving (optional)
Special Equipment:
4 toothpicks (optional), soaked in water for at least 30 minutes

Directions:

Make the filling: Combine the egg, egg whites, avocado, red bell pepper, cheese, and salsa in a medium bowl and stir until blended.   Assemble the burritos: Arrange the tortillas on a clean work surface and place ¼ of the prepared filling in the middle of each tortilla, leaving about 1½-inch on each end unfilled. Fold in the opposite sides of each tortilla and roll up. Secure with toothpicks through the center, if needed.   Transfer the burritos to the air fryer basket.   Put the air fryer basket on the baking pan and slide into Rack Position 2, select Air Fry, set temperature to 390°F (199°C) and set time to 4 minutes.   When cooking is complete, the burritos should be crisp and golden brown.   Allow to cool for 5 minutes and serve with salsa, if desired.

143. Easy French Toast Casserole

Servings: 6   Cooking Time: 12 Minutes

Ingredients:

3 large eggs, beaten
1 cup whole milk
1 tablespoon pure maple syrup
1 teaspoon vanilla extract
¼ teaspoon cinnamon
¼ teaspoon kosher salt
3 cups stale bread cubes

1 tablespoon unsalted butter, at room temperature
In a medium bowl, whisk together the eggs, milk, maple syrup, vanilla extract, cinnamon and salt.
Stir in the bread cubes to coat well.

Directions:

Grease the bottom of the baking pan with the butter. Spread the bread mixture into the pan in an even layer.   Slide the baking pan into Rack Position 2, select Roast, set temperature to 350°F (180°C) and set time to 12 minutes.   After about 10 minutes, remove the pan and check the casserole. The top should be browned and the middle of the casserole just set. If more time is needed, return the pan to the oven and continue cooking.   When cooking is complete, serve warm.

144. Zucchini Fritters

Servings: 4   Cooking Time: 7 Minutes

Ingredients:

10½ ounces zucchini, grated and squeezed
7 ounces Halloumi cheese
¼ cup all-purpose flour

2 eggs
1 teaspoon fresh dill, minced
Salt and black pepper, to taste

Directions:

Preheat the Air fryer to 360F and grease a baking dish.   Mix together all the ingredients in a large bowl.   Make small fritters from this mixture and place them on the prepared baking dish.   Transfer the dish in the Air Fryer basket and cook for about 7 minutes.   Dish out and serve warm.

Nutrition Info: Calories: 250 Cal Total Fat: 17.2 g Saturated Fat: 0 g   Cholesterol: 0 mg   Sodium: 330 mg   Total Carbs: 10 g   Fiber: 0 g   Sugar: 2.7 g   Protein: 15.2 g

145. Grilled Cheese Sandwich

Servings: 1 Person   Cooking Time: 12 Minutes

Ingredients:

2 slices of bread
2 pieces of bacon
½ tsp of olive oil side

Tomatoes
Jack cheese
Peach preserves

Directions:

If you have left over bacon from air fried bacon recipe you can get two pieces. However, if you do not have any leftover bacon you can get two pieces and fry them at 200 degree Celsius.   Place olive oil on the side of the bread slices. Layer the rest of the ingredients on the non-oiled side following the following steps, peach preserves, tomatoes, jack cheese and cooked bacon.   Press down the bread to allow it to cook a little bit and peach side down too to allow the bread and the peel to spread evenly. Place the sandwich in an air fryer and cook it for 12 minutes   at 393 degrees Fahrenheit.   Serve once you are done.

Nutrition Info: Calories 282 Fats 18g, Carbs 18g, Proteins 12g, Sodium: 830 Mg, Potassium: 250mg

146. Garlic And Cheese Bread Rolls

Servings: 2   Cooking Time: 5 Minutes

Ingredients:

8 tablespoons of grated cheese
6 tsp.s of melted margarine

Garlic bread spice mix
2 bread rolls

Directions:

Slice the bread rolls from top in a crisscross pattern but not cut through at the bottom.   Put all the cheese into the slits and brush the tops of the bread rolls with melted margarine. Sprinkle the garlic mix on the rolls.   Heat the air fryer to 350°F. Place the rolls into the basket and cook until cheese is melted for about 5 minutes.

Nutrition Info: Calories 113   Fat 8.2 g Carbohydrates 0.3 g   Sugar 0.2 g   Protein 5.4 g Cholesterol 18 mg

147. Stylish Ham Omelet

Servings: 2   Cooking Time: 30 Minutes

Ingredients:

4 small tomatoes, chopped	2 tablespoons cheddar cheese
4 eggs	Salt and black pepper, to taste
2 ham slices	
1 onion, chopped	

Directions:

Preheat the Air fryer to 390F and grease an Air fryer pan. Place the tomatoes in the Air fryer pan and cook for about 10 minutes. Heat a nonstick skillet on medium heat and add onion and ham. Stir fry for about 5 minutes and transfer into the Air fryer pan. Whisk together eggs, salt and black pepper in a bowl and pour in the Air fryer pan. Set the Air fryer to 335F and cook for about 15 minutes. Dish out and serve warm.

Nutrition Info: Calories: 255 Cal Total Fat: 13.9 g Saturated Fat: 0 g Cholesterol: 0 mg Sodium: 543 mg Total Carbs: 14.1 g Fiber: 0 g Sugar: 7.8 g Protein: 19.7 g

---

148. Cheesy Hash Brown Cups

Servings: 6 Cooking Time: 9 Minutes

Ingredients:

4 eggs, beaten	1 cup diced ham
2¼ cups frozen hash browns, thawed	½ teaspoon Cajun seasoning
½ cup shredded Cheddar cheese	Cooking spray

Directions:

Lightly spritz a 12-cup muffin tin with cooking spray. Combine the beaten eggs, hash browns, diced ham, cheese, and Cajun seasoning in a medium bowl and stir until well blended. Spoon a heaping 1½ tablespoons of egg mixture into each muffin cup. Put the muffin tin into Rack Position 1, select Convection Bake, set temperature to 350°F (180°C) and set time to 9 minutes. When cooked, the muffins will be golden brown. Allow to cool for 5 to 10 minutes on a wire rack and serve warm.

---

149. Herby Parmesan Bagel

Servings: 1 Cooking Time: 10 Minutes

Ingredients:

2 tbsp butter, softened	1 tbsp Parmesan cheese
1 tsp dried basil	Salt and black pepper to taste
1 tsp dried parsley	
1 tsp garlic powder	1 bagel

Directions:

Preheat Cuisinart on Bake function to 370 degrees. Cut the bagel in half. Combine the butter, Parmesan cheese, garlic, basil, and parsley in a small bowl. Season with salt and pepper. Spread the mixture onto the bagel. Place the bagel in a baking pan and cook for 5 minutes. Serve. Top each slice with 2 mozzarella slices. Return to the oven and cook for 1 minute more. Drizzle the caprese toasts with olive oil and top with chopped basil.

---

150. Pigs In A Blanket

Servings: 6 Cooking Time: 25 Minutes

Ingredients:

| 12 breakfast sausage links, cooked | ¾ cup Southwest hash browns, thawed |

| 6 eggs, scrambled | 2 tubes French bread loaf, refrigerated |
| ½ cup sharp cheddar cheese, grated | |

Directions:

Spray the baking pan with cooking spray. Open up can of bread loaf. Divide the dough in half. On a lightly floured surface, roll one half into a 5x12-inch rectangle. Place 3 sausage links along the dough, leaving room in between. Cut dough into 3 equal pieces. Top each sausage with a tablespoon of hash browns, tablespoon of egg, and a sprinkling of cheese. Roll up and seal the edges. Place seam side down on prepared pan. Repeat with remaining dough and filling ingredients. Set oven to convection bake at 325°F for 30 minutes. After 5 minutes, place the pan in position 1 of the oven. Bake for 25 minutes, or until bread is golden brown and cooked through. Let cool on wire rack 5 minutes before serving.

Nutrition Info: Calories 718, Total Fat 14g, Saturated Fat 5g, Total Carbs 74g, Net Carbs 71g, Protein 24g, Sugar 7g, Fiber 3g, Sodium 1115mg, Potassium 321mg, Phosphorus 261mg

---

151. Easy Cheesy Breakfast Casserole

Servings: 8 Cooking Time: 30 Minutes

Ingredients:

| 6 eggs, lightly beaten | 2 cups cheddar cheese, shredded |
| 8 oz can crescent rolls | 1 lb breakfast sausage, cooked |

Directions:

Fit the Cuisinart oven with the rack in position Spray a 9*13-inch baking dish with cooking spray and set aside. Spread crescent rolls in the bottom of the prepared baking dish and top with sausage, egg, and cheese. Set to bake at 350 F for 35 minutes. After 5 minutes place the baking dish in the preheated oven. Serve and enjoy.

Nutrition Info: Calories 465 Fat 34.6 g Carbohydrates 11.8 g Sugar 2.4 g Protein 24.2 g Cholesterol 200 mg

---

152. Golden Cod Tacos With Salsa

Servings: 4 Cooking Time: 15 Minutes

Ingredients:

2 eggs	1 tablespoon cumin
1¼ cups Mexican beer	Salt, to taste
1½ cups coconut flour	4 toasted corn tortillas
1½ cups almond flour	4 large lettuce leaves, chopped
½ tablespoon chili powder	¼ cup salsa
1 pound (454 g) cod fillet, slice into large pieces	Cooking spray

Directions:

Spritz the air fryer basket with cooking spray. Break the eggs in a bowl, then pour in the beer. Whisk to combine well. Combine the coconut flour, almond flour, chili powder, cumin, and salt in a separate bowl. Stir to mix well. Dunk the cod pieces in the egg mixture, then shake the excess off and dredge into the flour mixture to coat well. Arrange the cod in the pan. Put the air fryer basket on the baking pan and slide into Rack Position 2, select Air Fry, set temperature to 375°F (190°C) and set time to 15 minutes. Flip the cod halfway through the cooking time. When cooking is complete, the cod should be golden brown. Unwrap the toasted tortillas on a large plate, then divide the cod and lettuce leaves on top. Baste with salsa and wrap to serve.

153. Carrot Banana Bread

Servings: 12   Cooking Time: 55 Minutes

Ingredients:

1 egg	1 tsp baking soda
1/2 cup carrots, shredded	3/4 cup sugar
1/4 cup flaked coconut	1 1/2 cups flour
1/4 cup walnuts, chopped	1/2 cup mayonnaise
	3 bananas, mashed
	1/2 tsp salt

Directions:
Fit the Cuisinart oven with the rack in position In a bowl, whisk egg, mayonnaise, and mashed bananas. Add flour, baking soda, sugar, and salt and mix until well combined. Add carrots, coconut, and walnut and fold well. Pour mixture into the greased loaf pan. Set to bake at 350 F for 60 minutes. After 5 minutes place the loaf pan in the preheated oven. Serve and enjoy.
Nutrition Info: Calories 197 Fat 6 g Carbohydrates 34.5 g Sugar 17.2 g Protein 3.2 g Cholesterol 16 mg

154. Zucchini Breakfast Bread

Servings: 10   Cooking Time: 50 Minutes

Ingredients:

2 eggs	1/2 tsp baking powder
1 1/2 cups zucchini, grated	1/2 cup applesauce
1 tsp vanilla extract	1/4 cup coconut sugar
1/4 cup yogurt	1 tsp ground cinnamon
1 1/2 cups whole wheat flour	1/2 tsp baking soda
	1/2 cup apple, grated
	1/4 tsp sea salt

Directions:
Fit the Cuisinart oven with the rack in position In a bowl, mix all dry ingredients. In another bowl, whisk eggs, coconut sugar, vanilla, yogurt, and applesauce. Add dry ingredients mixture into the wet mixture and stir until well combined. Add apples and zucchini and stir well. Pour batter into the 9*5-inch greased loaf pan. Set to bake at 350 F for 55 minutes, after 5 minutes, place the loaf pan in the oven. Slice and serve.
Nutrition Info: Calories 103 Fat 1.2 g Carbohydrates 19.1 g Sugar 3.3 g Protein 3.7 g Cholesterol 33 mg

155. Creamy Quesadillas With Blueberries

Servings: 2   Cooking Time: 4 Minutes

Ingredients:

1/4 cup nonfat Ricotta cheese	1/2 teaspoon cinnamon
1/4 cup plain nonfat Greek yogurt	1/4 teaspoon vanilla extract
2 tablespoons finely ground flaxseeds	2 (8-inch) low-carb whole-wheat tortillas
1 tablespoon granulated stevia	1/2 cup fresh blueberries, divided

Directions:
Line the baking pan with aluminum foil. In a small bowl, whisk together the Ricotta cheese, yogurt, flaxseeds, stevia, cinnamon and vanilla. Place the tortillas on the prepared pan. Spread half of the yogurt mixture on each tortilla, almost to the edges. Top each tortilla with 1/4 cup of blueberries. Fold the tortillas in half. Slide the baking pan into Rack Position 1, select Convection Bake, set temperature to 400°F (205°C) and set time to 4 minutes. When cooking is complete, remove the pan from the oven. Serve immediately.

156. Spicy Egg Casserole

Servings: 8   Cooking Time: 45 Minutes

Ingredients:

10 eggs	4.5 oz can green chilies, chopped
1 cup Colby jack cheese, shredded	1/2 small onion, minced
1 cup cottage cheese	2 tbsp butter
1 tsp baking powder	1 tsp seasoned salt
1/3 cup flour	
1/2 cup milk	

Directions:
Fit the Cuisinart oven with the rack in position Spray 9*13-inch casserole dish with cooking spray and set aside. Melt butter in a pan over medium heat. Add onion and green chilies and sauté for 5 minutes. Remove pan from heat and set aside. In a small bowl, whisk milk, baking powder, and flour until smooth. In a mixing bowl, whisk eggs with cheese, cottage cheese, and seasoned salt. Add sautéed onion and green chilies, milk, and flour mixture to the eggs and whisk until well combined. Pour egg mixture into the prepared casserole dish. Set to bake at 350 F for 50 minutes. After 5 minutes place the casserole dish in the preheated oven. Serve and enjoy.
Nutrition Info: Calories 219 Fat 13.8 g Carbohydrates 8.4 g Sugar 1.4 g Protein 14.9 g Cholesterol 228 mg

157. Bacon And Cheddar Cheese Frittata

Ingredients:

8 slices bacon, chopped	Coarse salt, freshly ground pepper, to taste
1/2 cup grated cheddar cheese	1/4 cup Romano cheese
12 large eggs	Dash of hot sauce
3 Tbsp milk	

Directions:

Preheat oven to 375°F.   Heat Cuisinart oven and cook bacon over medium heat, stirring until crisp. Set aside on a plate.   In a bowl, whisk eggs, milk, salt, pepper, cheeses and hot sauce.   Add cooked bacon to egg mixture.   Pour eggs into Cuisinart oven. When eggs are half set and edges begin to pull away, place frittata in oven and bake for about 10 minutes, or until   center is no longer jiggly. Cut into wedges inside pot or slide out onto serving plate.

158.   Apricot & Almond Scones

Servings: 4   Cooking Time: 30 Minutes

Ingredients:

2 cups flour	¼ cup cold butter,
⅓ cup sugar	cut into cubes
2 tsp baking powder	½ cup milk
½ cup sliced almonds	1 egg
¾ cup dried apricots, chopped	1 tsp vanilla extract

Directions:

reheat Cuisinart on AirFry function to 370 F. Line a baking dish with parchment paper. Mix together flour, sugar, baking powder, almonds, and apricots. Rub the butter into the dry ingredients with hands to form a sandy, crumbly texture. Whisk together egg, milk, and vanilla extract.   Pour into the dry ingredients and stir to combine. Sprinkle a working board with flour, lay the dough onto the board and give it a few kneads. Shape into a rectangle and cut into 8 squares. Arrange the squares on the baking dish and press Start. Bake for 25 minutes. Serve chilled.

159.   Cheddar Eggs With Potatoes

Servings: 3   Cooking Time: 24 Minutes

Ingredients:

3 potatoes, thinly sliced	2 eggs, beaten
2 oz cheddar cheese, shredded	1 tbsp all-purpose flour
	½ cup coconut cream

Directions:

Preheat Cuisinart on AirFry function to 390 F. Place the potatoes the basket and press Start. Cook for 12 minutes. Mix the eggs, coconut cream, and flour until the cream mixture thickens.   Remove the potatoes from the oven, line them in the ramekin and top with the cream mixture. Top with the cheddar cheese. Cook for 12 more minutes.

160.   Whole-wheat Muffins With Blueberries

Servings: 8 Muffins   Cooking Time: 25 Minutes

Ingredients:

½ cup unsweetened applesauce	2 cups whole-wheat flour
½ cup plant-based milk	½ teaspoon baking soda
½ cup maple syrup	1 cup blueberries
1 teaspoon vanilla extract	Cooking spray

Directions:

Spritz a 8-cup muffin pan with cooking spray.   In a large bowl, stir together the applesauce, milk, maple syrup and vanilla extract. Whisk in the flour and baking soda until no dry flour is left and the batter is smooth. Gently mix in the blueberries until they are evenly distributed throughout the batter. Spoon the batter into the muffin cups, three-quarters full.   Put the muffin pan into Rack Position 1, select Convection Bake, set temperature to 375°F (190ºC) and set time to 25 minutes. When cooking is complete, remove from the oven and check the muffins. You can stick a knife into the center of a muffin and it should come out clean. Let rest for 5 minutes before serving.

161. Peppery Sausage & Parsley Patties

Servings: 4   Cooking Time: 20 Minutes

Ingredients:

1 lb ground Italian sausage	1 tsp dried parsley
¼ cup breadcrumbs	½ tsp salt
1 tsp red pepper flakes	¼ tsp black pepper
	¼ tsp garlic powder
	1 egg, beaten

Directions:

Preheat Cuisinart on Bake function to 350 F. Combine all of the ingredients in a large bowl. Line a baking sheet with parchment paper. Make patties out of the sausage mixture and arrange them on the baking sheet. Cook for 15 minutes, flipping once halfway through cooking. Serve.

162.   Avocado Oil Gluten Free Banana Bread Recipe

Ingredients:

1/2 cup Granulated Sugar	1 teaspoon Baking Powder
1 cup Mashed Banana	1/2 teaspoon Baking Soda
1/2 cup Light Brown Sugar	1/2 teaspoon Fine Sea Salt
1/3 cup Avocado Oil, (or canola oil)	2 large Eggs, room temperature
2 cups All-Purpose Gluten Free Flour, (see notes)	2/3 cup Milk, (dairy free or regular milk), room temperature
3/4 teaspoon Xanthan Gum, (omit if your flour blend contains it)	1 teaspoon Pure Vanilla Extract

Directions:

Preheat oven to 350°F and spray a 9x9 inch square pan with non-stick spray and line with parchment paper.   In a large bowl, whisk together the flour, xanthan gum, baking powder, baking soda, salt, and granulated sugar.   In a separate bowl, whisk together the mashed banana, brown sugar, oil, eggs, milk, and vanilla extract. Pour the wet ingredients into the dry ingredients and stir to combine.   Pour the batter into the prepared pan and bake at 350°F for 25-30 minutes or until a toothpick or cake tester comes out clean or with a few moist crumbs attached. Cooking time will vary depending on your oven - mine took 29 minutes.   Cool the bread in the pan on a cooling rack. Cut into 16 pieces and serve slightly warm or room temperature.   To store, wrap tightly in foil or store slices in an air-tight container. It will stay fresh up to 3 days. This bread also freezes well. To freeze, slice into individual pieces and freeze in a freezer bag.

163.   Healthy Bran Muffins

Servings: 12   Cooking Time: 20 Minutes

Ingredients:

2 eggs	1/2 cup raisins
1 cup milk	1/4 tsp cinnamon
1 1/2 cups wheat bran	1/2 tsp baking soda
1/4 cup molasses	1 1/2 tsp baking
1/4 cup white sugar	powder
1/4 cup brown sugar	1 cup flour
1/4 cup shortening	1/2 tsp salt

Directions:

Fit the Cuisinart oven with the rack in position Line a 12-cup muffin tray with cupcake liners and set aside.   In a bowl, mix flour, raisins, cinnamon, baking soda, baking powder, flour, and salt.   In a separate bowl, beat sugar and shortening using a hand mixer until fluffy.   Add eggs and molasses and beat until well combined. Add bran and milk and stir well.   Add flour mixture and mix until just combined.   Pour mixture into the prepared muffin tray.   Set to bake at 400 F for 25 minutes. After 5 minutes place the muffin tray in the preheated oven.   Serve and enjoy.

Nutrition Info: Calories 178 Fat 5.9 g Carbohydrates 31 g Sugar 15.5 g Protein 4 g Cholesterol 29 mg

164.   Mozzarella Endives And Tomato Salad

Servings: 4   Cooking Time: 20 Minutes

Ingredients:

2 endives, shredded	Salt and black pepper
½ pound cherry	to the taste
tomatoes, halved	1 teaspoon sweet
1 tablespoon olive oil	paprika
4 eggs, whisked	½ cup mozzarella,
	shredded

Directions:

Preheat the air fryer with the oil at 350 degrees F, add the tomatoes, endives and the other ingredients except the mozzarella and toss.   Sprinkle the mozzarella on top, cook for 20 minutes, divide into bowls and serve for breakfast.

Nutrition Info: calories 229, fat 13, fiber 3, carbs 4, protein 7

165.   Fried Cheese Grits

Servings: 4   Cooking Time: 11 Minutes

Ingredients:

⅔ cup instant grits	1 teaspoon salt
1 teaspoon freshly	1 large egg, beaten
ground black pepper	1 tablespoon butter,
¾ cup whole or 2%	melted
milk	1 cup shredded mild
3 ounces (85 g)	Cheddar cheese
cream cheese, at	Cooking spray
room temperature	

Directions:

Mix the grits, salt, and black pepper in a large bowl. Add the milk, cream cheese, beaten egg, and melted butter and whisk to combine. Fold in the Cheddar cheese and stir well.   Spray the baking pan with cooking spray. Spread the grits mixture into the baking pan.   Put the air fryer basket on the baking pan and slide into Rack Position 2, select Air Fry, set temperature to 400ºF (205ºC) and set time to 11 minutes.   Stir the mixture halfway through the cooking time.   When done, a knife inserted in the center should come out clean.   Rest for 5 minutes and serve warm.

166.   Simple Apple Crisp

Servings: 8   Cooking Time: 35 Minutes

Ingredients:

4 medium apples,	For topping:
peel & slice	1/2 cup brown sugar
1 tsp cinnamon	3/4 cup all-purpose
4 tbsp sugar	flour
1/3 cup butter,	3/4 cup rolled oats
melted	

Directions:

Fit the Cuisinart oven with the rack in position Add sliced apples, cinnamon, and sugar in a greased 9-inch baking dish and mix well.   In a bowl, mix oats, brown sugar, and flour. Add melted butter and mix well.   Sprinkle oat mixture over sliced apples. Set to bake at 375 F for 40 minutes. After 5 minutes place the baking dish in the preheated oven. Serve and enjoy.

Nutrition Info: Calories 255 Fat 8.5 g Carbohydrates 44.7 g Sugar 26.5 g Protein 2.6 g Cholesterol 20 mg

167.   Breakfast Tater Tot Casserole

Servings: 4   Cooking Time: 17 To 18 Minutes

Ingredients:

4 eggs	1 pound (454 g)
1 cup milk	frozen tater tots,
Salt and pepper, to	thawed
taste	¾ cup grated
12 ounces (340 g)	Cheddar cheese
ground chicken	Cooking spray
sausage	

Directions:

Whisk together the eggs and milk in a medium bowl. Season with salt and pepper to taste and stir until mixed. Set aside.   Place a skillet over medium-high heat and spritz with cooking spray. Place the ground sausage in the skillet and break it into smaller pieces with a spatula or spoon. Cook for 3 to 4 minutes until the sausage starts to brown, stirring occasionally. Remove from heat and set aside. Coat the baking pan with cooking spray. Arrange the tater tots in the baking pan.   Slide the baking pan into Rack Position 1, select Convection Bake, set temperature to 400ºF (205ºC) and set time to 14 minutes.   After 6 minutes, remove the pan from the oven. Stir the tater tots and add the egg mixture and cooked sausage. Return the pan to the oven and continue cooking.   After 6 minutes, remove the pan from the oven. Scatter the cheese on top of the tater tots. Return the pan to the oven and continue to cook for another 2 minutes. When done, the cheese should be bubbly and melted. Let the mixture cool for 5 minutes and serve warm.

168. Smoked Sausage Breakfast Mix

Servings: 4   Cooking Time: 30 Minutes
Ingredients:

1 and 1/2 pounds smoked sausage, diced and browned	4 and 1/2 cups water
A pinch of salt and black pepper	1 cup milk
	¼ tsp. garlic powder
1 and 1/2 cups grits	1 and 1/2 tsp.s thyme, diced
16 ounces cheddar cheese, shredded	Cooking spray
	4 eggs, whisked

Directions:
Put the water in a pot, bring to a boil over medium heat, add grits, stir, cover, cook for 5 minutes and take off heat.   Add cheese, stir until it melts and mix with milk, thyme, salt, pepper, garlic powder and eggs and whisk really well.   Heat up your air fryer at 300 °F, grease with cooking spray and add browned sausage.   Add grits mix, spread and cook for 25 minutes.   Divide among plates and serve for breakfast.
Nutrition Info: Calories 113   Fat 8.2 g
Carbohydrates 0.3 g   Protein 5.4 g

169. Banana & Peanut Butter Cake

Servings: 4   Cooking Time: 30 Minutes
Ingredients:

1 cup flour	1 egg, beaten
¼ tsp baking soda	1 tsp vanilla extract
1 tsp baking powder	¾ cup chopped walnuts
⅓ cup sugar	
2 mashed bananas	¼ tsp salt
¼ cup vegetable oil	2 tbsp peanut butter
	2 tbsp sour cream

Directions:
Preheat Cuisinart on Bake function to 350 F. Spray a 9-inch baking pan with cooking spray or grease with butter. Combine the flour, salt, baking powder, and baking soda in a bowl.   In another bowl, combine bananas, oil, egg, peanut butter, vanilla, sugar, and sour cream. Combine both mixtures gently. Stir in the chopped walnuts. Pour the batter into the pan. Cook for 20 minutes. Let cool completely and serve sliced.

170. Hash Browns

Servings: 3   Cooking Time: 18 Minutes
Ingredients:

1 tsp flour	½ tsp Cajun seasoning
1 ½ pound potatoes peeled	
½ shallot	1 egg white
	½ tsp black pepper
	1 tsp coconut oil

Directions:
Keep the peeled potatoes in a bowl of water and mix them with Cajun seasoning as well as flour. Grate the potatoes and pour some cold water with a little salt to reduce the starch content. Set this mixture aside. Grate the shallot and set it aside, strain your potatoes using a fine strainer or cheesecloth. Ensure all the water has been strained out of the potatoes. Mix the ingredients in a bowl except the potatoes and ensure that they are well combined. Add the potatoes and mix them thoroughly. Form several patties.   Place your instant air fryer at 400 degrees Fahrenheit. Once the fryer indicates add food, add the patties on the pan. Flip every time the panel indicates turn food.   Serve while hot.
Nutrition Info: Calories 145 Fat 9g, Carbohydrates 15g, Proteins 1g, Sodium: 1990 Mg.

171. Italian Sandwich

Servings: 1   Cooking Time: 7 Minutes
Ingredients:

2 bread slices	1 tbsp fresh basil, chopped
4 tomato slices	
4 mozzarella cheese slices	Salt and black pepper to taste
1 tbsp olive oil	

Directions:
Preheat Cuisinart on Toast function to 350 F. Place the bread slices in the toaster oven and toast for 5 minutes. Arrange two tomato slices on each bread slice. Season with salt and pepper.   Top each slice with 2 mozzarella slices. Return to the oven and cook for 1 more minute. Drizzle the caprese toasts with olive oil and top with chopped basil.

172. Fluffy Frittata With Bell Pepper

Ingredients:

8 eggs	1 Tbsp butter
2 Tbsp whole milk	½ zucchini diced
Coarse salt, freshly ground pepper, to taste	1 bell Pepper seeded and diced

Directions:
Preheat oven to 400°F.   Heat Cuisinart oven over medium heat. Add butter.   In a bowl, add remaining ingredients. Pour mixture into Cuisinart oven.   When eggs are half set and edges begin to pull away, place frittata in   the oven and bake for about 10 minutes, or until center is no longer jiggly. Cut into wedges or slide out onto serving plate.

173. Oatmeal Muffins

Servings: 2-4   Cooking Time: 15 Minutes
Ingredients:

2 Eggs	1/2 cup flour
31/2 ounce oats	1/2 cup icing sugar
3 ounce margarine, melted	Pinch baking powder
	1 tablespoon raisins
1/4 tsp. vanilla essence	Cooking spray

Directions:
Combine sugar and margarine until soft. Whisk together the eggs and vanilla essence. Add it to the sugar/margarine mix until soft peaks forms. Combine flour, raisins, baking powder and oats in a separate bowl. Add it to the mixed ingredients. Grease the muffin molds lightly with cooking spray and fill with the batter mixture. Preheat the Air fryer

at 350°F.   Place the muffin molds into the air fryer tray. Let it cook for 12 minutes.
Nutrition Info: Calories 108   Fat 9.0 g Carbohydrates 0.3 g   Sugar 0.3 g   Protein 6.3 g Cholesterol 21 mg

174.   Healthy Tofu Omelet

Servings: 2   Cooking Time: 29 Minutes
Ingredients:

¼ of onion, chopped
12-ounce silken tofu, pressed and sliced
3 eggs, beaten
1 tablespoon chives, chopped

1 garlic clove, minced
2 teaspoons olive oil
Salt and black pepper, to taste

Directions:
Preheat the Air fryer to 355F and grease an Air fryer pan with olive oil.   Add onion and garlic to the greased pan and cook for about 4 minutes.   Add tofu, mushrooms and chives and season with salt and black pepper.   Beat the eggs and pour over the tofu mixture.   Cook for about 25 minutes, poking the eggs twice in between   Dish out and serve warm.
Nutrition Info: Calories: 248 Cal Total Fat: 15.9 g Saturated Fat: 0 g   Cholesterol: 0 mg   Sodium: 155 mg   Total Carbs: 6.5 g   Fiber: 0 g   Sugar: 3.3 g   Protein: 20.4 g

175.Spinach And Ricotta Pockets

Servings: 8 Pockets   Cooking Time: 10 Minutes
Ingredients:

2 large eggs, divided
1 tablespoon water
1 cup baby spinach, roughly chopped
¼ cup sun-dried tomatoes, finely chopped
1 cup ricotta cheese
1 cup basil, chopped

¼ teaspoon red pepper flakes
¼ teaspoon kosher salt
2 refrigerated rolled pie crusts
2 tablespoons sesame seeds

Directions:
Spritz the air fryer basket with cooking spray. Whisk an egg with water in a small bowl. Combine the spinach, tomatoes, the other egg, ricotta cheese, basil, red pepper flakes, and salt in a large bowl. Whisk to mix well.   Unfold the pie crusts on a clean work surface and slice each crust into 4 wedges. Scoop up 3 tablespoons of the spinach mixture on each crust and leave ½ inch space from edges.   Fold the crust wedges in half to wrap the filling and press the edges with a fork to seal. Arrange the wraps in the pan and spritz with cooking spray. Sprinkle with sesame seeds.   Put the air fryer basket on the baking pan and slide into Rack Position 2, select Air Fry, set temperature to 380°F (193°C) and set time to 10 minutes.   Flip the wraps halfway through the cooking time.   When cooked, the wraps will be crispy and golden. Serve immediately.

176.   Balsamic Chicken With Spinach & Kale

Servings: 1   Cooking Time: 20 Minutes

Ingredients:

½ cup baby spinach
½ cup romaine lettuce, shredded
3 large kale leaves, chopped
1 chicken breast, cut into cubes

2 tbsp olive oil
1 tsp balsamic vinegar
1 garlic clove, minced
Salt and black pepper to taste

Directions:
Place the chicken, some olive oil, garlic, salt, and pepper in a bowl; toss to combine. Put on a lined baking dish and cook in the Cuisinart for 14 minutes at 390F on Bake function.   Meanwhile, place the greens in a large bowl. Add the remaining olive oil and balsamic vinegar. Season with salt and pepper and toss to combine. Top with the sliced chicken and serve.

177. Honey Banana Pastry With Berries

Servings: 2   Cooking Time: 15 Minutes
Ingredients:

3 bananas, sliced
2 puff pastry sheets, cut into thin strips

3 tbsp honey
Fresh berries to serve

Directions:
Preheat Cuisinart on Bake function to 340 F. Place the banana slices into a baking dish. Cover with the pastry strips and top with honey. Cook for 12 minutes. Serve with berries.

178.   Potato Hash

Servings: 2   Cooking Time: 25 Minutes
Ingredients:

5 big potatoes
1 medium onion
2 eggs
½ tsp of thyme

½ green pepper
½ tsp savory
½ tsp black pepper
2 tsp duck fat

Directions:
Melt the duck fat in the fryer for 2 minutes   and then peal your onion then dice it. Add to the fryer, wash and seed the green pepper to add a sumptuous taste. Cook for 5 minutes.   Wash your potatoes and peel them according to your taste and preference. Dice the potatoes into small cubes and add to the fryer along with the seasonings set the timer to 20 minutes   and allow it to cook.   Spray a nonstick pan with cooking spray and grind some pepper before adding it in. let the pepper heat for a minute before adding your egg. Cook until the egg becomes solid. Take the pan out and set it aside. Chop up the eggs.   Add the egg to the potato mixture once the timer runs out.
Nutrition Info: Calories 266 Fat 10g, Carbohydrates 39 g, Proteins 5g, Sodium: 5mg

179.   Avocado And Tomato Egg Rolls

Servings: 5   Cooking Time: 5 Minutes
Ingredients:

10 egg roll wrappers
3 avocados, peeled and pitted
1 tomato, diced
Salt and ground black pepper, to taste
Cooking spray

Directions:
Spritz the air fryer basket with cooking spray. Put the tomato and avocados in a food processor. Sprinkle with salt and ground black pepper. Pulse to mix and coarsely mash until smooth. Unfold the wrappers on a clean work surface, then divide the mixture in the center of each wrapper. Roll the wrapper up and press to seal. Transfer the rolls to the pan and spritz with cooking spray. Put the air fryer basket on the baking pan and slide into Rack Position 2, select Air Fry, set temperature to 350°F (180°C) and set time to 5 minutes. Flip the rolls halfway through the cooking time. When cooked, the rolls should be golden brown. Serve immediately.

---

180.   Air Fryer Breakfast Frittata

Servings: 2   Cooking Time: 20 Minutes
Ingredients:
¼ pound breakfast sausage, fully cooked and crumbled
4 eggs, lightly beaten
½ cup Monterey Jack cheese, shredded
2 tablespoons red bell pepper, diced
1 green onion, chopped
1 pinch cayenne pepper

Directions:
Preheat the Air fryer to 365F and grease a nonstick 6x2-inch cake pan. Whisk together eggs with sausage, green onion, bell pepper, cheese and cayenne in a bowl. Transfer the egg mixture in the prepared cake pan and place in the Air fryer. Cook for about 20 minutes and serve warm.
Nutrition Info: Calories: 464, Fat: 33.7g, Carbohydrates: 10.4g, Sugar: 7g, Protein: 30.4g, Sodium: 704mg

---

181.French Toast Sticks

Servings: 4   Cooking Time: 12 Minutes
Ingredients:
3 slices low-sodium whole-wheat bread, each cut into 4 strips
1 tablespoon unsalted butter, melted
1 tablespoon 2 percent milk
1 tablespoon sugar
1 egg, beaten
1 egg white
1 cup sliced fresh strawberries
1 tablespoon freshly squeezed lemon juice

Directions:
Arrange the bread strips on a plate and drizzle with the melted butter. In a bowl, whisk together the milk, sugar, egg and egg white. Dredge the bread strips into the egg mixture and place on a wire rack to let the batter drip off. Arrange half the coated bread strips in the air fryer basket. Put the air fryer basket on the baking pan and slide into Rack Position 2, select Air Fry, set temperature to 380°F (193°C) and set time to 6 minutes. After 3 minutes, remove from the oven and turn the strips over. Return to the oven to continue cooking. When cooking is complete, the strips should be golden brown. Repeat with the remaining strips. In a small bowl, mash the strawberries with a fork and stir in the lemon juice. Serve the French toast sticks with the strawberry sauce.

---

182.   Aromatic Potato Hash

Servings: 4   Cooking Time: 42 Minutes
Ingredients:
2 teaspoons butter, melted
½ of green bell pepper, seeded and chopped
1½ pound russet potatoes, peeled and cubed
5 eggs, beaten
1 medium onion, chopped
½ teaspoon dried thyme, crushed
½ teaspoon dried savory, crushed
Salt and black pepper, to taste

Directions:
Preheat the Air fryer to 390F and grease an Air fryer pan with melted butter. Put onion and bell pepper in the Air fryer pan and cook for about 5 minutes. Add the potatoes, thyme, savory, salt and black pepper and cook for about 30 minutes. Meanwhile, heat a greased skillet on medium heat and stir in the beaten eggs. Cook for about 1 minute on each side and remove from the skillet. Cut it into small pieces and transfer the egg pieces into the Air fryer pan. Cook for about 5 more minutes and serve warm.
Nutrition Info: Calories: 229 Cal Total Fat: 7.6 g Saturated Fat: 0 g Cholesterol: 0 mg Sodium: 103 mg Total Carbs: 30.8 g Fiber: 0 g Sugar: 4.2 g Protein: 10.3 g

---

183.   Easy Grilled Pork Chops With Sweet & Tangy Mustard Glaze

Servings: 4   Cooking Time: 45 Minutes
Ingredients:
For the glace 1 ½ tsp cider
1 tsp Dijon mustard
2 tsp brown sugar for the brine
3 cups light brown
2 bay leaves
2 tsp of salt
2 cloves smashed
1 ½ cups of ice cubes
4 boneless pork chops

Directions:
Make the glaze by placing all the ingredients in a small bowl and set them aside. Brine your pork by placing it inside water with bay leaves, brown sugar, and garlic and heat it on medium heat. Cover and bring the mixture to boil. Uncover and stir it until the sugar is completely dissolved in the mixture. Add ice cubes to cool into it is slightly warm to the touch. Once it is cooled submerge the pork chops and set aside for 15 minutes. Prepare your grill. Put the instant vortex fryer on GRILL mode and wait for it to attain the desired temperature. once it has attained 400 degree Celsius then it is time to add your pork chops. Usually the appliance will be indicated 'add food'. Remove the pork chops from the salt mixture and pat them with paper towels. Place them on the grill and cover. Do not remove until they are well cooked. Once the instant fryer indicates TURN FOOD. flip your food and glaze it twice before allowing it to cook some more.

Transfer the pork to a clean cutting board once the appliance has indicated end. Serve while hot.
Nutrition Info: Calories 355.9 Fat 20.7g, Carbs 21.2g, Fiber 0.3%, Protein 21.2g, Sodium:1086.5mg

184. Zucchini Squash Pita Sandwiches Recipe

Ingredients:

1 small Zucchini Squash, (5-6 ounces)	1 1/2 cups Fresh Spinach, (2 handfuls)
Salt and Pepper, to taste	2 teaspoons Olive Oil
2 Whole Wheat Pitas	1/4 teaspoon Dried Oregano
1/2 cup Hummus	1/4 teaspoon Dried Thyme
1/2 cup Diced Red Bell Pepper, (about half a large pepper)	1/4 teaspoon Garlic Powder
1/2 cup Chopped Red Onion, (about 1/4 a large onion)	2 tablespoons Crumbled Feta Cheese, (about 1 ounce)

Directions:
Adjust the cooking rack to the lowest placement and preheat toaster oven to 425°F on the BAKE setting. While the oven preheats, quarter the zucchini lengthwise and then cut into 1/2-inch thick pieces. Cut the bell pepper and onion into 1-inch thick pieces.   Add the vegetables to a roasting pan. Drizzle with oil and sprinkle over the oregano, garlic powder, and salt and pepper, to taste. Toss to combine.   Roast vegetables for 10 minutes. Carefully remove the pan and stir. Return pan to oven and continue cooking until the vegetables have softened and started to brown, about 5 minutes more. Remove from the toaster oven and set aside. Reduce the temperature to 375°F and warm the pitas by placing them directly on the cooking rack for 1 to 2 minutes.   Spread warm pitas with hummus. Layer with spinach, roasted vegetables, and crumbled feta.

185. Buttery Chocolate Toast

Servings: 1   Cooking Time: 5 Minutes
Ingredients:

Whole wheat bread slices	Pure maple syrup
Coconut oil	Cacao powder

Directions:
Toast the bread in toaster oven.   Spread coconut oil over the toast.   Drizzle maple syrup in lines over the toast.   Sprinkle cacao powder and serve.
Nutrition Info: Calories: 101, Sodium: 133 mg, Dietary Fiber: 2.4 g, Total Fat: 3.5 g, Total Carbs: 14.8 g, Protein: 4.0 g.

186. Eggplant Hoagies

Servings: 3 Hoagies   Cooking Time: 12 Minutes
Ingredients:

6 peeled eggplant slices (about ½ inch thick and 3 inches in diameter)	6 tablespoons grated Parmesan cheese
¼ cup jarred pizza sauce	3 Italian sub rolls, split open lengthwise, warmed
	Cooking spray

Directions:
Spritz the air fryer basket with cooking spray. Arrange the eggplant slices in the pan and spritz with cooking spray.   Put the air fryer basket on the baking pan and slide into Rack Position 2, select Air Fry, set temperature to 350°F (180ºC) and set time to 10 minutes.   Flip the slices halfway through the cooking time.   When cooked, the eggplant slices should be lightly wilted and tender.   Divide and spread the pizza sauce and cheese on top of the eggplant slice   Put the air fryer basket on the baking pan and slide into Rack Position 2, select Air Fry, set temperature to 375°F (190ºC) and set time to 2 minutes.   When cooked, the cheese will be melted.   Assemble each sub roll with two slices of eggplant and serve immediately.

187. Yogurt & Cream Cheese Zucchini Cakes

Servings: 4   Cooking Time: 20 Minutes
Ingredients:

1 ½ cups flour	2 tbsp butter, melted
1 tsp cinnamon	1 tbsp yogurt
3 eggs	½ cup shredded zucchini
2 tsp baking powder	
2 tbsp sugar	2 tbsp cream cheese
1 cup milk	

Directions:
In a bowl, whisk the eggs along with the sugar, salt, cinnamon, cream cheese, flour, and baking powder. In another bowl, combine all of the liquid ingredients. Gently combine the dry and liquid mixtures. Stir in zucchini.   Line muffin tins with baking paper, and pour the batter inside them. Arrange on the Air Fryer tray and cook for 15-18 minutes on Bake function at 380 F. Serve chilled.

188. Cheesy Potato Taquitos

Servings: 12 Taquitos   Cooking Time: 6 Minutes
Ingredients:

2 cups mashed potatoes	½ cup shredded Mexican cheese
12 corn tortillas	Cooking spray

Directions:
Line the baking pan with parchment paper.   In a bowl, combine the potatoes and cheese until well mixed. Microwave the tortillas on high heat for 30 seconds, or until softened. Add some water to another bowl and set alongside.   On a clean work surface, lay the tortillas. Scoop 3 tablespoons of the potato mixture in the center of each tortilla. Roll up tightly and secure with toothpicks if necessary. Arrange the filled tortillas, seam side down, in the prepared baking pan. Spritz the tortillas with cooking spray.   Put the air fryer basket on the baking pan and slide into Rack Position 2, select Air Fry, set temperature to 400°F (205ºC) and set time to 6 minutes.   Flip the tortillas halfway through the cooking time.   When cooked, the tortillas should be crispy and golden brown.   Serve hot.

189. Corned Beef Hash With Eggs

Servings: 4   Cooking Time: 25 Minutes
Ingredients:

1 medium onion, chopped
1/3 cup diced red bell pepper
3 tablespoons vegetable oil
1/2 teaspoon dried thyme
1/2 teaspoon kosher salt, divided

2 medium Yukon Gold potatoes, peeled and cut into 1/4-inch cubes
1/2 teaspoon freshly ground black pepper, divided
3/4 pound (340 g) corned beef, cut into 1/4-inch pieces
4 large eggs

Directions:
In a large bowl, stir together the potatoes, onion, red pepper, vegetable oil, thyme, 1/4 teaspoon of the salt and 1/4 teaspoon of the pepper. Spread the vegetable mixture into the baking pan in an even layer. Slide the baking pan into Rack Position 2, select Roast, set temperature to 375°F (190°C) and set time to 25 minutes. After 15 minutes, remove the pan from the oven and add the corned beef. Stir the mixture to incorporate the corned beef. Return the pan to the oven and continue cooking. After 5 minutes, remove the pan from the oven. Using a large spoon, create 4 circles in the hash to hold the eggs. Gently crack an egg into each circle. Season the eggs with the remaining 1/4 teaspoon of the salt and 1/4 teaspoon of the pepper. Return the pan to the oven. Continue cooking for 3 to 5 minutes, depending on how you like your eggs. When cooking is complete, remove the pan from the oven. Serve immediately.

190.	**Giant Strawberry Pancake**

Servings: 3   Cooking Time: 30 Minutes
Ingredients:
3 eggs, beaten
2 tbsp butter, melted
2 tbsp sugar, powdered

1/2 cup flour
1/2 cup milk
1 1/2 cups fresh strawberries, sliced

Directions:
Preheat Cuisinart on Bake function to 350 F. In a bowl, mix flour, milk, eggs, and vanilla until fully incorporated. Add the mixture a greased with melted butter pan. Place the pan in your toaster oven and cook for 12-16 minutes until the pancake is fluffy and golden brown. Drizzle powdered sugar and toss sliced strawberries on top.

191.	**Fried Apple Lemon & Vanilla Turnovers**

Ingredients:
2 sheets frozen puff pastry (17-ounce/480g package), thawed (keep
3 medium Granny Smith apples, peeled and diced (about 3 cups)
2 tablespoons (30g)

cold until use)
1 teaspoon vanilla extract
1 teaspoon lemon juice
3/4 teaspoon ground cinnamon
1/4 teaspoon kosher salt

unsalted butter
L cup (70g) dark brown sugar

1 egg
1 tablespoon water
Turbinado sugar for sprinkling

Directions:
Combine filling ingredients in a medium saucepan and cook over medium heat, stirring occasionally, until apples are tender and syrup is thick, about 10 minutes. Transfer apple mixture to a plate and chill in the refrigerator until cool to the touch, about 20 minutes. Scramble egg and water in a small bowl. Place 1 sheet of puff pastry on a clean cutting board; reserve second sheet in the refrigerator. Divide pastry into 4 equal squares. Spoon 2 tablespoons apple mixture onto the center of each square. Brush the edges of each square with egg wash. Fold pastry diagonally over apple mixture and seal the edges with a fork. Place turnovers on a plate and refrigerate while preparing remaining turnovers. Repeat steps 4 to 6 with second sheet of puff pastry. Select AIRFRY/325°F (165°C)/SUPER CONVECTION/20 minutes and press START to preheat oven. Place turnovers on air fry rack. Brush tops with egg wash and sprinkle with turbinado sugar. Make 3 small slits in each turnover. Cook in rack position 4 until puffed and golden brown, about 20 minutes. Serve warm or at room temperature.

192.	**Sausage And Cheese Quiche**

Servings: 4   Cooking Time: 25 Minutes
Ingredients:
12 large eggs
1 cup heavy cream
12 ounces (340 g) sugar-free breakfast sausage

Salt and black pepper, to taste
2 cups shredded Cheddar cheese
Cooking spray

Directions:
Coat the baking pan with cooking spray. Beat together the eggs, heavy cream, salt and pepper in a large bowl until creamy. Stir in the breakfast sausage and Cheddar cheese. Pour the sausage mixture into the prepared pan. Slide the baking pan into Rack Position 1, select Convection Bake, set temperature to 375°F (190°C) and set time to 25 minutes. When done, the top of the quiche should be golden brown and the eggs will be set. Remove from the oven and let sit for 5 to 10 minutes before serving.

193.	**Mediterranean Spinach Frittata**

Servings: 6   Cooking Time: 20 Minutes
Ingredients:
1/2 cup frozen spinach, drained the excess liquid
1/4 cup feta cheese, crumbled
1/4 cup olives, chopped
1/4 cup kalamata olives, chopped

6 eggs
1/2 cup tomatoes, diced
1/2 tsp garlic powder
1 tsp oregano
1/4 cup milk
1/2 tsp pepper
1/4 tsp salt

Directions:

Fit the Cuisinart oven with the rack in position Spray 9-inch pie pan with cooking spray and set aside. In a bowl, whisk eggs with oregano, garlic powder, milk, pepper, and salt until well combined. Add olives, feta cheese, tomatoes, and spinach and mix well. Pour egg mixture into the prepared pie pan. Set to bake at 400 F for 25 minutes. After 5 minutes place the pie pan in the preheated oven. Serve and enjoy.

Nutrition Info: Calories 103 Fat 7.2 g Carbohydrates 2.9 g Sugar 1.5 g Protein 7.2 g Cholesterol 170 mg

194. Oats, Chocolate Chip, Pecan Cookies

Ingredients:

½ cup (115g) butter, softened	½ cup (100g) sugar
1 cup (170g) chocolate chips	1 large egg
½ cup (60g) pecan halves, chopped	1L cup (160g) all-purpose flour
½ cup (100g) firmly packed brown sugar	2 teaspoons baking powder
1 teaspoon vanilla extract	½ teaspoon kosher salt
	¼ cup (20g) rolled oats

Directions:
Line 2 baking pans with parchment paper. Assemble Cuisinart bench mixer with beater attachment. Place butter, sugar, brown sugar and vanilla in the mixing bowl. Mix on medium speed for 2 minutes until pale and creamy. Add egg and beat until just combined. Sift flour, baking powder and salt, then add to egg mixture on low speed, mixing until just combined. Add chocolate chips, pecans and oats and mix on low speed until just combined. Roll heaping tablespoons of dough into balls and place 6 balls, 2 inches (4cm) apart, on each prepared pan. Insert wire racks in rack positions 3 and Select COOKIES/315°F (155°C)/SUPER CONVECTION/12 minutes. Press START to preheat oven. Bake cookies for 12 minutes, rotating halfway through baking (change top to bottom and front to back). Let cool on baking pans for 5 minutes then transfer to a wire rack to cool completely. 9. Repeat with remaining dough.

195. Breakfast Sweet Potato Hash

Servings: 6   Cooking Time: 65 Minutes

Ingredients:

6 cups sweet potatoes, peeled and diced	1 onion, diced
	1/3 cup olive oil
1 tsp thyme	1/2 tsp paprika
1 tsp onion powder	1 tbsp garlic powder
8 garlic cloves, minced	1/2 tsp pepper
	2 tsp salt

Directions:
Fit the Cuisinart oven with the rack in position Add sweet potatoes to a casserole dish and sprinkle with paprika, thyme, onion powder, garlic powder, pepper, and salt. Drizzle oil over sweet potatoes and toss well. Set to bake at 450 F for 60 minutes, after 5 minutes, place the casserole dish in the oven. Heat 1 tbsp of olive oil in a pan over medium heat. Add onion and garlic and sauté for 10 minutes. Add onion and garlic mixture to the sweet potatoes and mix well. Serve and enjoy.

Nutrition Info: Calories 294 Fat 11.6 g Carbohydrates 46.5 g Sugar 2.1 g Protein 3.1 g Cholesterol 0 mg

196. Sweet Pineapple Oatmeal

Servings: 6   Cooking Time: 45 Minutes

Ingredients:

2 cups old-fashioned oats	1/3 cup yogurt
	1/3 cup butter, melted
1/2 cup coconut flakes	1/2 tsp baking powder
1 cup pineapple, crushed	1/3 cup brown sugar
2 eggs, lightly beaten	1/2 tsp vanilla
	2/3 cup milk
	1/2 tsp salt

Directions:
Fit the Cuisinart oven with the rack in position In a mixing bowl, mix together oats, baking powder, brown sugar, and salt. In a separate bowl, beat eggs with vanilla, milk, yogurt, and butter. Add egg mixture into the oat mixture and stir to combine. Add coconut and pineapple and stir to combine. Pour oat mixture into the greased 8-inch baking dish. Set to bake at 350 F for 50 minutes, after 5 minutes, place the baking dish in the oven. Serve and enjoy.

Nutrition Info: Calories 304 Fat 16.4 g Carbohydrates 33.2 g Sugar 13.6 g Protein 7.5 g Cholesterol 85 mg

197. Perfect Sausage-hash Brown Casserole

Servings: 12   Cooking Time: 45 Minutes

Ingredients:

6 eggs	1/2 cup milk
16 oz frozen hash browns, defrosted	1 lb breakfast sausage, browned
2 cups cheddar cheese, shredded	1/2 tsp pepper
	1 tsp kosher salt

Directions:
Fit the Cuisinart oven with the rack in position Layer hash browns in a greased 9*9-inch casserole dish. Spread sausage on top of hash browns. Sprinkle cheese on top. In a mixing bowl, whisk eggs with milk, pepper, and salt. Pour egg mixture over hash brown mixture. Set to bake at 350 F for 50 minutes. After 5 minutes place the casserole dish in the preheated oven. Serve and enjoy.

Nutrition Info: Calories 323 Fat 24.4 g Carbohydrates 11.7 g Sugar 0.7 g Protein 15.8 g Cholesterol 134 mg

198. Basil Parmesan Bagel

Servings: 1   Cooking Time: 6 Minutes

Ingredients:

2 tbsp butter, softened	1 tsp garlic powder
	Salt and black pepper

¼ tsp dried basil
1 tbsp Parmesan cheese, grated

to taste
1 bagel

Directions:
Preheat Cuisinart on Bake function to 370 F. Cut the bagel in half. Combine the butter, Parmesan cheese, garlic, and basil in a small bowl. Season with salt and pepper. Spread the mixture onto the halved bagel. Place the bagel in the basket and press Start. Cook for 5-6 minutes.

199.	**Buttery Cheese Sandwich**

Servings: 1   Cooking Time: 10 Minutes
Ingredients:
2 tbsp butter
2 slices bread

3 slices American cheese

Directions:
Preheat Cuisinart on Bake function to 370 F. Spread one tsp of butter on the outside of each of the bread slices. Place the cheese on the inside of one bread slice. Top with the other slice. Cook in the toaster oven for 4 minutes. Flip the sandwich over and cook for an additional 4 minutes. Serve sliced diagonally.

200.	**Crunchy Vanilla Granola**

Servings: 10   Cooking Time: 30 Minutes
Ingredients:
4 cups old fashioned oats
1 1/2 tsp vanilla

1/4 cup coconut oil
1/2 cup honey
1/2 tsp cinnamon

Directions:
Fit the Cuisinart oven with the rack in position   In a mixing bowl, mix oats and cinnamon and set aside. In a small saucepan, add honey and coconut oil and heat over medium-low heat until oil is melted. Remove saucepan from heat. Add vanilla and stir well.   Pour honey mixture over oats and stir well. Pour oats mixture onto the parchment-lined baking pan and spread evenly.   Set to bake at 300 F for 35 minutes. After 5 minutes place the baking pan in the preheated oven.   Serve and enjoy.
Nutrition Info: Calories 350 Fat 9.6 g Carbohydrates 57.1 g Sugar 15.7 g Protein 8.1 g Cholesterol 0 mg

201.	**Easy Parsnip Hash Browns**

Servings: 2   Cooking Time: 20 Minutes
Ingredients:
1 large parsnip, grated
3 eggs, beaten
½ tsp garlic powder
¼ tsp nutmeg

1 tbsp olive oil
1 cup flour
Salt and black pepper to taste

Directions:
In a bowl, combine flour, eggs, parsnip, nutmeg, and garlic powder. Season with salt and pepper. Form patties out of the mixture. Drizzle the basket with olive oil and arrange the patties inside. Press Start. Cook for 15 minutes on AirFry function at 360 F. Serve with garlic mayo.

202.	**Egg English Muffin With Bacon**

Servings: 1   Cooking Time: 10 Minutes

Ingredients:
1 egg
1 English muffin
2 slices of bacon

Salt and black pepper to taste

Directions:
Preheat Cuisinart on Bake function to 395 F. Crack the egg into a ramekin. Place the muffin, egg and bacon in the oven. Cook for 9 minutes. Let cool slightly so you can assemble the sandwich.   Cut the muffin in half. Place the egg on one half and season with salt and pepper. Arrange the bacon on top. Top with the other muffin half.

203.	**Tomato Oatmeal**

Servings: 4   Cooking Time: 20 Minutes
Ingredients:
1 cup tomatoes, cubed
1 cup old fashioned oats
A drizzle of avocado oil
A pinch of salt and black pepper

2 cups almond milk
1 teaspoon cilantro, chopped
1 teaspoon basil, chopped
2 spring onions, chopped

Directions:
In your air fryer, combine the tomatoes with the oats and the other ingredients, toss and cook at 360 degrees F for 20 minutes.   Divide the oatmeal into bowls and serve for breakfast.
Nutrition Info:calories 140, fat 2, fiber 3, carbs 8, protein 4

204.	**Air Fried Crispy Spring Rolls**

Servings: 4   Cooking Time: 18 Minutes
Ingredients:
4 spring roll wrappers
½ cup cooked vermicelli noodles
1 tablespoon freshly minced ginger
1 tablespoon soy sauce
1 clove garlic, minced

1 teaspoon sesame oil
½ red bell pepper, deseeded and chopped
½ cup chopped carrot
½ cup chopped mushrooms
¼ cup chopped scallions
Cooking spray

Directions:
Spritz the air fryer basket with cooking spray and set aside.   Heat the sesame oil in a saucepan on medium heat. Sauté the ginger and garlic in the sesame oil for 1 minute, or until fragrant. Add soy sauce, red bell pepper, carrot, mushrooms and scallions. Sauté for 5 minutes or until the vegetables become tender. Mix in vermicelli noodles. Turn off the heat and remove them from the saucepan. Allow to cool for 10 minutes.   Lay out one spring roll wrapper with a corner pointed toward you. Scoop the noodle mixture on spring roll wrapper and fold corner up over the mixture. Fold left and right corners toward the center and continue to roll to make firmly sealed rolls.   Arrange the spring rolls in the pan and spritz with cooking spray.   Put the air fryer basket on the baking pan and slide into

Rack Position 2, select Air Fry, set temperature to 340°F (171°C) and set time to 12 minutes. Flip the spring rolls halfway through the cooking time. When done, the spring rolls will be golden brown and crispy. Serve warm.

205. Eggs In Bell Pepper Rings

Servings: 4   Cooking Time: 7 Minutes

Ingredients:

1 large red, yellow, or orange bell pepper, cut into four ¾-inch rings	Salt and freshly ground black pepper, to taste
4 eggs	2 teaspoons salsa
	Cooking spray

Directions:
Coat the baking pan lightly with cooking spray. Put 4 bell pepper rings in the prepared baking pan. Crack one egg into each bell pepper ring and sprinkle with salt and pepper. Top each egg with ½ teaspoon of salsa. Put the air fryer basket on the baking pan and slide into Rack Position 2, select Air Fry, set temperature to 350°F (180°C) and set time

to 7 minutes.   When done, the eggs should be cooked to your desired doneness.   Remove the rings from the pan to a plate and serve warm.

206. Zucchini And Carrot Pudding

Servings: 4   Cooking Time: 15 Minutes

Ingredients:

1 cup carrots, shredded	2 cups coconut milk
1 cup zucchinis, grated	1 teaspoon cardamom, ground
1 cup heavy cream	2 teaspoons sugar
1 cup wild rice	Cooking spray

Directions:
Spray your air fryer with cooking spray, add the carrots, zucchinis and the other ingredients, toss, cover and cook at 365 degrees F for 15 minutes. Divide the pudding into bowls and serve for breakfast.

Nutrition Info: calories 172, fat 7, fiber 4, carbs 14, protein 5

Lunch Recipes

207. Zucchini And Cauliflower Stew

Servings: 4   Cooking Time: 12 Minutes

Ingredients:

- 1 cauliflower head, florets separated
- 1 ½ cups zucchinis; sliced
- 1 handful parsley leaves; chopped.
- ½ cup tomato puree
- 2 green onions; chopped.
- 1 tbsp. balsamic vinegar
- 1 tbsp. olive oil
- Salt and black pepper to taste.

Directions:

In a pan that fits your air fryer, mix the zucchinis with the rest of the ingredients except the parsley, toss, introduce the pan in the air fryer and cook at 380°F for 20 minutes   Divide into bowls and serve for lunch with parsley sprinkled on top.

Nutrition Info: Calories: 193; Fat: 5g; Fiber: 2g; Carbs: 4g; Protein: 7g

208. Roasted Stuffed Peppers

Servings: 4   Cooking Time: 20 Minutes

Ingredients:

- 4 ounces shredded cheddar cheese
- ½ tsp. Pepper
- ½ tsp. Salt
- 1 tsp. Worcestershire sauce
- ½ c. Tomato sauce
- 8 ounces lean ground beef
- 1 tsp. Olive oil
- 1 minced garlic clove
- ½ chopped onion
- 2 green peppers

Directions:

Preparing the ingredients. Ensure your instant crisp air fryer is preheated to 390 degrees. Spray with olive oil.   Cut stems off bell peppers and remove seeds. Cook in boiling salted water for 3 minutes. Sauté garlic and onion together in a skillet until golden in color.   Take skillet off the heat. Mix pepper, salt, Worcestershire sauce, ¼ cup of tomato sauce, half of cheese and beef together.   Divide meat mixture into pepper halves. Top filled peppers with remaining cheese and tomato sauce.   Place filled peppers in the instant crisp air fryer.   Air frying. Close air fryer lid. Set temperature to 390°f, and set time to 20 minutes, bake 15-20 minutes.

Nutrition Info: Calories: 295; Fat: 8g; Protein:23g; Sugar:2g

209. Squash And Zucchini Mini Pizza

Servings: 4   Cooking Time: 15 Minutes

Ingredients:

- 1 pizza crust
- 1/2 cup parmesan cheese
- 4 tablespoons oregano
- 1 zucchini
- 1 yellow summer squash
- Olive oil
- Salt and pepper

Directions:

Start by preheating toaster oven to 350°F.   If you are using homemade crust, roll out 8 mini portions; if crust is store-bought, use a cookie cutter to cut out the portions.   Sprinkle parmesan and oregano equally on each piece. Layer the zucchini and squash in a circle – one on top of the other – around the entire circle.   Brush with olive oil and sprinkle salt and pepper to taste.   Bake for 15 minutes and serve.

Nutrition Info: Calories: 151, Sodium: 327 mg, Dietary Fiber: 3.1 g, Total Fat: 8.6 g, Total Carbs: 10.3 g, Protein: 11.4 g.

210. Saucy Chicken With Leeks

Servings: 6   Cooking Time: 10 Minutes

Ingredients:

- 2 large-sized tomatoes, chopped
- 3 cloves garlic, minced
- ½ teaspoon dried oregano
- 6 chicken legs, boneless and skinless
- 2 leeks, sliced
- ½ teaspoon smoked cayenne pepper
- 2 tablespoons olive oil
- A freshly ground nutmeg

Directions:

In a mixing dish, thoroughly combine all ingredients, minus the leeks. Place in the refrigerator and let it marinate overnight.   Lay the leeks onto the bottom of an Air Fryer cooking basket. Top with the chicken legs.   Roast chicken legs at 375 degrees F for 18 minutes, turning halfway through. Serve with hoisin sauce.

Nutrition Info:390 Calories; 16g Fat; 2g Carbs; 59g Protein; 8g Sugars; 4g Fiber

211. Tomato And Avocado

Servings: 4   Cooking Time: 12 Minutes

Ingredients:

- ½ lb. cherry tomatoes; halved
- 2 avocados, pitted; peeled and cubed
- 1 ¼ cup lettuce; torn
- 1/3 cup coconut cream
- A pinch of salt and black pepper
- Cooking spray

Directions:

Grease the air fryer with cooking spray, combine the tomatoes with avocados, salt, pepper and the cream and cook at 350°F for 5 minutes shaking once   In a salad bowl, mix the lettuce with the tomatoes and avocado mix, toss and serve.

Nutrition Info: Calories: 226; Fat: 12g; Fiber: 2g; Carbs: 4g; Protein: 8g

212. Buttered Duck Breasts

Servings: 4   Cooking Time: 22 Minutes

Ingredients:

- 2: 12-ouncesduck breasts
- Salt and ground black pepper, as required
- ½ teaspoon dried thyme, crushed
- 3 tablespoons unsalted butter, melted
- ¼ teaspoon star anise powder

Directions:

Preheat the Air fryer to 390 degree F and grease an Air fryer basket. Season the duck breasts generously with salt and black pepper. Arrange the duck breasts into the prepared Air fryer basket and cook for about 10 minutes. Dish out the duck breasts and drizzle with melted butter. Season with thyme and star anise powder and place the duck breasts again into the Air fryer basket. Cook for about 12 more minutes and dish out to serve warm.

Nutrition Info: Calories: 296, Fat: 15.5g, Carbohydrates: 0.1g, Sugar: 0g, Protein: 37.5g, Sodium: 100mg

213.	**Kalamta Mozarella Pita Melts**

Servings: 2   Cooking Time: 5 Minutes
Ingredients:

2 (6-inch) whole wheat pitas	1/4 small red onion
1 teaspoon extra-virgin olive oil	1/4 cup pitted Kalamata olives
1 cup grated part-skim mozzarella cheese	2 tablespoons chopped fresh herbs such as parsley, basil, or oregano

Directions:
Start by preheating toaster oven to 425°F. Brush the pita on both sides with oil and warm in the oven for one minute. Dice onions and halve olives. Sprinkle mozzarella over each pita and top with onion and olive. Return to the oven for another 5 minutes or until the cheese is melted. Sprinkle herbs over the pita and serve.

Nutrition Info: Calories: 387, Sodium: 828 mg, Dietary Fiber: 7.4 g, Total Fat: 16.2 g, Total Carbs: 42.0 g, Protein: 23.0 g.

214.	**Air Fryer Beef Steak**

Servings: 4   Cooking Time: 15 Minutes
Ingredients:

1 tbsp. Olive oil	2 pounds of ribeye steak
Pepper and salt	

Directions:
Preparing the ingredients. Season meat on both sides with pepper and salt. Rub all sides of meat with olive oil. Preheat instant crisp air fryer to 356 degrees and spritz with olive oil. Air frying. Close air fryer lid. Set temperature to 356°f, and set time to 7 minutes. Cook steak 7 minutes. Flip and cook an additional 6 minutes. Let meat sit 2-5 minutes to rest. Slice and serve with salad.

Nutrition Info: Calories: 233; Fat: 19g; Protein:16g; Sugar:0g

215.	**Rosemary Lemon Chicken**

Servings: 8   Cooking Time: 45 Minutes
Ingredients:

4-lb. chicken, cut into pieces	2 large garlic cloves, minced
Salt and black pepper, to taste	1 1/2 teaspoons rosemary leaves
Flour for dredging 3 tablespoons olive oil	1 tablespoon honey
1 large onion, sliced	1/4 cup lemon juice
Peel of ½ lemon	1 cup chicken broth

Directions:
Dredges the chicken through the flour then place in the baking pan. Whisk broth with the rest of the Ingredients: in a bowl. Pour this mixture over the dredged chicken in the pan. Press "Power Button" of Air Fry Oven and turn the dial to select the "Bake" mode. Press the Time button and again turn the dial to set the cooking time to 45 minutes. Now push the Temp button and rotate the dial to set the temperature at 400 degrees F. Once preheated, place the baking pan inside and close its lid. Baste the chicken with its sauce every 15 minutes. Serve warm.

Nutrition Info: Calories 405 Total Fat 22.7 g Saturated Fat 6.1 g Cholesterol 4 mg Sodium 227 mg Total Carbs 26.1 g Fiber 1.4 g Sugar 0.9 g Protein 45.2 g

216.	**Roasted Mini Peppers**

Servings: 6   Cooking Time: 15 Minutes
Ingredients:

1 bag mini bell peppers	Salt and pepper to taste
Cooking spray	

Directions:
Start by preheating toaster oven to 400°F. Wash and dry the peppers, then place flat on a baking sheet. Spray peppers with cooking spray and sprinkle with salt and pepper. Roast for 15 minutes.

Nutrition Info: Calories: 19, Sodium: 2 mg, Dietary Fiber: 1.3 g, Total Fat: 0.3 g, Total Carbs: 3.6 g, Protein: 0.6 g.

217.	**Herbed Duck Legs**

Servings: 2   Cooking Time: 30 Minutes
Ingredients:

½ tablespoon fresh thyme, chopped	2 duck legs
½ tablespoon fresh parsley, chopped	1 teaspoon five spice powder
1 garlic clove, minced	Salt and black pepper, as required

Directions:
Preheat the Air fryer to 340 degree F and grease an Air fryer basket. Mix the garlic, herbs, five spice powder, salt, and black pepper in a bowl. Rub the duck legs with garlic mixture generously and arrange into the Air fryer basket. Cook for about 25 minutes and set the Air fryer to 390 degree F. Cook for 5 more minutes and dish out to serve hot.

Nutrition Info: Calories: 138, Fat: 4.5g, Carbohydrates: 1g, Sugar: 0g, Protein: 25g, Sodium: 82mg

218.	**Creamy Green Beans And Tomatoes**

Servings: 4   Cooking Time: 20 Minutes
Ingredients:

1 pound green beans, trimmed and halved	1 teaspoon basil, dried
½ pound cherry tomatoes, halved	Salt and black pepper to the taste
2 tablespoons olive oil	1 cup heavy cream

1 teaspoon oregano, dried

½ tablespoon cilantro, chopped

Directions:
In your air fryer's pan, combine the green beans with the tomatoes and the other Ingredients:, toss and cook at 360 degrees F for 20 minutes. Divide the mix between plates and serve.
Nutrition Info: Calories 174, fat 5, fiber 7, carbs 11, protein 4

219.   Turkey And Almonds

Servings: 2   Cooking Time: 10 Minutes
Ingredients:

1 big turkey breast, skinless; boneless and halved
1/3 cup almonds; chopped

2 shallots; chopped
1 tbsp. sweet paprika
2 tbsp. olive oil
Salt and black pepper to taste.

Directions:
In a pan that fits the air fryer, combine the turkey with all the other ingredients, toss. Put the pan in the machine and cook at 370°F for 25 minutes Divide everything between plates and serve.
Nutrition Info: Calories: 274; Fat: 12g; Fiber: 3g; Carbs: 5g; Protein: 14g

220.   Air Fryer Marinated Salmon

Servings: 4   Cooking Time: 12 Minutes
Ingredients:

4 salmon fillets or 1 1lb fillet cut into 4 pieces
1 Tbsp brown sugar
½ Tbsp Minced Garlic

6 Tbsps Soy Sauce
¼ cup Dijon Mustard
1 Green onions finely chopped

Directions:
Take a bowl and whisk together soy sauce, dijon mustard, brown sugar, and minced garlic. Pour this mixture over salmon fillets, making sure that all the fillets are covered. Refrigerate and marinate for 20-30 minutes. Remove salmon fillets from marinade and place them in greased or lined on the tray in the Instant Pot Duo Crisp Air Fryer basket, close the lid. Select the Air Fry option and Air Fry for around 12 minutes at 400°F. Remove from Instant Pot Duo Crisp Air Fryer and top with chopped green onions.
Nutrition Info: Calories 267, Total Fat 11g, Total Carbs 5g, Protein 37g

221.   Air Fried Sausages

Servings: 6   Cooking Time: 13 Minutes
Ingredients:

6 sausage   olive oil spray

Directions:
Pour 5 cup of water into Instant Pot Duo Crisp Air Fryer. Place air fryer basket inside the pot, spray inside with nonstick spray and put sausage links inside. Close the Air Fryer lid and steam for about 5 minutes. Remove the lid once done. Spray links with olive oil and close air crisp lid. Set to air crisp at 400°F for 8 min flipping halfway through so both sides get browned.

Nutrition Info: Calories 267, Total Fat 23g, Total Carbs 2g, Protein 13g

222.   Easy Prosciutto Grilled Cheese

Servings: 1   Cooking Time: 5 Minutes
Ingredients:

2 slices muenster cheese
Four thinly-shaved pieces of prosciutto

2 slices white bread
1 tablespoon sweet and spicy pickles

Directions:
Set toaster oven to the Toast setting. Place one slice of cheese on each piece of bread. Put prosciutto on one slice and pickles on the other. Transfer to a baking sheet and toast for 4 minutes or until the cheese is melted. Combine the sides, cut, and serve.
Nutrition Info: Calories: 460, Sodium: 2180 mg, Dietary Fiber: 0 g, Total Fat: 25.2 g, Total Carbs: 11.9 g, Protein: 44.2 g.

223.   Turkey Meatloaf

Servings: 4   Cooking Time: 20 Minutes
Ingredients:

1 pound ground turkey
1 cup kale leaves, trimmed and finely chopped
½ cup fresh breadcrumbs
1 cup Monterey Jack cheese, grated
2 garlic cloves, minced

1 cup onion, chopped
¼ cup salsa verde
1 teaspoon red chili powder
½ teaspoon ground cumin
½ teaspoon dried oregano, crushed
Salt and ground black pepper, as required

Directions:
Preheat the Air fryer to 400 degree F and grease an Air fryer basket. Mix all the ingredients in a bowl and divide the turkey mixture into 4 equal-sized portions. Shape each into a mini loaf and arrange the loaves into the Air fryer basket. Cook for about 20 minutes and dish out to serve warm.
Nutrition Info: Calories: 435, Fat: 23.1g, Carbohydrates: 18.1g, Sugar: 3.6g, Protein: 42.2g, Sodium: 641mg

224.   Boneless Air Fryer Turkey Breasts

Servings: 4   Cooking Time: 50 Minutes
Ingredients:

3 lb boneless breast
¼ cup mayonnaise
2 tsp poultry seasoning

1 tsp salt
½ tsp garlic powder
¼ tsp black pepper

Directions:
Choose the Air Fry option on the Instant Pot Duo Crisp Air fryer. Set the temperature to 360°F and push start. The preheating will start. Season your boneless turkey breast with mayonnaise, poultry seasoning, salt, garlic powder, and black pepper. Once preheated, Air Fry the turkey breasts on 360°F

for 1 hour, turning every 15 minutes or until internal temperature has reached a temperature of 165°F.
Nutrition Info: Calories 558, Total Fat 18g, Total Carbs 1g, Protein 98g

225. Rolled Salmon Sandwich

Servings: 1   Cooking Time: 5 Minutes
Ingredients:

1 piece of flatbread	Pinch of salt
1 salmon filet	1/2 teaspoon thyme
1 tablespoon green onion, chopped	1/2 teaspoon sesame seeds
1/4 teaspoon dried sumac	1/4 English cucumber
	1 tablespoon yogurt

Directions:
Start by peeling and chopping the cucumber. Cut the salmon at a 45-degree angle into 4 slices and lay them flat on the flatbread.   Sprinkle salmon with salt to taste. Sprinkle onions, thyme, sumac, and sesame seeds evenly over the salmon.   Broil the salmon for at least 3 minutes, but longer if you want a more well-done fish.   While you broil your salmon, mix together the yogurt and cucumber. Remove your flatbread from the toaster oven and put it on a plate, then spoon the yogurt mix over the salmon.   Fold the sides of the flatbread in and roll it up for a gourmet lunch that you can take on the go.
Nutrition Info: Calories: 347, Sodium: 397 mg, Dietary Fiber: 1.6 g, Total Fat: 12.4 g, Total Carbs: 20.6 g, Protein: 38.9 g.

226. Roasted Delicata Squash With Kale

Servings: 2   Cooking Time: 10 Minutes
Ingredients:

1 medium delicata squash	2 tablespoons olive oil
1 bunch kale	Salt and pepper
1 clove garlic	

Directions:
Start by preheating toaster oven to 425°F.   Clean squash and cut off each end. Cut in half and remove the seeds. Quarter the halves.   Toss the squash in 1 tablespoon of olive oil.   Place the squash on a greased baking sheet and roast for 25 minutes, turning halfway through.   Rinse kale and remove stems. Chop garlic.   Heat the leftover oil in a medium skillet and add kale and salt to taste. Sauté the kale until it darkens, then mix in the garlic. Cook for another minute then remove from heat and add 2 tablespoons of water.   Remove squash from oven and lay it on top of the garlic kale.   Top with salt and pepper to taste and serve.
Nutrition Info: Calories: 159, Sodium: 28 mg, Dietary Fiber: 1.8 g, Total Fat: 14.2 g, Total Carbs: 8.2 g, Protein: 2.6 g.

227. Eggplant And Leeks Stew

Servings: 4   Cooking Time: 12 Minutes
Ingredients:

2 big eggplants, roughly cubed	3 leeks; sliced
½ bunch cilantro; chopped.	2 tbsp. olive oil
	1 tbsp. hot sauce
	1 tbsp. sweet paprika
1 cup veggie stock	1 tbsp. tomato puree
2 garlic cloves; minced	Salt and black pepper to taste.

Directions:
In a pan that fits the air fryer, mix all the ingredients, toss, introduce in the fryer and cook at 380°F for 20 minutes   Divide the stew into bowls and serve for lunch.
Nutrition Info: Calories: 183; Fat: 4g; Fiber: 2g; Carbs: 4g; Protein: 12g

228. Sweet Potato Chips

Servings: 2   Cooking Time: 40 Minutes
Ingredients:

2 sweet potatoes	Olive oil
Salt and pepper to taste	Cinnamon

Directions:
Start by preheating toaster oven to 400°F.   Cut off each end of potato and discard.   Cut potatoes into 1/2-inch slices.   Brush a pan with olive oil and lay potato slices flat on the pan.   Bake for 20 minutes, then flip and bake for another 20.
Nutrition Info: Calories: 139, Sodium: 29 mg, Dietary Fiber: 8.2 g, Total Fat: 0.5 g, Total Carbs: 34.1 g, Protein: 1.9 g.

229. Fried Chicken Tacos

Servings: 4   Cooking Time: 10 Minutes
Ingredients:

Chicken	Coleslaw
1 lb. chicken tenders or breast chopped into 2-inch pieces	¼ tsp red pepper flakes
1 tsp garlic powder	2 cups coleslaw mix
½ tsp onion powder	1 Tbsp brown sugar
1 large egg	½ tsp salt
1 ½ tsp salt	2 Tbsp apple cider vinegar
1 tsp paprika	1 Tbsp water
3 Tbsp buttermilk	Spicy Mayo
¾ cup All-purpose flour	½ tsp salt
3 Tbsp corn starch	
½ tsp black pepper	¼ cup mayonnaise
½ tsp cayenne pepper	1 tsp garlic powder
oil for spraying	2 Tbsp hot sauce
	1 Tbsp buttermilk
	Tortilla wrappers

Directions:
Take a large bowl and mix together coleslaw mix, water, brown sugar, salt, apple cider vinegar, and red pepper flakes. Set aside.   Take another small bowl and combine mayonnaise, hot sauce, buttermilk, garlic powder, and salt. Set this mixture aside.   Select the Instant Pot Duo Crisp Air Fryer option, adjust the temperature to 360°F and push start. Preheating will start.   Create a clear station by placing two large flat pans side by side. Whisk together egg and buttermilk with salt and pepper in one of them. In the second, whisk flour, corn starch, black pepper, garlic powder, onion powder, salt, paprika, and cayenne pepper.   Cut the chicken tenders into 1-inch pieces. Season all pieces with a little salt and pepper.   Once the Instant Pot Duo Crisp Air Fryer is preheated, remove the tray and

lightly spray it with oil. Coat your chicken with egg mixture while shaking off any excess egg, followed by the flour mixture, and place it on the tray and tray in the basket, making sure your chicken pieces don't overlap. Close the Air Fryer lid, and cook on 360°F for 10 minutes while flipping and spraying halfway through cooking. Once the chicken is done, remove and place chicken into warmed tortilla shells. Top with coleslaw and spicy mayonnaise.

Nutrition Info: Calories 375, Total Fat 15g, Total Carbs 31g, Protein 29g

230. Fried Whole Chicken

Servings: 4   Cooking Time: 70 Minutes

Ingredients:

1 Whole chicken	1 tsp Italian
2 Tbsp or spray of oil	seasoning
of choice	2 Tbsp Montreal
1 tsp garlic powder	Steak Seasoning (or
1 tsp onion powder	salt and pepper to
1 tsp paprika	taste)
	1.5 cup chicken broth

Directions:
Truss and wash the chicken. Mix the seasoning and rub a little amount on the chicken. Pour the broth inside the Instant Pot Duo Crisp Air Fryer. Place the chicken in the air fryer basket. Select the option Air Fry and Close the Air Fryer lid and cook for 25 minutes. Spray or rub the top of the chicken with oil and rub it with half of the seasoning. Close the air fryer lid and air fry again at 400°F for 10 minutes. Flip the chicken, spray it with oil, and rub with the remaining seasoning. Again air fry it for another ten minutes. Allow the chicken to rest for 10 minutes.

Nutrition Info: Calories 436, Total Fat 28g, Total Carbs 4g, Protein 42g

231. Crisp Chicken Casserole

Servings: 4   Cooking Time: 15 Minutes

Ingredients:

3 cup chicken,	1 tsp garlic powder
shredded	salt and pepper to
12 oz bag egg noodles	taste
1/2 large onion	1 cup cheddar cheese,
1/2 cup chopped	shredded
carrots	1 package French's
1/4 cup frozen peas	onions
1/4 cup frozen	1/4 cup sour cream
broccoli pieces	1 can cream of
2 stalks celery	chicken and
chopped	mushroom soup
5 cup chicken broth	

Directions:
Place the chicken, vegetables, garlic powder, salt and pepper, and broth and stir. Then place it into the Instant Pot Duo Crisp Air Fryer Basket. Press or lightly stir the egg noodles into the mix until damp/wet. Select the option Air Fryer and cook for 4 minutes. Stir in the sour cream, can of soup, cheese, and 1/3 of the French's onions. Top with the remaining French's onions and close the Air Fryer lid and cook for about 10 more minutes.

Nutrition Info: Calories 301, Total Fat 17g, Total Carbs 17g, Protein 20g

232. Turkey-stuffed Peppers

Servings: 6   Cooking Time: 35 Minutes

Ingredients:

1 pound lean ground	1/3 onion, minced
turkey	1/2 teaspoon salt
1 tablespoon olive oil	Pepper to taste
2 cloves garlic,	3 large red bell
minced	peppers
1 tablespoon cilantro	1 cup chicken broth
(optional)	1/4 cup tomato sauce
1 teaspoon garlic	1-1/2 cups cooked
powder	brown rice
1 teaspoon cumin	1/4 cup shredded
powder	cheddar
	6 green onions

Directions:
Start by preheating toaster oven to 400°F. Heat a skillet on medium heat. Add olive oil to the skillet, then mix in onion and garlic. Sauté for about 5 minutes, or until the onion starts to look opaque. Add the turkey to the skillet and season with cumin, garlic powder, salt, and pepper. Brown the meat until thoroughly cooked, then mix in chicken broth and tomato sauce. Reduce heat and simmer for about 5 minutes, stirring occasionally. Add the brown rice and continue stirring until it is evenly spread through the mix. Cut the bell peppers lengthwise down the middle and remove all of the seeds. Grease a pan or line it with parchment paper and lay all peppers in the pan with the outside facing down. Spoon the meat mixture evenly into each pepper and use the back of the spoon to level. Bake for 30 minutes. Remove pan from oven and sprinkle cheddar over each pepper, then put it back in for another 3 minutes, or until the cheese is melted. While the cheese melts, dice the green onions. Remove pan from oven and sprinkle onions over each pepper and serve.

Nutrition Info: Calories: 394, Sodium: 493 mg, Dietary Fiber: 4.1 g, Total Fat: 12.9 g, Total Carbs: 44.4 g, Protein: 27.7 g.

233. Parmigiano Reggiano And Prosciutto Toasts With Balsamic Glaze

Servings: 8   Cooking Time: 15 Minutes

Ingredients:

3 ounces thinly sliced	1/2 cup balsamic
prosciutto, cut	vinegar
crosswise into 1/4-	1 medium red onion,
inch-wide strips	thinly sliced
1 (3-ounce) piece	1 tablespoon extra-
Parmigiano Reggiano	virgin olive oil
cheese	1 clove garlic
1 loaf ciabatta, cut	Black pepper to taste
into 3/4-inch-thick	
slices	

Directions:
Preheat toaster oven to 350°F. Place onion in a bowl of cold water and let sit for 10 minutes. Bring vinegar to a boil, then reduce heat and simmer for 5 minutes. Remove from heat completely and set aside to allow the vinegar to thicken. Drain the onion. Brush the tops of each bun with oil, rub

with garlic, and sprinkle with pepper.   Use a vegetable peeler to make large curls of Parmigiano Reggiano cheese and place them on the bun.   Bake for 15 minutes or until the bread just starts to crisp. Sprinkle prosciutto and onions on top, then drizzle vinegar and serve.
Nutrition Info: Calories: 154, Sodium: 432 mg, Dietary Fiber: 1.0 g, Total Fat: 5.6 g, Total Carbs: 17.3 g, Protein: 8.1 g.

234.	Dijon And Swiss Croque Monsieur

Servings: 2   Cooking Time: 13 Minutes
Ingredients:

4 slices white bread	1/2 cup whole milk
2 tablespoons unsalted butter	1/4 teaspoon freshly ground black pepper
1 tablespoon all-purpose flour	1/8 teaspoon salt
3/4 cups shredded Swiss cheese	1 tablespoon Dijon mustard
	4 slices ham

Directions:
Start by cutting crusts off bread and placing them on a pan lined with parchment paper.   Melt 1 tablespoon of butter in a sauce pan, then dab the top sides of each piece of bread with butter.   Toast bread in oven for 3-5 minutes until each piece is golden brown.   Melt the second tablespoon of butter in the sauce pan and add the flour, mix together until they form a paste.   Add the milk and continue to mix until the sauce begins to thicken. Remove from heat and mix in 1 tablespoon of Swiss cheese, salt, and pepper; continue stirring until cheese is melted.   Flip the bread over in the pan so the untoasted side is facing up.   Set two slices aside and spread Dijon on the other two slices. Add ham and sprinkle 1/4 cup Swiss over each piece. Broil for about 3 minutes.   Top the sandwiches off with the other slices of bread, soft-side down.   Top with sauce and sprinkle with remaining Swiss. Toast for another 5 minutes or until the cheese is golden brown.   Serve immediately.
Nutrition Info: Calories: 452, Sodium: 1273 mg, Dietary Fiber: 1.6 g, Total Fat: 30.5 g, Total Carbs: 19.8 g, Protein: 24.4 g.

235.	Chicken Wings With Prawn Paste

Servings: 6   Cooking Time: 8 Minutes
Ingredients:

Corn flour, as required	1½ teaspoons sugar
2 pounds mid-joint chicken wings	2 teaspoons sesame oil
2 tablespoons prawn paste	1 teaspoon Shaoxing wine
4 tablespoons olive oil	2 teaspoons fresh ginger juice

Directions:
Preheat the Air fryer to 360 degree F and grease an Air fryer basket.   Mix all the ingredients in a bowl except wings and corn flour.   Rub the chicken wings generously with marinade and refrigerate overnight.   Coat the chicken wings evenly with

corn flour and keep aside.   Set the Air fryer to 390 degree F and arrange the chicken wings in the Air fryer basket.   Cook for about 8 minutes and dish out to serve hot.
Nutrition Info: Calories: 416, Fat: 31.5g, Carbohydrates: 11.2g, Sugar: 1.6g, Protein: 24.4g, Sodium: 661mg

236.	Buttermilk Brined Turkey Breast

Servings: 8   Cooking Time: 20 Minutes
Ingredients:

¾ cup brine from a can of olives	2 fresh thyme sprigs
3½ pounds boneless, skinless turkey breast	1 fresh rosemary sprig
	½ cup buttermilk

Directions:
Preheat the Air fryer to 350 degree F and grease an Air fryer basket.   Mix olive brine and buttermilk in a bowl until well combined.   Place the turkey breast, buttermilk mixture and herb sprigs in a resealable plastic bag.   Seal the bag and refrigerate for about 12 hours.   Remove the turkey breast from bag and arrange the turkey breast into the Air fryer basket.   Cook for about 20 minutes, flipping once in between.   Dish out the turkey breast onto a cutting board and cut into desired size slices to serve.
Nutrition Info: Calories: 215, Fat: 3.5g, Carbohydrates: 9.4g, Sugar: 7.7g, Protein: 34.4g, Sodium: 2000mg

237.	Roasted Beet Salad With Oranges & Beet Greens

Servings: 6   Cooking Time: 1-1/2 Hours
Ingredients:

6 medium beets with beet greens attached	1/4 cup extra-virgin olive oil
2 large oranges	2 garlic cloves, minced
1 small sweet onion, cut into wedges	1/2 teaspoon grated orange peel
1/3 cup red wine vinegar	

Directions:
Start by preheating toaster oven to 400°F.   Trim leaves from beets and chop, then set aside.   Pierce beets with a fork and place in a roasting pan. Roast beets for 1-1/2 hours.   Allow beets to cool, peel, then cut into 8 wedges and put into a bowl. Place beet greens in a sauce pan and cover with just enough water to cover.   Heat until water boils, then immediately remove from heat.   Drain greens and press to remove liquid from greens, then add to beet bowl.   Remove peel and pith from orange and segment, adding each segment to the bowl.   Add onion to beet mixture. In a separate bowl mix together vinegar, oil, garlic and orange peel. Combine both bowls and toss, sprinkle with salt and pepper.   Let stand for an hour before serving.
Nutrition Info: Calories: 214, Sodium: 183 mg, Dietary Fiber: 6.5 g, Total Fat: 8.9 g, Total Carbs: 32.4 g, Protein: 4.7 g.

238. Ranch Chicken Wings

Servings: 3   Cooking Time: 10 Minutes

Ingredients:

1/4 cup almond meal	1/4 cup flaxseed meal
2 tablespoons butter, melted	1 tablespoon Ranch seasoning mix
6 tablespoons parmesan cheese, preferably freshly grated	2 tablespoons oyster sauce
	6 chicken wings, bone-in

Directions:

Start by preheating your Air Fryer to 370 degrees F. In a resealable bag, place the almond meal, flaxseed meal, butter, parmesan, Ranch seasoning mix, andoyster sauce. Add the chicken wings and shake to coat on all sides.   Arrange the chicken wings in the Air Fryer basket. Spritz the chicken wings with a nonstick cooking spray.   Cook for 11 minutes. Turn them over and cook an additional 11 minutes. Serve warm with your favorite dipping sauce, if desired. Enjoy!

Nutrition Info:285 Calories; 22g Fat; 3g Carbs; 12g Protein; 5g Sugars; 6g Fiber

239. Chicken And Celery Stew

Servings: 6   Cooking Time: 12 Minutes

Ingredients:

1 lb. chicken breasts, skinless; boneless and cubed	2 red bell peppers; chopped.
4 celery stalks; chopped.	2 tsp. garlic; minced
1/2 cup coconut cream	1 tbsp. butter, soft
	Salt and black pepper to taste.

Directions:

Grease a baking dish that fits your air fryer with the butter, add all the ingredients in the pan and toss them.   Introduce the dish in the fryer, cook at 360°F for 30 minutes, divide into bowls and serve

Nutrition Info: Calories: 246; Fat: 12g; Fiber: 2g; Carbs: 6g; Protein: 12g

240. Roasted Fennel, Ditalini, And Shrimp

Servings: 4   Cooking Time: 30 Minutes

Ingredients:

1 pound extra large, thawed, tail-on shrimp	1 teaspoon salt
1 teaspoon fennel seeds	2 tablespoons olive oil
1 fennel bulb, halved and sliced crosswise	1/2 teaspoon freshly ground black pepper
4 garlic cloves, chopped	Grated zest of 1 lemon
	1/2 pound whole wheat ditalini

Directions:

Start by preheating toaster oven to 450°F.   Toast the seeds in a medium pan over medium heat for about 5 minutes, then toss with shrimp.   Add water and 1/2 teaspoon salt to the pan and bring the mixture to a boil.   Reduce heat and simmer for 30 minutes.   Combine fennel, garlic, oil, pepper, and remaining salt in a roasting pan.   Roast for 20 minutes, then add shrimp mixture and roast for another 5 minutes or until shrimp are cooked.

While the fennel is roasting, cook pasta per the directions on the package, drain, and set aside. Remove the shrimp mixture and mix in pasta, roast for another 5 minutes.

Nutrition Info: Calories: 420, Sodium: 890 mg, Dietary Fiber: 4.2 g, Total Fat: 10.2 g, Total Carbs: 49.5 g, Protein: 33.9 g.

241. Air Fried Steak Sandwich

Servings: 4   Cooking Time: 16 Minutes

Ingredients:

Large hoagie bun, sliced in half	1 tablespoon of fresh bleu cheese, crumbled
6 ounces of sirloin or flank steak, sliced into bite-sized pieces	8 medium-sized cherry tomatoes, sliced in half
1/2 tablespoon of mustard powder	1 cup of fresh arugula, rinsed and patted dry
1/2 tablespoon of soy sauce	

Directions:

Preparing the ingredients. In a small mixing bowl, combine the soy sauce and onion powder; stir with a fork until thoroughly combined.   Lay the raw steak strips in the soy-mustard mixture, and fully immerse each piece to marinate.   Set the instant crisp air fryer to 320 degrees for 10 minutes. Arrange the soy-mustard marinated steak pieces on a piece of tin foil, flat and not overlapping, and set the tin foil on one side of the instant crisp air fryer basket. The foil should not take up more than half of the surface.   Lay the hoagie-bun halves, crusty-side up and soft-side down, on the other half of the air-fryer.   Air frying. Close air fryer lid.   After 10 minutes, the instant crisp air fryer will shut off; the hoagie buns should be starting to crisp and the steak will have begun to cook.   Carefully, flip the hoagie buns so they are now crusty-side down and soft-side up; crumble a layer of the bleu cheese on each hoagie half.   With a long spoon, gently stir the marinated steak in the foil to ensure even coverage.   Set the instant crisp air fryer to 360 degrees for 6 minutes. After 6 minutes, when the fryer shuts off, the bleu cheese will be perfectly melted over the toasted bread, and the steak will be juicy on the inside and crispy on the outside.   Remove the cheesy hoagie halves first, using tongs, and set on a serving plate; then cover one side with the steak, and top with the cherry-tomato halves and the arugula. Close with the other cheesy hoagie-half, slice into two pieces, and enjoy.

Nutrition Info: Calories 284 Total fat 7.9 g Saturated fat 1.4 g Cholesterol 36 mg Sodium 704 mg Total carbs 46 g Fiber 3.6 g Sugar 5.5 g Protein 17.9 g

242. Portobello Pesto Burgers

Servings: 4   Cooking Time: 26 Minutes

Ingredients:

4 portobello mushrooms	1 large ripe tomato
1/4 cup sundried tomato pesto	1 log fresh goat cheese
4 whole-grain hamburger buns	8 large fresh basil leaves

Directions:
Start by preheating toaster oven to 425°F.   Place mushrooms on a pan, round sides facing up.   Bake for 14 minutes.   Pull out tray, flip the mushrooms and spread 1 tablespoon of pesto on each piece. Return to oven and bake for another 10 minutes. Remove the mushrooms and toast the buns for 2 minutes.   Remove the buns and build the burger by placing tomatoes, mushroom, 2 slices of cheese, and a sprinkle of basil, then topping with the top bun.
Nutrition Info: Calories: 297, Sodium: 346 mg, Dietary Fiber: 1.8 g, Total Fat: 18.1 g, Total Carbs: 19.7 g, Protein: 14.4 g.

---

243.   Pecan Crunch Catfish And Asparagus

Servings: 4   Cooking Time: 12 Minutes
Ingredients:

1 cup whole wheat panko breadcrumbs	3 teaspoons chopped fresh thyme
1/4 cup chopped pecans	Salt and pepper to taste
1-1/2 tablespoons extra-virgin olive oil, plus more for the pan	1-1/4 pounds asparagus
1 tablespoon honey	4 (5- to 6-ounce each) catfish filets

Directions:
Start by preheating toaster oven to 425°F. Combine breadcrumbs, pecans, 2 teaspoons thyme, 1 tablespoon oil, salt, pepper and 2 tablespoons water.   In another bowl combine asparagus, the rest of the thyme, honey, salt, and pepper.   Spread the asparagus in a flat layer on a baking sheet. Sprinkle a quarter of the breadcrumb mixture over the asparagus.   Lay the catfish over the asparagus and press the rest of the breadcrumb mixture into each piece. Roast for 12 minutes.
Nutrition Info: Calories: 531, Sodium: 291 mg, Dietary Fiber: 6.1 g, Total Fat: 30.4 g, Total Carbs: 31.9 g, Protein: 34.8 g.

---

244.   Ricotta Toasts With Salmon

Servings: 2   Cooking Time: 4 Minutes
Ingredients:

4 bread slices	1 teaspoon lemon zest
1 garlic clove, minced	Freshly ground black pepper, to taste
8 oz. ricotta cheese	4 oz. smoked salmon

Directions:
In a food processor, add the garlic, ricotta, lemon zest and black pepper and pulse until smooth. Spread ricotta mixture over each bread slices evenly. Press "Power Button" of Air Fry Oven and turn the dial to select the "Air Fry" mode.   Press the Time button and again turn the dial to set the cooking time to 4 minutes.   Now push the Temp button and rotate the dial to set the temperature at 355 degrees F.   Press "Start/Pause" button to start. When the unit beeps to show that it is preheated, open the lid and lightly, grease the sheet pan. Arrange the bread slices into "Air Fry Basket" and insert in the oven.   Top with salmon and serve.
Nutrition Info: Calories: 274 Cal Total Fat: 12 g Saturated Fat: 6.3 g   Cholesterol: 48 mg   Sodium:

1300 mg   Total Carbs: 15.7 g   Fiber: 0.5 g Sugar: 1.2 g   Protein: 24.8 g

---

245.   Parmesan Chicken Meatballs

Servings: 4   Cooking Time: 12 Minutes
Ingredients:

1-lb. ground chicken	1 teaspoon paprika
1 large egg, beaten	1 teaspoon kosher salt
½ cup Parmesan cheese, grated	½ teaspoon pepper
½ cup pork rinds, ground	Crust:
1 teaspoon garlic powder	½ cup pork rinds, ground

Directions:
Toss all the meatball Ingredients: in a bowl and mix well.   Make small meatballs out this mixture and roll them in the pork rinds.   Place the coated meatballs in the air fryer basket.   Press "Power Button" of Air Fry Oven and turn the dial to select the "Bake" mode.   Press the Time button and again turn the dial to set the cooking time to 12 minutes.   Now push the Temp button and rotate the dial to set the temperature at 400 degrees F. Once preheated, place the air fryer basket inside and close its lid.   Serve warm.
Nutrition Info: Calories 529 Total Fat 17 g Saturated Fat 3 g Cholesterol 65 mg Sodium 391 mg Total Carbs 55 g Fiber 6 g Sugar 8 g Protein 41g

---

246.   Vegetarian Philly Sandwich

Servings: 2   Cooking Time: 20 Minutes
Ingredients:

2 tablespoons olive oil	1 green bell pepper, thinly sliced
8 ounces sliced portabello mushrooms	1 red bell pepper, thinly sliced
1 vidalia onion, thinly sliced	4 slices 2% provolone cheese
Salt and pepper	4 rolls

Directions:
Preheat toaster oven to 475°F.   Heat the oil in a medium sauce pan over medium heat.   Sauté mushrooms about 5 minutes, then add the onions and peppers and sauté another 10 minutes.   Slice rolls lengthwise and divide the vegetables into each roll.   Add the cheese and toast until the rolls start to brown and the cheese melts.
Nutrition Info: Calories: 645, Sodium: 916 mg, Dietary Fiber: 7.2 g, Total Fat: 33.3 g, Total Carbs: 61.8 g, Protein: 27.1 g.

---

247.   Nutmeg Chicken Thighs

Servings: 4   Cooking Time: 10 Minutes
Ingredients:

2 lb. chicken thighs	A pinch of salt and black pepper
2 tbsp. olive oil	
½ tsp. nutmeg, ground	

Directions:
Season the chicken thighs with salt and pepper and rub with the rest of the ingredients   Put the chicken thighs in air fryer's basket, cook at 360°F for

15 minutes on each side, divide between plates and serve.
Nutrition Info: Calories: 271; Fat: 12g; Fiber: 4g; Carbs: 6g; Protein: 13g

248. Onion Omelet

Servings: 2   Cooking Time: 15 Minutes
Ingredients:

4 eggs	1 teaspoon butter
¼ teaspoon low-sodium soy sauce	1 medium yellow onion, sliced
Ground black pepper, as required	¼ cup Cheddar cheese, grated

Directions:
In a skillet, melt the butter over medium heat and cook the onion and cook for about 8-10 minutes. Remove from the heat and set aside to cool slightly. Meanwhile, in a bowl, add the eggs, soy sauce and black pepper and beat well.   Add the cooked onion and gently, stir to combine.   Place the zucchini mixture into a small baking pan.   Press "Power Button" of Air Fry Oven and turn the dial to select the "Air Fry" mode.   Press the Time button and again turn the dial to set the cooking time to 5 minutes.   Now push the Temp button and rotate the dial to set the temperature at 355 degrees F. Press "Start/Pause" button to start.   When the unit beeps to show that it is preheated, open the lid. Arrange pan over the "Wire Rack" and insert in the oven.   Cut the omelet into 2 portions and serve hot.
Nutrition Info: Calories: 222 Cal Total Fat: 15.4 g Saturated Fat: 6.9 g   Cholesterol: 347 mg Sodium: 264 mg   Total Carbs: 6.1 g   Fiber: 1.2 g Sugar: 3.1 g   Protein: 15.3 g

249. Bok Choy And Butter Sauce(1)

Servings: 4   Cooking Time: 12 Minutes
Ingredients:

2 bok choy heads; trimmed and cut into strips	2 tbsp. chicken stock
	1 tsp. lemon juice
	1 tbsp. olive oil
1 tbsp. butter; melted	A pinch of salt and black pepper

Directions:
In a pan that fits your air fryer, mix all the ingredients, toss, introduce the pan in the air fryer and cook at 380°F for 15 minutes.   Divide between plates and serve as a side dish
Nutrition Info: Calories: 141; Fat: 3g; Fiber: 2g; Carbs: 4g; Protein: 3g

250. Crispy Breaded Pork Chop

Servings: 6   Cooking Time: 12 Minutes
Ingredients:

olive oil spray	1 large egg, beaten
6 3/4-inch thick center-cut boneless pork chops, fat trimmed (5 oz each)	2 tbsp grated parmesan cheese
	1 1/4 tsp sweet paprika
kosher salt	1/2 tsp garlic powder
1/2 cup panko crumbs, check labels for GF	1/2 tsp onion powder
	1/4 tsp chili powder
	1/8 tsp black pepper

1/3 cup crushed cornflakes crumbs
Directions:
Preheat the Instant Pot Duo Crisp Air Fryer for 12 minutes at 400°F.   On both sides, season pork chops with half teaspoon kosher salt.   Then combine cornflake crumbs, panko, parmesan cheese, 3/4 tsp kosher salt, garlic powder, paprika, onion powder, chili powder, and black pepper in a large bowl.   Place the egg beat in another bowl. Dip the pork in the egg & then crumb mixture.   When the air fryer is ready, place 3 of the chops into the Instant Pot Duo Crisp Air Fryer Basket and spritz the top with oil.   Close the Air Fryer lid and cook for 12 minutes turning halfway, spritzing both sides with oil.   Set aside and repeat with the remaining.
Nutrition Info: Calories 281, Total Fat 13g, Total Carbs 8g, Protein 33g

251. Chicken Legs With Dilled Brussels Sprouts

Servings: 2   Cooking Time: 10 Minutes
Ingredients:

2 chicken legs	1/2 teaspoon paprika
1/2 teaspoon kosher salt	1/2 pound Brussels sprouts
1/2 teaspoon black pepper	1 teaspoon dill, fresh or dried

Directions:
Start by preheating your Air Fryer to 370 degrees F. Now, season your chicken with paprika, salt, and pepper. Transfer the chicken legs to the cooking basket. Cook for 10 minutes.   Flip the chicken legs and cook an additional 10 minutes. Reserve.   Add the Brussels sprouts to the cooking basket; sprinkle with dill. Cook at 380 degrees F for 15 minutes, shaking the basket halfway through.   Serve with the reserved chicken legs.
Nutrition Info:365 Calories; 21g Fat; 3g Carbs; 36g Protein; 2g Sugars; 3g Fiber

252. Lemon Chicken Breasts

Servings: 4   Cooking Time: 30 Minutes
Ingredients:

1/4 cup olive oil	1 1/2 teaspoons dried oregano, crushed
3 tablespoons garlic, minced	1 teaspoon thyme leaves, minced
1/3 cup dry white wine	Salt and black pepper
1 tablespoon lemon zest, grated	4 skin-on boneless chicken breasts
2 tablespoons lemon juice	1 lemon, sliced

Directions:
Whisk everything in a baking pan to coat the chicken breasts well.   Place the lemon slices on top of the chicken breasts.   Spread the mustard mixture over the toasted bread slices.   Press "Power Button" of Air Fry Oven and turn the dial to select the "Bake" mode.   Press the Time button and again turn the dial to set the cooking time to 30 minutes.   Now push the Temp button and rotate the dial to set the temperature at 370 degrees F.

Once preheated, place the baking pan inside and close its lid.   Serve warm.
Nutrition Info: Calories 388 Total Fat 8 g Saturated Fat 1 g Cholesterol 153mg sodium 339 mg Total Carbs 8 g Fiber 1 g Sugar 2 g Protein 13 g

253.	**Garlic Chicken Potatoes**

Servings: 4   Cooking Time: 30 Minutes
Ingredients:

2 lbs. red potatoes, quartered	4 garlic cloves, chopped
3 tablespoons olive oil	2 tablespoons brown sugar
1/2 teaspoon cumin seeds	Pinch of red pepper flakes
Salt and black pepper, to taste	4 skinless, boneless chicken breasts
1 lemon (1/2 juiced and 1/2 cut into wedges)	2 tablespoons cilantro, chopped

Directions:
Place the chicken, lemon, garlic, and potatoes in a baking pan.   Toss the spices, herbs, oil, and sugar in a bowl.   Add this mixture to the chicken and veggies then toss well to coat.   Press "Power Button" of Air Fry Oven and turn the dial to select the "Bake" mode.   Press the Time button and again turn the dial to set the cooking time to 30 minutes.   Now push the Temp button and rotate the dial to set the temperature at 400 degrees F. Once preheated, place the baking pan inside and close its lid.   Serve warm.
Nutrition Info: Calories 545 Total Fat 36.4 g Saturated Fat 10.1 g Cholesterol 200 mg Sodium 272 mg Total Carbs 40.7 g Fiber 0.2 g Sugar 0.1 g Protein 42.5 g

254.	**Easy Turkey Breasts With Basil**

Servings: 4   Cooking Time: 10 Minutes
Ingredients:

2 pounds turkey breasts, bone-in skin-on	2 tablespoons olive oil
Coarse sea salt and ground black pepper, to taste	1 teaspoon fresh basil leaves, chopped
	2 tablespoons lemon zest, grated

Directions:
Rub olive oil on all sides of the turkey breasts; sprinkle with salt, pepper, basil, and lemon zest. Place the turkey breasts skin side up on a parchment-lined cooking basket.   Cook in the preheated Air Fryer at 330 degrees F for 30 minutes. Now, turn them over and cook an additional 28 minutes.   Serve with lemon wedges, if desired.
Nutrition Info:416 Calories; 26g Fat; 0g Carbs; 49g Protein; 0g Sugars; 2g Fiber

255.	**Baked Shrimp Scampi**

Servings: 4   Cooking Time: 10 Minutes
Ingredients:

1 lb large shrimp	1/2 tsp salt
8 tbsp butter	1/4 tsp cayenne pepper
1 tbsp minced garlic	

(use 2 for extra garlic flavor) / 1/4 tsp paprika
1/4 cup white wine or cooking sherry / 1/2 tsp onion powder
3/4 cup bread crumbs

Directions:
Take a bowl and mix the bread crumbs with dry seasonings.   On the stovetop (or in the Instant Pot on saute), melt the butter with the garlic and the white wine.   Remove from heat and add the shrimp and the bread crumb mix.   Transfer the mix to a casserole dish.   Choose the Bake operation and add food to the Instant Pot Duo Crisp Air Fryer. Close the lid and Bake at 350°F for 10 minutes or until they are browned.   Serve and enjoy.
Nutrition Info: Calories 422, Total Fat 26g, Total Carbs 18g, Protein 29 g

256.	**Butter Fish With Sake And Miso**

Servings: 4   Cooking Time: 11 Minutes
Ingredients:

4 (7-ounce) pieces of butter fish	1/3 cup mirin
1/3 cup sake	2/3 cup sugar
	1 cup white miso

Directions:
Start by combining sake, mirin, and sugar in a sauce pan and bring to a boil.   Allow to boil for 5 minutes, then reduce heat and simmer for another 10 minutes.   Remove from heat completely and mix in miso.   Marinate the fish in the mixture for as long as possible, up to 3 days if possible. Preheat toaster oven to 450°F and bake fish for 8 minutes.   Switch your setting to Broil and broil another 2-3 minutes, until the sauce is caramelized.
Nutrition Info: Calories: 529, Sodium: 2892 mg, Dietary Fiber: 3.7 g, Total Fat: 5.8 g, Total Carbs: 61.9 g, Protein: 53.4 g.

257.	**Cheddar & Cream Omelet**

Servings: 2   Cooking Time: 8 Minutes
Ingredients:

4 eggs	1/4 cup cream
Salt and ground black pepper, as required	1/4 cup Cheddar cheese, grated

Directions:
In a bowl, add the eggs, cream, salt, and black pepper and beat well.   Place the egg mixture into a small baking pan.   Press "Power Button" of Air Fry Oven and turn the dial to select the "Air Fry" mode.   Press the Time button and again turn the dial to set the cooking time to 8 minutes.   Now push the Temp button and rotate the dial to set the temperature at 350 degrees F.   Press "Start/Pause" button to start.   When the unit beeps to show that it is preheated, open the lid.   Arrange pan over the "Wire Rack" and insert in the oven.   After 4 minutes, sprinkle the omelet with cheese evenly. Cut the omelet into 2 portions and serve hot.   Cut into equal-sized wedges and serve hot.
Nutrition Info: Calories: 202 Cal Total Fat: 15.1 g Saturated Fat: 6.8 g   Cholesterol: 348 mg

Sodium: 298 mg   Total Carbs: 1.8 g   Fiber: 0 g
Sugar: 1.4 g   Protein: 14.8 g

258.   Tomato Avocado Melt

Servings: 2   Cooking Time: 4 Minutes

Ingredients:

4 slices of bread	1 small Roma tomato
1-2 tablespoons mayonnaise	1/2 avocado
Cayenne pepper	8 slices of cheese of your choice

Directions:
Start by slicing avocado and tomato and set aside. Spread mayonnaise on the bread.   Sprinkle cayenne pepper over the mayo to taste.   Layer tomato and avocado on top of cayenne pepper. Top with cheese and put on greased baking sheet. Broil on high for 2–4 minutes, until the cheese is melted and bread is toasted.

Nutrition Info: Calories: 635, Sodium: 874 mg, Dietary Fiber: 4.1 g, Total Fat: 50.1 g, Total Carbs: 17.4 g, Protein: 30.5 g.

259.   Duck Breast With Figs

Servings: 2   Cooking Time: 45 Minutes

Ingredients:

1 pound boneless duck breast	2 tablespoons lemon juice
6 fresh figs, halved	3 tablespoons brown sugar
1 tablespoon fresh thyme, chopped	1 teaspoon olive oil
2 cups fresh pomegranate juice	Salt and black pepper, as required

Directions:
Preheat the Air fryer to 400 degree F and grease an Air fryer basket.   Put the pomegranate juice, lemon juice, and brown sugar in a medium saucepan over medium heat.   Bring to a boil and simmer on low heat for about 25 minutes.   Season the duck breasts generously with salt and black pepper. Arrange the duck breasts into the Air fryer basket, skin side up and cook for about 14 minutes, flipping once in between.   Dish out the duck breasts onto a cutting board for about 10 minutes.   Meanwhile, put the figs, olive oil, salt, and black pepper in a bowl until well mixed.   Set the Air fryer to 400 degree F and arrange the figs into the Air fryer basket. Cook for about 5 more minutes and dish out in a platter.   Put the duck breast with the roasted figs and drizzle with warm pomegranate juice mixture. Garnish with fresh thyme and serve warm.

Nutrition Info: Calories: 699, Fat: 12.1g, Carbohydrates: 90g, Sugar: 74g, Protein: 519g, Sodium: 110mg

260.   Juicy Turkey Burgers

Servings: 8   Cooking Time: 25 Minutes

Ingredients:

1 lb ground turkey 85% lean / 15% fat	2 tsp Worcestershire Sauce
1/4 cup unsweetened apple sauce	1 tsp minced garlic
1/2 onion grated	1/4 cup plain breadcrumbs
1 Tbsp ranch seasoning	Salt and pepper to taste

Directions:
Combine the onion, ground turkey, unsweetened apple sauce, minced garlic, breadcrumbs, ranch seasoning, Worchestire sauce, and salt and pepper. Mix them with your hands until well combined. Form 4 equally sized hamburger patties with them. Place these burgers in the refrigerator for about 30 minutes to have them firm up a bit.   While preparing for cooking, select the Air Fry option. Set the temperature of 360°F and the cook time as required. Press start to begin preheating.   Once the preheating temperature is reached, place the burgers on the tray in the Air fryer basket, making sure they don't overlap or touch. Cook on for 15 minutes   flipping halfway through.

Nutrition Info: Calories 183, Total Fat 3g, Total Carbs 11g, Protein 28g

261.   Delicious Chicken Burgers

Servings: 4   Cooking Time: 30 Minutes

Ingredients:

4 boneless, skinless chicken breasts	1/2 teaspoon paprika
1¾ ounces plain flour	1/4 teaspoon dried tarragon
2 eggs	1/4 teaspoon dried oregano
4 hamburger buns, split and toasted	1 teaspoon dried garlic
4 mozzarella cheese slices	1 teaspoon chicken seasoning
1 teaspoon mustard powder	1/2 teaspoon cayenne pepper
1 teaspoon Worcestershire sauce	Salt and black pepper, as required
1/4 teaspoon dried parsley	

Directions:
Preheat the Air fryer to 355 degree F and grease an Air fryer basket.   Put the chicken breasts, mustard, paprika, Worcestershire sauce, salt, and black pepper in a food processor and pulse until minced. Make 4 equal-sized patties from the mixture. Place the flour in a shallow bowl and whisk the egg in a second bowl.   Combine dried herbs and spices in a third bowl.   Coat each chicken patty with flour, dip into whisked egg and then coat with breadcrumb mixture.   Arrange the chicken patties into the Air fryer basket in a single layer and cook for about 30 minutes, flipping once in between.   Place half bun in a plate, layer with lettuce leaf, patty and cheese slice.   Cover with bun top and dish out to serve warm.

Nutrition Info: Calories: 562, Fat: 20.3g, Carbohydrates: 33g, Sugar: 3.3g, Protein: 58.7g, Sodium: 560mg

262.   Spicy Green Crusted Chicken

Servings: 6   Cooking Time: 40 Minutes

Ingredients:

6 eggs, beaten	6 teaspoons oregano
6 teaspoons parsley	Salt and freshly ground black pepper, to taste
4 teaspoons thyme	
1 pound chicken pieces	4 teaspoons paprika

Directions:

Preheat the Air fryer to 360 degree F and grease an Air fryer basket. Whisk eggs in a bowl and mix all the ingredients in another bowl except chicken pieces. Dip the chicken in eggs and then coat generously with the dry mixture. Arrange half of the chicken pieces in the Air fryer basket and cook for about 20 minutes. Repeat with the remaining mixture and dish out to serve hot.
Nutrition Info: Calories: 218, Fat: 10.4g, Carbohydrates: 2.6g, Sugar: 0.6g, Protein: 27.9g, Sodium: 128mg

263.	Okra Casserole

Servings: 4   Cooking Time: 12 Minutes
Ingredients:

2 red bell peppers; cubed
2 tomatoes; chopped.
3 garlic cloves; minced
3 cups okra
½ cup cheddar; shredded

¼ cup tomato puree
1 tbsp. cilantro; chopped.
1 tsp. olive oil
2 tsp. coriander, ground
Salt and black pepper to taste.

Directions:
Grease a heat proof dish that fits your air fryer with the oil, add all the ingredients except the cilantro and the cheese and toss them really gently Sprinkle the cheese and the cilantro on top, introduce the dish in the fryer and cook at 390°F for 20 minutes. Divide between plates and serve for lunch.
Nutrition Info: Calories: 221; Fat: 7g; Fiber: 2g; Carbs: 4g; Protein: 9g

264.	Marinated Chicken Parmesan

Servings: 4   Cooking Time: 20 Minutes
Ingredients:

2 cups breadcrumbs
1 teaspoon dried oregano
1/2 teaspoon garlic powder
4 teaspoons paprika
1/2 teaspoon salt
1/2 teaspoon black pepper
2 egg whites

1/2 cup skim milk
1/2 cup flour
4 (6 oz.) chicken breast halves, lb.ed
Cooking spray
1 jar marinara sauce
3/4 cup mozzarella cheese, shredded
2 tablespoons Parmesan, shredded

Directions:
Whisk the flour with all the spices in a bowl and beat the eggs in another. Coat the pounded chicken with flour then dip in the egg whites. Dredge the chicken breast through the crumbs well. Spread marinara sauce in a baking dish and place the crusted chicken on it. Drizzle cheese on top of the chicken. Press "Power Button" of Air Fry Oven and turn the dial to select the "Bake" mode. Press the Time button and again turn the dial to set the cooking time to 20 minutes. Now push the Temp button and rotate the dial to set the temperature at 400 degrees F. Once preheated, place the baking pan inside and close its lid. Serve warm.
Nutrition Info: Calories 361 Total Fat 16.3 g Saturated Fat 4.9 g Cholesterol 114 mg Sodium 515

mg Total Carbs 19.3 g Fiber 0.1 g Sugar 18.2 g Protein 33.3 g

265.	Turkey Meatballs With Manchego Cheese

Servings: 4   Cooking Time: 10 Minutes
Ingredients:

1 pound ground turkey
1/2 pound ground pork
1 egg, well beaten
1 teaspoon dried basil
1 teaspoon dried rosemary
1/4 cup Manchego cheese, grated

2 tablespoons yellow onions, finely chopped
1 teaspoon fresh garlic, finely chopped
Sea salt and ground black pepper, to taste

Directions:
In a mixing bowl, combine all the ingredients until everything is well incorporated. Shape the mixture into 1-inch balls. Cook the meatballs in the preheated Air Fryer at 380 degrees for 7 minutes. Shake halfway through the cooking time. Work in batches. Serve with your favorite pasta.
Nutrition Info:386 Calories; 24g Fat; 9g Carbs; 41g Protein; 3g Sugars; 2g Fiber

266.	Balsamic Roasted Chicken

Servings: 4   Cooking Time: 1 Hour
Ingredients:

1/2 cup balsamic vinegar
1/4 cup Dijon mustard
1/3 cup olive oil
Juice and zest from 1 lemon
3 minced garlic cloves

1 teaspoon salt
1 teaspoon pepper
4 bone-in, skin-on chicken thighs
4 bone-in, skin-on chicken drumsticks
1 tablespoon chopped parsley

Directions:
Mix vinegar, lemon juice, mustard, olive oil, garlic, salt, and pepper in a bowl, then pour into a sauce pan. Roll chicken pieces in the pan, then cover and marinate for at least 2 hours, but up to 24 hours. Preheat the toaster oven to 400°F and place the chicken on a fresh baking sheet, reserving the marinade for later. Roast the chicken for 50 minutes. Remove the chicken and cover it with foil to keep it warm. Place the marinade in the toaster oven for about 5 minutes until it simmers down and begins to thicken. Pour marinade over chicken and sprinkle with parsley and lemon zest.
Nutrition Info: Calories: 1537, Sodium: 1383 mg, Dietary Fiber: 0.8 g, Total Fat: 70.5 g, Total Carbs: 2.4 g, Protein: 210.4 g.

267.	Herbed Radish Sauté(3)

Servings: 4   Cooking Time: 12 Minutes
Ingredients:

2 bunches red radishes; halved
2 tbsp. parsley; chopped.
1 tbsp. olive oil

2 tbsp. balsamic vinegar
Salt and black pepper to taste.

Directions:

Take a bowl and mix the radishes with the remaining ingredients except the parsley, toss and put them in your air fryer's basket. Cook at 400°F for 15 minutes, divide between plates, sprinkle the parsley on top and serve as a side dish

Nutrition Info: Calories: 180; Fat: 4g; Fiber: 2g; Carbs: 3g; Protein: 5g

---

268. Roasted Grape And Goat Cheese Crostinis

Servings: 10   Cooking Time: 5 Minutes

Ingredients:

1 pound seedless red grapes	1 rustic French baguette
1 teaspoon chopped rosemary	2 tablespoons unsalted butter
4 tablespoons olive oil	8 ounces goat cheese
1 cup sliced shallots	1 tablespoon honey

Directions:

Start by preheating toaster oven to 400°F. Toss grapes, rosemary, and 1 tablespoon of olive oil in a large bowl. Transfer to a roasting pan and roast for 20 minutes. Remove the pan from the oven and set aside to cool. Slice the baguette into 1/2-inch-thick pieces. Brush each slice with olive oil and place on baking sheet. Bake for 8 minutes, then remove from oven and set aside. In a medium skillet add butter and one tablespoon of olive oil. Add shallots and sauté for about 10 minutes. Mix goat cheese and honey in a medium bowl, then add contents of shallot pan and mix thoroughly. Spread shallot mixture onto baguette, top with grapes, and serve.

Nutrition Info: Calories: 238, Sodium: 139 mg, Dietary Fiber: 0.6 g, Total Fat: 16.3 g, Total Carbs: 16.4 g, Protein: 8.4 g.

---

269. Chili Chicken Sliders

Servings: 4   Cooking Time: 10 Minutes

Ingredients:

1/3 teaspoon paprika	1 ½ cups chicken,minced
1/3 cup scallions, peeled and chopped	
3 cloves garlic, peeled and minced	1 ½ tablespoons coconut aminos
1 teaspoon ground black pepper, or to taste	1/2 teaspoon grated fresh ginger
1/2 teaspoon fresh basil, minced	1/2 tablespoon chili sauce
	1 teaspoon salt

Directions:

Thoroughly combine all ingredients in a mixing dish. Then, form into 4 patties. Cook in the preheated Air Fryer for 18 minutes at 355 degrees F. Garnish with toppings of choice.

Nutrition Info:366 Calories; 6g Fat; 4g Carbs; 66g Protein; 3g Sugars; 9g Fiber

---

270. Coriander Artichokes(3)

Servings: 4   Cooking Time: 12 Minutes

Ingredients:

12 oz. artichoke hearts	½ tsp. cumin seeds
1 tbsp. lemon juice	½ tsp. olive oil
1 tsp. coriander, ground	Salt and black pepper to taste.

Directions:

In a pan that fits your air fryer, mix all the ingredients, toss, introduce the pan in the fryer and cook at 370°F for 15 minutes Divide the mix between plates and serve as a side dish.

Nutrition Info: Calories: 200; Fat: 7g; Fiber: 2g; Carbs: 5g; Protein: 8g

---

271.Jicama Fries(1)

Servings: 4   Cooking Time: 12 Minutes

Ingredients:

1 small jicama; peeled.	¼ tsp. ground black pepper
¼ tsp. onion powder.	
¾tsp. chili powder	¼ tsp. garlic powder.

Directions:

Cut jicama into matchstick-sized pieces. Place pieces into a small bowl and sprinkle with remaining ingredients. Place the fries into the air fryer basket Adjust the temperature to 350 Degrees F and set the timer for 20 minutes. Toss the basket two or three times during cooking. Serve warm.

Nutrition Info: Calories: 37; Protein: 8g; Fiber: 7g; Fat: 1g; Carbs: 7g

---

272. Chicken & Rice Casserole

Servings: 6   Cooking Time: 40 Minutes

Ingredients:

2 lbs. bone-in chicken thighs	1 teaspoon hot Hungarian paprika
Salt and black pepper	2 tablespoons tomato paste
1 teaspoon olive oil	
5 cloves garlic, chopped	2 cups chicken broth
2 large onions, chopped	3 cups brown rice, thawed
2 large red bell peppers, chopped	2 tablespoons parsley, chopped
1 tablespoon sweet Hungarian paprika	6 tablespoons sour cream

Directions:

Mix broth, tomato paste, and all the spices in a bowl. Add chicken and mix well to coat. Spread the rice in a casserole dish and add chicken along with its marinade. Top the casserole with the rest of the Ingredients:. Press "Power Button" of Air Fry Oven and turn the dial to select the "Bake" mode. Press the Time button and again turn the dial to set the cooking time to 40 minutes. Now push the Temp button and rotate the dial to set the temperature at 350 degrees F. Once preheated, place the baking pan inside and close its lid. Serve warm.

Nutrition Info: Calories 440 Total Fat 7.9 g Saturated Fat 1.8 g Cholesterol 5 mg Sodium 581 mg Total Carbs 21.8 g Sugar 7.1 g Fiber 2.6 g Protein 37.2 g

273. Simple Turkey Breast

Servings: 10   Cooking Time: 40 Minutes

Ingredients:

1: 8-poundsbone-in turkey breast
Salt and black pepper, as required

2 tablespoons olive oil

Directions:

Preheat the Air fryer to 360 degree F and grease an Air fryer basket. Season the turkey breast with salt and black pepper and drizzle with oil. Arrange the turkey breast into the Air Fryer basket, skin side down and cook for about 20 minutes. Flip the side and cook for another 20 minutes. Dish out in a platter and cut into desired size slices to serve.

Nutrition Info: Calories: 719, Fat: 35.9g, Carbohydrates: 0g, Sugar: 0g, Protein: 97.2g, Sodium: 386mg

274. Tomato Frittata

Servings: 2   Cooking Time: 30 Minutes

Ingredients:

4 eggs
¼ cup onion, chopped
½ cup tomatoes, chopped

½ cup milk
1 cup Gouda cheese, shredded
Salt, as required

Directions:

In a small baking pan, add all the ingredients and mix well. Press "Power Button" of Air Fry Oven and turn the dial to select the "Air Fry" mode. Press the Time button and again turn the dial to set the cooking time to 30 minutes. Now push the Temp button and rotate the dial to set the temperature at 340 degrees F. Press "Start/Pause" button to start. When the unit beeps to show that it is preheated, open the lid. Arrange the baking pan over the "Wire Rack" and insert in the oven. Cut into 2 wedges and serve.

Nutrition Info: Calories: 247 Cal Total Fat: 16.1 g Saturated Fat: 7.5 g   Cholesterol: 332 mg Sodium: 417 mg   Total Carbs: 7.30 g   Fiber: 0.9 g Sugar: 5.2 g   Protein: 18.6 g

275. Beef Steaks With Beans

Servings: 4   Cooking Time: 10 Minutes

Ingredients:

4 beef steaks, trim the fat and cut into strips
1 cup green onions, chopped
2 cloves garlic, minced
1 red bell pepper, seeded and thinly sliced
1 can tomatoes, crushed

1 can cannellini beans
3/4 cup beef broth
1/4 teaspoon dried basil
1/2 teaspoon cayenne pepper
1/2 teaspoon sea salt
1/4 teaspoon ground black pepper, or to taste

Directions:

Preparing the ingredients. Add the steaks, green onions and garlic to the instant crisp air fryer basket. Air frying. Close air fryer lid. Cook at 390 degrees f for 10 minutes, working in batches.   Stir in the remaining ingredients and cook for an additional 5 minutes.

Nutrition Info: Calories 284 Total fat 7.9 g Saturated fat 1.4 g Cholesterol 36 mg Sodium 704 mg Total carbs 46 g Fiber 3.6 g Sugar 5.5 g Protein 17.9 g

276. Deviled Chicken

Servings: 8   Cooking Time: 40 Minutes

Ingredients:

2 tablespoons butter
2 cloves garlic, chopped
1 cup Dijon mustard
1/2 teaspoon cayenne pepper
1 1/2 cups panko breadcrumbs

3/4 cup Parmesan, freshly grated
1/4 cup chives, chopped
2 teaspoons paprika
8 small bone-in chicken thighs, skin removed

Directions:

Toss the chicken thighs with crumbs, cheese, chives, butter, and spices in a bowl and mix well to coat. Transfer the chicken along with its spice mix to a baking pan.   Press "Power Button" of Air Fry Oven and turn the dial to select the "Air Fry" mode. Press the Time button and again turn the dial to set the cooking time to 40 minutes.   Now push the Temp button and rotate the dial to set the temperature at 350 degrees F.   Once preheated, place the baking pan inside and close its lid.   Serve warm.

Nutrition Info: Calories 380 Total Fat 20 g Saturated Fat 5 g Cholesterol 151 mg Sodium 686 mg Total Carbs 33 g Fiber 1 g Sugar 1.2 g Protein 21 g

277. Roasted Garlic(2)

Servings: 12 Cloves   Cooking Time: 12 Minutes

Ingredients:

1 medium head garlic   2 tsp. avocado oil

Directions:

Remove any hanging excess peel from the garlic but leave the cloves covered. Cut off ¼ of the head of garlic, exposing the tips of the cloves   Drizzle with avocado oil. Place the garlic head into a small sheet of aluminum foil, completely enclosing it. Place it into the air fryer basket. Adjust the temperature to 400 Degrees F and set the timer for 20 minutes. If your garlic head is a bit smaller, check it after 15 minutes   When done, garlic should be golden brown and very soft   To serve, cloves should pop out and easily be spread or sliced. Store in an airtight container in the refrigerator up to 5 days.   You may also freeze individual cloves on a baking sheet, then store together in a freezer-safe storage bag once frozen.

Nutrition Info: Calories: 11; Protein: 2g; Fiber: 1g; Fat: 7g; Carbs: 0g

278. Pork Stew

Servings: 4   Cooking Time: 12 Minutes

Ingredients:

2 lb. pork stew meat; cubed

½ tsp. smoked paprika

1 eggplant; cubed
½ cup beef stock
2 zucchinis; cubed

Salt and black pepper to taste.
A handful cilantro; chopped.

Directions:
In a pan that fits your air fryer, mix all the ingredients, toss, introduce in your air fryer and cook at 370°F for 30 minutes   Divide into bowls and serve right away.
Nutrition Info: Calories: 245; Fat: 12g; Fiber: 2g; Carbs: 5g; Protein: 14g

279.   Ground Chicken Meatballs

Servings: 4   Cooking Time: 10 Minutes
Ingredients:

1-lb. ground chicken	1/2 teaspoon garlic
1/3 cup panko	powder
1 teaspoon salt	1 teaspoon thyme
2 teaspoons chives	1 egg

Directions:
Toss all the meatball Ingredients: in a bowl and mix well.   Make small meatballs out this mixture and place them in the air fryer basket.   Press "Power Button" of Air Fry Oven and turn the dial to select the "Air Fry" mode.   Press the Time button and again turn the dial to set the cooking time to 10 minutes.   Now push the Temp button and rotate the dial to set the temperature at 350 degrees F. Once preheated, place the air fryer basket inside and close its lid.   Serve warm.
Nutrition Info: Calories 453 Total Fat 2.4 g Saturated Fat 3 g Cholesterol 21 mg Sodium 216 mg Total Carbs 18 g Fiber 2.3 g Sugar 1.2 g Protein 23.2 g

280.   Country Comfort Corn Bread

Servings: 12   Cooking Time: 20 Minutes
Ingredients:

1 cup yellow cornmeal	2 teaspoons baking powder
1-1/2 cups oatmeal	1 cup milk
1/4 teaspoon salt	1 large egg
1/4 cup granulated sugar	1/2 cup applesauce

Directions:
Start by blending oatmeal into a fine powder. Preheat toaster oven to 400°F.   Mix oatmeal, cornmeal, salt, sugar, and baking powder, and stir to blend.   Add milk, egg, and applesauce, and mix well.   Pour into a pan and bake for 20 minutes.
Nutrition Info: Calories: 113, Sodium: 71 mg, Dietary Fiber: 1.9 g, Total Fat: 1.9 g, Total Carbs: 21.5 g, Protein: 3.4 g.

281.   Chicken Breast With Rosemary

Servings: 4   Cooking Time: 60 Minutes
Ingredients:

4 bone-in chicken breast halves	1/4 teaspoon pepper
3 tablespoons softened butter	1 tablespoon rosemary
1/2 teaspoon salt	1 tablespoon extra-virgin olive oil

Directions:

Start by preheating toaster oven to 400°F.   Mix butter, salt, pepper, and rosemary in a bowl.   Coat chicken with the butter mixture and place in a shallow pan.   Drizzle oil over chicken and roast for 25 minutes.   Flip chicken and roast for another 20 minutes.   Flip chicken one more time and roast for a final 15 minutes.
Nutrition Info: Calories: 392, Sodium: 551 mg, Dietary Fiber: 0 g, Total Fat: 18.4 g, Total Carbs: 0.6 g, Protein: 55.4 g.

282.   Green Bean Casserole(2)

Servings: 4   Cooking Time: 12 Minutes
Ingredients:

1 lb. fresh green beans, edges trimmed	¼ cup diced yellow onion
½ oz. pork rinds, finely ground	½ cup chopped white mushrooms
1 oz. full-fat cream cheese	½ cup chicken broth
½ cup heavy whipping cream.	4 tbsp. unsalted butter.
	¼ tsp. xanthan gum

Directions:
In a medium skillet over medium heat, melt the butter. Sauté the onion and mushrooms until they become soft and fragrant, about 3–5 minutes. Add the heavy whipping cream, cream cheese and broth to the pan. Whisk until smooth. Bring to a boil and then reduce to a simmer. Sprinkle the xanthan gum into the pan and remove from heat   Chop the green beans into 2-inch pieces and place into a 4-cup round baking dish. Pour the sauce mixture over them and stir until coated. Top the dish with ground pork rinds. Place into the air fryer basket   Adjust the temperature to 320 Degrees F and set the timer for 15 minutes. Top will be golden and green beans fork tender when fully cooked. Serve warm.
Nutrition Info: Calories: 267; Protein: 6g; Fiber: 2g; Fat: 24g; Carbs: 7g

283.   Lemon Pepper Turkey

Servings: 6   Cooking Time: 45 Minutes
Ingredients:

3 lbs. turkey breast	1 teaspoon lemon pepper
2 tablespoons oil	
1 tablespoon Worcestershire sauce	1/2 teaspoon salt

Directions:
Whisk everything in a bowl and coat the turkey liberally.   Place the turkey in the Air fryer basket. Press "Power Button" of Air Fry Oven and turn the dial to select the "Air Fry" mode.   Press the Time button and again turn the dial to set the cooking time to 45 minutes.   Now push the Temp button and rotate the dial to set the temperature at 375 degrees F.   Once preheated, place the air fryer basket inside and close its lid.   Serve warm.
Nutrition Info: Calories 391 Total Fat 2.8 g Saturated Fat 0.6 g Cholesterol 330 mg Sodium 62 mg Total Carbs 36.5 g Fiber 9.2 g Sugar 4.5 g Protein 6.6

284. Amazing Mac And Cheese

Servings: Cooking Time: 12 Minutes

Ingredients:

1 cup cooked macaroni	1 cup grated cheddar cheese
1/2 cup warm milk	salt and pepper; to taste
1 tablespoon parmesan cheese	

Directions:

Preheat the Air Fryer to 350 - degrees Fahrenheit. Stir all of the ingredients; except Parmesan, in a baking dish.   Place the dish inside the Air Fryer and cook for 10 minutes. Top with the Parmesan cheese.

285. Fried Paprika Tofu

Servings: Cooking Time: 12 Minutes

Ingredients:

1 block extra firm tofu; pressed to remove excess water and cut into cubes	1 tablespoon smoked paprika
1/4 cup cornstarch	salt and pepper to taste

Directions:

Line the Air Fryer basket with aluminum foil and brush with oil. Preheat the Air Fryer to 370 - degrees Fahrenheit.   Mix all ingredients in a bowl. Toss to combine. Place in the Air Fryer basket and cook for 12 minutes.

286. Herb-roasted Turkey Breast

Servings: 8   Cooking Time: 60 Minutes

Ingredients:

3 lb turkey breast	2 tsp kosher salt
Rub Ingredients:	1 tsp pepper
2 tbsp olive oil	1 tsp dried rosemary
2 tbsp lemon juice	1 tsp dried thyme
1 tbsp minced Garlic	1 tsp ground sage
2 tsp ground mustard	

Directions:

Take a small bowl and thoroughly combine the Rub Ingredients: in it. Rub this on the outside of the turkey breast and under any loose skin.   Place the coated turkey breast keeping skin side up on a cooking tray.   Place the drip pan at the bottom of the cooking chamber of the Instant Pot Duo Crisp Air Fryer. Select Air Fry option, post this, adjust the temperature to 360°F and the time to one hour, then touch start.   When preheated, add the food to the cooking tray in the lowest position. Close the lid for cooking.   When the Air Fry program is complete, check to make sure that the thickest portion of the meat reads at least 160°F, remove the turkey and let it rest for 10 minutes before slicing and serving.
Nutrition Info: Calories 214, Total Fat 10g, Total Carbs 2g, Protein 29g

287. Skinny Black Bean Flautas

Servings: 10   Cooking Time: 25 Minutes

Ingredients:

2 (15-ounce) cans black beans	2 teaspoons taco seasoning
1 cup shredded cheddar	10 (8-inch) whole
1 (4-ounce) can diced green chilies	wheat flour tortillas Olive oil

Directions:

Start by preheating toaster oven to 350°F.   Drain black beans and mash in a medium bowl with a fork. Mix in cheese, chilies, and taco seasoning until all ingredients are thoroughly combined.   Evenly spread the mixture over each tortilla and wrap tightly.   Brush each side lightly with olive oil and place on a baking sheet.   Bake for 12 minutes, turn, and bake for another 13 minutes.
Nutrition Info: Calories: 367, Sodium: 136 mg, Dietary Fiber: 14.4 g, Total Fat: 2.8 g, Total Carbs: 64.8 g, Protein: 22.6 g.

288. Mushroom Meatloaf

Servings: 4   Cooking Time: 25 Minutes

Ingredients:

14-ounce lean ground beef	3 tablespoons breadcrumbs
1 chorizo sausage, chopped finely	Salt and freshly ground black pepper, to taste
1 small onion, chopped	2 tablespoons fresh mushrooms, sliced thinly
1 garlic clove, minced	
2 tablespoons fresh cilantro, chopped	3 tablespoons olive oil
1 egg	

Directions:

Preparing the ingredients. Preheat the instant crisp air fryer to 390 degrees f.   In a large bowl, add all ingredients except mushrooms and mix till well combined.   In a baking pan, place the beef mixture.   With the back of spatula, smooth the surface.   Top with mushroom slices and gently, press into the meatloaf.   Drizzle with oil evenly. Air frying. Arrange the pan in the instant crisp air fryer basket, close air fryer lid and cook for about 25 minutes.   Cut the meatloaf in desires size wedges and serve.
Nutrition Info: Calories 284 Total fat 7.9 g Saturated fat 1.4 g Cholesterol 36 mg Sodium 704 mg Total carbs 46 g Fiber 3.6 g Sugar 5.5 g Protein 17.9 g

289. Turkey Legs

Servings: 2   Cooking Time: 40 Minutes

Ingredients:

2 large turkey legs	1 tsp season salt
1 1/2 tsp smoked paprika	½ tsp garlic powder
1 tsp brown sugar	oil for spraying avocado, canola, etc.

Directions:

Mix the smoked paprika, brown sugar, seasoned salt, garlic powder thoroughly.   Wash and pat dry the turkey legs.   Rub the made seasoning mixture all over the turkey legs making sure to get under the skin also.   While preparing for cooking, select the Air Fry option. Press start to begin preheating. Once the preheating temperature is reached, place the turkey legs on the tray in the Instant Pot Duo Crisp Air Fryer basket. Lightly spray them with oil. Air Fry the turkey legs on 400°F for 20 minutes. Then, open the Air Fryer lid and flip the turkey legs

and lightly spray with oil. Close the Instant Pot Duo Crisp Air Fryer lid and cook for 20 more minutes. Remove and Enjoy.
Nutrition Info: Calories 958, Total Fat 46g, Total Carbs 3g, Protein 133g

290.	**Chicken Caprese Sandwich**

Servings: 2   Cooking Time: 3 Minutes
Ingredients:

2 leftover chicken breasts, or pre-cooked breaded chicken	4 slices of whole grain bread
	1/4 cup olive oil
1 large ripe tomato	1/3 cup fresh basil leaves
4 ounces mozzarella cheese slices	Salt and pepper to taste

Directions:
Start by slicing tomatoes into thin slices.   Layer tomatoes then cheese over two slices of bread and place on a greased baking sheet.   Toast in the toaster oven for about 2 minutes or until the cheese is melted.   Heat chicken while the cheese melts. Remove from oven, sprinkle with basil, and add chicken.   Drizzle with oil and add salt and pepper. Top with other slice of bread and serve.
Nutrition Info: Calories: 808, Sodium: 847 mg, Dietary Fiber: 5.2 g, Total Fat: 43.6 g, Total Carbs: 30.7 g, Protein: 78.4 g.

291.	**Simple Lamb Bbq With Herbed Salt**

Servings: 8   Cooking Time: 1 Hour 20 Minutes
Ingredients:

2 ½ tablespoons herb salt	4 pounds boneless leg of lamb, cut into 2-inch chunks
2 tablespoons olive oil	

Directions:
Preheat the air fryer to 390F.   Place the grill pan accessory in the air fryer.   Season the meat with the herb salt and brush with olive oil.   Grill the meat for 20 minutes per batch.   Make sure to flip the meat every 10 minutes for even cooking.
Nutrition Info: Calories: 347 kcal Total Fat: 17.8 g Saturated Fat: 0 g   Cholesterol: 0 mg   Sodium: 0 mg   Total Carbs: 0 g   Fiber: 0 g   Sugar: 0 g Protein: 46.6 g

292.	**Carrot And Beef Cocktail Balls**

Servings: 10   Cooking Time: 20 Minutes
Ingredients:

1-pound ground beef	1 teaspoon dried oregano
2 carrots	
1 red onion, peeled and chopped	1 egg
	3/4 cup breadcrumbs
2 cloves garlic	1/2 teaspoon salt
1/2 teaspoon dried rosemary, crushed	1/2 teaspoon black pepper, or to taste
1/2 teaspoon dried basil	1 cup plain flour

Directions:
Preparing the ingredients. Place ground beef in a large bowl.   In a food processor, pulse the carrot,

onion and garlic; transfer the vegetable mixture to a large-sized bowl.   Then, add the rosemary, basil, oregano, egg, breadcrumbs, salt, and black pepper. Shape the mixture into even balls; refrigerate for about 30 minutes.   Roll the balls into the flour. Air frying. Close air fryer lid.   Then, air-fry the balls at 350 degrees f for about 20 minutes, turning occasionally; work with batches. Serve with toothpicks.
Nutrition Info: Calories 284 Total fat 7.9 g Saturated fat 1.4 g Cholesterol 36 mg Sodium 704 mg Total carbs 46 g Fiber 3.6 g Sugar 5.5 g Protein 17.9 g

293.	**Lime And Mustard Marinated Chicken**

Servings: 4   Cooking Time: 10 Minutes
Ingredients:

1/2 teaspoon stone-ground mustard	1/3 cup freshly squeezed lime juice
1/2 teaspoon minced fresh oregano	2 small-sized chicken breasts, skin-on
1teaspoon freshly cracked mixed peppercorns	1 teaspoon kosher salt

Directions:
Preheat your Air Fryer to 345 degrees F.   Toss all of the above ingredients in a medium-sized mixing dish; allow it to marinate overnight.   Cook in the preheated Air Fryer for 26 minutes.
Nutrition Info:255 Calories; 15g Fat; 7g Carbs; 33g Protein; 8g Sugars; 3g Fiber

294.	**Orange Chicken Rice**

Servings: 4   Cooking Time: 55 Minutes
Ingredients:

3 tablespoons olive oil	Salt to taste
	4 (6-oz.) boneless, skinless chicken thighs
1 medium onion, chopped	
1 3/4 cups chicken broth	Black pepper, to taste
	2 tablespoons fresh mint, chopped
1 cup brown basmati rice	
Zest and juice of 2 oranges	2 tablespoons pine nuts, toasted

Directions:
Spread the rice in a casserole dish and place the chicken on top.   Toss the rest of the Ingredients: in a bowl and liberally pour over the chicken. Press "Power Button" of Air Fry Oven and turn the dial to select the "Bake" mode.   Press the Time button and again turn the dial to set the cooking time to 55 minutes.   Now push the Temp button and rotate the dial to set the temperature at 350 degrees F.   Once preheated, place the casserole dish inside and close its lid.   Serve warm.
Nutrition Info: Calories 231 Total Fat 20.1 g Saturated Fat 2.4 g Cholesterol 110 mg Sodium 941 mg Total Carbs 30.1 g Fiber 0.9 g Sugar 1.4 g Protein 14.6 g

295.	**Spice-roasted Almonds**

Servings: 32   Cooking Time: 10 Minutes

Ingredients:
1 tablespoon chili powder
1 tablespoon olive oil
1/2 teaspoon salt
1/2 teaspoon ground cumin
1/2 teaspoon ground coriander
1/4 teaspoon ground cinnamon
1/4 teaspoon black pepper
2 cups whole almonds

Directions:
Start by preheating toaster oven to 350°F. Mix olive oil, chili powder, coriander, cinnamon, cumin, salt, and pepper. Add almonds and toss together. Transfer to a baking pan and bake for 10 minutes.
Nutrition Info: Calories: 39, Sodium: 37 mg, Dietary Fiber: 0.8 g, Total Fat: 3.5 g, Total Carbs: 1.4 g, Protein: 1.3 g.

296. Turkey And Broccoli Stew
Servings: 4   Cooking Time: 12 Minutes
Ingredients:
1 broccoli head, florets separated
1 turkey breast, skinless; boneless and cubed
1 cup tomato sauce
1 tbsp. parsley; chopped.
1 tbsp. olive oil
Salt and black pepper to taste.

Directions:
In a baking dish that fits your air fryer, mix the turkey with the rest of the ingredients except the parsley, toss, introduce the dish in the fryer, bake at 380°F for 25 minutes Divide into bowls, sprinkle the parsley on top and serve.
Nutrition Info: Calories: 250; Fat: 11g; Fiber: 2g; Carbs: 6g; Protein: 12g

297. Turkey And Mushroom Stew
Servings: 4   Cooking Time: 12 Minutes
Ingredients:
½ lb. brown mushrooms; sliced
1 turkey breast, skinless, boneless; cubed and browned
¼ cup tomato sauce
1 tbsp. parsley; chopped.
Salt and black pepper to taste.

Directions:
In a pan that fits your air fryer, mix the turkey with the mushrooms, salt, pepper and tomato sauce, toss, introduce in the fryer and cook at 350°F for 25 minutes Divide into bowls and serve for lunch with parsley sprinkled on top.
Nutrition Info: Calories: 220; Fat: 12g; Fiber: 2g; Carbs: 5g; Protein: 12g

298. Herb-roasted Chicken Tenders
Servings: 2   Cooking Time: 10 Minutes
Ingredients:
7 ounces chicken tenders
1 tablespoon olive oil
1 tablespoon honey
1/2 teaspoon Herbes de Provence
2 tablespoons Dijon mustard
Salt and pepper

Directions:
Start by preheating toaster oven to 450°F. Brush bottom of pan with 1/2 tablespoon olive oil. Season the chicken with herbs, salt, and pepper. Place the chicken in a single flat layer in the pan and drizzle the remaining olive oil over it. Bake for about 10 minutes. While the chicken is baking, mix together the mustard and honey for a tasty condiment.
Nutrition Info: Calories: 297, Sodium: 268 mg, Dietary Fiber: 0.8 g, Total Fat: 15.5 g, Total Carbs: 9.6 g, Protein: 29.8 g.

299. Perfect Size French Fries
Servings: 1   Cooking Time: 30 Minutes
Ingredients:
1 medium potato
1 tablespoon olive oil
Salt and pepper to taste

Directions:
Start by preheating your oven to 425°F. Clean the potato and cut it into fries or wedges. Place fries in a bowl of cold water to rinse. Lay the fries on a thick sheet of paper towels and pat dry. Toss in a bowl with oil, salt, and pepper. Bake for 30 minutes.
Nutrition Info: Calories: 284, Sodium: 13 mg, Dietary Fiber: 4.7 g, Total Fat: 14.2 g, Total Carbs: 37.3 g, Protein: 4.3 g.

300. Spicy Avocado Cauliflower Toast
Servings: 2   Cooking Time: 15 Minutes
Ingredients:
1/2 large head of cauliflower, leaves removed
3 1/4 teaspoons olive oil
1 small jalapeño
1 tablespoon chopped cilantro leaves
2 slices whole grain bread
1 medium avocado
Salt and pepper
5 radishes
1 green onion
2 teaspoons hot sauce
1 lime

Directions:
Start by preheating toaster oven to 450°F. Cut cauliflower into thick pieces, about 3/4-inches-thick, and slice jalapeño into thin slices. Place cauliflower and jalapeño in a bowl and mix together with 2 teaspoons olive oil. Add salt and pepper to taste and mix for another minute. Coat a pan with another teaspoon of olive oil, then lay the cauliflower mixture flat across the pan. Cook for 20 minutes, flipping in the last 5 minutes. Reduce heat to toast. Sprinkle cilantro over the mix while it is still warm, and set aside. Brush bread with remaining oil and toast until golden brown, about 5 minutes. Dice onion and radish. Mash avocado in a bowl, then spread on toast and sprinkle salt and pepper to taste. Put cauliflower mix on toast and cover with onion and radish. Drizzle with hot sauce and serve with a lime wedge.
Nutrition Info: Calories: 359, Sodium: 308 mg, Dietary Fiber: 11.1 g, Total Fat: 28.3 g, Total Carbs: 26.4 g, Protein: 6.6 g.

301. Sweet Potato And Parsnip Spiralized Latkes

Servings: 12   Cooking Time: 20 Minutes

Ingredients:

1 medium sweet potato	1/2 teaspoon garlic powder
1 large parsnip	1/2 teaspoon sea salt
4 cups water	1/2 teaspoon ground pepper
1 egg + 1 egg white	
2 scallions	

Directions:

Start by spiralizing the sweet potato and parsnip and chopping the scallions, reserving only the green parts.   Preheat toaster oven to 425°F.   Bring 4 cups of water to a boil. Place all of your noodles in a colander and pour the boiling water over the top, draining well.   Let the noodles cool, then grab handfuls and place them in a paper towel; squeeze to remove as much liquid as possible.   In a large bowl, beat egg and egg white together. Add noodles, scallions, garlic powder, salt, and pepper, mix well. Prepare a baking sheet; scoop out 1/4 cup of mixture at a time and place on sheet.   Slightly press down each scoop with your hands, then bake for 20 minutes, flipping halfway through.

Nutrition Info: Calories: 24, Sodium: 91 mg, Dietary Fiber: 1.0 g, Total Fat: 0.4 g, Total Carbs: 4.3 g, Protein: 0.9 g.

302. Cheese-stuffed Meatballs

Servings: 4   Cooking Time: 10 Minutes

Ingredients:

⅓ cup soft bread crumbs	Freshly ground black pepper
3 tablespoons milk	1-pound 95 percent lean ground beef
1 tablespoon ketchup	
1 egg	20 ½-inch cubes of cheese
½ teaspoon dried marjoram	
Pinch salt	Olive oil for misting

Directions:

Preparing the ingredients. In a large bowl, combine the bread crumbs, milk, ketchup, egg, marjoram, salt, and pepper, and mix well. Add the ground beef and mix gently but thoroughly with your hands. Form the mixture into 20 meatballs. Shape each meatball around a cheese cube. Mist the meatballs with olive oil and put into the instant crisp air fryer basket.   Air frying. Close air fryer lid. Bake for 10 to 13 minutes or until the meatballs register 165°f on a meat thermometer.

Nutrition Info: Calories: 393; Fat: 17g; Protein:50g; Fiber:0g

303. Bbq Chicken Breasts

Servings: 4   Cooking Time: 15 Minutes

Ingredients:

4 boneless skinless chicken breast about 6 oz each	1-2 Tbsp bbq seasoning

Directions:

Cover both sides of chicken breast with the BBQ seasoning.   Cover and marinate the in the refrigerator for 45 minutes.   Choose the Air Fry option and set the temperature to 400°F. Push start and let it preheat for 5 minutes.   Upon preheating, place the chicken breast in the Instant Pot Duo Crisp Air Fryer basket, making sure they do not overlap. Spray with oil.   Cook for 13-14 minutes   flipping halfway.   Remove chicken when the chicken reaches an internal temperature of 160°F. Place on a plate and allow to rest for 5 minutes before slicing.

Nutrition Info: Calories 131, Total Fat 3g, Total Carbs 2g, Protein 24g

304. Seven-layer Tostadas

Servings: 6   Cooking Time: 5 Minutes

Ingredients:

1 (16-ounce) can refried pinto beans	1-1/2 cups guacamole
1 cup light sour cream	1/2 cup thinly sliced green onions
1/2 teaspoon taco seasoning	1/2 cup sliced black olives
1 cup shredded Mexican cheese blend	6-8 whole wheat flour tortillas small enough to fit in your oven
1 cup chopped tomatoes	Olive oil

Directions:

Start by placing baking sheet into toaster oven while preheating it to 450°F.   Remove pan and drizzle with olive oil.   Place tortillas on pan and cook in oven until they are crisp, turn at least once, this should take about 5 minutes or less.   In a medium bowl, mash refried beans to break apart any chunks, then microwave for 2 1/2 minutes.   Stir taco seasoning into the sour cream. Chop vegetables and halve olives.   Top tortillas with ingredients in this order: refried beans, guacamole, sour cream, shredded cheese, tomatoes, onions, and olives.

Nutrition Info: Calories: 657, Sodium: 581 mg, Dietary Fiber: 16.8 g, Total Fat: 31.7 g, Total Carbs: 71.3 g, Protein: 28.9 g.

Dinner Recipes

305. Creole Beef Meatloaf

Servings: 6   Cooking Time: 15 Minutes

Ingredients:

- 1 lb. ground beef
- 1/2 tablespoon butter
- 1 red bell pepper diced
- 1/3 cup red onion diced
- 1/3 cup cilantro diced
- 1/3 cup zucchini diced
- 1 tablespoon creole seasoning
- 1/2 teaspoon turmeric
- 1/2 teaspoon cumin
- 1/2 teaspoon coriander
- 2 garlic cloves minced
- Salt and black pepper to taste

Directions:

Mix the beef minced with all the meatball ingredients in a bowl.   Make small meatballs out of this mixture and place them in the Air fryer basket. Press "Power Button" of Air Fry Oven and turn the dial to select the "Air Fry" mode.   Press the Time button and again turn the dial to set the cooking time to 15 minutes.   Now push the Temp button and rotate the dial to set the temperature at 370 degrees F.   Once preheated, place the Air fryer basket in the oven and close its lid.   Slice and serve warm.

Nutrition Info: Calories: 331 Cal Total Fat: 2.5 g Saturated Fat: 0.5 g Cholesterol: 35 mg Sodium: 595 mg   Total Carbs: 69 g   Fiber: 12.2 g   Sugar: 12.5 g   Protein: 26.7 g

306. Shrimp Scampi

Servings: 6   Cooking Time: 7 Minutes

Ingredients:

- 4 tablespoons salted butter
- 1 pound shrimp, peeled and deveined
- 2 tablespoons fresh basil, chopped
- 2 teaspoons red pepper flakes, crushed
- 1 tablespoon fresh chives, chopped
- 1 tablespoon fresh lemon juice
- 1 tablespoon garlic, minced
- 2 tablespoons dry white wine

Directions:

Preheat the Air fryer to 325F and grease an Air fryer pan.   Heat butter, lemon juice, garlic, and red pepper flakes in a pan and return the pan to Air fryer basket.   Cook for about 2 minutes and stir in shrimp, basil, chives and wine.   Cook for about 5 minutes and dish out the mixture onto serving plates. Serve hot.

Nutrition Info: Calories: 250, Fat: 13.7g, Carbohydrates: 3.3g, Sugar: 0.3g, Protein: 26.3g, Sodium: 360mg

307. Beef Sausage With Grilled Broccoli

Servings: 4   Cooking Time: 20 Minutes

Ingredients:

- 1 pound beef Vienna sausage
- 1/2 cup mayonnaise
- 1 teaspoon garlic
- 1 teaspoon yellow mustard
- 1 tablespoon fresh lemon juice
- powder
- 1/4 teaspoon black pepper
- 1 pound broccoli

Directions:

Start by preheating your Air Fryer to 380 degrees F. Spritz the grill pan with cooking oil.   Cut the sausages into serving sized pieces. Cook the sausages for 15 minutes, shaking the basket occasionally to get all sides browned. Set aside.   In the meantime, whisk the mayonnaise with mustard, lemon juice, garlic powder, and black pepper. Toss the broccoli with the mayo mixture.   Turn up temperature to 400 degrees F. Cook broccoli for 6 minutes, turning halfway through the cooking time. Serve the sausage with the grilled broccoli on the side.

Nutrition Info: 477 Calories; 42g Fat; 3g Carbs; 19g Protein; 7g Sugars; 6g Fiber

308. Smoked Ham With Pears

Servings: 2   Cooking Time: 30 Minutes

Ingredients:

- 15 oz pears, halved
- 8 pound smoked ham
- 1 1/2 cups brown sugar
- 3/4 tbsp allspice
- 1 tbsp apple cider vinegar
- 1 tsp black pepper
- 1 tsp vanilla extract

Directions:

Preheat your air fryer to 330 f. In a bowl, mix pears, brown sugar, cider vinegar, vanilla extract, pepper, and allspice. Place the mixture in a frying pan and fry for 2-3 minutes. Pour the mixture over ham. Add the ham to the air fryer cooking basket and cook for 15 minutes. Serve ham with hot sauce, to enjoy!

Nutrition Info: Calories: 550 Cal Total Fat: 29 g Saturated Fat: 0 g   Cholesterol: 0 mg   Sodium: 0 mg   Total Carbs: 46 g   Fiber: 0 g   Sugar: 0 g Protein: 28 g

309. Roasted Garlic Zucchini Rolls

Servings: 4   Cooking Time: 20 Minutes

Ingredients:

- 2 medium zucchinis
- 1/2 cup full-fat ricotta cheese
- 1/4 white onion; peeled. And diced
- 2 cups spinach; chopped
- 1/2 cup sliced baby portobello mushrooms
- 3/4 cup shredded mozzarella cheese, divided.
- 1/4 cup heavy cream
- 2 tbsp. unsalted butter.
- 2 tbsp. vegetable broth.
- 1/2 tsp. finely minced roasted garlic
- 1/4 tsp. dried oregano.
- 1/8 tsp. xanthan gum
- 1/4 tsp. salt
- 1/2 tsp. garlic powder.

Directions:

Using a mandoline or sharp knife, slice zucchini into long strips lengthwise. Place strips between paper towels to absorb moisture. Set aside   In a medium saucepan over medium heat, melt butter. Add onion

and sauté until fragrant. Add garlic and sauté 30 seconds. Pour in heavy cream, broth and xanthan gum. Turn off heat and whisk mixture until it begins to thicken, about 3 minutes. Take a medium bowl, add ricotta, salt, garlic powder and oregano and mix well. Fold in spinach, mushrooms and ½ cup mozzarella Pour half of the sauce into a 6-inch round baking pan. To assemble the rolls, place two strips of zucchini on a work surface. Spoon 2 tbsp. of ricotta mixture onto the slices and roll up. Place seam side down on top of sauce. Repeat with remaining ingredients Pour remaining sauce over the rolls and sprinkle with remaining mozzarella. Cover with foil and place into the air fryer basket. Adjust the temperature to 350 Degrees F and set the timer for 20 minutes. In the last 5 minutes, remove the foil to brown the cheese. Serve immediately.
Nutrition Info: Calories: 245; Protein: 15g; Fiber: 8g; Fat: 19g; Carbs: 1g

310. One-pan Shrimp And Chorizo Mix Grill

Servings: 4   Cooking Time: 15 Minutes
Ingredients:

1 ½ pounds large shrimps, peeled and deveined	6 links fresh chorizo sausage
Salt and pepper to taste	2 bunches asparagus spears, trimmed
	Lime wedges

Directions:
Place the instant pot air fryer lid on and preheat the instant pot at 390 degrees F.   Place the grill pan accessory in the instant pot.   Season the shrimps with salt and pepper to taste. Set aside.   Place the chorizo on the grill pan and the sausage.   Place the asparagus on top.   Close the air fryer lid and grill for 15 minutes.   Serve with lime wedges.
Nutrition Info: Calories:124 ; Carbs: 9.4g; Protein: 8.2g; Fat: 7.1g

311. Indian Meatballs With Lamb

Servings: 8   Cooking Time: 14 Minutes
Ingredients:

1 garlic clove	¼ tablespoon turmeric
1 tablespoon butter	
4 oz chive stems	¼ teaspoon bay leaf
1/3 teaspoon cayenne pepper	1 teaspoon salt
1 teaspoon ground coriander	1-pound ground lamb
	1 egg
	1 teaspoon ground black pepper

Directions:
Peel the garlic clove and mince it   Combine the minced garlic with the ground lamb.   Then sprinkle the meat mixture with the turmeric, cayenne pepper, ground coriander, bay leaf, salt, and ground black pepper.   Beat the egg in the forcemeat.   Then grate the chives and add them in the lamb forcemeat too.   Mix it up to make the smooth mass.   Then preheat the air fryer to 400 F. Put the butter in the air fryer basket tray and melt it. Then make the meatballs from the lamb mixture and

place them in the air fryer basket tray.   Cook the dish for 14 minutes.   Stir the meatballs twice during the cooking.   Serve the cooked meatballs immediately.   Enjoy!
Nutrition Info:calories 134, fat 6.2, fiber 0.4, carbs 1.8, protein 16.9

312. Spiced Salmon Kebabs

Servings: 3   Cooking Time: 15 Minutes
Ingredients:

2 tablespoons chopped fresh oregano	1 ½ pounds salmon fillets
2 teaspoons sesame seeds	2 tablespoons olive oil
1 teaspoon ground cumin	2 lemons, sliced into rounds
Salt and pepper to taste	

Directions:
Place the instant pot air fryer lid on and preheat the instant pot at 390 degrees F.   Place the grill pan accessory in the instant pot.   Create dry rub by combining the oregano, sesame seeds, cumin, salt, and pepper.   Rub the salmon fillets with the dry rub and brush with oil.   Place on the grill pan, close the air fryer lid and grill the salmon for 15 minutes.   Serve with lemon slices once cooked.
Nutrition Info: Calories per serving 447 ; Carbs: 4.1g; Protein:47.6 g; Fat:26.6 g

313. Beef With Apples And Plums

Servings: 4   Cooking Time: 30 Minutes
Ingredients:

2pounds beef stew meat, cubed	2tablespoons butter, melted
1cup apples, cored and cubed	Salt and black pepper to the taste
1cup plums, pitted and halved	1tablespoon chives, chopped
½ cup red wine	

Directions:
In the air fryer's pan, mix the beef with the apples and the other ingredients, toss, put the pan in the machine and cook at 390 degrees F for 30 minutes. Divide the mix between plates and serve right away.
Nutrition Info: Calories 290, Fat 12, Fiber 5, Carbs 19, Protein 28

314. Breaded Shrimp With Lemon

Servings: 3   Cooking Time: 14 Minutes
Ingredients:

½ cup plain flour	¼ teaspoon lemon zest
2 egg whites	
1 cup breadcrumbs	¼ teaspoon cayenne pepper
1 pound large shrimp, peeled and deveined	
Salt and ground black pepper, as required	¼ teaspoon red pepper flakes, crushed
	2 tablespoons vegetable oil

Directions:

68

Preheat the Air fryer to 400 degree F and grease an Air fryer basket. Mix flour, salt, and black pepper in a shallow bowl. Whisk the egg whites in a second bowl and mix the breadcrumbs, lime zest and spices in a third bowl. Coat each shrimp with the flour, dip into egg whites and finally, dredge in the breadcrumbs. Drizzle the shrimp evenly with olive oil and arrange half of the coated shrimps into the Air fryer basket. Cook for about 7 minutes and dish out the coated shrimps onto serving plates. Repeat with the remaining mixture and serve hot.
Nutrition Info: Calories: 432, Fat: 11.3g, Carbohydrates: 44.8g, Sugar: 2.5g, Protein: 37.7g, Sodium: 526mg

315. Cocktail Franks In Blanket

Servings: 4   Cooking Time: 20 Minutes
Ingredients:
  8 oz can crescent rolls   12 oz cocktail franks
Directions:
Use a paper towel to pat the cocktail franks to drain completely. Cut the dough in 1 by 5-inch rectangles using a knife. Gently roll the franks in the strips, making sure the ends are visible place in freezer for 5 minutes. Preheat the fryer to 330 f. Take the franks out of the freezer and place them in the air fryer's basket and cook for 6-8 minutes. Increase the temperature to 390 f. Cook for another 3 minutes until a fine golden texture appears.
Nutrition Info: Calories: 60 Cal Total Fat: 4.8 g Saturated Fat: 1.6 g Cholesterol: 2 mg Sodium: 136 mg Total Carbs: 2.4 g Fiber: 0.2 g Sugar: 0.1 g Protein: 1.6 g

316. Salmon With Crisped Topped Crumbs

Servings: 2   Cooking Time: 15 Minutes
Ingredients:

1-1/2 cups soft bread crumbs	1 teaspoon grated lemon zest
2 tablespoons minced fresh parsley	1/4 teaspoon lemon-pepper seasoning
1 tablespoon minced fresh thyme or 1 teaspoon dried thyme	1/4 teaspoon paprika
	1 tablespoon butter, melted
2 garlic cloves, minced	2 salmon fillets (6 ounces each)
1/2 teaspoon salt	

Directions:
In a medium bowl mix well bread crumbs, fresh parsley thyme, garlic, lemon zest, salt, lemon-pepper seasoning, and paprika. Place the instant pot air fryer lid on, lightly grease baking pan of the instant pot with cooking spray. Add salmon fillet with skin side down. Evenly sprinkle crumbs on tops of salmon and place the baking pan in the instant pot. Close the air fryer lid and cook at 390F for 10 minutes. Let it rest for 5 minutes. Serve and enjoy.
Nutrition Info: Calories: 331; Carbs: 9.0g; Protein: 31.0g; Fat: 19.0g

317. Tasty Sausage Bacon Rolls

Servings: 4   Cooking Time: 1 Hour 44 Minutes
Ingredients:

Sausage:	3 tbsp chopped parsley
8 bacon strips	
8 pork sausages	A pinch of salt
Relish:	A pinch of pepper
8 large tomatoes	2 tbsp sugar
1 clove garlic, peeled	1 tsp smoked paprika
1 small onion, peeled	1 tbsp white wine vinegar

Directions:
Start with the relish; add the tomatoes, garlic, and onion in a food processor. Blitz them for 10 seconds until the mixture is pulpy. Pour the pulp into a saucepan, add the vinegar, salt, pepper, and place it over medium heat. Bring to simmer for 10 minutes; add the paprika and sugar. Stir with a spoon and simmer for 10 minutes until pulpy and thick. Turn off the heat, transfer the relish to a bowl and chill it for an hour. In 30 minutes after putting the relish in the refrigerator, move on to the sausages. Wrap each sausage with a bacon strip neatly and stick in a bamboo skewer at the end of the sausage to secure the bacon ends. Open the Air Fryer, place 3 to 4 wrapped sausages in the fryer basket and cook for 12 minutes at 350 F. Ensure that the bacon is golden and crispy before removing them. Repeat the cooking process for the remaining wrapped sausages. Remove the relish from the refrigerator. Serve the sausages and relish with turnip mash.
Nutrition Info:346 Calories; 11g Fat; 4g Carbs; 32g Protein; 1g Sugars; 1g Fiber

318. Pesto & White Wine Salmon

Servings: 4   Cooking Time: 10 Minutes
Ingredients:

1-1/4 pounds salmon filet	2 tablespoons white wine
2 tablespoons pesto	1 lemon

Directions:
Cut the salmon into 4 pieces and place on a greased baking sheet. Slice the lemon into quarters and squeeze 1 quarter over each piece of salmon. Drizzle wine over salmon and set aside to marinate while preheating the toaster oven on broil. Spread pesto over each piece of salmon. Broil for at least 10 minutes, or until the fish is cooked to desired doneness and the pesto is browned.
Nutrition Info: Calories: 236, Sodium: 111 mg, Dietary Fiber: 0.9 g, Total Fat: 12.1 g, Total Carbs: 3.3 g, Protein: 28.6 g.

319. Fennel & Tomato Chicken Paillard

Servings: 1   Cooking Time: 12 Minutes
Ingredients:

1/4 cup olive oil	1/4 cup sliced mushrooms
1 boneless skinless chicken breast	2 tablespoons sliced black olives
Salt and pepper	
1 garlic clove, thinly sliced	1-1/2 teaspoons capers
1 small diced Roma tomato	2 sprigs fresh thyme

1/2 fennel bulb, shaved | 1 tablespoon chopped fresh parsley

Directions:
Start by pounding the chicken until it is about 1/2-inch thick. Preheat the toaster oven to 400°F and brush the bottom of a baking pan with olive oil. Sprinkle salt and pepper on both sides of the chicken and place it in the baking pan. In a bowl, mix together all other ingredients, including the remaining olive oil. Spoon mixture over chicken and bake for 12 minutes.

Nutrition Info: Calories: 797, Sodium: 471 mg, Dietary Fiber: 6.0 g, Total Fat: 63.7 g, Total Carbs: 16.4 g, Protein: 45.8 g.

320. Broccoli And Avocado Tacos

Servings: 3   Cooking Time: 5 Minutes

Ingredients:
6-10 authentic Mexican corn tortillas
1 large ripe avocado
6-8 white mushrooms, sliced

1 large head broccoli
1/2 bunch cilantro
1/2 teaspoon garlic powder
Sea salt and pepper
Olive oil

Directions:
Start by preheating toaster oven to 400°F. Slice avocado into thin slices and chop the broccoli into bite-sized florets. Arrange the broccoli and mushrooms on a baking sheet; drizzle oil and sprinkle salt, pepper, and garlic powder over the veggies. Bake for 20 minutes. Warm the tortillas, then fill with mushrooms and broccoli, and top with avocado. Sprinkle cilantro over tacos and serve.

Nutrition Info: Calories: 313, Sodium: 99 mg, Dietary Fiber: 12.6 g, Total Fat: 15.3 g, Total Carbs: 40.5 g, Protein: 10.4 g.

321. Roasted Lamb

Servings: 4   Cooking Time: 1 Hour 30 Minutes

Ingredients:
2½ pounds half lamb leg roast, slits carved
1 tablespoon dried rosemary
1 tablespoon olive oil

2 garlic cloves, sliced into smaller slithers
Cracked Himalayan rock salt and cracked peppercorns, to taste

Directions:
Preheat the Air fryer to 400 degree F and grease an Air fryer basket. Insert the garlic slithers in the slits and brush with rosemary, oil, salt, and black pepper. Arrange the lamb in the Air fryer basket and cook for about 15 minutes. Set the Air fryer to 350 degree F on the Roast mode and cook for 1 hour and 15 minutes. Dish out the lamb chops and serve hot.

Nutrition Info: Calories: 246, Fat: 7.4g, Carbohydrates: 9.4g, Sugar: 6.5g, Protein: 37.2g, Sodium: 353mg

322. Sage Beef

Servings: 4   Cooking Time: 30 Minutes

Ingredients:
2pounds beef stew meat, cubed
1tablespoon sage,

½ tablespoon garlic powder
1teaspoon Italian

chopped
2tablespoons butter, melted
½ teaspoon coriander, ground

seasoning
Salt and black pepper to the taste

Directions:
In the air fryer's pan, mix the beef with the sage, melted butter and the other ingredients, introduce the pan in the fryer and cook at 360 degrees F for 30 minutes. Divide everything between plates and serve.

Nutrition Info: Calories 290, Fat 11, Fiber 6, Carbs 20, Protein 29

323. Christmas Filet Mignon Steak

Servings: 6   Cooking Time: 20 Minutes

Ingredients:
1/3 stick butter, at room temperature
1/2 medium-sized garlic bulb, peeled and pressed
2 teaspoons mixed peppercorns, freshly cracked

1/2 cup heavy cream
6 filet mignon steaks
1 ½ tablespoons apple cider
A dash of hot sauce
1 ½ teaspoons sea salt flakes

Directions:
Season the mignon steaks with the cracked peppercorns and salt flakes. Roast the mignon steaks in the preheated Air Fryer for 24 minutes at 385 degrees F, turning once. Check for doneness and set aside, keeping it warm. In a small nonstick saucepan that is placed over a moderate flame, mash the garlic to a smooth paste. Whisk in the rest of the above ingredients. Whisk constantly until it has a uniform consistency. To finish, lay the filet mignon steaks on serving plates; spoon a little sauce onto each filet mignon.

Nutrition Info:452 Calories; 32g Fat; 8g Carbs; 26g Protein; 6g Sugars; 1g Fiber

324. Lemon Duck Legs

Servings: 6   Cooking Time: 25 Minutes

Ingredients:
1 lemon
2-pound duck legs
1 teaspoon ground coriander
1 teaspoon ground nutmeg
1 teaspoon kosher salt

½ teaspoon dried rosemary
1 tablespoon olive oil
1 teaspoon stevia extract
¼ teaspoon sage

Directions:
Squeeze the juice from the lemon and grate the zest. Combine the lemon juice and lemon zest together in the big mixing bowl. Add the ground coriander, ground nutmeg, kosher salt, dried rosemary, and sage. Sprinkle the liquid with the olive oil and stevia extract. Whisk it carefully and put the duck legs there. Stir the duck legs and leave them for 15 minutes to marinate. Meanwhile, preheat the air fryer to 380 F. Put the marinated duck legs in the air fryer and cook them for 25 minutes. Turn the duck legs into another side after 15 minutes of cooking. When the duck legs are cooked – let them cool little. Serve and enjoy!

Nutrition Info:calories 296, fat 11.5, fiber 0.5, carbs 1.6, protein 44.2

325. Sirloin Steak With Cremini Mushroom Sauce

Servings: 5   Cooking Time: 20 Minutes

Ingredients:

2 tablespoons butter	1/2 teaspoon dried
2 pounds sirloin, cut	dill
into four pieces	1/4 teaspoon dried
Salt and cracked	thyme
black pepper, to taste	1 pound Cremini
1 teaspoon cayenne	mushrooms, sliced
pepper	1 cup sour cream
1/2 teaspoon dried	1 teaspoon mustard
rosemary	1/2 teaspoon curry
	powder

Directions:

Start by preheating your Air Fryer to 396 degrees F. Grease a baking pan with butter.   Add the sirloin, salt, black pepper, cayenne pepper, rosemary, dill, and thyme to the baking pan. Cook for 9 minutes. Next, stir in the mushrooms, sour cream, mustard, and curry powder. Continue to cook another 5 minutes or until everything is heated through. Spoon onto individual serving plates.

Nutrition Info:349 Calories; 12g Fat; 4g Carbs; 49g Protein; 6g Sugars; 4g Fiber

326. Keto Lamb Kleftiko

Servings: 6   Cooking Time: 30 Minutes

Ingredients:

2 oz. garlic clove, peeled	½ lemon
1 tablespoon dried	18 oz. leg of lamb
oregano	1 cup heavy cream
¼ tablespoon ground	1 teaspoon bay leaf
cinnamon	1 teaspoon dried mint
3 tablespoon butter, frozen	1 tablespoon olive oil

Directions:

Crush the garlic cloves and combine them with the dried oregano, and ground cinnamon. Mix it. Then chop the lemon.   Sprinkle the leg of lamb with the crushed garlic mixture.   Then rub it with the chopped lemon.   Combine the heavy cream, bay leaf, and dried mint together.   Whisk the mixture well.   After this, add the olive oil and whisk it one more time more.   Then pour the cream mixture on the leg of lamb and stir it carefully. Leave the leg of lamb for 10 minutes to marinate. Preheat the air fryer to 380 F.   Chop the butter and sprinkle the marinated lamb.   Then place the leg of lamb in the air fryer basket tray and sprinkle it with the remaining cream mixture.   Then sprinkle the meat with the chopped butter.   Cook the meat for 30 minutes.   When the time is over – remove the meat from the air fryer and sprinkle it gently with the remaining cream mixture.   Serve it!

Nutrition Info:calories 318, fat 21.9, fiber 0.9, carbs 4.9, protein 25.1

327. Scallops With Capers Sauce

Servings: 2   Cooking Time: 6 Minutes

Ingredients:

10: 1-ouncesea	2 tablespoons fresh
scallops, cleaned and	parsley, finely
patted very dry	chopped
2 teaspoons capers,	1 teaspoon fresh
finely chopped	lemon zest, finely
Salt and ground black	grated
pepper, as required	½ teaspoon garlic,
¼ cup extra-virgin	finely chopped
olive oil	

Directions:

Preheat the Air fryer to 390 degree F and grease an Air fryer basket.   Season the scallops evenly with salt and black pepper.   Arrange the scallops in the Air fryer basket and cook for about 6 minutes. Mix parsley, capers, olive oil, lemon zest and garlic in a bowl.   Dish out the scallops in a platter and top with capers sauce.

Nutrition Info: Calories: 344, Fat: 26.3g, Carbohydrates: 4.2g, Sugar: 0.1g, Protein: 24g, Sodium: 393mg

328. Chat Masala Grilled Snapper

Servings: 5   Cooking Time: 25 Minutes

Ingredients:

2 ½ pounds whole	1/3 cup chat masala
fish	5 tablespoons olive
Salt to taste	oil
3 tablespoons fresh	
lime juice	

Directions:

Place the instant pot air fryer lid on and preheat the instant pot at 390 degrees F.   Place the grill pan accessory in the instant pot.   Season the fish with salt, chat masala and lime juice.   Brush with oil Place the fish on a foil basket and place it inside the grill.   Close the air fryer lid and cook for 25 minutes.

Nutrition Info: Calories:308; Carbs: 0.7g; Protein: 35.2g; Fat: 17.4g

329. Artichoke Spinach Casserole

Servings: 4   Cooking Time: 20 Minutes

Ingredients:

⅓cup full-fat	2 cups fresh spinach;
mayonnaise	chopped
oz. full-fat cream	2 cups cauliflower
cheese; softened.	florets; chopped
¼ cup diced yellow	1 cup artichoke
onion	hearts; chopped
⅓cup full-fat sour	1 tbsp. salted butter;
cream.	melted.
¼ cup chopped	
pickled jalapeños.	

Directions:

Take a large bowl, mix butter, onion, cream cheese, mayonnaise and sour cream. Fold in jalapeños, spinach, cauliflower and artichokes.   Pour the mixture into a 4-cup round baking dish. Cover with foil and place into the air fryer basket   Adjust the temperature to 370 Degrees F and set the timer for

15 minutes. In the last 2 minutes of cooking, remove the foil to brown the top. Serve warm.
Nutrition Info: Calories: 423; Protein: 7g; Fiber: 3g; Fat: 33g; Carbs: 11g

---

330. Broccoli With Olives

Servings: 4   Cooking Time: 19 Minutes
Ingredients:

2 pounds broccoli, stemmed and cut into 1-inch florets	1/3 cup Kalamata olives, halved and pitted
¼ cup Parmesan cheese, grated	Salt and ground black pepper, as required
2 tablespoons olive oil	2 teaspoons fresh lemon zest, grated

Directions:
Preheat the Air fryer to 400F and grease an Air fryer basket.   Boil the broccoli for about 4 minutes and drain well.   Mix broccoli, oil, salt, and black pepper in a bowl and toss to coat well.   Arrange broccoli into the Air fryer basket and cook for about 15 minutes.   Stir in the olives, lemon zest and cheese and dish out to serve.
Nutrition Info: Calories: 169, Fat: 10.2g, Carbohydrates: 16g, Sugar: 3.9g, Protein: 8.5g, Sodium: 254mg

---

331. Rich Meatloaf With Mustard And Peppers

Servings: 5   Cooking Time: 20 Minutes
Ingredients:

1 pound beef, ground	1 onion, chopped
1/2 pound veal, ground	2 tablespoons soy sauce
1 egg	1 (1-ouncepackage ranch dressing mix
4 tablespoons vegetable juice	
1/2 cup pork rinds	Sea salt, to taste
2 bell peppers, chopped	1/2 teaspoon ground black pepper, to taste
2 garlic cloves, minced	7 ounces tomato puree
2 tablespoons tomato paste	1 tablespoon Dijon mustard

Directions:
Start by preheating your Air Fryer to 330 degrees F. In a mixing bowl, thoroughly combine the ground beef, veal, egg, vegetable juice, pork rinds, bell peppers, onion, garlic, tomato paste, soy sauce, ranch dressing mix, salt, and ground black pepper. Mix until everything is well incorporated and press into a lightly greased meatloaf pan.   Cook approximately 25 minutes in the preheated Air Fryer. Whisk the tomato puree with the mustard and spread the topping over the top of your meatloaf. Continue to cook 2 minutes more. Let it stand on a cooling rack for 6 minutes before slicing and serving. Enjoy!
Nutrition Info:398 Calories; 24g Fat; 9g Carbs; 32g Protein; 3g Sugars; 6g Fiber

---

332. Venetian Liver

Servings: 6   Cooking Time: 15-30;
Ingredients:

500g veal liver	2 tbsp vinegar
2 white onions	Salt and pepper to taste
100g of water	

Directions:
Chop the onion and put it inside the pan with the water. Set the air fryer to 1800C and cook for 20 minutes.   Add the liver cut into small pieces and vinegar, close the lid, and cook for an additional 10 minutes.   Add salt and pepper.
Nutrition Info: Calories 131, Fat 14.19 g, Carbohydrates 16.40 g, Sugars 5.15 g, Protein 25.39 g, Cholesterol 350.41 mg

---

333. Irish Whisky Steak

Servings: 6   Cooking Time: 20 Minutes
Ingredients:

2 pounds sirloin steaks	2 garlic cloves, thinly sliced
1 ½tablespoons tamari sauce	2 tablespoons Irish whiskey
1/3 teaspoon cayenne pepper	2 tablespoons olive oil
1/3 teaspoon ground ginger	Fine sea salt, to taste

Directions:
Firstly, add all the ingredients, minus the olive oil and the steak, to a resealable plastic bag.   Throw in the steak and let it marinate for a couple of hours. After that, drizzle the sirloin steaks with 2 tablespoons olive oil.   Roast for approximately 22 minutesat 395 degrees F, turning it halfway through the time.
Nutrition Info:260 Calories; 17g Fat; 8g Carbs; 35g Protein; 2g Sugars; 1g Fiber

---

334. Garlic Parmesan Shrimp

Servings: 2   Cooking Time: 10 Minutes
Ingredients:

1 pound shrimp, deveined and peeled	1 teaspoon salt
½ cup parmesan cheese, grated	1 teaspoon fresh cracked pepper
¼ cup cilantro, diced	1 tablespoon lemon juice
1 tablespoon olive oil	6 garlic cloves, diced

Directions:
Preheat the Air fryer to 350 degree F and grease an Air fryer basket.   Drizzle shrimp with olive oil and lemon juice and season with garlic, salt and cracked pepper.   Cover the bowl with plastic wrap and refrigerate for about 3 hours.   Stir in the parmesan cheese and cilantro to the bowl and transfer to the Air fryer basket.   Cook for about 10 minutes and serve immediately.
Nutrition Info: Calories: 602, Fat: 23.9g, Carbohydrates: 46.5g, Sugar: 2.9g, Protein: 11.3g, Sodium: 886mg

---

335. Greek Souvlaki With Eggplant

Servings: 4   Cooking Time: 20 Minutes
Ingredients:

1 ½ pounds beef stew meat cubes	1 cup pearl onions
1/4 cup mayonnaise	1 small-sized
1/4 cup sour cream	eggplant, 1 ½-inch cubes

1 tablespoon yellow mustard
1 tablespoon Worcestershire sauce

Sea salt and ground black pepper, to taste

Directions:
In a mixing bowl, toss all ingredients until everything is well coated. Place in your refrigerator, cover, and let it marinate for 1 hour. Soak wooden skewers in water for 15 minutes Thread the beef cubes, pearl onions and eggplant onto skewers. Cook in preheated Air Fryer at 395 degrees F for 12 minutes, flipping halfway through the cooking time. Serve warm.

Nutrition Info: 372 Calories; 22g Fat; 2g Carbs; 33g Protein; 6g Sugars; 7g Fiber

336. Almond Pork Bites

Servings: 10   Cooking Time: 40 Minutes

Ingredients:

16 oz sausage meat	2 tbsp dried sage
1 whole egg, beaten	½ tsp pepper
3 ½ oz onion, chopped	3 ½ oz apple, sliced
2 tbsp almonds, chopped	½ tsp salt

Directions:
Preheat your air fryer to 350 f. In a bowl, mix onion, almonds, sliced apples, egg, pepper and salt. Add the almond mixture and sausage in a ziploc bag. Mix to coat well and set aside for 15 minutes. Use the mixture to form cutlets. Add cutlets to your fryer's basket and cook for 25 minutes. Serve with heavy cream and enjoy!

Nutrition Info: Calories: 491.7 Cal Total Fat: 25.9 g   Saturated Fat: 4.4 g   Cholesterol: 42 mg Sodium: 364.3 mg   Total Carbs: 40.4 g   Fiber: 3.3 g   Sugar: 0.7 g   Protein: 21.8 g

337. Spicy Cauliflower Rice

Servings: 2   Cooking Time: 22 Minutes

Ingredients:

1 cauliflower head, cut into florets 1/2 tsp cumin	1 zucchini, trimmed and cut into cubes 1/2 tsp paprika
1/2 tsp chili powder	1/2 tsp garlic powder
6 onion spring, chopped 2 jalapenos, chopped	1/2 tsp cayenne pepper 1/2 tsp pepper
4 tbsp olive oil	1/2 tsp salt

Directions:
Preheat the air fryer to 370 F. Add cauliflower florets into the food processor and process until it looks like rice. Transfer cauliflower rice into the air fryer baking pan and drizzle with half oil. Place pan in the air fryer and cook for 12 minutes, stir halfway through. Heat remaining oil in a small pan over medium heat. Add zucchini and cook for 5-8 minutes. Add onion and jalapenos and cook for 5 minutes. Add spices and stir well. Set aside. Add cauliflower rice in the zucchini mixture and stir well. Serve and enjoy.

Nutrition Info: Calories 254   Fat 28 g Carbohydrates 12.3 g   Sugar 5 g

338. Roasted Tuna On Linguine

Servings: 2   Cooking Time: 20 Minutes

Ingredients:

1pound fresh tuna fillets	1 tablespoon olive oil
Salt and pepper to taste	2 cups parsley leaves, chopped
12 ounces linguine, cooked according to package Directions:	1 tablespoon capers, chopped Juice from 1 lemon

Directions:
Place the instant pot air fryer lid on and preheat the instant pot at 390 degrees F. Place the grill pan accessory in the instant pot. Season the tuna with salt and pepper. Brush with oil. Place on the grill pan, close the air fryer lid and grill for 20 minutes. Once the tuna is cooked, shred using forks and place on top of cooked linguine. Add parsley and capers. Season with salt and pepper and add lemon juice.

Nutrition Info: Calories: 520; Carbs: 60.6g; Protein: 47.7g; Fat: 9.6g

339. Basil Tomatoes

Servings: 2   Cooking Time: 10 Minutes

Ingredients:

1 tablespoon fresh basil, chopped	2 tomatoes, halved Salt and black
Olive oil cooking spray	pepper, as required

Directions:
Preheat the Air fryer to 320 degree F and grease an Air fryer basket. Spray the tomato halves evenly with olive oil cooking spray and season with salt, black pepper and basil. Arrange the tomato halves into the Air fryer basket, cut sides up. Cook for about 10 minutes and dish out onto serving plates.

Nutrition Info: Calories: 22, Fat: 4.8g, Carbohydrates: 4.8g, Sugar: 3.2g, Protein: 1.1g, Sodium: 84mg

340. Delicious Beef Roast With Red Potatoes

Servings: 3   Cooking Time: 25 Minutes

Ingredients:

2 tbsp olive oil	½ tsp fresh rosemary, chopped
4 pound top round roast beef	3 pounds red potatoes, halved
1 tsp salt	Olive oil, black pepper and salt for garnish
¼ tsp fresh ground black pepper	
1 tsp dried thyme	

Directions:
Preheat your Air Fryer to 360 F. In a small bowl, mix rosemary, salt, pepper and thyme; rub oil onto beef. Season with the spice mixture. Place the prepared meat in your Air Fryer's cooking basket and cook for 20 minutes. Give the meat a turn and add potatoes, more pepper and oil. Cook for 20 minutes more. Take the steak out and set aside to cool for 10 minutes. Cook the potatoes in your Air Fryer for 10 more minutes at 400 F. Serve hot.

Nutrition Info: 346 Calories; 11g Fat; 4g Carbs; 32g Protein; 1g Sugars; 1g Fiber

341. Grilled Halibut With Tomatoes And Hearts Of Palm

Servings: 4   Cooking Time: 15 Minutes

Ingredients:

4 halibut fillets	2 tablespoons oil
Juice from 1 lemon	½ cup hearts of palm, rinse and drained
Salt and pepper to taste	
	1 cup cherry tomatoes

Directions:

Place the instant pot air fryer lid on and preheat the instant pot at 390 degrees F.   Place the grill pan accessory in the instant pot.   Season the halibut fillets with lemon juice, salt, and pepper. Brush with oil.   Place the fish on the grill pan.   Arrange the hearts of palms and cherry tomatoes on the side and sprinkle with more salt and pepper.   Close the air fryer lid and cook for 15 minutes.

Nutrition Info: Calories: 208; Carbs: 7g; Protein: 21 g; Fat: 11g

342. Roasted Butternut Squash With Brussels Sprouts & Sweet Potato Noodles

Servings: 2   Cooking Time: 15 Minutes

Ingredients:

Squash:	2 cloves garlic
3 cups chopped butternut squash	A small pinch red pepper flakes
2 teaspoons extra light olive oil	1 tablespoon extra light olive oil
1/8 teaspoon sea salt	1 teaspoon sesame oil
Veggies:	1 teaspoon onion powder
5-6 Brussels sprouts	1 teaspoon garlic powder
5 fresh shiitake mushrooms	1/4 teaspoon sea salt
1/2 teaspoon black sesame seeds	Noodles:
1/2 teaspoon white sesame seeds	1 bundle sweet potato vermicelli
A few sprinkles ground pepper	2-3 teaspoons low-sodium soy sauce

Directions:

Start by soaking potato vermicelli in water for at least 2 hours.   Preheat toaster oven to 375°F. Place squash on a baking sheet with edges, then drizzle with olive oil and sprinkle with salt and pepper. Mix together well on pan.   Bake the squash for 30 minutes, mixing and flipping half way through.   Remove the stems from the mushrooms and chop the Brussels sprouts.   Chop garlic and mix the veggies.   Drizzle sesame and olive oil over the mixture, then add garlic powder, onion powder, sesame seeds, red pepper flakes, salt, and pepper. Bake veggie mix for 15 minutes.   While the veggies bake, put noodles in a small sauce pan and add just enough water to cover.   Bring water to a rolling boil and boil noodles for about 8 minutes.   Drain noodles and combine with squash and veggies in a large bowl.   Drizzle with soy sauce, sprinkle with sesame seeds, and serve.

Nutrition Info: Calories: 409, Sodium: 1124 mg, Dietary Fiber: 12.2 g, Total Fat: 15.6 g, Total Carbs: 69.3 g, Protein: 8.8 g.

343. Stuffed Potatoes

Servings: 4   Cooking Time: 31 Minutes

Ingredients:

4 potatoes, peeled	1 tablespoon butter
½ of brown onion, chopped	½ cup Parmesan cheese, grated
2 tablespoons chives, chopped	3 tablespoons canola oil

Directions:

Preheat the Air fryer to 390F and grease an Air fryer basket.   Coat the potatoes with canola oil and arrange into the Air fryer basket.   Cook for about 20 minutes and transfer into a platter.   Cut each potato in half and scoop out the flesh from each half. Heat butter in a frying pan over medium heat and add onions.   Sauté for about 5 minutes and dish out in a bowl.   Mix the onions with the potato flesh, chives, and half of cheese.   Stir well and stuff the potato halves evenly with the onion potato mixture. Top with the remaining cheese and arrange the potato halves into the Air fryer basket.   Cook for about 6 minutes and dish out to serve warm.

Nutrition Info: Calories: 328, Fat: 11.3g, Carbohydrates: 34.8g, Sugar: 3.1g, Protein: 5.8g, Sodium: 77mg

344. Tomato Stuffed Pork Roll

Servings: 4   Cooking Time: 15 Minutes

Ingredients:

¼ cup sun-dried tomatoes, chopped finely	1 scallion, chopped
	Salt and freshly ground black pepper, to taste
2 tablespoons fresh parsley, chopped	2 teaspoons paprika
4: 6-ounce pork cutlets, pounded slightly	½ tablespoon olive oil

Directions:

Preheat the Air fryer to 390 degree F and grease an Air fryer basket.   Mix scallion, tomatoes, parsley, salt and black pepper in a bowl.   Coat each cutlet with tomato mixture and roll up the cutlet, securing with cocktail sticks.   Coat the rolls with oil and rub with paprika, salt and black pepper.   Arrange the rolls in the Air fryer basket and cook for about 15 minutes, flipping once in between.   Dish out in a platter and serve warm.

Nutrition Info: Calories: 244, Fat: 14.5g, Carbohydrates: 20.1g, Sugar: 1.7g, Protein: 8.2g, Sodium: 670mg

345. Spicy Paprika Steak

Servings: 2   Cooking Time: 20 Minutes

Ingredients:

1/2 Ancho chili pepper, soaked in hot water before using	1 tablespoon brandy
	2 beef steaks
2 teaspoons smoked paprika	Kosher salt, to taste
	1 teaspoon ground allspice
	3 cloves garlic, sliced

1 1/2 tablespoons olive oil

Directions:
Sprinkle the beef steaks with salt, paprika, and allspice. Add the steak to a baking dish that fits your fryer. Scatter the sliced garlic over the top. Now, drizzle it with brandy and olive oil; spread minced Ancho chili pepper over the top. Bake at 385 degrees F for 14 minutes, turning halfway through. Serve warm.
Nutrition Info:450 Calories; 26g Fat; 4g Carbs; 58g Protein; 3g Sugars; 3g Fiber

---

346. Smoked Sausage And Bacon Shashlik

Servings: 4   Cooking Time: 20 Minutes
Ingredients:

1 pound smoked Polish beef sausage, sliced	1 tablespoon mustard
	2 bell peppers, sliced
1 tablespoon olive oil	Salt and ground black pepper, to taste
2 tablespoons Worcestershire sauce	

Directions:
Toss the sausage with the mustard, olive, and Worcestershire sauce. Thread sausage and peppers onto skewers. Sprinkle with salt and black pepper. Cook in the preheated Air Fryer at 360 degrees Ffor 11 minutes. Brush the skewers with the reserved marinade.
Nutrition Info:422 Calories; 36g Fat; 9g Carbs; 18g Protein; 6g Sugars; 7g Fiber

---

347. Veggie Stuffed Bell Peppers

Servings: 6   Cooking Time: 25 Minutes
Ingredients:

1 carrot, peeled and finely chopped	6 large bell peppers, tops and seeds removed
1 potato, peeled and finely chopped	2 garlic cloves, minced
½ cup fresh peas, shelled	Salt and black pepper, to taste
1/3 cup cheddar cheese, grated	

Directions:
Preheat the Air fryer to 350F and grease an Air fryer basket. Mix vegetables, garlic, salt and black pepper in a bowl. Stuff the vegetable mixture in each bell pepper and arrange in the Air fryer pan. Cook for about 20 minutes and top with cheddar cheese. Cook for about 5 more minutes and dish out to serve warm.
Nutrition Info: Calories: 101, Fat: 2.5g, Carbohydrates: 17.1g, Sugar: 7.4g, Protein: 4.1g, Sodium: 51mg

---

348. Miso-glazed Salmon

Servings: 4   Cooking Time: 5 Minutes
Ingredients:

1/4 cup red or white miso	2 tablespoons vegetable oil
1/3 cup sake	1/4 cup sugar
1 tablespoon soy sauce	4 skinless salmon filets

Directions:
In a shallow bowl, mix together the miso, sake, oil, soy sauce, and sugar. Toss the salmon in the mixture until thoroughly coated on all sides. Preheat your toaster oven to "high" on broil mode. Place salmon in a broiling pan and broil until the top is well charred—about 5 minutes.
Nutrition Info: Calories: 401, Sodium: 315 mg, Dietary Fiber: 0 g, Total Fat: 19.2 g, Total Carbs: 14.1 g, Protein: 39.2 g.

---

349. Chinese-style Spicy And Herby Beef

Servings: 4   Cooking Time: 20 Minutes
Ingredients:

1 pound flank steak, cut into small pieces	1/8 teaspoon xanthum gum
1 teaspoon fresh sage leaves, minced	1 teaspoon seasoned salt
1/3 cup olive oil	3 cloves garlic,minced
3 teaspoons sesame oil	1 teaspoon fresh rosemary leaves, finely minced
3 tablespoons Shaoxing wine	
2 tablespoons tamari	1/2 teaspoon freshly cracked black pepper
1 teaspoon hot sauce	

Directions:
Warm the oil in a sauté pan over a moderate heat. Now, sauté the garlic until just tender and fragrant. Now, add the remaining ingredients. Toss to coat well. Then, roast for about 18 minutes at 345 degrees F. Check doneness and serve warm.
Nutrition Info:354 Calories; 24g Fat; 8g Carbs; 21g Protein; 3g Sugars; 3g Fiber

---

350. Zucchini Muffins

Servings: 8   Cooking Time: 20 Minutes
Ingredients:

6 eggs	3/4 cup coconut flour
4 drops stevia 1/4 cup Swerve	1/4 tsp ground nutmeg 1 tsp ground cinnamon 1/2 tsp baking soda
1/3 cup coconut oil, melted 1 cup zucchini, grated	

Directions:
Preheat the air fryer to 325 F. Add all ingredients except zucchini in a bowl and mix well. Add zucchini and stir well. Pour batter into the silicone muffin molds and place into the air fryer basket. Cook muffins for 20 minutes. Serve and enjoy.
Nutrition Info: Calories 136   Fat 12 g Carbohydrates 1 g   Sugar 0.6 g   Protein 4 g Cholesterol 123 mg

---

351. Bacon Pork Bites

Servings: 6   Cooking Time: 14 Minutes
Ingredients:

1-pound pork brisket	½ teaspoon red pepper
6 oz. bacon, sliced	
1 teaspoon salt	1 teaspoon olive oil
1 teaspoon turmeric	1 tablespoon apple cider vinegar

Directions:

Cut the pork brisket into the medium bites. Then put the pork bites in the big mixing bowl. Sprinkle the meat with the turmeric, salt, red pepper, and apple cider vinegar. Mix the pork bites carefully and leave them for 10 minutes to marinate. Then wrap the pork bites in the sliced bacon. Secure the pork bites with the toothpicks. Preheat the air fryer to 370 F. Put the prepared bacon pork bites on the air fryer tray. Cook the pork bites for 8 minutes. After this, turn the pork bites into another side. Cook the dish for 6 minutes more. When the bacon pork bites are cooked – let them in the air fryer for 2 minutes. Then transfer the dish to the serving plate. Enjoy!
Nutrition Info:calories 239, fat 13.7, fiber 0.2, carbs 2.8, protein 26.8

352. Salmon Steak Grilled With Cilantro Garlic Sauce

Servings: 2   Cooking Time: 15 Minutes
Ingredients:

2 salmon steaks	2 cloves of garlic, minced
Salt and pepper to taste	1 cup cilantro leaves
2 tablespoons vegetable oil	½ cup Greek yogurt
	1 teaspoon honey

Directions:
Place the instant pot air fryer lid on and preheat the instant pot at 390 degrees F. Place the grill pan accessory in the instant pot. Season the salmon steaks with salt and pepper. Brush with oil. Place on the grill pan, close the air fryer lid and grill for 15 minutes and make sure to flip halfway through the cooking time. In a food processor, mix the garlic, cilantro leaves, yogurt, and honey. Season with salt and pepper to taste. Pulse until smooth. Serve the salmon steaks with the cilantro sauce.
Nutrition Info: Calories: 485; Carbs: 6.3g; Protein: 47.6g; Fat: 29.9g

353. Bbq Pork Ribs

Servings: 2 To 3   Cooking Time: 5 Hrs 30 Minutes
Ingredients:

1 lb pork ribs	1 tsp oregano
1 tsp soy sauce	3 tbsp barbecue sauce
Salt and black pepper to taste	2 cloves garlic, minced
1 tbsp + 1 tbsp maple syrup	1 tbsp cayenne pepper
	1 tsp sesame oil

Directions:
Put the chops on a chopping board and use a knife to cut them into smaller pieces of desired sizes. Put them in a mixing bowl, add the soy sauce, salt, pepper, oregano, one tablespoon of maple syrup, barbecue sauce, garlic, cayenne pepper, and sesame oil. Mix well and place the pork in the fridge to marinate in the spices for 5 hours. Preheat the Air Fryer to 350 F. Open the Air Fryer and place the ribs in the fryer basket. Slide the fryer basket in and cook for 15 minutes. Open the Air fryer, turn the ribs using tongs, apply the remaining maple syrup with a

brush, close the Air Fryer, and continue cooking for 10 minutes.
Nutrition Info:346 Calories; 11g Fat; 4g Carbs; 32g Protein; 1g Sugars; 1g Fiber

354. Flank Steak Beef

Servings: 4   Cooking Time: 20 Minutes
Ingredients:

1 pound flank steaks, sliced	½ cup soy sauce
¼ cup xanthum gum	1 tablespoon garlic, minced
2 teaspoon vegetable oil	½ cup water
½ teaspoon ginger	¾ cup swerve, packed

Directions:
Preheat the Air fryer to 390 degree F and grease an Air fryer basket. Coat the steaks with xanthum gum on both the sides and transfer into the Air fryer basket. Cook for about 10 minutes and dish out in a platter. Meanwhile, cook rest of the ingredients for the sauce in a saucepan. Bring to a boil and pour over the steak slices to serve.
Nutrition Info: Calories: 372, Fat: 11.8g, Carbohydrates: 1.8g, Sugar: 27.3g, Protein: 34g, Sodium: 871mg

355. Traditional English Fish And Chips

Servings: 4   Cooking Time: 17 Minutes
Ingredients:

1 3/4 pounds potatoes	8 sprigs fresh thyme
4 tablespoons olive oil	4 (6-ounce) pieces cod
1-1/4 teaspoons kosher salt	1 lemon
1-1/4 teaspoons black pepper	1 clove garlic
	2 tablespoons capers

Directions:
Start by preheating toaster oven to 450°F. Cut potatoes into 1-inch chunks. Place potatoes, 2 tablespoons oil, salt, and thyme in a baking tray and toss to combine. Spread in a flat layer and bake for 30 minutes. Wrap mixture in foil to keep warm. Wipe tray with a paper towel and then lay cod in the tray. Slice the lemon and top cod with lemon, salt, pepper, and thyme. Drizzle rest of the oil over the cod and bake for 12 minutes. Place cod and potatoes on separate pans and bake together for an additional 5 minutes. Combine and serve.
Nutrition Info: Calories: 442, Sodium: 1002 mg, Dietary Fiber: 5.4 g, Total Fat: 15.8 g, Total Carbs: 32.7 g, Protein: 42.5 g.

356. Portuguese Bacalao Tapas

Servings: 4   Cooking Time: 26 Minutes
Ingredients:

1-pound codfish fillet, chopped	2 tablespoon butter
2 Yukon Gold potatoes, peeled and diced	1/4 cup olive oil
	3/4 teaspoon red pepper flakes
	freshly ground black

1 yellow onion, thinly sliced
1 clove garlic, chopped, divided
1/4 cup chopped fresh parsley, divided

pepper to taste
2 hard-cooked eggs, chopped
5 pitted green olives
5 pitted black olives

Directions:
Place the instant pot air fryer lid on, lightly grease baking pan of the instant pot with cooking spray. Add butter and place the baking pan in the instant pot. Close the air fryer lid and melt butter at 360F. Stir in onions and cook for 6 minutes until caramelized. Stir in black pepper, red pepper flakes, half of the parsley, garlic, olive oil, diced potatoes, and chopped fish. For 10 minutes, cook on 360F. Halfway through cooking time, stir well to mix. Cook for 10 minutes at 390F until tops are lightly browned. Garnish with remaining parsley, eggs, black and green olives. Serve and enjoy with chips.
Nutrition Info: Calories: 691; Carbs: 25.2g; Protein: 77.1g; Fat: 31.3g

357. Grandma's Meatballs With Spicy Sauce

Servings: 4   Cooking Time: 20 Minutes
Ingredients:

4 tablespoons pork rinds
1/3 cup green onion
1 pound beef sausage meat
3 garlic cloves, minced
1/3 teaspoon ground black pepper
Sea salt, to taste
For the sauce:

2 tablespoons Worcestershire sauce
1/3 yellow onion, minced
Dash of Tabasco sauce
1/3 cup tomato paste
1 teaspoon cumin powder
1/2 tablespoon balsamic vinegar

Directions:
Knead all of the above ingredients until everything is well incorporated. Roll into balls and cook in the preheated Air Fryer at 365 degrees for 13 minutes. In the meantime, in a saucepan, cook the ingredients for the sauce until thoroughly warmed. Serve your meatballs with the tomato sauce and enjoy!
Nutrition Info: 360 Calories; 23g Fat; 6g Carbs; 23g Protein; 4g Sugars; 2g Fiber

358. Scallops With Spinach

Servings: 2   Cooking Time: 10 Minutes
Ingredients:

1: 12-ouncespackage frozen spinach, thawed and drained
8 jumbo sea scallops
Olive oil cooking spray
1 tablespoon fresh basil, chopped

Salt and ground black pepper, as required
3/4 cup heavy whipping cream
1 tablespoon tomato paste
1 teaspoon garlic, minced

Directions:
Preheat the Air fryer to 350 degree F and grease an Air fryer pan. Season the scallops evenly with salt and black pepper. Mix cream, tomato paste,

garlic, basil, salt, and black pepper in a bowl. Place spinach at the bottom of the Air fryer pan, followed by seasoned scallops and top with the cream mixture. Transfer into the Air fryer and cook for about 10 minutes. Dish out in a platter and serve hot.
Nutrition Info: Calories: 203, Fat: 18.3g, Carbohydrates: 12.3g, Sugar: 1.7g, Protein: 26.4g, Sodium: 101mg

359. Hot Pork Skewers

Servings: 3 To 4   Cooking Time: 1 Hour 20 Minutes
Ingredients:

1 lb pork steak, cut in cubes
1/4 cup soy sauce
2 tsp smoked paprika
1 tsp powdered chili
1 tsp garlic salt
1 tsp red chili flakes
1 tbsp white wine vinegar
3 tbsp steak sauce
Skewing:

1 green pepper, cut in cubes
1 red pepper, cut in cubes
1 yellow squash, seeded and cut in cubes
1 green squash, seeded and cut in cubes
Salt and black pepper to taste to season

Directions:
In a mixing bowl, add the pork cubes, soy sauce, smoked paprika, powdered chili, garlic salt, red chili flakes, white wine vinegar, and steak sauce. Mix them using a ladle. Refrigerate to marinate them for 1 hour. After one hour, remove the marinated pork from the fridge and preheat the Air Fryer to 370 F. On each skewer, stick the pork cubes and vegetables in the order that you prefer. Have fun doing this. Once the pork cubes and vegetables are finished, arrange the skewers in the fryer basket and grill them for 8 minutes. You can do them in batches. Once ready, remove them onto the serving platter and serve with salad.
Nutrition Info: 456 Calories; 37g Fat; 1g Carbs; 21g Protein; 5g Sugars; 6g Fiber

360. Carrot Beef Cake

Servings: 10   Cooking Time: 60 Minutes
Ingredients:

3 eggs, beaten
1/2 cup almond milk
1-oz. onion soup mix
1 cup dry bread crumbs

2 cups shredded carrots
2 lbs. lean ground beef
1/2-lb. ground pork

Directions:
Thoroughly mix ground beef with carrots and all other ingredients in a bowl. Grease a meatloaf pan with oil or butter and spread the minced beef in the pan. Press "Power Button" of Air Fry Oven and turn the dial to select the "Bake" mode. Press the Time button and again turn the dial to set the cooking time to 60 minutes. Now push the Temp button and rotate the dial to set the temperature at 350 degrees F. Once preheated, place the beef baking pan in the oven and close its lid. Slice and serve.
Nutrition Info: Calories: 212 Cal Total Fat: 11.8 g Saturated Fat: 2.2 g Cholesterol: 23 mg Sodium:

321 mg   Total Carbs: 14.6 g   Fiber: 4.4 g   Sugar: 8 g   Protein: 17.3 g

361.   Ham Pinwheels

Servings: 4   Cooking Time: 11 Minutes

Ingredients:

1 puff pastry sheet
1 cup Gruyere cheese, shredded plus more for sprinkling
10 ham slices
4 teaspoons Dijon mustard

Directions:

Preheat the Air fryer to 375 degree F and grease an Air fryer basket.   Place the puff pastry onto a smooth surface and spread evenly with the mustard. Top with the ham and ¾ cup cheese and roll the puff pastry.   Wrap the roll in plastic wrap and freeze for about 30 minutes.   Remove from the freezer and slice into ½-inch rounds.   Arrange the pinwheels in the Air fryer basket and cook for about 8 minutes.   Top with remaining cheese and cook for 3 more minutes.   Dish out in a platter and serve warm.

Nutrition Info: Calories: 294, Fat: 19.4g, Carbohydrates: 8.4g, Sugar: 0.2g, Protein: 20.8g, Sodium: 1090mg

362.   Chargrilled Halibut Niçoise With Vegetables

Servings: 6   Cooking Time: 15 Minutes

Ingredients:

1 ½ pounds halibut fillets
Salt and pepper to taste
2 tablespoons olive oil
2 pounds mixed vegetables
4 cups torn lettuce leaves
1 cup cherry tomatoes, halved
4 large hard-boiled eggs, peeled and sliced

Directions:

Place the instant pot air fryer lid on and preheat the instant pot at 390 degrees F.   Place the grill pan accessory in the instant pot.   Rub the halibut with salt and pepper. Brush the fish with oil.   Place on the grill.   Surround the fish fillet with the mixed vegetables, close the air fryer lid and grill for 15 minutes.   Assemble the salad by serving the fish fillet with mixed grilled vegetables, lettuce, cherry tomatoes, and hard-boiled eggs.

Nutrition Info: Calories: 312; Carbs:16.8 g; Protein: 19.8g; Fat: 18.3g

363.   Clam With Lemons On The Grill

Servings: 6   Cooking Time: 6 Minutes

Ingredients:

4 pounds littleneck clams
Salt and pepper to taste
1 clove of garlic, minced
½ cup parsley, chopped
1 teaspoon crushed red pepper flakes
5 tablespoons olive oil
1 loaf crusty bread, halved
½ cup Parmesan cheese, grated

Directions:

Place the instant pot air fryer lid on and preheat the instant pot at 390 degrees F.   Place the grill pan accessory in the instant pot.   Place the clams on the grill pan, close the air fryer lid and cook for 6 minutes.   Once the clams have opened, take them out and extract the meat.   Transfer the meat into a bowl and season with salt and pepper.   Stir in the garlic, parsley, red pepper flakes, and olive oil. Serve on top of bread and sprinkle with Parmesan cheese.

Nutrition Info: Calories: 341; Carbs: 26g; Protein:48.3g; Fat: 17.2g

364.   Fried Spicy Tofu

Servings: 4   Cooking Time: 20 Minutes

Ingredients:

16 ounces firm tofu, pressed and cubed
1 tablespoon vegan oyster sauce
1 tablespoon tamari sauce
1 teaspoon cider vinegar
1 teaspoon pure maple syrup
1 teaspoon sriracha
1/2 teaspoon shallot powder
1/2 teaspoon porcini powder
1 teaspoon garlic powder
1 tablespoon sesame oil
2 tablespoons golden flaxseed meal

Directions:

Toss the tofu with the oyster sauce, tamari sauce, vinegar, maple syrup, sriracha, shallot powder, porcini powder, garlic powder, and sesame oil. Let it marinate for 30 minutes.   Toss the marinated tofu with the flaxseed meal.   Cook at 360 degrees F for 10 minutes; turn them over and cook for 12 minutes more.

Nutrition Info: 173 Calories; 13g Fat; 5g Carbs; 12g Protein; 8g Sugars; 1g Fiber

365.   Air Fryer Veggie Quesdillas

Servings: 4   Cooking Time: 40 Minutes

Ingredients:

4 sprouted whole-grain flour tortillas (6-in.)
1 cup sliced red bell pepper
4 ounces reduced-fat Cheddar cheese, shredded
1 cup sliced zucchini
1 cup canned black beans, drained and rinsed (no salt)
Cooking spray
2 ounces plain 2% reduced-fat Greek yogurt
1 teaspoon lime zest
1 Tbsp. fresh juice (from 1 lime)
¼ tsp. ground cumin
2 tablespoons chopped fresh cilantro
1/2 cup drained refrigerated pico de gallo

Directions:

Place tortillas on work surface, sprinkle 2 tablespoons shredded cheese over half of each tortilla and top with cheese on each tortilla with 1/4 cup each red pepper slices, zucchini slices, and black beans.   Sprinkle evenly with remaining 1/2 cup cheese.   Fold tortillas over to form half-moon shaped quesadillas, lightly coat with cooking spray, and secure with toothpicks.   Lightly spray air fryer basket with cooking spray. Place 2 quesadillas in the

basket, and cook at 400°F for 10 minutes until tortillas are golden brown and slightly crispy, cheese is melted, and vegetables are slightly softened. Turn quesadillas over halfway through cooking. Repeat with remaining quesadillas. Meanwhile, stir yogurt, lime juice, lime zest and cumin in a small bowl. Cut each quesadilla into wedges and sprinkle with cilantro. Serve with 1 tablespoon cumin cream and 2 tablespoons pico de gallo each.
Nutrition Info: Calories 291 Fat 8g Saturated fat 4g Unsaturated fat 3g Protein 17g Carbohydrate 36g Fiber 8g Sugars 3g Sodium 518mg Calcium 30% DV Potassium 6% DV

366. Garlic Butter Pork Chops

Servings: 4   Cooking Time: 8 Minutes
Ingredients:

4 pork chops	2 teaspoons parsley
1 tablespoon coconut butter	2 teaspoons garlic, grated
1 tablespoon coconut oil	Salt and black pepper, to taste

Directions:
Preheat the Air fryer to 350 degree F and grease an Air fryer basket. Mix all the seasonings, coconut oil, garlic, butter, and parsley in a bowl and coat the pork chops with it. Cover the chops with foil and refrigerate to marinate for about 1 hour. Remove the foil and arrange the chops in the Air fryer basket. Cook for about 8 minutes and dish out in a bowl to serve warm.
Nutrition Info: Calories: 311, Fat: 25.5g, Carbohydrates: 1.4g, Sugar: 0.3g, Protein: 18.4g, Sodium: 58mg

367. Fish Cakes With Horseradish Sauce

Servings: 4   Cooking Time: 20 Minutes
Ingredients:

Halibut Cakes:	2 garlic cloves, minced
1 pound halibut	
2 tablespoons olive oil	1 cup Romano cheese, grated
1/2 teaspoon cayenne pepper	1 egg, whisked
1/4 teaspoon black pepper	1 tablespoon Worcestershire sauce
Salt, to taste	Mayo Sauce:
2 tablespoons cilantro, chopped	1 teaspoon horseradish, grated
1 shallot, chopped	1/2 cup mayonnaise

Directions:
Start by preheating your Air Fryer to 380 degrees F. Spritz the Air Fryer basket with cooking oil. Mix all ingredients for the halibut cakes in a bowl; knead with your hands until everything is well incorporated. Shape the mixture into equally sized patties. Transfer your patties to the Air Fryer basket. Cook the fish patties for 10 minutes, turning them over halfway through. Mix the horseradish and mayonnaise. Serve the halibut cakes with the horseradish mayo.
Nutrition Info:532 Calories; 32g Fat; 3g Carbs; 28g Protein; 3g Sugars; 6g Fiber

368. Five Spice Pork

Servings: 4   Cooking Time: 20 Minutes
Ingredients:

1-pound pork belly	2 tablespoons swerve
2 tablespoons dark soy sauce	2 teaspoons ginger, minced
1 tablespoon Shaoxing: cooking wine	1 tablespoon hoisin sauce
2 teaspoons garlic, minced	1 teaspoon Chinese Five Spice

Directions:
Preheat the Air fryer to 390 degree F and grease an Air fryer basket. Mix all the ingredients in a bowl and place in the Ziplock bag. Seal the bag, shake it well and refrigerate to marinate for about 1 hour. Remove the pork from the bag and arrange it in the Air fryer basket. Cook for about 15 minutes and dish out in a bowl to serve warm.
Nutrition Info: Calories: 604, Fat: 30.6g, Carbohydrates: 1.4g, Sugar: 20.3g, Protein: 19.8g, Sodium: 834mg

369. Crispy Scallops

Servings: 4   Cooking Time: 6 Minutes
Ingredients:

18 sea scallops, cleaned and patted very dry	½ egg
1/8 cup all-purpose flour	¼ cup cornflakes, crushed
1 tablespoon 2% milk	½ teaspoon paprika
	Salt and black pepper, as required

Directions:
Preheat the Air fryer to 400 degree F and grease an Air fryer basket. Mix flour, paprika, salt, and black pepper in a bowl. Whisk egg with milk in another bowl and place the cornflakes in a third bowl. Coat each scallop with the flour mixture, dip into the egg mixture and finally, dredge in the cornflakes. Arrange scallops in the Air fryer basket and cook for about 6 minutes. Dish out the scallops in a platter and serve hot.
Nutrition Info: Calories: 150, Fat: 1.7g, Carbohydrates: 8g, Sugar: 0.4g, Protein: 24g, Sodium: 278mg

370. Curried Eggplant

Servings: 2   Cooking Time: 10 Minutes
Ingredients:

1 garlic clove, minced	1 large eggplant, cut into ½-inch thick slices
½ fresh red chili, chopped	
1 tablespoon vegetable oil	¼ teaspoon curry powder
	Salt, to taste

Directions:
Preheat the Air fryer to 300 degree F and grease an Air fryer basket. Mix all the ingredients in a bowl and toss to coat well. Arrange the eggplant slices in the Air fryer basket and cook for about 10 minutes,

tossing once in between.   Dish out onto serving plates and serve hot.
Nutrition Info: Calories: 121, Fat: 7.3g, Carbohydrates: 14.2g, Sugar: 7g, Protein: 2.4g, Sodium: 83mg

371.Homemade Pork Ratatouille

Servings: 4   Cooking Time: 25 Minutes
Ingredients:

4 pork sausages	1 tbsp olive oil
For ratatouille	15 oz tomatoes,
1 pepper, chopped	chopped
2 zucchinis, chopped	2 sprigs fresh thyme
1 eggplant, chopped	1 tbsp balsamic
1 medium red onion,	vinegar
chopped	2 garlic cloves,
1-ounce butterbean,	minced
drained	1 red chili, chopped

Directions:
Preheat your air fryer to 392 f. Mix pepper, eggplant, oil, onion, zucchinis, and add to the cooking basket. Roast for 20 minutes. Set aside to cool. Reduce air fryer temperature to 356 f. In a saucepan, mix prepared vegetables and the remaining ratatouille ingredients, and bring to a boil over medium heat. Let the mixture simmer for 10 minutes; season with salt and pepper. Add sausages to your air fryer's basket and cook for 10-15 minutes. Serve the sausages with ratatouille.
Nutrition Info: Calories: 232.3 Cal Total Fat: 11.5 g Saturated Fat: 4.0 g Cholesterol: 58.2 mg Sodium: 611 mg Total Carbs: 9.2 g Fiber: 1.7 g Sugar: 4.4 g Protein: 23.1 g

372.   Award Winning Breaded Chicken

Servings: 4   Cooking Time: 20 Minutes
Ingredients:

1 1/2 tsp.s olive oil	1½ tablespoons
1 tsp. red pepper flakes, crushed 1/3 tsp. chicken bouillon granules 1/3 tsp. shallot powder	mayo 1 tsp. kosher salt
	For the chicken:
	2 beaten eggs
1 1/2 tablespoons tamari soy sauce 1/3 tsp. cumin powder	Breadcrumbs
	1½ chicken breasts, boneless and skinless
	1 ½ tablespoons plain flour

Directions:
Margarine fly the chicken breasts, and then, marinate them for at least 55 minutes. Coat the chicken with plain flour; then, coat with the beaten eggs; finally, roll them in the breadcrumbs. Lightly grease the cooking basket. Air-fry the breaded chicken at 345 °F for 12 minutes, flipping them halfway.
Nutrition Info:262 Calories;   14.9g Fat;   2.7g Carbs;   27.5g Protein;   0.3g Sugars

373.   Chili Pepper Lamb Chops

Servings: 6   Cooking Time: 10 Minutes
Ingredients:

1 teaspoon chili pepper	21 oz. lamb chops
½ teaspoon chili flakes	1 teaspoon cayenne pepper
1 teaspoon onion powder	1 tablespoon olive oil
	1 tablespoon butter
1 teaspoon garlic powder	½ teaspoon lime zest

Directions:
Melt the butter and combine it with the olive oil. Whisk the liquid and add chili pepper, chili flakes, onion powder, garlic powder, cayenne pepper, and lime zest.   Whisk it well   Then sprinkle the lamb chops with the prepared oily marinade.   Leave the meat for at least 5 minutes in the fridge.   Preheat the air fryer to 400 F.   Place the marinated lamb chops in the air fryer and cook them for 5 minutes. After this, open the air fryer and turn the lamb chops into another side.   Cook the lamb chops for 5 minutes more.   When the meat is cooked – transfer it to the serving plates.   Enjoy!
Nutrition Info:calories 227, fat 11.6, fiber 0.2, carbs 1, protein 28.1

374.   Pepper Pork Chops

Servings: 2   Cooking Time: 6 Minutes
Ingredients:

2 pork chops	¼ teaspoon freshly ground black pepper
1 egg white	
¾ cup xanthum gum	1 oil mister
½ teaspoon sea salt	

Directions:
Preheat the Air fryer to 400 degree F and grease an Air fryer basket.   Whisk egg white with salt and black pepper in a bowl and dip the pork chops in it. Cover the bowl and marinate for about 20 minutes. Pour the xanthum gum over both sides of the chops and spray with oil mister.   Arrange the chops in the Air fryer basket and cook for about 6 minutes. Dish out in a bowl and serve warm.
Nutrition Info: Calories: 541, Fat: 34g, Carbohydrates: 3.4g, Sugar: 1g, Protein: 20.3g, Sodium: 547mg

375.   Beef Pieces With Tender Broccoli

Servings: 4   Cooking Time: 13 Minutes
Ingredients:

6 oz. broccoli	1 teaspoon butter
10 oz. beef brisket	1 tablespoon flax seeds
4 oz chive stems	
1 teaspoon paprika	½ teaspoon chili flakes
1/3 cup water	
1 teaspoon olive oil	

Directions:
Cut the beef brisket into the medium/convenient pieces.   Sprinkle the beef pieces with the paprika and chili flakes.   Mix the meat up with the help of the hands.   Then preheat the air fryer to 360 F. Spray the air fryer basket tray with the olive oil. Put the beef pieces in the air fryer basket tray and cook the meat for 7 minutes.   Stir it once during the cooking.   Meanwhile, separate the broccoli into the florets.   When the time is over – add the

broccoli florets in the air fryer basket tray. Sprinkle the ingredients with the flax seeds and butter. Add water. Dice the chives and add them in the air fryer basket tray too. Stir it gently using the wooden spatula. Then cook the dish at 265 F for 6 minutes more. When the broccoli is tender – the dish is cooked. Serve the dish little bit chilled. Enjoy!

Nutrition Info: calories 187, fat 7.3, fiber 2.4, carbs 6.2, protein 23.4

376. Tasty Grilled Red Mullet

Servings: 8   Cooking Time: 15 Minutes

Ingredients:

8 whole red mullets, gutted and scales removed	Salt and pepper to taste
Juice from 1 lemon	1 tablespoon olive oil

Directions:

Place the instant pot air fryer lid on and preheat the instant pot at 390 degrees F. Place the grill pan accessory in the instant pot. Season the red mullet with salt, pepper, and lemon juice. Place red mullets on the grill pan and brush with olive oil. Close the air fryer lid and grill for 15 minutes.

Nutrition Info: Calories: 152; Carbs: 0.9g; Protein: 23.1g; Fat: 6.2g

377. Pollock With Kalamata Olives And Capers

Servings: 3   Cooking Time: 20 Minutes

Ingredients:

2 tablespoons olive oil	2 ripe tomatoes, diced
1 red onion, sliced	12 Kalamata olives, pitted and chopped
2 cloves garlic, chopped	2 tablespoons capers
1 Florina pepper, deveined and minced	1 teaspoon oregano
3 pollock fillets, skinless	1 teaspoon rosemary
	Sea salt, to taste
	1/2 cup white wine

Directions:

Start by preheating your Air Fryer to 360 degrees F. Heat the oil in a baking pan. Once hot, sauté the onion, garlic, and pepper for 2 to 3 minutes or until fragrant. Add the fish fillets to the baking pan. Top with the tomatoes, olives, and capers. Sprinkle with the oregano, rosemary, and salt. Pour in white wine and transfer to the cooking basket. Turn the temperature to 395 degrees F and bake for 10 minutes. Taste for seasoning and serve on individual plates, garnished with some extra Mediterranean herbs if desired. Enjoy!

Nutrition Info: 480 Calories; 37g Fat; 9g Carbs; 49g Protein; 5g Sugars; 2g Fiber

378. Greek-style Monkfish With Vegetables

Servings: 2   Cooking Time: 20 Minutes

Ingredients:

2 teaspoons olive oil	2 monkfish fillets
1 cup celery, sliced	2 tablespoons lime juice
2 bell peppers, sliced	
1 teaspoon dried thyme	Coarse salt and ground black pepper, to taste
1/2 teaspoon dried marjoram	1 teaspoon cayenne pepper
1/2 teaspoon dried rosemary	1/2 cup Kalamata olives, pitted and sliced
1 tablespoon soy sauce	

Directions:

In a nonstick skillet, heat the olive oil for 1 minute. Once hot, sauté the celery and peppers until tender, about 4 minutes. Sprinkle with thyme, marjoram, and rosemary and set aside. Toss the fish fillets with the soy sauce, lime juice, salt, black pepper, and cayenne pepper. Place the fish fillets in a lightly greased cooking basket and bake at 390 degrees F for 8 minutes. Turn them over, add the olives, and cook an additional 4 minutes. Serve with the sautéed vegetables on the side.

Nutrition Info: 292 Calories; 11g Fat; 1g Carbs; 22g Protein; 9g Sugars; 6g Fiber

379. Green Beans And Lime Sauce

Servings: 4   Cooking Time: 20 Minutes

Ingredients:

1 lb. green beans, trimmed	1 tsp. chili powder
2 tbsp. ghee; melted	A pinch of salt and black pepper
1 tbsp. lime juice	

Directions:

Take a bowl and mix the ghee with the rest of the ingredients except the green beans and whisk really well. Mix the green beans with the lime sauce, toss Put them in your air fryer's basket and cook at 400°F for 8 minutes. Serve right away.

Nutrition Info: Calories: 151; Fat: 4g; Fiber: 2g; Carbs: 4g; Protein: 6g

380. Korean Beef Bowl

Servings: 4   Cooking Time: 18 Minutes

Ingredients:

1 tablespoon minced garlic	1 teaspoon stevia extract
1 teaspoon ground ginger	1 tablespoon flax seeds
4 oz chive stems, chopped	1 teaspoon olive oil
2 tablespoon apple cider vinegar	1-pound ground beef
1 teaspoon olive oil	4 tablespoon chicken stock

Directions:

Sprinkle the ground beef with the apple cider vinegar and stir the meat with the help of the spoon. After this, sprinkle the ground beef with the ground ginger, minced garlic, and olive oil. Mix it up. Preheat the air fryer to 370 F. Put the ground beef in the air fryer basket tray and cook it for 8 minutes. After this, stir the ground beef carefully and sprinkle with the chopped chives, flax seeds, olive oil, and chicken stock. Mix the dish up and cook it for 10 minutes more. When the time is over – stir the dish carefully. Serve Korean beef bowl immediately. Enjoy!

Nutrition Info: calories 258, fat 10.1, fiber 1.2, carbs 4.2, protein 35.3

381. Cheese Zucchini Boats

Servings: 2   Cooking Time: 20 Minutes

Ingredients:

2 medium zucchinis	2 tbsp. grated
¼ cup full-fat ricotta cheese	vegetarian Parmesan cheese
¼ cup shredded mozzarella cheese	1 tbsp. avocado oil
¼ cup low-carb, no-sugar-added pasta sauce.	¼ tsp. garlic powder.
	½ tsp. dried parsley.
	¼ tsp. dried oregano.

Directions:

Cut off 1-inch from the top and bottom of each zucchini.   Slice zucchini in half lengthwise and use a spoon to scoop out a bit of the inside, making room for filling. Brush with oil and spoon 2 tbsp. pasta sauce into each shell   Take a medium bowl, mix ricotta, mozzarella, oregano, garlic powder and parsley   Spoon the mixture into each zucchini shell. Place stuffed zucchini shells into the air fryer basket.   Adjust the temperature to 350 Degrees F and set the timer for 20 minutes   To remove from the fryer basket, use tongs or a spatula and carefully lift out. Top with Parmesan. Serve immediately.

Nutrition Info: Calories: 215; Protein: 15g; Fiber: 7g; Fat: 19g; Carbs: 3g

382. Broccoli And Tomato Sauce

Servings: 4   Cooking Time: 7 Minutes

Ingredients:

1 broccoli head, florets separated	1 tbsp. olive oil
¼ cup scallions; chopped	1 tbsp. sweet paprika
½ cup tomato sauce	Salt and black pepper to taste.

Directions:

In a pan that fits the air fryer, combine the broccoli with the rest of the Ingredients: toss.   Put the pan in the fryer and cook at 380°F for 15 minutes   Divide between plates and serve.

Nutrition Info: Calories: 163; Fat: 5g; Fiber: 2g; Carbs: 4g; Protein: 8g

383. Air Fryer Roasted Broccoli

Servings: 4   Cooking Time: 10 Minutes

Ingredients:

1 tsp. herbes de provence seasoning (optional)	1 tablespoon olive oil
	Salt and pepper to taste
4 cups fresh broccoli	

Directions:

Drizzle or spray broccoli with olive and sprinkle seasoning throughout   Spray air fryer basket with cooking oil, place broccoli and cook for 5-8 minutes on 360F   Open air fryer and examine broccoli after 5 minutes because different fryer brands cook at different rates.

Nutrition Info: Calories 61 Fat 4g protein 3g net carbs 4g

384. Beef, Mushrooms And Noodles Dish

Servings: 5   Cooking Time: 35 Minutes

Ingredients:

1½ pounds beef steak	2 cups mushrooms, sliced
1 package egg noodles, cooked	1 whole onion, chopped
1 ounce dry onion soup mix	½ cup beef broth
1 can (15 oz cream mushroom soup	3 garlic cloves, minced?

Directions:

Preheat your Air Fryer to 360 F. Drizzle onion soup mix all over the meat. In a mixing bowl, mix the sauce, garlic cloves, beef broth, chopped onion, sliced mushrooms and mushroom soup. Top the meat with the prepared sauce mixture. Place the prepared meat in the air fryer's cooking basket and cook for 25 minutes. Serve with cooked egg noodles.

Nutrition Info:346 Calories; 11g Fat; 4g Carbs; 32g Protein; 1g Sugars; 1g Fiber

385. Cheesy Shrimp

Servings: 4   Cooking Time: 20 Minutes

Ingredients:

2/3 cup Parmesan cheese, grated	½ teaspoon dried oregano
2 pounds shrimp, peeled and deveined	1 teaspoon onion powder
4 garlic cloves, minced	½ teaspoon red pepper flakes, crushed
2 tablespoons olive oil	
1 teaspoon dried basil	Ground black pepper, as required
	2 tablespoons fresh lemon juice

Directions:

Preheat the Air fryer to 350 degree F and grease an Air fryer basket.   Mix Parmesan cheese, garlic, olive oil, herbs, and spices in a large bowl. Arrange half of the shrimp into the Air fryer basket in a single layer and cook for about 10 minutes. Dish out the shrimps onto serving plates and drizzle with lemon juice to serve hot.

Nutrition Info: Calories: 386, Fat: 14.2g, Carbohydrates: 5.3g, Sugar: 0.4g, Protein: 57.3g, Sodium: 670mg

386. Cheddar & Dijon Tuna Melt

Servings: 1   Cooking Time: 7 Minutes

Ingredients:

1 (6-ounce) can tuna, drained and flaked	1 pinch salt
2 tablespoons mayonnaise	2 slices whole wheat bread
1 teaspoon balsamic vinegar	2 teaspoons chopped dill pickle
1 teaspoon Dijon mustard	1/4 cup shredded sharp cheddar cheese

Directions:

Start by preheating toaster oven to 375°F.   Put bread in toaster while it warms.   Mix together tuna, mayo, salt, vinegar, mustard, and pickle in a small bowl.   Remove bread from oven and put tuna mixture on one side and the cheese on the other.

Return to toaster oven and bake for 7 minutes. Combine slices, then cut and serve.
Nutrition Info: Calories: 688, Sodium: 1024 mg, Dietary Fiber: 4.1 g, Total Fat: 35.0 g, Total Carbs: 31.0 g, Protein: 59.9 g.

387. Lobster Lasagna Maine Style

Servings: 6   Cooking Time: 50 Minutes
Ingredients:

1/2 (15 ounces) container ricotta cheese	1 egg
1 cup shredded Cheddar cheese	1 tablespoon chopped fresh parsley
1/2 cup shredded mozzarella cheese	1/2 teaspoon freshly ground black pepper
1/2 cup grated Parmesan cheese	1 (16 ounces) jar Alfredo pasta sauce
1/2 medium onion, minced	8 no-boil lasagna noodles
1-1/2 teaspoons minced garlic	1 pound cooked and cubed lobster meat
	5-ounce package baby spinach leaves

Directions:
Mix well half of Parmesan, half of the mozzarella, half of cheddar, egg, and ricotta cheese in a medium bowl. Stir in pepper, parsley, garlic, and onion. Place the instant pot air fryer lid on, lightly grease baking pan of the instant pot with cooking spray. On the bottom of the pan, spread ½ of the Alfredo sauce, top with a single layer of lasagna noodles. Followed by 1/3 of lobster meat, 1/3 of ricotta cheese mixture, 1/3 of spinach. Repeat layering process until all ingredients are used up.   Sprinkle remaining cheese on top. Shake pan to settle lasagna and burst bubbles. Cover pan with foil and place the baking pan in the instant pot.   Close the air fryer lid and cook at 360F for 30 minutes   Remove foil and cook for 10 minutes at 390F until tops are lightly browned.   Let it stand for 10 minutes.   Serve and enjoy.
Nutrition Info: Calories: 558; Carbs: 20.4g; Protein: 36.8g; Fat: 36.5g

388. Coconut Crusted Shrimp

Servings: 3   Cooking Time: 40 Minutes
Ingredients:

8 ounces coconut milk	1 pound large shrimp, peeled and deveined
1/2 cup sweetened coconut, shredded	Salt and black pepper, to taste
1/2 cup panko breadcrumbs	

Directions:
Preheat the Air fryer to 350-degree F and grease an Air fryer basket.   Place the coconut milk in a shallow bowl.   Mix coconut, breadcrumbs, salt, and black pepper in another bowl.   Dip each shrimp into coconut milk and finally, dredge in the coconut mixture.   Arrange half of the shrimps into the Air fryer basket and cook for about 20 minutes. Dish out the shrimps onto serving plates and repeat with the remaining mixture to serve.

Nutrition Info: Calories: 408, Fats: 23.7g, Carbohydrates: 11.7g, Sugar: 3.4g, Proteins: 31g, Sodium: 253mg

389. Herbed Eggplant

Servings: 2   Cooking Time: 15 Minutes
Ingredients:

1 large eggplant, cubed	1/2 teaspoon garlic powder
1/2 teaspoon dried marjoram, crushed	Salt and black pepper, to taste
1/2 teaspoon dried oregano, crushed	Olive oil cooking spray
1/2 teaspoon dried thyme, crushed	

Directions:
Preheat the Air fryer to 390 degree F and grease an Air fryer basket.   Mix herbs, garlic powder, salt, and black pepper in a bowl.   Spray the eggplant cubes with cooking spray and rub with the herb mixture.   Arrange the eggplant cubes in the Air fryer basket and cook for about 15 minutes, flipping twice in between.   Dish out onto serving plates and serve hot.
Nutrition Info: Calories: 62, Fat: 0.5g, Carbohydrates: 14.5g, Sugar: 7.1g, Protein: 2.4g, Sodium: 83mg

390. Zingy Dilled Salmon

Servings: 2   Cooking Time: 20 Minutes
Ingredients:

2 salmon steaks	1 tablespoon fresh lemon juice
Coarse sea salt, to taste	1 teaspoon garlic, minced
1/4 teaspoon freshly ground black pepper, or more to taste	1/2 teaspoon smoked cayenne pepper
1 tablespoon sesame oil	1/2 teaspoon dried dill
Zest of 1 lemon	

Directions:
Preheat your Air Fryer to 380 degrees F. Pat dry the salmon steaks with a kitchen towel.   In a ceramic dish, combine the remaining ingredients until everything is well whisked.   Add the salmon steaks to the ceramic dish and let them sit in the refrigerator for 1 hour. Now, place the salmon steaks in the cooking basket. Reserve the marinade. Cook for 12 minutes, flipping halfway through the cooking time.   Meanwhile, cook the marinade in a small sauté pan over a moderate flame. Cook until the sauce has thickened.   Pour the sauce over the steaks and serve.
Nutrition Info:476 Calories; 18g Fat; 2g Carbs; 47g Protein; 8g Sugars; 4g Fiber

391. Coconut-crusted Haddock With Curried Pumpkin Seeds

Servings: 4   Cooking Time: 10 Minutes
Ingredients:

2 teaspoons canola oil
2 teaspoons honey
1 teaspoon curry powder
1/4 teaspoon ground cinnamon
1 teaspoon salt
1 cup pumpkin seeds
1-1/2 pounds haddock or cod filets

1/2 cup roughly grated unsweetened coconut
3/4 cups panko-style bread crumbs
2 tablespoons butter, melted
3 tablespoons apricot fruit spread
1 tablespoon lime juice

Directions:
Start by preheating toaster oven to 350°F. In a medium bowl, mix honey, oil, curry powder, 1/2 teaspoon salt, and cinnamon. Add pumpkin seeds to the bowl and toss to coat, then lay flat on a baking sheet. Toast for 14 minutes, then transfer to a bowl to cool. Increase the oven temperature to 450°F. Brush a baking sheet with oil and lay filets flat. In another medium mixing bowl, mix together bread crumbs, butter, and remaining salt. In a small bowl mash together apricot spread and lime juice. Brush each filet with apricot mixture, then press bread crumb mixture onto each piece. Bake for 10 minutes. Transfer to a plate and top with pumpkin seeds to serve.
Nutrition Info: Calories: 273, Sodium: 491 mg, Dietary Fiber: 6.1 g, Total Fat: 8.4 g, Total Carbs: 47.3 g, Protein: 7.0 g.

392.	Almond Asparagus

Servings: 3   Cooking Time: 6 Minutes
Ingredients:

1 pound asparagus
1/3 cup almonds, sliced
2 tablespoons olive oil

2 tablespoons balsamic vinegar
Salt and black pepper, to taste

Directions:
Preheat the Air fryer to 400F and grease an Air fryer basket. Mix asparagus, oil, vinegar, salt, and black pepper in a bowl and toss to coat well. Arrange asparagus into the Air fryer basket and sprinkle with the almond slices. Cook for about 6 minutes and dish out to serve hot.
Nutrition Info: Calories: 173, Fat: 14.8g, Carbohydrates: 8.2g, Sugar: 3.3g, Protein: 5.6g, Sodium: 54mg

393.	Sautéed Green Beans

Servings: 2   Cooking Time: 10 Minutes
Ingredients:

8 ounces fresh green beans, trimmed and cut in half
1 teaspoon sesame oil
1 tablespoon soy sauce

Directions:
Preheat the Air fryer to 390F and grease an Air fryer basket. Mix green beans, soy sauce, and sesame oil in a bowl and toss to coat well. Arrange green beans into the Air fryer basket and cook for about 10 minutes, tossing once in between. Dish out onto serving plates and serve hot.
Nutrition Info: Calories: 59, Fats: 2.4g, Carbohydrates: 59g, Sugar: 1.7g, Proteins: 2.6g, Sodium: 458mg

394.	Beef Roast

Servings: 4
Ingredients:

1 tbsp. smoked paprika
3 tbsp. garlic; minced

2 lbs. beef roast
3 tbsp. olive oil
Salt and black pepper to taste

Directions:
In a bowl, combine all the ingredients and coat the roast well. Place the roast in your air fryer and cook at 390°F for 55 minutes. Slice the roast, divide it between plates and serve with a side salad

395.	Air Fryer Buffalo Mushroom Poppers

Servings: 8   Cooking Time: 50 Minutes
Ingredients:

1 pound fresh whole button mushrooms
1/2 teaspoon kosher salt
3 tablespoons 1/3-less-fat cream cheese,
1/4 cup all-purpose flour
Softened 1 jalapeño chile, seeded and minced
1/4 teaspoon black pepper
1 cup panko breadcrumbs

Cooking spray
2 large eggs, lightly beaten
1/4 cup buffalo-style hot sauce
2 tablespoons chopped fresh chives
1/2 cup low-fat buttermilk
1/2 cup plain fat-free yogurt
2 ounces blue cheese, crumbled (about 1/2 cup)
3 tablespoons apple cider vinegar

Directions:
Remove stems from mushroom caps, chop stems and set caps aside. Stir together chopped mushroom stems, cream cheese, jalapeño, salt, and pepper. Stuff about 1 teaspoon of the mixture into each mushroom cap, rounding the filling to form a smooth ball. Place panko in a bowl, place flour in a second bowl, and eggs in a third Coat mushrooms in flour, dip in egg mixture, and dredge in panko, pressing to adhere. Spray mushrooms well with cooking spray. Place half of the mushrooms in air fryer basket, and cook for 20 minutes at 350°F. Transfer cooked mushrooms to a large bowl. Drizzle buffalo sauce over mushrooms; toss to coat then sprinkle with chives. Stir buttermilk, yogurt, blue cheese, and cider vinegar in a small bowl. Serve mushroom poppers with blue cheese sauce.
Nutrition Info: Calories 133 Fat 4g Saturated fat 2g Unsaturated fat 2g Protein 7g Carbohydrate 16g Fiber 1g Sugars 3g Sodium 485mg Calcium 10% DV Potassium 7% DV

396. Homemade Beef Stroganoff

Servings: 3   Cooking Time: 20 Minutes

Ingredients:

1 pound thin steak	8 oz mushrooms, sliced
4 tbsp butter	
1 whole onion, chopped	4 cups beef broth
	16 oz egg noodles, cooked
1 cup sour cream	

Directions:

Preheat your Air Fryer to 400 F. Using a microwave proof bowl, melt butter in a microwave oven. In a mixing bowl, mix the melted butter, sliced mushrooms, cream, onion, and beef broth. Pour the mixture over steak and set aside for 10 minutes. Place the marinated beef in your fryer's cooking basket, and cook for 10 minutes. Serve with cooked egg noodles and enjoy!

Nutrition Info: 456 Calories; 37g Fat; 1g Carbs; 21g Protein; 5g Sugars; 6g Fiber

397. Filet Mignon With Chili Peanut Sauce

Servings: 4   Cooking Time: 20 Minutes

Ingredients:

2 pounds filet mignon, sliced into bite-sized strips	1 tablespoon ginger-garlic paste
1 tablespoon oyster sauce	1 teaspoon chili powder
2 tablespoons sesame oil	1/4 cup peanut butter
2 tablespoons tamari sauce	2 tablespoons lime juice
1 tablespoon mustard	1 teaspoon red pepper flakes
	2 tablespoons water

Directions:

Place the beef strips, oyster sauce, sesame oil, tamari sauce, ginger-garlic paste, mustard, and chili powder in a large ceramic dish.   Cover and allow it to marinate for 2 hours in your refrigerator. Cook in the preheated Air Fryer at 400 degrees F for 18 minutes, shaking the basket occasionally.   Mix the peanut butter with lime juice, red pepper flakes, and water. Spoon the sauce onto the air fried beef strips and serve warm.

Nutrition Info: 420 Calories; 21g Fat; 5g Carbs; 50g Protein; 7g Sugars; 1g Fiber

398. Crumbly Oat Meatloaf

Servings: 8   Cooking Time: 60 Minutes

Ingredients:

2 lbs. ground beef	1 tablespoon Worcestershire sauce
1 cup of salsa	
3/4 cup Quaker Oats	Salt and black pepper to taste
1/2 cup chopped onion	
1 large egg, beaten	

Directions:

Thoroughly mix ground beef with salsa, oats, onion, egg, and all the ingredients in a bowl.   Grease a meatloaf pan with oil or butter and spread the minced beef in the pan.   Press "Power Button" of Air Fry Oven and turn the dial to select the "Bake" mode.   Press the Time button and again turn the dial to set the cooking time to 60 minutes.   Now push the Temp button and rotate the dial to set the temperature at 350 degrees F.   Once preheated, place the beef baking pan in the oven and close its lid.   Slice and serve.

Nutrition Info: Calories: 412 Cal Total Fat: 24.8 g Saturated Fat: 12.4 g   Cholesterol: 3 mg   Sodium: 132 mg   Total Carbs: 43.8 g   Fiber: 3.9 g Sugar: 2.5 g   Protein: 18.9 g

399. Lamb Skewers

Servings: 4   Cooking Time: 20 Minutes

Ingredients:

2 lb. lamb meat; cubed	2 tbsp. lemon juice
	1 tbsp. red vinegar
2 red bell peppers; cut into medium pieces	1 tbsp. garlic; minced
	1/2 tsp. rosemary; dried
1/4 cup olive oil	
1 tbsp. oregano; dried	A pinch of salt and black pepper

Directions:

Take a bowl and mix all the ingredients and toss them well.   Thread the lamb and bell peppers on skewers, place them in your air fryer's basket and cook at 380°F for 10 minutes on each side. Divide between plates and serve with a side salad

Nutrition Info: Calories: 274; Fat: 12g; Fiber: 3g; Carbs: 6g; Protein: 16g

400. Hasselback Potatoes

Servings: 4   Cooking Time: 30 Minutes

Ingredients:

4 potatoes	1 tablespoon fresh chives, chopped
2 tablespoons Parmesan cheese, shredded	2 tablespoons olive oil

Directions:

Preheat the Air fryer to 355F and grease an Air fryer basket.   Cut slits along each potato about 1/4-inch apart with a sharp knife, making sure slices should stay connected at the bottom.   Coat the potatoes with olive oil and arrange into the Air fryer basket. Cook for about 30 minutes and dish out in a platter. Top with chives and Parmesan cheese to serve.

Nutrition Info: Calories: 218, Fat: 7.9g, Carbohydrates: 33.6g, Sugar: 2.5g, Protein: 4.6g, Sodium: 55mg

401. Cheddar Pork Meatballs

Servings: 4 To 6   Cooking Time: 25 Minutes

Ingredients:

1 lb ground pork	2 tsp mustard
1 large onion, chopped	Salt and black pepper to taste
1/2 tsp maple syrup	2 tbsp. grated cheddar cheese
1/2 cup chopped basil leaves	

Directions:

In a mixing bowl, add the ground pork, onion, maple syrup, mustard, basil leaves, salt, pepper, and cheddar cheese; mix well. Use your hands to form bite-size balls. Place in the fryer basket and cook at 400 f for 10 minutes. Slide out the fryer basket and shake it to toss the meatballs. Cook further for 5 minutes. Remove them onto a wire rack and serve with zoodles and marinara sauce.

Nutrition Info: Calories: 300 Cal Total Fat: 24 g Saturated Fat: 9 g Cholesterol: 70 mg Sodium: 860 mg Total Carbs: 3 g Fiber: 0 g Sugar: 0 g Protein: 16 g

402.	Spicy Sesame-honey Chicken

Servings: 4   Cooking Time: 30 Minutes

Ingredients:

1 package of chicken thighs/wings	1 tablespoon ketchup
1 tablespoon sugar	1 tablespoon honey
1-1/3 tablespoons chili garlic sauce	1 tablespoon soy sauce
1/4 cup soy sauce	1 teaspoon sugar or brown sugar
1 tablespoon sesame oil	1 teaspoon cornstarch

Directions:

Create marinade by combining 1 tablespoon chili sauce, soy sauce, and sesame oil. Toss chicken in marinade and refrigerate for at least 30 minutes, but up to a day. Preheat toaster oven to 375°F. Place chicken on a baking sheet with a little space between each piece and bake for 30 minutes. While the chicken bakes, create the sauce by combining all the leftover ingredients, including the 1/3 tablespoon of chili sauce. Mix well and microwave in 30-second intervals until the sauce starts to thicken. Toss chicken in sauce and serve.

Nutrition Info: Calories: 401, Sodium: 1439 mg, Dietary Fiber: 0 g, Total Fat: 16.0 g, Total Carbs: 11.2 g, Protein: 50.6 g.

403.	Asparagus Frittata

Servings: 4   Cooking Time: 10 Minutes

Ingredients:

6 eggs	2 tsp butter, melted
3 mushrooms, sliced	1 cup mozzarella cheese, shredded 1
10 asparagus, chopped 1/4 cup half and half	tsp pepper
	1 tsp salt

Directions:

Toss mushrooms and asparagus with melted butter and add into the air fryer basket. Cook mushrooms and asparagus at 350 F for 5 minutes. Shake basket twice. Meanwhile, in a bowl, whisk together eggs, half and half, pepper, and salt. Transfer cook mushrooms and asparagus into the air fryer baking dish. Pour egg mixture over mushrooms and asparagus. Place dish in the air fryer and cook at 350 F for 5 minutes or until eggs are set. Slice and serve.

Nutrition Info: Calories 211   Fat 13 g Carbohydrates 4 g   Sugar 1 g   Protein 16 g Cholesterol 272 mg

404.	Creamy Lemon Turkey

Servings: 4   Cooking Time: 20 Minutes

Ingredients:

2 cloves garlic, finely minced 1/3 tsp. lemon zest	1/3 cup sour cream Salt and freshly cracked mixed peppercorns, to taste
2 small-sized turkey breasts, skinless and cubed 1/3 cup thickened cream	1/2 cup scallion, chopped
2 tablespoons lemon juice	1/2 can tomatoes, diced
1 tsp. fresh marjoram, chopped	1½ tablespoons canola oil

Directions:

Firstly, pat dry the turkey breast. Mix the remaining items; marinate the turkey for 2 hours. Set the air fryer to cook at 355 °F. Brush the turkey with a nonstick spray; cook for 23 minutes, turning once. Serve with naan and enjoy!

Nutrition Info:260 Calories;   15.3g Fat;   8.9g Carbs;   28.6g Protein;   1.9g Sugars

405.	Adobe Turkey Chimichangas

Servings: 4   Cooking Time: 15 Minutes

Ingredients:

1 pound thickly-sliced smoked turkey from deli counter, chopped	3 chopped scallions Salt and pepper
1 tablespoon chili powder	4 (12-inch) flour tortillas
2 cups shredded slaw cabbage	1-1/2 cups pepper jack cheese
1 to 2 chipotles in adobo sauce	2 tablespoons olive oil
1 cup tomato sauce	1 cup sour cream
	2 tablespoons chopped cilantro

Directions:

Start by preheating toaster oven to 400°F. In a medium bowl mix together turkey and chili powder. Add cabbage, chipotles, tomato sauce, and scallions; mix well. Season cabbage mixture with salt and pepper and turn a few times. Warm tortillas in a microwave or on a stove top. Lay cheese flat in each tortilla and top with turkey mixture. Fold in the top and bottom of the tortilla, then roll to close. Brush baking tray with oil, then place chimichangas on tray and brush with oil. Bake for 15 minutes or until tortilla is golden brown. Top with sour cream and cilantro and serve.

Nutrition Info: Calories: 638, Sodium: 1785 mg, Dietary Fiber: 4.2 g, Total Fat: 44.0 g, Total Carbs: 23.9 g, Protein: 38.4 g.

406.	Cod With Avocado Mayo Sauce

Servings: 2   Cooking Time: 20 Minutes

Ingredients:

2 cod fish fillets

1 egg

Sea salt, to taste

1/2 avocado, peeled, pitted, and mashed

1 tablespoon mayonnaise

3 tablespoons sour cream

1/2 teaspoon yellow mustard

2 teaspoons olive oil

1 teaspoon lemon juice

1 garlic clove, minced

¼ teaspoon black pepper

¼ teaspoon salt

¼ teaspoon hot pepper sauce

Directions:

Start by preheating your Air Fryer to 360 degrees F. Spritz the Air Fryer basket with cooking oil. Pat dry the fish fillets with a kitchen towel. Beat the egg in a shallow bowl. Add in the salt and olive oil. Dip the fish into the egg mixture, making sure to coat thoroughly. Cook in the preheated Air Fryer approximately 12 minutes. Meanwhile, make the avocado sauce by mixing the remaining ingredients in a bowl. Place in your refrigerator until ready to serve. Serve the fish fillets with chilled avocado sauce on the side.

Nutrition Info:344 Calories; 27g Fat; 8g Carbs; 21g Protein; 8g Sugars; 7g Fiber

407.	Vegetable Cane

Servings: 4   Cooking Time: More Than 60 Minutes;

Ingredients:

2 calf legs

4 carrots

4 medium potatoes

1 clove garlic

300ml Broth

Leave to taste

Pepper to taste

Directions:

Place the ears, garlic, and half of the broth in the greased basket. Set the temperature to 1800C. Cook the stems for 40 minutes, turning them in the middle of cooking. Add the vegetables in pieces, salt, pepper, pour the rest of the broth and cook for another 50 minutes (time may vary depending on the size of the hocks). Mix the vegetables and the ears 2 to 3 times during cooking.

Nutrition Info: Calories 7.9, Fat 0.49g, Carbohydrate 0.77g, Sugar 0.49g, Protein 0.08mg, Cholesterol 0mg

Fish & Seafood Recipes

408. Marinated Salmon

Servings: 2   Cooking Time: 10 Minutes

Ingredients:

2 salmon fillets, skinless and boneless	2 garlic cloves, minced
For marinade:	2 tbsp mirin
2 tbsp scallions, minced	2 tbsp soy sauce
1 tbsp ginger, grated	1 tbsp olive oil

Directions:

Fit the Cuisinart oven with the rack in position 2. Add all marinade ingredients into the zip-lock bag and mix well.   Add salmon in the bag. The sealed bag shakes well and places it in the fridge for 30 minutes.   Arrange marinated salmon fillets in an air fryer basket then place an air fryer basket in the baking pan.   Place a baking pan on the oven rack. Set to air fry at 360 F for 10 minutes.   Serve and enjoy.

Nutrition Info: Calories 345 Fat 18.2 g Carbohydrates 11.6 g Sugar 4.5 g Protein 36.1 g Cholesterol 78 mg

409. Basil Tomato Salmon

Servings: 2   Cooking Time: 20 Minutes

Ingredients:

2 salmon fillets	2 tbsp parmesan cheese, grated
1 tomato, sliced	
1 tbsp dried basil	1 tbsp olive oil

Directions:

Fit the Cuisinart oven with the rack in position Place salmon fillets in a baking dish.   Sprinkle basil on top of salmon fillets.   Arrange tomato slices on top of salmon fillets. Drizzle with oil and top with cheese.   Set to bake at 375 F for 25 minutes. After 5 minutes place the baking dish in the preheated oven.   Serve and enjoy.

Nutrition Info: Calories 324 Fat 19.6 g Carbohydrates 1.5 g Sugar 0.8 g Protein 37.1 g Cholesterol 83 mg

410. Spicy Halibut

Servings: 4   Cooking Time: 12 Minutes

Ingredients:

1 lb halibut fillets	1/4 cup olive oil
1/2 tsp chili powder	1/4 tsp garlic powder
1/2 tsp smoked paprika	Pepper
	Salt

Directions:

Fit the Cuisinart oven with the rack in position Place halibut fillets in a baking dish.   In a small bowl, mix oil, garlic powder, paprika, pepper, chili powder, and salt.   Brush fish fillets with oil mixture.   Set to bake at 425 F for 17 minutes. After 5 minutes place the baking dish in the preheated oven.   Serve and enjoy.

Nutrition Info: Calories 236 Fat 15.3 g Carbohydrates 0.5 g Sugar 0.1 g Protein 24 g Cholesterol 36 mg

411. Rosemary Garlic Shrimp

Servings: 4   Cooking Time: 10 Minutes

Ingredients:

1 lb shrimp, peeled and deveined	1/2 tbsp fresh rosemary, chopped
2 garlic cloves, minced	Pepper
1 tbsp olive oil	Salt

Directions:

Fit the Cuisinart oven with the rack in position Add shrimp and remaining ingredients in a large bowl and toss well.   Pour shrimp mixture into the baking dish.   Set to bake at 400 F for 15 minutes. After 5 minutes place the baking dish in the preheated oven.   Serve and enjoy.

Nutrition Info: Calories 168 Fat 5.5 g Carbohydrates 2.5 g Sugar 0 g Protein 26 g Cholesterol 239 mg

412. Old Bay Shrimp

Servings: 4   Cooking Time: 10 Minutes

Ingredients:

1 lb jumbo shrimp	1/3 tsp smoked paprika
Salt to taste	
1/4 tsp old bay seasoning	1/4 tsp chili powder
	1 tbsp olive oil

Directions:

Preheat Cuisinart on AirFry function to 390 F. In a bowl, add the shrimp, paprika, oil, salt, old bay seasoning, and chili powder; mix well. Place the shrimp in the oven and cook for 5 minutes.

413. Dill Salmon Patties

Servings: 2   Cooking Time: 10 Minutes

Ingredients:

14 oz can salmon, drained and discard bones	1/4 tsp garlic powder
	1/2 cup breadcrumbs
1 tsp dill, chopped	1/4 cup onion, diced
1 egg, lightly beaten	Pepper
	Salt

Directions:

Fit the Cuisinart oven with the rack in position 2. Add all ingredients into the large bowl and mix well. Make equal shapes of patties from mixture and place in the air fryer basket then place the air fryer basket in the baking pan.   Place a baking pan on the oven rack. Set to air fry at 370 F for 10 minutes.   Serve and enjoy.

Nutrition Info: Calories 422 Fat 15.7 g Carbohydrates 21.5 g Sugar 2.5 g Protein 46 g Cholesterol 191 mg

414. Lemon Pepper Tilapia Fillets

Servings: 4   Cooking Time: 15 Minutes

Ingredients:

1 lb tilapia fillets	2 tbsp lemon pepper
1 tbsp Italian seasoning	Salt to taste
2 tbsp canola oil	2-3 butter buds

Directions:
Preheat your Cuisinart oven to 400 F on Bake function. Drizzle tilapia fillets with canola oil. In a bowl, mix salt, lemon pepper, butter buds, and Italian seasoning; spread on the fish. Place the fillet on a baking tray and press Start. Cook for 10 minutes until tender and crispy. Serve warm.

415.	**Browned Shrimp Patties**

Servings: 4   Cooking Time: 12 Minutes
Ingredients:

½ pound (227 g) raw shrimp, shelled, deveined, and chopped finely	2 teaspoons Worcestershire sauce
2 cups cooked sushi rice	½ teaspoon salt
¼ cup chopped red bell pepper	½ teaspoon garlic powder
¼ cup chopped celery	½ teaspoon Old Bay seasoning
¼ cup chopped green onion	½ cup plain bread crumbs
	Cooking spray

Directions:
Put all the ingredients except the bread crumbs and oil in a large bowl and stir to incorporate.   Scoop out the shrimp mixture and shape into 8 equal-sized patties with your hands, no more than ½-inch thick. Roll the patties in the bread crumbs on a plate and spray both sides with cooking spray. Place the patties in the air fryer basket.   Put the air fryer basket on the baking pan and slide into Rack Position 2, select Air Fry, set temperature to 390°F (199°C), and set time to 12 minutes.   Flip the patties halfway through the cooking time.   When cooking is complete, the outside should be crispy brown. Divide the patties among four plates and serve warm.

416.	**Lemon Pepper White Fish Fillets**

Servings: 2   Cooking Time: 12 Minutes
Ingredients:

12 oz white fish fillets	1/2 tsp lemon pepper seasoning
Pepper	Salt

Directions:
Fit the Cuisinart oven with the rack in position 2. Spray fish fillets with cooking spray and season with lemon pepper seasoning, pepper, and salt.   Place fish fillets in the air fryer basket then place an air fryer basket in the baking pan.   Place a baking pan on the oven rack. Set to air fry at 360 F for 12 minutes.   Serve and enjoy.
Nutrition Info: Calories 294 Fat 12.8 g Carbohydrates 0.4 g Sugar 0 g Protein 41.7 g Cholesterol 131 mg

417.	**Prawn Grandma's Easy To Cook Wontons**

Ingredients:

1 ½ cup all-purpose flour	2 tbsp. oil
½ tsp. salt	2 tsp. ginger-garlic paste

5 tbsp. water	2 tsp. soya sauce
2 cups minced prawn	2 tsp. vinegar

Directions:
Squeeze the dough and cover it with plastic wrap and set aside. Next, cook the ingredients for the filling and try to ensure that the prawn is covered well with the sauce. Roll the dough and place the filling in the center.   Now, wrap the dough to cover the filling and pinch the edges together. Pre heat the Cuisinart oven at 200° F for 5 minutes. Place the wontons in the fry basket and close it. Let them cook at the same temperature for another 20 minutes. Recommended sides are chili sauce or ketchup.

418.	**Easy Shrimp Fajitas**

Servings: 10   Cooking Time: 20 Minutes
Ingredients:

1 lb shrimp	2 tbsp taco seasoning
1 tbsp olive oil	1/2 cup onion, diced
2 bell peppers, diced	

Directions:
Fit the Cuisinart oven with the rack in position 2. Add shrimp and remaining ingredients into the bowl and toss well.   Add shrimp mixture to the air fryer basket then place an air fryer basket in baking pan. Place a baking pan on the oven rack. Set to air fry at 390 F for 20 minutes.   Serve and enjoy.
Nutrition Info: Calories 76 Fat 2.2 g Carbohydrates 3 g Sugar 1.4 g Protein 10.6 g Cholesterol 96 mg

419.	**Tuna Sandwich**

Ingredients:

2 slices of white bread	½ flake garlic crushed
1 tbsp. softened butter	¼ cup chopped onion
1 tin tuna	½ tbsp. sugar
1 small capsicum	1 tbsp. tomato ketchup
For Barbeque Sauce:	
¼ tbsp. Worcestershire sauce	½ cup water.
½ tsp. olive oil	¼ tbsp. red chili sauce
¼ tsp. mustard powder	A pinch of salt and black pepper to taste

Directions:
Take the slices of bread and remove the edges. Now cut the slices horizontally. Cook the ingredients for the sauce and wait till it thickens. Now, add the lamb to the sauce and stir till it obtains the flavors. Roast the capsicum and peel the skin off. Cut the capsicum into slices. Mix the ingredients together and apply it to the bread slices.   Pre-heat the Cuisinart oven for 5 minutes at 300 Fahrenheit. Open the basket of the Fryer and place the prepared Classic Sandwiches in it such that no two Classic Sandwiches are touching each other. Now keep the fryer at 250 degrees for around 15 minutes. Turn the Classic Sandwiches in between the cooking process to cook both slices. Serve the Classic Sandwiches with tomato ketchup or mint sauce.

420. Caesar Shrimp Salad

Servings: 4   Cooking Time: 15 Minutes

Ingredients:

½ baguette, cut into 1-inch cubes (about 2½ cups)
¼ teaspoon granulated garlic
¼ teaspoon kosher salt
2 romaine lettuce hearts, cut in half lengthwise and ends trimmed

4 tablespoons extra-virgin olive oil, divided
¾ cup Caesar dressing, divided
1 pound (454 g) medium shrimp, peeled and deveined
2 ounces (57 g) Parmesan cheese, coarsely grated

Directions:

Make the croutons: Put the bread cubes in a medium bowl and drizzle 3 tablespoons of olive oil over top. Season with granulated garlic and salt and toss to coat. Transfer to the air fryer basket in a single layer. Put the air fryer basket on the baking pan and slide into Rack Position 2, select Air Fry, set temperature to 400°F (205°C), and set time to 4 minutes. Toss the croutons halfway through the cooking time. When done, remove from the oven and set aside. Brush 2 tablespoons of Caesar dressing on the cut side of the lettuce. Set aside.   Toss the shrimp with the ¼ cup of Caesar dressing in a large bowl until well coated. Set aside.   Coat the baking pan with the remaining 1 tablespoon of olive oil. Arrange the romaine halves on the coated pan, cut side down. Brush the tops with the remaining 2 tablespoons of Caesar dressing.   Slide the baking pan into Rack Position 2, select Roast, set temperature to 375°F (190°C), and set time to 10 minutes.   After 5 minutes, remove from the oven and flip the romaine halves. Spoon the shrimp around the lettuce. Return the pan to the oven and continue cooking.   When done, remove from the oven. If they are not quite cooked through, roast for another 1 minute.   On each of four plates, put a romaine half. Divide the shrimp among the plates and top with croutons and grated Parmesan cheese. Serve immediately.

421. Squab Oregano Fingers

Ingredients:

½ lb. squab Oregano Fingers
2 cups of dry breadcrumbs
1 cup oil for frying
1 ½ tbsp. ginger-garlic paste
3 tbsp. lemon juice

2 tsp salt
1 ½ tsp pepper powder
1 tsp red chili flakes or to taste
3 eggs
5 tbsp. corn flour
2 tsp tomato ketchup

Directions:

Make the marinade and transfer the Oregano Fingers into the marinade. Leave them on a plate to dry for fifteen minutes. Now cover the Oregano Fingers with the crumbs and set aside to dry for fifteen minutes.   Pre heat the Cuisinart oven at 160 degrees Fahrenheit for 5 minutes or so. Keep the fish in the fry basket now and close it properly. Let the Oregano Fingers cook at the same temperature for another 25 minutes. In between the cooking

process, toss the fish once in a while to avoid burning the food. Serve either with tomato ketchup or chili sauce. Mint sauce also works well with the fish.

422. Breaded Scallops

Servings: 4   Cooking Time: 7 Minutes

Ingredients:

1 egg
3 tablespoons flour
1 cup bread crumbs
1 pound (454 g) fresh scallops

2 tablespoons olive oil
Salt and black pepper, to taste

Directions:

In a bowl, lightly beat the egg. Place the flour and bread crumbs into separate shallow dishes. Dredge the scallops in the flour and shake off any excess. Dip the flour-coated scallops in the beaten egg and roll in the bread crumbs.   Brush the scallops generously with olive oil and season with salt and pepper, to taste. Transfer the scallops to the air fryer basket.   Put the air fryer basket on the baking pan and slide into Rack Position 2, select Air Fry, set temperature to 360°F (182°C), and set time to 7 minutes.   Flip the scallops halfway through the cooking time.   When cooking is complete, the scallops should reach an internal temperature of just 145°F (63°C) on a meat thermometer. Remove from the oven. Let the scallops cool for 5 minutes and serve.

423. Goat Cheese Shrimp

Servings: 2   Cooking Time: 8 Minutes

Ingredients:

1 pound (454 g) shrimp, deveined
1½ tablespoons olive oil
1½ tablespoons balsamic vinegar
1 tablespoon coconut aminos
Sea salt flakes, to taste
1 teaspoon Dijon mustard

½ tablespoon fresh parsley, roughly chopped
½ teaspoon smoked cayenne pepper
½ teaspoon garlic powder
Salt and ground black peppercorns, to taste
1 cup shredded goat cheese

Directions:

Except for the cheese, stir together all the ingredients in a large bowl until the shrimp are evenly coated.   Place the shrimp in the air fryer basket.   Put the air fryer basket on the baking pan and slide into Rack Position 2, select Roast, set temperature to 385°F (196°C), and set time to 8 minutes.   When cooking is complete, the shrimp should be pink and cooked through. Remove from the oven and serve with the shredded goat cheese sprinkled on top.

424. Breaded Calamari With Lemon

Servings: 4   Cooking Time: 12 Minutes

Ingredients:

2 large eggs
2 garlic cloves,

1 pound (454 g) calamari rings

minced
½ cup cornstarch
1 cup bread crumbs

Cooking spray
1 lemon, sliced

Directions:
In a small bowl, whisk the eggs with minced garlic. Place the cornstarch and bread crumbs into separate shallow dishes.   Dredge the calamari rings in the cornstarch, then dip in the egg mixture, shaking off any excess, finally roll them in the bread crumbs to coat well. Let the calamari rings sit for 10 minutes in the refrigerator.   Spritz the air fryer basket with cooking spray. Transfer the calamari rings to the pan. Put the air fryer basket on the baking pan and slide into Rack Position 2, select Air Fry, set temperature to 390°F (199°C), and set time to 12 minutes.   Stir the calamari rings once halfway through the cooking time.   When cooking is complete, remove from the oven. Serve the calamari rings with the lemon slices sprinkled on top.

425.   Spicy Lemon Garlic Tilapia

Servings: 2   Cooking Time: 15 Minutes
Ingredients:

4 tilapia fillets
1 lemon, cut into slices
1/2 tsp pepper
1/2 tsp chili powder

1 tsp garlic, minced
3 tbsp butter, melted
1 tbsp fresh lemon juice
Salt

Directions:
Fit the Cuisinart oven with the rack in position Place fish fillets into the baking dish.   Arrange lemon slices on top of fish fillets.   Mix together the remaining ingredients and pour over fish fillets. Set to bake at 350 F for 20 minutes. After 5 minutes place the baking dish in the preheated oven. Serve and enjoy.
Nutrition Info: Calories 354 Fat 19.6 g Carbohydrates 4 g Sugar 1 g Protein 42.8 g Cholesterol 156 mg

426.   Crusty Scallops

Servings: 4   Cooking Time: 20 Minutes
Ingredients:

12 fresh scallops
Salt and black pepper to taste

3 tbsp flour
1 egg, lightly beaten
1 cup breadcrumbs

Directions:
Coat the scallops with flour. Dip into the egg, then into the breadcrumbs. Arrange them on the frying basket and spray with cooking spray. Cook for 12 minutes at 360 F on AirFry function.

427.   Crispy Paprika Fish Fillets(1)

Servings: 4   Cooking Time: 15 Minutes
Ingredients:

1/2 cup seasoned breadcrumbs
1 tablespoon balsamic vinegar
1/2 teaspoon seasoned salt
1 teaspoon paprika

1/2 teaspoon ground black pepper
1 teaspoon celery seed
2 fish fillets, halved
1 egg, beaten

Directions:

Preparing the Ingredients. Add the breadcrumbs, vinegar, salt, paprika, ground black pepper, and celery seeds to your food processor. Process for about 30 seconds.   Coat the fish fillets with the beaten egg; then, coat them with the breadcrumbs mixture.   Air Frying. Cook at 350 degrees F for about 15 minutes.

428.   Crispy Cheesy Fish Fingers

Servings: 4   Cooking Time: 20 Minutes
Ingredients:

Large codfish filet, approximately 6-8 ounces, fresh or frozen and thawed, cut into 1 ½-inch strips
½ cup of breadcrumbs (we like Panko, but any brand or home recipe will do)

2 raw eggs
2 tablespoons of shredded or powdered parmesan cheese
1 tablespoons of shredded cheddar cheese
Pinch of salt and pepper

Directions:
Preparing the Ingredients. Cover the basket of the Cuisinart air fryer oven with a lining of tin foil, leaving the edges uncovered to allow air to circulate through the basket.   Preheat the air fryer oven to 350 degrees.   In a large mixing bowl, beat the eggs until fluffy and until the yolks and whites are fully combined.   Dunk all the fish strips in the beaten eggs, fully submerging.   In a separate mixing bowl, combine the bread crumbs with the parmesan, cheddar, and salt and pepper, until evenly mixed. One by one, coat the egg-covered fish strips in the mixed dry ingredients so that they're fully covered, and place on the foil-lined Oven rack/basket. Place the Rack on the middle-shelf of the Cuisinart air fryer oven.   Air Frying. Set the air-fryer timer to 20 minutes.   Halfway through the cooking time, shake the handle of the air-fryer so that the breaded fish jostles inside and fry-coverage is even.   After 20 minutes, when the fryer shuts off, the fish strips will be perfectly cooked and their breaded crust golden-brown and delicious! Using tongs, remove from the air fryer oven and set on a serving dish to cool.

429.   Baked Pesto Salmon

Servings: 4   Cooking Time: 15 Minutes
Ingredients:

4 salmon fillets
1/3 cup parmesan cheese, grated

1/3 cup breadcrumbs
6 tbsp pesto

Directions:
Fit the Cuisinart oven with the rack in position Place fish fillets into the baking dish.   Pour pesto over fish fillets.   Mix together breadcrumbs and parmesan cheese and sprinkle over fish.   Set to bake at 325 F for 20 minutes. After 5 minutes place the baking dish in the preheated oven.   Serve and enjoy.
Nutrition Info: Calories 396 Fat 22.8 g Carbohydrates 8.3 g Sugar 2.1 g Protein 40.4 g Cholesterol 89 mg

430. Coconut-crusted Prawns

Servings: 4   Cooking Time: 8 Minutes

Ingredients:

12 prawns, cleaned and deveined
1 teaspoon fresh lemon juice
½ teaspoon cumin powder
Salt and ground black pepper, to taste
1 medium egg
⅓ cup beer
½ cup flour, divided
1 tablespoon curry powder
1 teaspoon baking powder
½ teaspoon grated fresh ginger
1 cup flaked coconut

Directions:

In a large bowl, toss the prawns with the lemon juice, cumin powder, salt, and pepper until well coated. Set aside.   In a shallow bowl, whisk together the egg, beer, ¼ cup of flour, curry powder, baking powder, and ginger until combined.   In a separate shallow bowl, put the remaining ¼ cup of flour, and on a plate, place the flaked coconut.   Dip the prawns in the flour, then in the egg mixture, finally roll in the flaked coconut to coat well. Transfer the prawns to a baking sheet.   Put the air fryer basket on the baking pan and slide into Rack Position 2, select Air Fry, set temperature to 350°F (180°C), and set time to 8 minutes.   After 5 minutes, remove from the oven and flip the prawns. Return to the oven and continue cooking for 3 minutes more. When cooking is complete, remove from the oven and serve warm.

431. Bacon Wrapped Shrimp

Servings: 4   Cooking Time: 5 Minutes

Ingredients:

1¼ pound tiger shrimp, peeled and deveined
1 pound bacon

Directions:

Preparing the Ingredients. Wrap each shrimp with a slice of bacon.   Refrigerate for about 20 minutes. Preheat the Cuisinart air fryer oven to 390 degrees F.   Air Frying. Arrange the shrimp in the Oven rack/basket. Place the Rack on the middle-shelf of the Cuisinart air fryer oven. Cook for about 5-7 minutes.

432. Shrimp Momo's Recipe

Ingredients:

1 ½ cup all-purpose flour
½ tsp. salt
5 tbsp. water
For filling:
2 cups minced shrimp
2 tbsp. oil
2 tsp. ginger-garlic paste
2 tsp. soya sauce
2 tsp. vinegar

Directions:

Squeeze the dough and cover it with plastic wrap and set aside. Next, cook the ingredients for the filling and try to ensure that the shrimp is covered well with the sauce. Roll the dough and cut it into a square. Place the filling in the center.   Now, wrap the dough to cover the filling and pinch the edges

together. Pre heat the Cuisinart oven at 200° F for 5 minutes. Place the wontons in the fry basket and close it. Let them cook at the same temperature for another 20 minutes. Recommended sides are chili sauce or ketchup.

433. Fired Shrimp With Mayonnaise Sauce

Servings: 4   Cooking Time: 7 Minutes

Ingredients:

Shrimp
12 jumbo shrimp
½ teaspoon garlic salt
¼ teaspoon freshly cracked mixed peppercorns
4 tablespoons mayonnaise
Sauce:
1 teaspoon grated lemon rind
1 teaspoon Dijon mustard
1 teaspoon chipotle powder
½ teaspoon cumin powder

Directions:

In a medium bowl, season the shrimp with garlic salt and cracked mixed peppercorns.   Place the shrimp in the air fryer basket.   Put the air fryer basket on the baking pan and slide into Rack Position 2, select Air Fry, set temperature to 395°F (202°C), and set time to 7 minutes.   After 5 minutes, remove from the oven and flip the shrimp. Return to the oven and continue cooking for 2 minutes more, or until they are pink and no longer opaque.   Meanwhile, stir together all the ingredients for the sauce in a small bowl until well mixed.   When cooking is complete, remove the shrimp from the oven and serve alongside the sauce.

434. Crab Cakes With Bell Peppers

Servings: 4   Cooking Time: 10 Minutes

Ingredients:

8 ounces (227 g) jumbo lump crab meat
1 egg, beaten
Juice of ½ lemon
⅓ cup bread crumbs
¼ cup diced green bell pepper
¼ cup diced red bell pepper
¼ cup mayonnaise
1 tablespoon Old Bay seasoning
1 teaspoon flour
Cooking spray

Directions:

Make the crab cakes: Place all the ingredients except the flour and oil in a large bowl and stir until well incorporated.   Divide the crab mixture into four equal portions and shape each portion into a patty with your hands. Top each patty with a sprinkle of ¼ teaspoon of flour.   Arrange the crab cakes in the air fryer basket and spritz them with cooking spray.   Put the air fryer basket on the baking pan and slide into Rack Position 2, select Air Fry, set temperature to 375°F (190°C), and set time to 10 minutes.   Flip the crab cakes halfway through. When cooking is complete, the cakes should be cooked through. Remove from the oven and divide the crab cakes among four plates and serve.

435. Sweet Cajun Salmon

Servings: 1   Cooking Time: 10 Minutes

Ingredients:

1 salmon fillet
¼ tsp brown sugar
1 tbsp cajun seasoning

Juice of ½ lemon
2 lemon wedges
1 tbsp chopped parsley

Directions:
Preheat Cuisinart on Bake function to 350 F. Combine sugar and lemon juice; coat the salmon with this mixture. Coat with the Cajun seasoning as well. Place a parchment paper on a baking tray and cook the fish in your Cuisinart for 10 minutes. Serve with lemon wedges and parsley.

436. Lemon Butter Shrimp

Servings: 4   Cooking Time: 12 Minutes

Ingredients:

1 1/4 lbs shrimp, peeled & deveined
2 tbsp fresh parsley, chopped
1 tbsp garlic, minced

2 tbsp fresh lemon juice
1/4 cup butter
Pepper
Salt

Directions:
Fit the Cuisinart oven with the rack in position Add shrimp into the baking dish.   Melt butter in a pan over low heat. Add garlic and sauté for 30 seconds. Stir in lemon juice.   Pour melted butter mixture over shrimp. Season with pepper and salt. Set to bake at 350 F for 17 minutes. After 5 minutes place the baking dish in the preheated oven. Garnish with parsley and serve.

Nutrition Info: Calories 276 Fat 14 g Carbohydrates 3.2 g Sugar 0.2 g Protein 32.7 g Cholesterol 329 mg

437. Pecan-crusted Catfish Fillets

Servings: 4   Cooking Time: 12 Minutes

Ingredients:

1 teaspoon fine sea salt
¼ teaspoon ground black pepper
4 (4-ounce / 113-g) catfish fillets

½ cup pecan meal
Avocado oil spray
For Garnish (Optional):
Fresh oregano
Pecan halves

Directions:
Spray the air fryer basket with avocado oil spray. Combine the pecan meal, sea salt, and black pepper in a large bowl. Dredge each catfish fillet in the meal mixture, turning until well coated. Spritz the fillets with avocado oil spray, then transfer to the basket. Put the air fryer basket on the baking pan and slide into Rack Position 2, select Air Fry, set temperature to 375°F (190°C), and set time to 12 minutes.   Flip the fillets halfway through the cooking time. When cooking is complete, the fish should be cooked through and no longer translucent. Remove from the oven and sprinkle the oregano sprigs and pecan halves on top for garnish, if desired. Serve immediately.

438. Shrimp And Cherry Tomato Kebabs

Servings: 4   Cooking Time: 5 Minutes

Ingredients:

1½ pounds (680 g) jumbo shrimp, cleaned, shelled and deveined
1 pound (454 g) cherry tomatoes
2 tablespoons butter, melted
1 tablespoons Sriracha sauce
Sea salt and ground black pepper, to taste

1 teaspoon dried parsley flakes
½ teaspoon dried basil
½ teaspoon dried oregano
½ teaspoon mustard seeds
½ teaspoon marjoram
Special Equipment:
4 to 6 wooden skewers, soaked in water for 30 minutes

Directions:
Put all the ingredients in a large bowl and toss to coat well.   Make the kebabs: Thread, alternating jumbo shrimp and cherry tomatoes, onto the wooden skewers. Place the kebabs in the air fryer basket.   Put the air fryer basket on the baking pan and slide into Rack Position 2, select Air Fry, set temperature to 400°F (205°C), and set time to 5 minutes.   When cooking is complete, the shrimp should be pink and the cherry tomatoes should be softened. Remove from the oven. Let the shrimp and cherry tomato kebabs cool for 5 minutes and serve hot.

439. Easy Shrimp And Vegetable Paella

Servings: 4   Cooking Time: 16 Minutes

Ingredients:

1 (10-ounce / 284-g) package frozen cooked rice, thawed
1 (6-ounce / 170-g) jar artichoke hearts, drained and chopped
½ teaspoon dried thyme

¼ cup vegetable broth
½ teaspoon turmeric
1 cup frozen cooked small shrimp
½ cup frozen baby peas
1 tomato, diced

Directions:
Mix together the cooked rice, chopped artichoke hearts, vegetable broth, thyme, and turmeric in the baking pan and stir to combine.   Slide the baking pan into Rack Position 1, select Convection Bake, set temperature to 340°F (171°C), and set time to 16 minutes.   After 9 minutes, remove from the oven and add the shrimp, baby peas, and diced tomato to the baking pan. Mix well. Return the pan to the oven and continue cooking for 7 minutes more, or until the shrimp are done and the paella is bubbling. When cooking is complete, remove from the oven. Cool for 5 minutes before serving.

440. Baked Halibut Steaks With Parsley

Servings: 4   Cooking Time: 10 Minutes

Ingredients:

1 pound (454 g) halibut steaks
¼ cup vegetable oil

2 tablespoons honey
1 tablespoon fresh parsley leaves,

2½ tablespoons Worcester sauce
2 tablespoons vermouth
1 tablespoon freshly squeezed lemon juice

coarsely chopped
Salt and pepper, to taste
1 teaspoon dried basil

Directions:

Put all the ingredients in a large mixing dish and gently stir until the fish is coated evenly. Transfer the fish to the baking pan.   Slide the baking pan into Rack Position 1, select Convection Bake, set temperature to 375°F (190°C), and set time to 10 minutes.   Flip the fish halfway through cooking time.   When cooking is complete, the fish should reach an internal temperature of at least 145°F (63°C) on a meat thermometer. Remove from the oven and let the fish cool for 5 minutes before serving.

---

441. Roasted Scallops With Snow Peas

Servings: 4   Cooking Time: 8 Minutes

Ingredients:

1 pound (454 g) sea scallops
3 tablespoons hoisin sauce
½ cup toasted sesame seeds
1 teaspoon soy sauce

6 ounces (170 g) snow peas, trimmed
3 teaspoons vegetable oil, divided
1 teaspoon sesame oil
1 cup roasted mushrooms

Directions:

Brush the scallops with the hoisin sauce. Put the sesame seeds in a shallow dish. Roll the scallops in the sesame seeds until evenly coated.   Combine the snow peas with 1 teaspoon of vegetable oil, the sesame oil, and soy sauce in a medium bowl and toss to coat.   Grease the baking pan with the remaining 2 teaspoons of vegetable oil. Put the scallops in the middle of the pan and arrange the snow peas around the scallops in a single layer.   Slide the baking pan into Rack Position 2, select Roast, set temperature to 375°F (190°C), and set time to 8 minutes.   After 5 minutes, remove the pan and flip the scallops. Fold in the mushrooms and stir well. Return the pan to the oven and continue cooking.   When done, remove from the oven and cool for 5 minutes. Serve warm.

---

442. Harissa Shrimp

Servings: 4   Cooking Time: 15 Minutes

Ingredients:

1 ¼ lb tiger shrimp
½ tsp old bay seasoning

¼ tsp harissa powder
Salt to taste
1 tbsp olive oil

Directions:

Preheat your Cuisinart oven to 390 F on AirFry function. In a bowl, mix the ingredients. Place the mixture in the cooking basket and cook for 5 minutes. Serve with a drizzle of lemon juice.

---

443. Crispy Crab And Fish Cakes

Servings: 4   Cooking Time: 12 Minutes

Ingredients:

8 ounces (227 g) imitation crab meat
4 ounces (113 g) leftover cooked fish (such as cod, pollock, or haddock)
2 tablespoons minced celery
2 tablespoons minced green onion
2 tablespoons light mayonnaise
1 tablespoon plus 2 teaspoons Worcestershire sauce

¾ cup crushed saltine cracker crumbs
2 teaspoons dried parsley flakes
1 teaspoon prepared yellow mustard
½ teaspoon garlic powder
½ teaspoon dried dill weed, crushed
½ teaspoon Old Bay seasoning
½ cup panko bread crumbs
Cooking spray

Directions:

Pulse the crab meat and fish in a food processor until finely chopped.   Transfer the meat mixture to a large bowl, along with the celery, green onion, mayo, Worcestershire sauce, cracker crumbs, parsley flakes, mustard, garlic powder, dill weed, and Old Bay seasoning. Stir to mix well.   Scoop out the meat mixture and form into 8 equal-sized patties with your hands.   Place the panko bread crumbs on a plate. Roll the patties in the bread crumbs until they are evenly coated on both sides. Put the patties in the baking pan and spritz them with cooking spray.   Slide the baking pan into Rack Position 1, select Convection Bake, set temperature to 390°F (199°C), and set time to 12 minutes.   Flip the patties halfway through the cooking time.   When cooking is complete, they should be golden brown and cooked through. Remove the pan from the oven. Divide the patties among four plates and serve.

---

444. Moist & Juicy Baked Cod

Servings: 2   Cooking Time: 10 Minutes

Ingredients:

1 lb cod fillets
1 1/2 tbsp olive oil
3 dashes cayenne pepper

1 tbsp fresh lemon juice
1/4 tsp salt

Directions:

Fit the Cuisinart oven with the rack in position Place fish fillets in a baking pan.   Drizzle with oil and lemon juice and sprinkle with cayenne pepper and salt.   Set to bake at 400 F for 15 minutes. After 5 minutes place the baking pan in the preheated oven.   Serve and enjoy.

Nutrition Info: Calories 275 Fat 12.7 g Carbohydrates 0.4 g Sugar 0.2 g Protein 40.6 g Cholesterol 111 mg

---

445. Shrimp With Smoked Paprika & Cayenne Pepper

Servings: 3   Cooking Time: 10 Minutes

Ingredients:

6 oz tiger shrimp, 12 to 16 pieces
1 tbsp olive oil

¼ a tbsp cayenne pepper
¼ a tbsp smoked

½ a tbsp old bay seasoning   paprika
A pinch of sea salt

Directions:
Preheat Cuisinart on Air Fry function to 380 F. Mix olive oil, old bay seasoning, cayenne pepper, smoked paprika, and sea salt in a large bowl. Add in the shrimp and toss to coat. Place the shrimp in the frying basket and fit in the baking tray; cook for 6-7 minutes, sahing once. Serve.

446. Tropical Shrimp Skewers

Servings: 4   Cooking Time: 5 Minutes

Ingredients:
1 tbsp. lime juice
1 tbsp. honey
¼ tsp red pepper flakes
¼ tsp pepper
¼ tsp ginger
1 lb. medium shrimp, peel, devein & leave tails on

Nonstick cooking spray
2 cups peaches, drain & chop
½ green bell pepper, chopped fine
¼ cup scallions, chopped

Directions:
Soak 8 small wooden skewers in water for 15 minutes.   In a small bowl, whisk together lime juice, honey and spices. Transfer 2 tablespoons of the mixture to a medium bowl.   Place the baking pan in position 2 of the oven. Lightly spray fryer basket with cooking spray. Set oven to broil on 400°F for 10 minutes.   Thread 5 shrimp on each skewer and brush both sides with marinade. Place in basket and after 5 minutes, place on the baking pan. Cook 4-5 minutes or until shrimp turn pink.   Add peaches, bell pepper, and scallions to reserved honey mixture, mix well. Divide salsa evenly between serving plates and top with 2 skewers each. Serve immediately.

Nutrition Info: Calories 181, Total Fat 1g, Saturated Fat 0g, Total Carbs 27g, Net Carbs 25g, Protein 16g, Sugar 21g, Fiber 2g, Sodium 650mg, Potassium 288mg, Phosphorus 297mg

447. Fish And Chips

Servings: 4   Cooking Time: 20 Minutes

Ingredients:
4 (4-ounce) fish fillets
Pinch salt
Freshly ground black pepper
½ teaspoon dried thyme
1 egg white

¾ cup crushed potato chips
2 tablespoons olive oil, divided
1 russet potatoes, peeled and cut into strips

Directions:
Preparing the Ingredients. Pat the fish fillets dry and sprinkle with salt, pepper, and thyme. Set aside. In a shallow bowl, beat the egg white until foamy. In another bowl, combine the potato chips and 1 tablespoon of olive oil and mix until combined. Dip the fish fillets into the egg white, then into the crushed potato chip mixture to coat.   Toss the fresh potato strips with the remaining 1 tablespoon olive oil.   Air Frying. Use your separator to divide the Oven rack/basket in half, then fry the chips and

fish. The chips will take about 20 minutes; the fish will take about 10 to 12 minutes to cook.
Nutrition Info:CALORIES: 374; FAT:16G; PROTEIN:30G; FIBER:4G

448. Chili Tuna Casserole

Servings: 4   Cooking Time: 16 Minutes

Ingredients:
½ tablespoon sesame oil
⅓ cup yellow onions, chopped
½ bell pepper, deveined and chopped
2 cups canned tuna, chopped
½ chili pepper, deveined and finely minced

Cooking spray
5 eggs, beaten
1½ tablespoons sour cream
⅓ teaspoon dried basil
⅓ teaspoon dried oregano
Fine sea salt and ground black pepper, to taste

Directions:
Heat the sesame oil in a nonstick skillet over medium heat until it shimmers.   Add the onions and bell pepper and sauté for 4 minutes, stirring occasionally, or until tender.   Add the canned tuna and keep stirring until the tuna is heated through.   Meanwhile, coat the baking pan lightly with cooking spray.   Transfer the tuna mixture to the baking pan, along with the beaten eggs, chili pepper, sour cream, basil, and oregano. Stir to combine well. Season with sea salt and black pepper. Slide the baking pan into Rack Position 1, select Convection Bake, set temperature to 325°F (160ºC), and set time to 12 minutes.   When cooking is complete, the eggs should be completely set and the top lightly browned. Remove from the oven and serve on a plate.

449. Salmon Beans & Mushrooms

Servings: 6   Cooking Time: 25 Minutes

Ingredients:
4 salmon fillets
2 tbsp fresh parsley, minced
1/4 cup fresh lemon juice
1 tsp garlic, minced
1/2 lb mushrooms, sliced

1 tbsp olive oil
1/2 lb green beans, trimmed
1/2 cup parmesan cheese, grated
Pepper
Salt

Directions:
Fit the Cuisinart oven with the rack in position Heat oil in a small saucepan over medium-high heat. Add garlic and sauté for 30 seconds.   Remove from heat and stir in lemon juice, parsley, pepper, and salt.   Arrange fish fillets, mushrooms, and green beans in baking pan and drizzle with oil mixture.   Sprinkle with grated parmesan cheese. Set to bake at 400 F for 30 minutes. After 5 minutes place the baking pan in the preheated oven.   Serve and enjoy.

Nutrition Info: Calories 225 Fat 11.5 g Carbohydrates 4.7 g Sugar 1.4 g Protein 27.5 g Cholesterol 58 mg

450. Tomato Garlic Shrimp

Servings: 4   **Cooking Time:** 25 Minutes
Ingredients:

1 lb shrimp, peeled	1 tbsp olive oil
1 tbsp garlic, sliced	Pepper
2 cups cherry tomatoes	Salt

Directions:
Fit the Cuisinart oven with the rack in position Add shrimp, oil, garlic, tomatoes, pepper, and salt into the large bowl and toss well.   Transfer shrimp mixture into the baking dish.   Set to bake at 400 F for 30 minutes. After 5 minutes place the baking dish in the preheated oven.   Serve and enjoy.
Nutrition Info: Calories 184 Fat 5.6 g Carbohydrates 5.9 g Sugar 2.4 g Protein 26.8 gCholesterol 239 mg

451. Roasted Halibut Steaks With Parsley

Servings: 4   **Cooking Time:** 10 Minutes
Ingredients:

1 pound (454 g) halibut steaks	2 tablespoons honey
¼ cup vegetable oil	1 tablespoon fresh parsley leaves, coarsely chopped
2½ tablespoons Worcester sauce	Salt and pepper, to taste
2 tablespoons vermouth	1 teaspoon dried basil
1 tablespoon freshly squeezed lemon juice	

Directions:
Put all the ingredients in a large mixing dish and gently stir until the fish is coated evenly. Transfer the fish to the air fryer basket.   Put the air fryer basket on the baking pan and slide into Rack Position 2, select Roast, set temperature to 390°F (199°C), and set time to 10 minutes.   Flip the fish halfway through cooking time.   When cooking is complete, the fish should reach an internal temperature of at least 145°F (63°C) on a meat thermometer. Remove from the oven and let the fish cool for 5 minutes before serving.

452. Baked Tilapia With Garlic Aioli

Servings: 4   **Cooking Time:** 15 Minutes
Ingredients:

Tilapia:	1 teaspoon paprika
4 tilapia fillets	Garlic Aioli:
1 tablespoon extra-virgin olive oil	2 garlic cloves, minced
1 teaspoon garlic powder	1 tablespoon mayonnaise
1 teaspoon dried basil	Juice of ½ lemon
A pinch of lemon-pepper seasoning	1 teaspoon extra-virgin olive oil
	Salt and pepper, to taste

Directions:
On a clean work surface, brush both sides of each fillet with the olive oil. Sprinkle with the garlic powder, paprika, basil, and lemon-pepper seasoning.

Place the fillets in the baking pan.   Slide the baking pan into Rack Position 1, select Convection Bake, set temperature to 400°F (205°C), and set time to 15 minutes.   Flip the fillets halfway through.   Meanwhile, make the garlic aioli: Whisk together the garlic, mayo, lemon juice, olive oil, salt, and pepper in a small bowl until smooth.   When cooking is complete, the fish should flake apart with a fork and no longer translucent in the center. Remove the fish from the oven and serve with the garlic aioli on the side.

453. Basil Salmon With Tomatoes

Servings: 4   **Cooking Time:** 15 Minutes
Ingredients:

4 (6-ounce / 170-g) salmon fillets, patted dry	1 teaspoon kosher salt, divided
2 pints cherry or grape tomatoes, halved if large, divided	2 garlic cloves, minced
	1 small red bell pepper, deseeded and chopped
3 tablespoons extra-virgin olive oil, divided	2 tablespoons chopped fresh basil, divided

Directions:
Season both sides of the salmon with ½ teaspoon of kosher salt.   Put about half of the tomatoes in a large bowl, along with the remaining ½ teaspoon of kosher salt, 2 tablespoons of olive oil, garlic, bell pepper, and 1 tablespoon of basil. Toss to coat and then transfer to the baking pan.   Arrange the salmon fillets in the pan, skin-side down. Brush them with the remaining 1 tablespoon of olive oil. Slide the baking pan into Rack Position 2, select Roast, set temperature to 375°F (190°C), and set time to 15 minutes.   After 7 minutes, remove the pan and fold in the remaining tomatoes. Return the pan to the oven and continue cooking.   When cooked, remove from the oven. Serve sprinkled with the remaining 1 tablespoon of basil.

454. Savory Cod Fish In Soy Sauce

Servings: 4   **Cooking Time:** 20 Minutes
Ingredients:

4 cod fish fillets	4 slices of ginger
4 tbsp chopped cilantro	4 tbsp light soy sauce
Salt to taste	3 tbsp oil
2 green onions, chopped	1 tsp dark soy sauce
1 cup water	4 cubes rock sugar

Directions:
Sprinkle the cod with salt and cilantro and drizzle with olive oil. Place in the cooking basket and fit in the baking tray; cook for 15 minutes at 360 F on Air Fry function.   Place the remaining ingredients in a frying pan over medium heat and cook for 5 minutes until sauce reaches desired consistency. Pour the sauce over the fish and serve.

455. Delightful Catfish Fillets

Servings: 4   **Cooking Time:** 25 Minutes
Ingredients:

| 4 catfish fillets | 1 tbsp olive oil |
| ¼ cup seasoned fish fry | 1 tbsp parsley, chopped |

Directions:
Add seasoned fish fry and catfish fillets in a large Ziploc bag and massage well to coat. Place the fillets in your Cuisinart Air Fryer basket and fit in the baking tray; cook for 10 minutes at 360 F on Air Fry function. Flip the fish and cook for 2-3 more minutes. Top with parsley and serve.

456. Old Bay Seasoned Scallops

Servings: 4   Cooking Time: 4 Minutes
Ingredients:

1 lb sea scallops	2 tbsp butter, melted
1/2 tsp garlic powder	1/2 tsp old bay seasoning
1/2 cup crushed crackers	

Directions:
Fit the Cuisinart oven with the rack in position 2. In a shallow dish, mix crushed crackers, garlic powder, and old bay seasoning.   Add melted butter in a separate shallow dish.   Dip scallops in melted butter and coat with crushed crackers. Place coated scallops in air fryer basket then place air fryer basket in baking pan.   Place a baking pan on the oven rack. Set to air fry at 390 F for 4 minutes. Serve and enjoy.
Nutrition Info: Calories 167 Fat 7.4 g Carbohydrates 4.8 g Sugar 0.5 g Protein 19.5 g Cholesterol 53 mg

457. Spicy Grilled Halibut

Servings: 4   Cooking Time: 10 Minutes
Ingredients:

½ cup fresh lemon juice	Nonstick cooking spray
2 jalapeno peppers, seeded & chopped fine	¼ cup cilantro, chopped
4 6 oz. halibut fillets	

Directions:
In a small bowl, combine lemon juice and chilies, mix well.   Place fish in a large Ziploc bag and add marinade. Toss to coat. Refrigerate 30 minutes. Lightly spray the baking pan with cooking spray. Set oven to broil on 400°F for 15 minutes.   After 5 minutes, lay fish on the pan and place in position 2 of the oven. Cook 10 minutes, or until fish flakes easily with a fork. Turn fish over and brush with marinade halfway through cooking time. Sprinkle with cilantro before serving.
Nutrition Info: Calories 328, Total Fat 24g, Saturated Fat 4g, Total Carbs 3g, Net Carbs 3g, Protein 25g, Sugar 1g, Fiber 0g, Sodium 137mg, Potassium 510mg, Phosphorus 284mg

458. Old Bay Tilapia Fillets

Servings: 4   Cooking Time: 15 Minutes
Ingredients:

1 pound tilapia fillets	2 tbsp canola oil
1 tbsp old bay seasoning	2 tbsp lemon pepper
	Salt to taste
	2-3 butter buds

Directions:
Preheat your Cuisinart oven to 400 F on Bake function. Drizzle tilapia fillets with canola oil. In a bowl, mix salt, lemon pepper, butter buds, and seasoning; spread on the fish. Place the fillet on the basket and fit in the baking tray. Cook for 10 minutes, flipping once until tender and crispy.

459. Speedy Fried Scallops

Servings: 4   Cooking Time: 5 Minutes
Ingredients:

12 fresh scallops	3 tbsp flour
Salt and black pepper to taste	1 egg, lightly beaten
	1 cup breadcrumbs

Directions:
Coat the scallops with flour. Dip into the egg, then into the breadcrumbs. Spray with olive oil and arrange them on the basket. Fit in the baking tray and cook for 6 minutes at 360 F on Air Fry function, turning once halfway through cooking. Serve.

460. Spicy Baked Shrimp

Servings: 4   Cooking Time: 8 Minutes
Ingredients:

2 lbs shrimp, peeled & deveined	1 tsp garlic powder
	2 tbsp chili powder
1/4 tsp cayenne pepper	2 tbsp olive oil
	1 tsp kosher salt

Directions:
Fit the Cuisinart oven with the rack in position Toss shrimp with remaining ingredients. Transfer shrimp into the baking pan.   Set to bake at 400 F for 13 minutes. After 5 minutes place the baking pan in the preheated oven.   Serve and enjoy.
Nutrition Info: Calories 344 Fat 11.5 g Carbohydrates 6.1 g Sugar 0.5 g Protein 52.3 g Cholesterol 478 mg

461. Basil White Fish

Servings: 4   Cooking Time: 20 Minutes
Ingredients:

2 tbsp fresh basil, chopped	Salt and black pepper to taste
2 garlic cloves, minced	2 tbsp pine nuts
	4 white fish fillets
1 tbsp Parmesan cheese, grated	2 tbsp olive oil

Directions:
Preheat Cuisinart on AirFry function to 350 F. Season the fillets with salt and pepper and place in the basket. Drizzle with some olive oil and press Start. Cook for 12-14 minutes. In a bowl, mix basil, remaining olive oil, pine nuts, garlic, and Parmesan cheese and spread on the fish. Serve.

462. Crispy Paprika Fish Fillets(2)

Servings: 4   Cooking Time: 15 Minutes
Ingredients:

1/2 cup seasoned breadcrumbs	1/2 teaspoon ground black pepper
1 tablespoon balsamic vinegar	1 teaspoon celery seed
1/2 teaspoon	

seasoned salt

1 teaspoon paprika

2 fish fillets, halved

1 egg, beaten

Directions:

Preparing the Ingredients. Add the breadcrumbs, vinegar, salt, paprika, ground black pepper, and celery seeds to your food processor. Process for about 30 seconds. Coat the fish fillets with the beaten egg; then, coat them with the breadcrumbs mixture. Air Frying. Cook at 350 degrees F for about 15 minutes.

---

463. Parmesan-crusted Salmon Patties

Servings: 4   Cooking Time: 13 Minutes

Ingredients:

1 pound (454 g) salmon, chopped into ½-inch pieces

2 tablespoons coconut flour

2 tablespoons grated Parmesan cheese

½ white onion, peeled and finely chopped

½ teaspoon butter, at room temperature

1½ tablespoons milk

½ teaspoon chipotle powder

½ teaspoon dried parsley flakes

⅓ teaspoon ground black pepper

⅓ teaspoon smoked cayenne pepper

1 teaspoon fine sea salt

Directions:

Put all the ingredients for the salmon patties in a bowl and stir to combine well. Scoop out 2 tablespoons of the salmon mixture and shape into a patty with your palm, about ½ inch thick. Repeat until all the mixture is used. Transfer to the refrigerator for about 2 hours until firm. When ready, arrange the salmon patties in the baking pan. Slide the baking pan into Rack Position 1, select Convection Bake, set temperature to 395°F (202°C), and set time to 13 minutes. Flip the patties halfway through the cooking time. When cooking is complete, the patties should be golden brown. Remove from the oven and cool for 5 minutes before serving.

---

464. Herb Fish Fillets

Servings: 2   Cooking Time: 5 Minutes

Ingredients:

2 salmon fillets

1/4 tsp smoked paprika

1 tsp herb de Provence

1 tbsp butter, melted

2 tbsp olive oil

Pepper

Salt

Directions:

Fit the Cuisinart oven with the rack in position 2. Brush salmon fillets with oil and sprinkle with paprika, herb de Provence, pepper, and salt. Place salmon fillets in the air fryer basket then place an air fryer basket in the baking pan. Place a baking pan on the oven rack. Set to air fry at 390 F for 5 minutes. Drizzle melted butter over salmon and serve.

Nutrition Info: Calories 413 Fat 31.1 g Carbohydrates 0.2 g Sugar 0 g Protein 35.4 g Cholesterol 94 mg

---

465. Cheese Carp Fries

Ingredients:

1 lb. carp Oregano Fingers ingredients for the marinade:

1 tbsp. olive oil

½ tsp. red chili flakes

1 tsp. mixed herbs

A pinch of salt to taste

1 tbsp. lemon juice

For the garnish:

1 cup melted cheddar cheese

Directions:

Take all the ingredients mentioned under the heading "For the marinade" and mix them well. Cook the carp Oregano Fingers and soak them in the marinade. Pre heat the Cuisinart oven for around 5 minutes at 300 Fahrenheit. Take out the basket of the fryer and place the carp in them. Close the basket. Now keep the fryer at 220 Fahrenheit for 20 or 25 minutes. In between the process, toss the fries twice or thrice so that they get cooked properly. Towards the end of the cooking process (the last 2 minutes or so), sprinkle the melted cheddar cheese over the fries and serve hot.

---

466. Paprika Cod

Servings: 4   Cooking Time: 15 Minutes

Ingredients:

4 cod fillets

1 tsp smoked paprika

1/2 cup parmesan cheese, grated

1/2 tbsp olive oil

1 tsp parsley

Pepper

Salt

Directions:

Fit the Cuisinart oven with the rack in position Brush fish fillets with oil and season with pepper and salt. In a shallow dish, mix parmesan cheese, paprika, and parsley. Coat fish fillets with cheese mixture and place into the baking dish. Set to bake at 400 F for 20 minutes. After 5 minutes place the baking dish in the preheated oven. Serve and enjoy.

Nutrition Info: Calories 125 Fat 5 g Carbohydrates 0.7 g Sugar 0.1 g Protein 19.8 g Cholesterol 52 mg

---

467. Garlic-butter Shrimp With Vegetables

Servings: 4   Cooking Time: 15 Minutes

Ingredients:

1 pound (454 g) small red potatoes, halved

2 ears corn, shucked and cut into rounds, 1 to 1½ inches thick

2 tablespoons Old Bay or similar seasoning

½ cup unsalted butter, melted

1 (12- to 13-ounce / 340- to 369-g) package kielbasa or other smoked sausages

3 garlic cloves, minced

1 pound (454 g) medium shrimp, peeled and deveined

Directions:

Place the potatoes and corn in a large bowl. Stir together the butter and Old Bay seasoning in a small bowl. Drizzle half the butter mixture over the potatoes and corn, tossing to coat. Spread out the vegetables in the baking pan. Slide the baking pan into Rack Position 2, select Roast, set temperature to 350ºF (180ºC), and set time to 15 minutes.   Meanwhile, cut the sausages into 2-inch lengths, then cut each piece in half lengthwise. Put the sausages and shrimp in a medium bowl and set aside.   Add the garlic to the bowl of remaining butter mixture and stir well.   After 10 minutes, remove the pan and pour the vegetables into the large bowl. Drizzle with the garlic butter and toss until well coated. Arrange the vegetables, sausages, and shrimp in the pan.   Return to the oven and continue cooking. After 5 minutes, check the shrimp for doneness. The shrimp should be pink and opaque. If they are not quite cooked through, roast for an additional 1 minute.   When done, remove from the oven and serve on a plate.

468.   Parmesan-crusted Halibut Fillets

Servings: 4   Cooking Time: 10 Minutes
Ingredients:

2 medium-sized halibut fillets	Kosher salt and freshly cracked mixed peppercorns, to taste
Dash of tabasco sauce	
1 teaspoon curry powder	2 eggs
½ teaspoon ground coriander	1½ tablespoons olive oil
½ teaspoon hot paprika	½ cup grated Parmesan cheese

Directions:
On a clean work surface, drizzle the halibut fillets with the tabasco sauce. Sprinkle with the curry powder, coriander, hot paprika, salt, and cracked mixed peppercorns. Set aside.   In a shallow bowl, beat the eggs until frothy. In another shallow bowl, combine the olive oil and Parmesan cheese.   One at a time, dredge the halibut fillets in the beaten eggs, shaking off any excess, then roll them over the Parmesan cheese until evenly coated.   Arrange the halibut fillets in the air fryer basket in a single layer.   Put the air fryer basket on the baking pan and slide into Rack Position 2, select Roast, set temperature to 365ºF (185ºC), and set time to 10 minutes.   When cooking is complete, the fish should be golden brown and crisp. Cool for 5 minutes before serving.

469.   Orange Fish Fillets

Servings: 2   Cooking Time: 25 Minutes
Ingredients:

1 lb salmon fillets	2 tbsp honey
1 orange juice	3 tbsp soy sauce
1 orange zest, grated	

Directions:
Fit the Cuisinart oven with the rack in position   In a small bowl, whisk together honey, soy sauce, orange juice, and orange zest.   Place salmon fillets in a baking dish and pour honey mixture over salmon fillets.   Set to bake at 425 F for 30 minutes. After 5 minutes place the baking dish in the preheated oven.   Serve and enjoy.
Nutrition Info: Calories 399 Fat 14.1 g Carbohydrates 24.4 g Sugar 21.3 g Protein 45.9 g Cholesterol 100 mg

470.   Mediterranean Sole

Servings: 6   Cooking Time: 20 Minutes
Ingredients:

Nonstick cooking spray	2 tbsp. fresh parsley, chopped fine
2 tbsp. olive oil	1 tsp oregano
8 scallions, sliced thin	1 tsp pepper
2 cloves garlic, diced fine	2 lbs. sole, cut in 6 pieces
4 tomatoes, chopped	4 oz. feta cheese, crumbled
½ cup dry white wine	

Directions:
Place the rack in position 1 of the oven. Spray an 8x11-inch baking dish with cooking spray.   Heat the oil in a medium skillet over medium heat. Add scallions and garlic and cook until tender, stirring frequently.   Add the tomatoes, wine, parsley, oregano, and pepper. Stir to mix. Simmer for 5 minutes, or until sauce thickens. Remove from heat. Pour half the sauce on the bottom of the prepared dish. Lay fish on top then pour remaining sauce over the top. Sprinkle with feta.   Set the oven to bake on 400ºF for 25 minutes. After 5 minutes, place the baking dish on the rack and cook 15-18 minutes or until fish flakes easily with a fork. Serve immediately.
Nutrition Info: Calories 220, Total Fat 12g, Saturated Fat 4g, Total Carbs 6g, Net Carbs 4g, Protein 22g, Sugar 4g, Fiber 2g, Sodium 631mg, Potassium 540mg, Phosphorus 478mg

471.   Delicious Crab Cakes

Servings: 5   Cooking Time: 10 Minutes
Ingredients:

18 oz can crab meat, drained	1 tbsp dried celery
2 1/2 tbsp mayonnaise	1 tsp Old bay seasoning
2 eggs, lightly beaten	1 1/2 tbsp Dijon mustard
1/4 cup breadcrumbs	Pepper
1 1/2 tsp dried parsley	Salt

Directions:
Fit the Cuisinart oven with the rack in position 2. Add all ingredients into the mixing bowl and mix until well combined.   Make patties from mixture and place in the air fryer basket then place an air fryer basket in the baking pan.   Place a baking pan on the oven rack. Set to air fry at 320 F for 10 minutes.   Serve and enjoy.
Nutrition Info: Calories 138 Fat 4.7 g Carbohydrates 7.8 g Sugar 2.7 g Protein 16.8 g Cholesterol 127 mg

472.   Panko Catfish Nuggets

Servings: 4   Cooking Time: 7 To 8 Minutes
Ingredients:

2 medium catfish fillets, cut into chunks (approximately 1 × 2 inch)	2 tablespoons skim milk
	½ cup cornstarch
Salt and pepper, to	1 cup panko bread crumbs
	Cooking spray

taste

2 eggs

Directions:

In a medium bowl, season the fish chunks with salt and pepper to taste. In a small bowl, beat together the eggs with milk until well combined. Place the cornstarch and bread crumbs into separate shallow dishes. Dredge the fish chunks one at a time in the cornstarch, coating well on both sides, then dip in the egg mixture, shaking off any excess, finally press well into the bread crumbs. Spritz the fish chunks with cooking spray. Arrange the fish chunks in the air fryer basket in a single layer. Put the air fryer basket on the baking pan and slide into Rack Position 2, select Air Fry, set temperature to 390°F (199°C), and set time to 8 minutes. Flip the fish chunks halfway through the cooking time. When cooking is complete, they should be no longer translucent in the center and golden brown. Remove the fish chunks from the oven to a plate. Serve warm.

473. Parmesan Fish With Pine Nuts

Servings: 4   Cooking Time: 15 Minutes

Ingredients:

2 tbsp fresh basil, chopped	2 tbsp olive oil
2 garlic cloves, minced	salt and black pepper to taste
1 tbsp Parmesan cheese, grated	2 tbsp pine nuts
	4 white fish fillets
	2 tbsp olive oil

Directions:

Preheat Cuisinart on Air Fry function to 350 F. Season the fish with salt and pepper. Place in the greased basket and fit in the baking tray. Cook the fillets for 8 minutes, flipping once. In a bowl, add basil, olive oil, pine nuts, garlic, and Parmesan cheese; mix well. Serve with the fish.

474. Baked Scallops

Servings: 4   Cooking Time: 15 Minutes

Ingredients:

1 lb scallops, frozen & thawed	1 lemon, cut into wedges
1 tbsp garlic, grated	1 tbsp olive oil
1/2 cup butter, melted	Pepper
	Salt

Directions:

Fit the Cuisinart oven with the rack in position Add scallops and lemon into the baking dish and spread well. Mix melted butter, oil, garlic, pepper, and salt and pour over scallops. Set to bake at 400 F for 20 minutes. After 5 minutes place the baking dish in the preheated oven. Serve and enjoy.

Nutrition Info: Calories 341 Fat 27.4 g Carbohydrates 4.8 g Sugar 0.4 g Protein 19.6 g Cholesterol 98 mg

475. Baked Buttery Shrimp

Servings: 4   Cooking Time: 15 Minutes

Ingredients:

1 lb shrimp, peel & deveined	4 tsp cayenne pepper
	1/2 cup butter,

2 tsp garlic powder	melted
2 tsp dry mustard	2 tsp onion powder
2 tsp cumin	1 tsp dried oregano
2 tsp paprika	1 tsp dried thyme
2 tsp black pepper	3 tsp salt

Directions:

Fit the Cuisinart oven with the rack in position Add shrimp, butter, and remaining ingredients into the mixing bowl and toss well. Transfer shrimp mixture into the baking pan. Set to bake at 400 F for 20 minutes. After 5 minutes place the baking pan in the preheated oven. Serve and enjoy.

Nutrition Info: Calories 372 Fat 26.2 g Carbohydrates 7.5 g Sugar 1.3 g Protein 27.6 g Cholesterol 300 mg

476. Crispy Coated Scallops

Servings: 4   Cooking Time: 10 Minutes

Ingredients:

Nonstick cooking spray	1 egg
1 lb. sea scallops, patted dry	1 tbsp. water
	¼ cup Italian bread crumbs
1 teaspoon onion powder	Paprika
½ tsp pepper	1 tbsp. fresh lemon juice

Directions:

Lightly spray fryer basket with cooking spray. Place baking pan in position 2 of the oven. Sprinkle scallops with onion powder and pepper. In a shallow dish, whisk together egg and water. Place bread crumbs in a separate shallow dish. Dip scallops in egg then bread crumbs coating them lightly. Place in fryer basket and lightly spray with cooking spray. Sprinkle with paprika. Place the basket on the baking pan and set oven to air fryer on 400°F. Bake 10-12 minutes until scallops are firm on the inside and golden brown on the outside. Drizzle with lemon juice and serve.

Nutrition Info: Calories 122, Total Fat 2g, Saturated Fat 1g, Total Carbs 10g, Net Carbs 9g, Protein 16g, Sugar 1g, Fiber 1g, Sodium 563mg, Potassium 282mg, Phosphorus 420mg

477. Herb Baked Catfish Fillets

Servings: 4   Cooking Time: 20 Minutes

Ingredients:

4 catfish fillets	1/2 tsp dried basil
1/2 tsp garlic powder	1/2 tsp dried thyme
2 tbsp butter, melted	3/4 tsp paprika
1 lemon juice	1/2 tsp dried oregano
1/2 tsp pepper	1 tsp salt

Directions:

Fit the Cuisinart oven with the rack in position Place fish fillets into the baking pan. Mix together garlic powder, pepper, basil, oregano, thyme, paprika, and salt and sprinkle over fish fillets. Pour lemon juice and melted butter over fish fillets. Set to bake at 350 F for 25 minutes. After 5 minutes place the baking pan in the preheated oven. Serve and enjoy.

Nutrition Info: Calories 274 Fat 18.1 g Carbohydrates 1.1 g Sugar 0.4 g Protein 25.2 g Cholesterol 90 mg

478. Crab Cakes

Servings: 4   Cooking Time: 10 Minutes

Ingredients:

8 ounces jumbo lump crabmeat

1 tablespoon Old Bay Seasoning

⅓ cup bread crumbs

¼ cup diced red bell pepper

¼ cup diced green bell pepper

1 egg

¼ cup mayonnaise

Juice of ½ lemon

1 teaspoon flour

Cooking oil

Directions:

Preparing the Ingredients. In a large bowl, combine the crabmeat, Old Bay Seasoning, bread crumbs, red bell pepper, green bell pepper, egg, mayo, and lemon juice. Mix gently to combine.   Form the mixture into 4 patties. Sprinkle ¼ teaspoon of flour on top of each patty.   Air Frying. Place the crab cakes in the Cuisinart air fryer oven. Spray them with cooking oil. Cook for 10 minutes.   Serve.

479. Lemon-honey Snapper With Fruit

Servings: 4   Cooking Time: 12 Minutes

Ingredients:

4 (4-ounce / 113-g) red snapper fillets

2 teaspoons olive oil

3 plums, halved and pitted

3 nectarines, halved and pitted

1 cup red grapes

1 tablespoon freshly squeezed lemon juice

1 tablespoon honey

½ teaspoon dried thyme

Directions:

Arrange the red snapper fillets in the air fryer basket and drizzle the olive oil over the top.   Put the air fryer basket on the baking pan and slide into Rack Position 2, select Air Fry, set temperature to 390°F (199°C), and set time to 12 minutes.   After 4 minutes, remove from the oven. Top the fillets with the plums and nectarines. Scatter the red grapes all over the fillets. Drizzle with the lemon juice and honey and sprinkle the thyme on top. Return the pan to the oven and continue cooking for 8 minutes, or until the fish is flaky.   When cooking is complete, remove from the oven and serve warm.

480. Rosemary & Garlic Prawns

Servings: 2   Cooking Time: 15 Minutes + Chilling Time

Ingredients:

2 garlic cloves, minced

1 rosemary sprig, chopped

8 large prawns

1 tbsp butter, melted

Salt and black pepper to taste

Directions:

Combine garlic, butter, rosemary, salt, and pepper in a bowl. Add in the prawns and mix to coat. Cover the bowl and refrigerate for 1 hour. Preheat Cuisinart on AirFry function to 350 F. Remove the prawns from the fridge and transfer to the frying basket. Cook for 6-8 minutes.

481. Teriyaki Salmon

Servings: 4   Cooking Time: 15 Minutes

Ingredients:

4 (6-ounce / 170-g) skinless salmon fillets

4 heads baby bok choy, root ends trimmed off and cut in half lengthwise through the root

¾ cup Teriyaki sauce, divided

1 teaspoon sesame oil

1 tablespoon vegetable oil

1 tablespoon toasted sesame seeds

Directions:

Set aside ¼ cup of Teriyaki sauce and pour the remaining sauce into a resealable plastic bag. Put the salmon into the bag and seal, squeezing as much air out as possible. Allow the salmon to marinate for at least 10 minutes.   Arrange the bok choy halves in the baking pan. Drizzle the oils over the vegetables, tossing to coat. Drizzle about 1 tablespoon of the reserved Teriyaki sauce over the bok choy, then push them to the sides of the pan. Put the salmon fillets in the middle of the pan. Slide the baking pan into Rack Position 2, select Roast, set temperature to 375°F (190°C), and set time to 15 minutes.   When done, remove the pan and brush the salmon with the remaining Teriyaki sauce. Serve garnished with the sesame seeds.

482. Easy Blackened Shrimp

Servings: 6   Cooking Time: 10 Minutes

Ingredients:

1 lb shrimp, deveined

1 tbsp olive oil

1/4 tsp pepper

2 tsp blackened seasoning

1/4 tsp salt

Directions:

Fit the Cuisinart oven with the rack in position Toss shrimp with oil, pepper, blackened seasoning, and salt.   Transfer shrimp into the baking pan. Set to bake at 400 F for 15 minutes. After 5 minutes place the baking pan in the preheated oven.   Serve and enjoy.

Nutrition Info: Calories 167 Fat 4.3 g Carbohydrates 10.5 g Sugar 0 g Protein 20.6 g Cholesterol 159 mg

483. Tasty Parmesan Shrimp

Servings: 4   Cooking Time: 10 Minutes

Ingredients:

1 lb shrimp, peeled and deveined

1/4 cup parmesan cheese, grated

4 garlic cloves, minced

1 tbsp olive oil

1/4 tsp oregano

1/2 tsp pepper

1/2 tsp onion powder

1/2 tsp basil

Directions:

Fit the Cuisinart oven with the rack in position 2. Add all ingredients into the large bowl and toss well. Add shrimp to the air fryer basket then place an air fryer basket in the baking pan.   Place a baking pan on the oven rack. Set to air fry at 350 F for 10 minutes.   Serve and enjoy.

Nutrition Info: Calories 189 Fat 6.7 g Carbohydrates 3.4 g Sugar 0.1 g Protein 27.9 g Cholesterol 243 mg

484. Italian Salmon

Servings: 4   Cooking Time: 20 Minutes
Ingredients:

1 3/4 lbs salmon fillet	1/4 cup olives, pitted
1/4 cup sun-dried	and chopped
tomatoes, drained	1/3 cup basil pesto
1 tbsp fresh dill,	1/3 cup artichoke
chopped	hearts
1/4 cup capers	1 tsp paprika
	1/4 tsp salt

Directions:
Fit the Cuisinart oven with the rack in position Arrange salmon fillet in a baking pan and season with paprika and salt.   Pour remaining ingredients on top of salmon.   Set to bake at 400 F for 25 minutes. After 5 minutes place the baking pan in the preheated oven.   Serve and enjoy.
Nutrition Info: Calories 286 Fat 13.4 g Carbohydrates 3.6 g Sugar 0.5 g Protein 39.6 g Cholesterol 88 mg

485. Soy And Ginger Shrimp

Servings: 4   Cooking Time: 10 Minutes
Ingredients:

2 tablespoons olive oil	1 tablespoon dry white wine
2 tablespoons scallions, finely chopped	1 tablespoon balsamic vinegar
2 cloves garlic, chopped	1/4 cup soy sauce
1 teaspoon fresh ginger, grated	1 tablespoon sugar
	1 pound shrimp
	Salt and ground black pepper, to taste

Directions:
Preparing the Ingredients. To make the marinade, warm the oil in a saucepan; cook all ingredients, except the shrimp, salt, and black pepper. Now, let it cool.   Marinate the shrimp, covered, at least an hour, in the refrigerator.   Air Frying. After that, bake the shrimp at 350 degrees F for 8 to 10 minutes (depending on the size), turning once or twice. Season prepared shrimp with salt and black pepper and serve right away.

486. Prawn Momo's Recipe

Ingredients:

1 1/2 cup all-purpose flour	2 tbsp. oil
1/2 tsp. salt	2 tsp. ginger-garlic paste
5 tbsp. water	2 tsp. soya sauce
For filling:	2 tsp. vinegar
2 cups minced prawn	

Directions:
Squeeze the dough and cover it with plastic wrap and set aside. Next, cook the ingredients for the filling and try to ensure that the prawn is covered well with the sauce. Roll the dough and cut it into a square.   Place the filling in the center. Now, wrap the dough to cover the filling and pinch the edges together. Pre heat the Cuisinart oven at 200° F for 5 minutes. Place the wontons in the fry basket and close it. Let them cook at the same temperature for another 20 minutes. Recommended sides are chili sauce or ketchup.

487. Simple Salmon Patties

Servings: 2   Cooking Time: 7 Minutes
Ingredients:

8 oz salmon fillet, minced	1/8 tsp paprika
1 egg, lightly beaten	2 tbsp breadcrumbs
1/4 tsp garlic powder	Pepper
1/4 tsp onion powder	Salt

Directions:
Fit the Cuisinart oven with the rack in position 2. Add all ingredients into the bowl and mix until well combined.   Make patties from mixture and place in the air fryer basket then place an air fryer basket in the baking pan.   Place a baking pan on the oven rack. Set to air fry at 390 F for 7 minutes.   Serve and enjoy.
Nutrition Info: Calories 211 Fat 9.6 g Carbohydrates 5.6 g Sugar 0.8 g Protein 25.8 g Cholesterol 132 mg

488. Lobster Grandma's Easy To Cook Wontons

Ingredients:

1 1/2 cup all-purpose flour	2 tbsp. oil
1/2 tsp. salt	2 tsp. ginger-garlic paste
5 tbsp. water	2 tsp. soya sauce
For filling:	2 tsp. vinegar
2 cups minced lobster	

Directions:
Squeeze the dough and cover it with plastic wrap and set aside. Next, cook the ingredients for the filling and try to ensure that the lobster is covered well with the sauce.   Roll the dough and place the filling in the center. Now, wrap the dough to cover the filling and pinch the edges together.   Pre heat the Cuisinart oven at 200° F for 5 minutes. Place the wontons in the fry basket and close it. Let them cook at the same temperature for another 20 minutes. Recommended sides are chili sauce or ketchup.

489. Maryland Crab Cakes

Servings: 6   Cooking Time: 10 Minutes
Ingredients:

Nonstick cooking spray	1/4 cup mozzarella cheese, grated
2 eggs	1 tsp Italian seasoning
1 cup Panko bread crumbs	1 tbsp. fresh parsley, chopped
1 stalk celery, chopped	1 tsp pepper
3 tbsp. mayonnaise	3/4 lb. lump
1 tsp Worcestershire sauce	crabmeat, drained

Directions:
Place baking pan in position 2 of the oven. Lightly spray the fryer basket with cooking spray.   In a large bowl, combine all ingredients except crab meat, mix well.   Fold in crab carefully so it retains some chunks. Form mixture into 12 patties.   Place patties in a single layer in the fryer basket. Place the basket on the baking pan.   Set oven to air fryer on 350°F for 10 minutes. Cook until golden brown,

turning over halfway through cooking time. Serve immediately.

Nutrition Info: Calories 172, Total Fat 8g, Saturated Fat 2g, Total Carbs 14g, Net Carbs 13g, Protein 16g, Sugar 1g, Fiber 1g, Sodium 527mg, Potassium 290mg, Phosphorus 201mg

490.   Air Fry Tuna Patties

Servings: 4   Cooking Time: 6 Minutes
Ingredients:

1 egg, lightly beaten	1 tbsp mustard
8 oz can tuna, drained	1/4 tsp garlic powder
1/4 cup breadcrumbs	Pepper
	Salt

Directions:
Fit the Cuisinart oven with the rack in position 2. Add all ingredients into the large bowl and mix until well combined.   Make four equal shapes of patties from the mixture and place in the air fryer basket then place an air fryer basket in the baking pan. Place a baking pan on the oven rack. Set to air fry at 400 F for 6 minutes.   Serve and enjoy.

Nutrition Info: Calories 122 Fat 2.7 g Carbohydrates 6.1 g Sugar 0.7 g Protein 17.5 g Cholesterol 58 mg

491.   Air Fryer Spicy Shrimp

Servings: 4   Cooking Time: 6 Minutes
Ingredients:

1 lb shrimp, peeled and deveined	2 tsp paprika
1/4 tsp chili powder	1/4 tsp cayenne
1 tsp dried oregano	2 tbsp olive oil
1 tsp garlic powder	Pepper
1 tsp onion powder	Salt

Directions:
Fit the Cuisinart oven with the rack in position 2. In a bowl, toss shrimp with remaining ingredients. Add shrimp to the air fryer basket then place an air fryer basket in the baking pan.   Place a baking pan on the oven rack. Set to air fry at 400 F for 6 minutes. Serve and enjoy.

Nutrition Info: Calories 204 Fat 9.2 g Carbohydrates 3.7 g Sugar 0.5 g Protein 26.2 g Cholesterol 239 mg

492.   Coconut Shrimp

Servings: 4   Cooking Time: 5 Minutes
Ingredients:

1 (8-ounce) can crushed pineapple	2/3 cup cornstarch
1/2 cup sour cream	1 cup panko bread crumbs
1/4 cup pineapple preserves	1 pound uncooked large shrimp, thawed if frozen, deveined and shelled
2 egg whites	Olive oil for misting
2/3 cup sweetened coconut	

Directions:
Preparing the Ingredients. Drain the crushed pineapple well, reserving the juice. In a small bowl, combine the pineapple, sour cream, and preserves, and mix well. Set aside. In a shallow bowl, beat the egg whites with 2 tablespoons of the reserved pineapple liquid. Place the cornstarch on a plate.

Combine the coconut and bread crumbs on another plate. Dip the shrimp into the cornstarch, shake it off, then dip into the egg white mixture and finally into the coconut mixture. Place the shrimp in the air fryer rack/basket and mist with oil.   Air Frying. Air-fry for 5 to 7 minutes or until the shrimp are crisp and golden brown.

Nutrition Info:CALORIES: 524; FAT: 14G; PROTEIN:33G; FIBER:4G

493.   Crispy Crab Legs

Servings: 4   Cooking Time: 15 Minutes
Ingredients:

3 pounds crab legs	1/2 cup butter, melted

Directions:
Preheat Cuisinart on Air Fry function to 380 F. Cover the crab legs with salted water and let them stay for a few minutes. Drain, pat them dry, and place the legs in the basket. Fit in the baking tray and brush with some butter; cook for 10 minutes, flipping once. Drizzle with the remaining butter and serve.

494.   Quick Shrimp Bowl

Servings: 4   Cooking Time: 15 Minutes
Ingredients:

1 1/4 pounds tiger shrimp	1/4 tsp cayenne pepper
1/2 tsp old bay seasoning	1/4 tsp smoked paprika
	A pinch of salt
	1 tbsp olive oil

Directions:
Preheat your Cuisinart oven to 390 F on Air Fry function. In a bowl, mix all the ingredients. Place the mixture in your the cooking basket and fit in the baking tray; cook for 5 minutes, flipping once. Serve drizzled with lemon juice.

495.   Parmesan Salmon & Asparagus

Servings: 4   Cooking Time: 20 Minutes
Ingredients:

4 salmon fillets	1 lb asparagus, ends trimmed
1 cup parmesan cheese, shredded	1/4 tsp pepper
1 tbsp garlic, minced	1/4 tsp salt
3 tbsp olive oil	

Directions:
Fit the Cuisinart oven with the rack in position Place fish fillets and asparagus in a parchment-lined baking pan.   Brush fish fillets with olive oil. Season with pepper and salt.   Sprinkle with garlic and shredded parmesan cheese on top.   Set to bake at 400 F for 25 minutes. After 5 minutes place the baking pan in the preheated oven.   Serve and enjoy.

Nutrition Info: Calories 424 Fat 26.5 g Carbohydrates 6 g Sugar 2.2 g Protein 44.4 g Cholesterol 95 mg

496. Perfect Baked Cod

Servings: 4   Cooking Time: 15 Minutes
Ingredients:

4 cod fillets	3/4 cup parmesan
1 tbsp olive oil	cheese, grated
1 tsp dried parsley	1/4 tsp salt
2 tsp paprika	

Directions:
Fit the Cuisinart oven with the rack in position   In a shallow dish, mix parmesan cheese, paprika, parsley, and salt.   Brush fish fillets with oil and coat with parmesan cheese mixture.   Place coated fish fillets into the baking dish.   Set to bake at 400 F for 20 minutes. After 5 minutes place the baking dish in the preheated oven.   Serve and enjoy.
Nutrition Info: Calories 160 Fat 8.1 g Carbohydrates 1.2 g Sugar 0.1 g Protein 21.7 g Cholesterol 56 mg

497. Citrus Cilantro Catfish

Servings: 2   Cooking Time: 20 Minutes
Ingredients:

2 catfish fillets	1 garlic clove, mashed
2 tsp blackening	2 tbsp fresh cilantro,
seasoning	chopped
Juice of 1 lime	
2 tbsp butter, melted	

Directions:
In a bowl, blend garlic, lime juice, cilantro, and butter. Pour half of the mixture over the fillets and sprinkle with blackening seasoning. Place the fillets in the basket and press Start. Cook for 15 minutes at 360 F on AirFry function. Serve the fish topped with the remaining sauce.

498. Baked Flounder Fillets

Servings: 2   Cooking Time: 12 Minutes
Ingredients:

2 flounder fillets, patted dry	½ teaspoon coarse sea salt
1 egg	
½ teaspoon Worcestershire sauce	½ teaspoon lemon pepper
¼ cup almond flour	¼ teaspoon chili powder
¼ cup coconut flour	Cooking spray

Directions:
In a shallow bowl, beat together the egg with Worcestershire sauce until well incorporated.   In another bowl, thoroughly combine the almond flour, coconut flour, sea salt, lemon pepper, and chili powder.   Dredge the fillets in the egg mixture, shaking off any excess, then roll in the flour mixture to coat well.   Spritz the baking pan with cooking spray. Place the fillets in the pan.   Slide the baking pan into Rack Position 1, select Convection Bake, set temperature to 390°F (199°C), and set time to 12 minutes.   After 7 minutes, remove from the oven and flip the fillets and spray with cooking spray. Return the pan to the oven and continue cooking for 5 minutes, or until the fish is flaky.   When cooking is complete, remove from the oven and serve warm.

499. Scallops And Spring Veggies

Servings: 4   Cooking Time: 8 Minutes
Ingredients:

½ pound asparagus ends trimmed, cut into 2-inch pieces	2 teaspoons olive oil
1 cup sugar snap peas	½ teaspoon dried thyme
1 pound sea scallops	Pinch salt
1 tablespoon lemon juice	Freshly ground black pepper

Directions:
Preparing the Ingredients. Place the asparagus and sugar snap peas in the Oven rack/basket. Place the Rack on the middle-shelf of the Cuisinart air fryer oven.   Air Frying. Cook for 2 to 3 minutes or until the vegetables are just starting to get tender. Meanwhile, check the scallops for a small muscle attached to the side, and pull it off and discard.   In a medium bowl, toss the scallops with the lemon juice, olive oil, thyme, salt, and pepper. Place into the Oven rack/basket on top of the vegetables. Place the Rack on the middle-shelf of the Cuisinart air fryer oven.   Air Frying.   Steam for 5 to 7 minutes. Until the scallops are just firm, and the vegetables are tender. Serve immediately.
Nutrition Info:CALORIES: 162; CARBS:10G; FAT: 4G; PROTEIN:22G; FIBER:3G

500. Salmon Tandoor

Ingredients:

2 lb. boneless salmon filets	4 tsp. tandoori masala
1st Marinade:	2 tbsp. dry fenugreek leaves
3 tbsp. vinegar or lemon juice	1 tsp. black salt
2 or 3 tsp. paprika	1 tsp. chat masala
1 tsp. black pepper	1 tsp. garam masala powder
1 tsp. salt	
3 tsp. ginger-garlic paste	1 tsp. red chili powder
2nd Marinade:	1 tsp. salt
1 cup yogurt	3 drops of red color

Directions:
Make the first marinade and soak the fileted salmon in it for four hours. While this is happening, make the second marinade and soak the salmon in it overnight to let the flavors blend. Pre heat the Cuisinart oven at 160 degrees Fahrenheit for 5 minutes.   Place the Oregano Fingers in the fry basket and close it. Let them cook at the same temperature for another 15 minutes or so. Toss the Oregano Fingers well so that they are cooked uniformly. Serve them with mint sauce.

501. Panko Crab Sticks With Mayo Sauce

Servings: 4   Cooking Time: 12 Minutes
Ingredients:

Crab Sticks:	1 cup flour
2 eggs	Cooking spray
⅓ cup panko bread crumbs	Mayo Sauce:
1 tablespoon old bay seasoning	½ cup mayonnaise
	1 lime, juiced

1 pound (454 g) crab sticks | 2 garlic cloves, minced

Directions:
In a bowl, beat the eggs. In a shallow bowl, place the flour. In another shallow bowl, thoroughly combine the panko bread crumbs and old bay seasoning. Dredge the crab sticks in the flour, shaking off any excess, then in the beaten eggs, finally press them in the bread crumb mixture to coat well. Arrange the crab sticks in the air fryer basket and spray with cooking spray. Put the air fryer basket on the baking pan and slide into Rack Position 2, select Air Fry, set temperature to 390°F (199°C), and set time to 12 minutes. Flip the crab sticks halfway through the cooking time. Meanwhile, make the sauce by whisking together the mayo, lime juice, and garlic in a small bowl. When cooking is complete, remove from the oven. Serve the crab sticks with the mayo sauce on the side.

502.   Fried Calamari

Servings: 6-8   Cooking Time: 7 Minutes
Ingredients:

½ tsp. salt
½ tsp. Old Bay seasoning
1/3 C. plain cornmeal | ½ C. semolina flour
½ C. almond flour
5-6 C. olive oil
1 ½ pounds baby squid

Directions:
Preparing the Ingredients. Rinse squid in cold water and slice tentacles, keeping just ¼-inch of the hood in one piece. Combine 1-2 pinches of pepper, salt, Old Bay seasoning, cornmeal, and both flours together. Dredge squid pieces into flour mixture and place into the Cuisinart air fryer oven. Air Frying. Spray liberally with olive oil. Cook 15 minutes at 345 degrees till coating turns a golden brown.
Nutrition Info:CALORIES: 211; CARBS:55; FAT: 6G; PROTEIN:21G; SUGAR:1G

503.   Spicy Lemon Cod

Servings: 2   Cooking Time: 10 Minutes
Ingredients:

1 lb cod fillets
1/4 tsp chili powder
1 tbsp fresh parsley, chopped
1 1/2 tbsp olive oil | 1 tbsp fresh lemon juice
1/8 tsp cayenne pepper
1/4 tsp salt

Directions:
Fit the Cuisinart oven with the rack in position Arrange fish fillets in a baking dish. Drizzle with oil and lemon juice. Sprinkle with chili powder, salt, and cayenne pepper. Set to bake at 400 F for 15 minutes. After 5 minutes place the baking dish in the preheated oven. Garnish with parsley and serve.
Nutrition Info: Calories 276 Fat 12.7 g Carbohydrates 0.5 g Sugar 0.2 g Protein 40.7 g Cholesterol 111 mg

504.   Breaded Seafood

Servings: 4   Cooking Time: 15 Minutes
Ingredients:

1 lb scallops, mussels, fish fillets, prawns, shrimp
2 eggs, lightly beaten | Salt and black pepper to taste
1 cup breadcrumbs mixed with zest of 1 lemon

Directions:
Dip the seafood pieces into the eggs and season with salt and black pepper. Coat in the crumbs and spray with cooking spray. Arrange them on the frying basket and press Start. Cook for 10 minutes at 400 F on AirFry function. Serve with lemon wedges.

505.   Lemon Tilapia

Servings: 4   Cooking Time: 12 Minutes
Ingredients:

1 tablespoon olive oil
1 tablespoon lemon juice
4 tilapia fillets | 1 teaspoon minced garlic
½ teaspoon chili powder

Directions:
Line the baking pan with parchment paper. In a shallow bowl, stir together the olive oil, lemon juice, garlic, and chili powder to make a marinade. Put the tilapia fillets in the bowl, turning to coat evenly. Place the fillets in the baking pan in a single layer. Put the air fryer basket on the baking pan and slide into Rack Position 2, select Air Fry, set temperature to 375°F (190°C), and set time to 12 minutes. When cooked, the fish will flake apart with a fork. Remove from the oven to a plate and serve hot.

506.   Party Cod Nuggets

Servings: 4   Cooking Time: 25 Minutes
Ingredients:

1 ¼ lb cod fillets, cut into 4 chunks each
½ cup flour
1 egg | 1 cup cornflakes
1 tbsp olive oil
Salt and black pepper to taste

Directions:
Place the oil and cornflakes in a food processor and process until crumbed. Season the fish chunks with salt and pepper. In a bowl, beat the egg with 1 tbsp of water. Dredge the chunks in flour first, then dip in the egg, and finally coat with cornflakes. Arrange on a lined sheet and press Start. Cook on AirFry function at 350 F for 15 minutes until crispy. Serve.

507.   Golden Beer-battered Cod

Servings: 4   Cooking Time: 15 Minutes
Ingredients:

2 eggs
1 cup malty beer
1 cup all-purpose flour
1 teaspoon garlic powder | ½ cup cornstarch
Salt and pepper, to taste
4 (4-ounce / 113-g) cod fillets
Cooking spray

Directions:
In a shallow bowl, beat together the eggs with the beer. In another shallow bowl, thoroughly combine the flour and cornstarch. Sprinkle with the garlic powder, salt, and pepper. Dredge each cod fillet in the flour mixture, then in the egg mixture. Dip

each piece of fish in the flour mixture a second time. Spritz the air fryer basket with cooking spray. Arrange the cod fillets in the pan in a single layer. Put the air fryer basket on the baking pan and slide into Rack Position 2, select Air Fry, set temperature to 400°F (205°C), and set time to 15 minutes. Flip the fillets halfway through the cooking time. When cooking is complete, the cod should reach an internal temperature of 145°F (63°C) on a meat thermometer and the outside should be crispy. Let the fish cool for 5 minutes and serve.

---

508.   Tasty Lemon Pepper Basa

Servings: 4   Cooking Time: 12 Minutes
Ingredients:
- 4 basa fish fillets
- 8 tsp olive oil
- 2 tbsp fresh parsley, chopped
- 1/4 cup green onion, sliced
- 1/2 tsp garlic powder
- 1/4 tsp lemon pepper seasoning
- 4 tbsp fresh lemon juice
- Pepper
- Salt

Directions:
Fit the Cuisinart oven with the rack in position Place fish fillets in a baking dish.   Pour remaining ingredients over fish fillets.   Set to bake at 425 F for 12 minutes. After 5 minutes place the baking dish in the preheated oven.   Serve and enjoy.
Nutrition Info: Calories 308 Fat 21.4 g Carbohydrates 5.5 g Sugar 3.4 g Protein 24.1 g Cholesterol 0 mg

---

509.   Quick Tuna Patties

Servings: 10   Cooking Time: 10 Minutes
Ingredients:
- 15 oz can tuna, drained and flaked
- 1/2 tsp dried mixed herbs
- 3 tbsp parmesan cheese, grated
- 1/2 cup breadcrumbs
- 1 tbsp lemon juice
- 2 eggs, lightly beaten
- 1/2 tsp garlic powder
- 2 tbsp onion, minced
- 1 celery stalk, chopped
- Pepper
- Salt

Directions:
Fit the Cuisinart oven with the rack in position 2. Add all ingredients into the mixing bowl and mix until well combined.   Make patties from mixture and place in the air fryer basket then place the air fryer basket in the baking pan.   Place a baking pan on the oven rack. Set to air fry at 360 F for 10 minutes.   Serve and enjoy.
Nutrition Info: Calories 90 Fat 1.8 g Carbohydrates 4.4 g Sugar 0.6 g Protein 13.2 g Cholesterol 47 mg

---

510.   Crispy Fish Sticks

Servings: 8   Cooking Time: 6 Minutes
Ingredients:
- 8 ounces (227 g) fish fillets (pollock or cod), cut into ½ × 3 inches strips
- Cooking spray
- Salt, to taste (optional)
- ½ cup plain bread crumbs

Directions:
Season the fish strips with salt to taste, if desired. Place the bread crumbs on a plate, then roll the fish in the bread crumbs until well coated. Spray all sides of the fish with cooking spray. Transfer to the air fryer basket in a single layer.   Put the air fryer basket on the baking pan and slide into Rack Position 2, select Air Fry, set temperature to 400°F (205°C), and set time to 6 minutes.   When cooked, the fish sticks should be golden brown and crispy. Remove from the oven to a plate and serve hot.

Meat Recipes

511. Quail Marinade Cutlet

Ingredients:

½ cup mint leaves
4 tsp. fennel
2 tbsp. ginger-garlic paste
1 small onion
6-7 flakes garlic (optional)
Salt to taste
2 cups sliced quail
1 big capsicum (Cut this capsicum into big cubes)
1 onion (Cut it into quarters. Now separate the layers carefully.)
5 tbsp. gram flour
A pinch of salt to taste
For the filling:
2 cup fresh green coriander
3 tbsp. lemon juice

Directions:

You will first need to make the sauce. Add the ingredients to a blender and make a thick paste. Slit the pieces of quail and stuff half the paste into the cavity obtained.   Take the remaining paste and add it to the gram flour and salt. Toss the pieces of quail in this mixture and set aside.   Apply a little bit of the mixture on the capsicum and onion. Place these on a stick along with the quail pieces.   Pre heat the Cuisinart oven at 290 Fahrenheit for around 5 minutes. Open the basket. Arrange the satay sticks properly. Close the basket. Keep the sticks with the quail at 180 degrees for around half an hour while the sticks with the vegetables are to be kept at the same temperature for only 7 minutes. Turn the sticks in between so that one side does not get burnt and also to provide a uniform cook.

512. Crispy Crusted Pork Chops

Servings: 2   Cooking Time: 15 Minutes

Ingredients:

2 pork chops, bone-in
1 cup pork rinds, crushed
1/2 tsp parsley
1 tbsp olive oil
1/2 tsp garlic powder
1/2 tsp onion powder
1/2 tsp paprika

Directions:

Fit the Cuisinart oven with the rack in position 2. In a large bowl, mix pork rinds, garlic powder, onion powder, parsley, and paprika.   Brush pork chops with oil and coat with pork rind mixture.   place coated pork chops in air fryer basket then place air fryer basket in baking pan.   Place a baking pan on the oven rack. Set to air fry at 400 F for 15 minutes. Serve and enjoy.

Nutrition Info: Calories 413 Fat 32.7 g Carbohydrates 1.3 g Sugar 0.4 g Protein 28.5 g Cholesterol 92 mg

513. Lemon-pepper Chicken Wings

Servings: 4   Cooking Time: 20 Minutes

Ingredients:

8 whole chicken wings
Juice of ½ lemon
½ teaspoon garlic powder
Pepper
¼ cup low-fat buttermilk
½ cup all-purpose
1 teaspoon onion powder
Salt
flour
Cooking oil

Directions:

Preparing the Ingredients. Place the wings in a sealable plastic bag. Drizzle the wings with the lemon juice. Season the wings with the garlic powder, onion powder, and salt and pepper to taste. Seal the bag. Shake thoroughly to combine the seasonings and coat the wings.   Pour the buttermilk and the flour into separate bowls large enough to dip the wings.   Spray the Oven rack/basket with cooking oil.   One at a time, dip the wings in the buttermilk and then the flour.   Air Frying.   Place the wings in the Oven rack/basket. It is okay to stack them on top of each other. Spray the wings with cooking oil, being sure to spray the bottom layer. Place the Rack on the middle-shelf of the Cuisinart air fryer oven. Cook for 5 minutes. Remove the basket and shake it to ensure all of the pieces will cook fully.   Return the basket to the Cuisinart air fryer oven and continue to cook the chicken. Repeat shaking every 5 minutes until a total of 20 minutes has passed.   Cool before serving.

Nutrition Info: CALORIES: 347; FAT: 12G; PROTEIN:46G; FIBER:1G

514. Italian Sausages And Red Grapes

Servings: 6   Cooking Time: 20 Minutes

Ingredients:

2 pounds (905 g) seedless red grapes
2 teaspoons fresh thyme
2 tablespoons olive oil
½ teaspoon kosher salt
3 shallots, sliced
Freshly ground black pepper, to taste
6 links (about 1½ pounds / 680 g) hot Italian sausage
3 tablespoons balsamic vinegar

Directions:

Place the grapes in a large bowl. Add the shallots, thyme, olive oil, salt, and pepper. Gently toss. Place the grapes in the baking pan. Arrange the sausage links evenly in the pan.   Slide the baking pan into Rack Position 2, select Roast, set temperature to 375°F (190°C), and set time to 20 minutes.   After 10 minutes, remove the pan. Turn over the sausages and sprinkle the vinegar over the sausages and grapes. Gently toss the grapes and move them to one side of the pan. Return the pan to the oven and continue cooking.   When cooking is complete, the grapes should be very soft and the sausages browned. Serve immediately.

515. Meatballs(14)

Servings: 4   Cooking Time: 25 Minutes

Ingredients:

1 lb ground beef
1 tsp fresh rosemary, chopped
1 tbsp garlic, chopped
1 tsp onion powder
1/4 cup breadcrumbs
2 eggs
1 lb ground pork

1/2 tsp pepper
1 tsp garlic powder

1/2 tsp pepper
1 tsp sea salt

Directions:
Fit the Cuisinart oven with the rack in position Add all ingredients into the mixing bowl and mix until well combined. Make small balls from the meat mixture and place it into the parchment-lined baking pan. Set to bake at 400 F for 30 minutes. After 5 minutes place the baking pan in the preheated oven. Serve and enjoy.
Nutrition Info: Calories 441 Fat 13.7 g Carbohydrates 7.2 g Sugar 1 g Protein 68.1 g Cholesterol 266 mg

---

516. Spicy Chicken Strips With Aioli Sauce

Servings: 4   Cooking Time: 15 Minutes
Ingredients:

3 chicken breasts, cut into strips
2 tbsp olive oil
Salt and black pepper to taste

1 cup breadcrumbs
½ tbsp garlic powder
½ cup mayonnaise
1 tbsp lemon juice
½ tbsp ground chili

Directions:
Mix breadcrumbs, salt, pepper, and garlic and spread onto a plate. Brush the chicken with olive oil then roll up in the breadcrumb mixture. Arrange on the oiled SirFryer basket and fit in the baking tray; cook for 10-12 minutes at 360 F on Air Fry function, turning once halfway through. To prepare the aioli: mix well mayonnaise with lemon juice and ground chili. Serve the chicken with hot aioli.

---

517. Bo Luc Lac

Servings: 4   Cooking Time: 4 Minutes
Ingredients:

For the Meat:
2 teaspoons soy sauce
4 garlic cloves, minced
1 teaspoon kosher salt
2 teaspoons sugar
¼ teaspoon ground black pepper
1 teaspoon toasted sesame oil
1½ pounds (680 g) top sirloin steak, cut into 1-inch cubes
Cooking spray
For the Salad:
1 head Bibb lettuce, leaves separated and torn into large pieces
¼ cup fresh mint leaves

½ cup halved grape tomatoes
½ red onion, halved and thinly sliced
2 tablespoons apple cider vinegar
1 garlic clove, minced
2 teaspoons sugar
¼ teaspoon kosher salt
¼ teaspoon ground black pepper
2 tablespoons vegetable oil
For Serving:
Lime wedges, for garnish
Coarse salt and freshly cracked black pepper, to taste

Directions:
Combine the ingredients for the meat, except for the steak, in a large bowl. Stir to mix well. Dunk the steak cubes in the bowl and press to coat. Wrap the bowl in plastic and marinate under room

temperature for at least 30 minutes. Spritz the air fryer basket with cooking spray. Discard the marinade and transfer the steak cubes in the prepared basket. Put the air fryer basket on the baking pan and slide into Rack Position 2, select Air Fry, set temperature to 450°F (235°C) and set time to 4 minutes. Flip the steak cubes halfway through. When cooking is complete, the steak cubes should be lightly browned but still have a little pink. Meanwhile, combine the ingredients for the salad in a separate large bowl. Toss to mix well. Pour the salad in a large serving bowl and top with the steak cubes. Squeeze the lime wedges over and sprinkle with salt and black pepper before serving.

---

518. Beef Kinking Coriander Powder

Ingredients:

3 tbsp. cream
2 tbsp. coriander powder
4 tbsp. fresh mint (chopped)
3 tbsp. chopped capsicum
2 tbsp. peanut flour
1 lb. boneless beef liver (Chop into cubes)
3 onions chopped

5 green chilies-roughly chopped
1 ½ tbsp. ginger paste
1 ½ tsp. garlic paste
1 ½ tsp. salt
3 tsp. lemon juice
2 tsp. garam masala
4 tbsp. chopped coriander
3 eggs

Directions:
Mix the dry ingredients in a bowl. Make the mixture into a smooth paste and coat the beef cubes with the mixture. Beat the eggs in a bowl and add a little salt to them. Dip the cubes in the egg mixture and coat them with sesame seeds and leave them in the refrigerator for an hour. Pre heat the Cuisinart oven at 290 Fahrenheit for around 5 minutes. Place the kebabs in the basket and let them cook for another 25 minutes at the same temperature. Turn the kebabs over in between the cooking process to get a uniform cook. Serve the kebabs with mint sauce.

---

519. Hot Curried Chicken Wings

Servings: 2   Cooking Time: 20 Minutes + Marinating Time
Ingredients:

8 chicken wings
1 tbsp water
4 tbsp potato starch

2 tbsp hot curry paste
½ tbsp baking powder

Directions:
In a bowl, combine curry paste with 1 tbsp of water. Add in the wings and toss to coat. Cover the bowl with cling film and refrigerate for 2 hours. Preheat Cuisinart on AirFry function to 370 degrees. In a bowl, mix baking powder and potato starch. Dip in the wings. Transfer to a lined baking dish, press Start, and cook for 14 minutes.

---

520. Sumptuous Beef And Pork Sausage Meatloaf

Servings: 4   Cooking Time: 25 Minutes

Ingredients:

¾ pound (340 g) ground chuck
4 ounces (113 g) ground pork sausage
2 eggs, beaten
1 cup Parmesan cheese, grated
1 cup chopped shallot
3 tablespoons plain milk
1 tablespoon oyster sauce
1 tablespoon fresh parsley
1 teaspoon garlic paste
1 teaspoon chopped porcini mushrooms
½ teaspoon cumin powder
Seasoned salt and crushed red pepper flakes, to taste

Directions:

In a large bowl, combine all the ingredients until well blended. Place the meat mixture in the baking pan. Use a spatula to press the mixture to fill the pan. Slide the baking pan into Rack Position 1, select Convection Bake, set temperature to 360°F (182°C) and set time to 25 minutes. When cooking is complete, the meatloaf should be well browned. Let the meatloaf rest for 5 minutes. Transfer to a serving dish and slice. Serve warm.

---

521. Turkey Burgers

Servings: 4   Cooking Time: 10 Minutes

Ingredients:

1 1/3 lb. ground turkey
½ cup gruyere cheese, grated
¼ cup bread crumbs
3 green onions, chopped fine
¼ cup Dijon mustard
½ tsp salt
½ tsp pepper

Directions:

In a large bowl, combine all ingredients until combined. Form into 4 patties. Lightly spray tops with cooking spray and put them in the fryer basket, sprayed side down. Spray patties again. Place the baking pan in position 2 of the oven and add basket. Set oven to air fry on 400°F for 10 minutes. Turn burgers over halfway through cooking time. Serve.

Nutrition Info: Calories 321, Total Fat 17g, Saturated Fat 6g, Total Carbs 7g, Net Carbs 6g, Protein 35g, Sugar 1g, Fiber 1g, Sodium 697mg, Potassium 436mg, Phosphorus 415mg

---

522. Beef Steak Momo's Recipe

Ingredients:

2 tsp. ginger-garlic paste
2 tsp. soya sauce
1 ½ cup all-purpose flour
½ tsp. salt
5 tbsp. water
For filling:
2 cups minced beef steak
2 tbsp. oil
2 tsp. vinegar

Directions:

Squeeze the dough and cover it with plastic wrap and set aside. Next, cook the ingredients for the filling and try to ensure that the beef is covered well with the sauce. Roll the dough and cut it into a square. Place the filling in the center. Now, wrap the dough to cover the filling and pinch the edges together. Pre heat the Cuisinart oven at 200° F for 5 minutes. Place the wontons in the fry basket and close it. Let them cook at the same temperature for

---

another 20 minutes. Recommended sides are chili sauce or ketchup.

523. Herby Stuffed Turkey Breast

Servings: 4   Cooking Time: 35 Minutes

Ingredients:

1 pound turkey breast
1 ham slice
1 slice cheddar cheese
2 oz breadcrumbs
1 tbsp cream cheese
½ tsp garlic powder
1 tbsp fresh thyme, chopped
1 tbsp fresh tarragon, chopped
1 egg, beaten
Salt and black pepper to taste

Directions:

Preheat Cuisinart on Air Fry function to 350 F. Cut the turkey in the middle; that way so you can add ingredients in the center. Season with salt, pepper, thyme, and tarragon. Combine cream cheese and garlic powder in a bowl. Spread the mixture on the inside of the breast. Place half cheddar slice and half ham slice in the center of each breast. Dip in the egg first, then sprinkle with breadcrumbs. Cook on the baking tray for 30 minutes, flipping once.

---

524. Onion & Pork Sausage Balls

Servings: 4   Cooking Time: 20 Minutes

Ingredients:

1 pound pork sausages, sliced
Salt and black pepper to taste
1 cup onions, chopped
1 cup breadcrumbs
½ tsp garlic puree
1 tsp dried sage

Directions:

In a bowl, mix onions, sausages, sage, garlic, salt, and pepper. In a plate, scatter the breadcrumbs. Form balls out of the mixture and roll in breadcrumbs. Add the balls to the cooking basket. Select AirFry function, adjust the temperature to 380 F, and press Start. Cook the balls for 15 minutes. Serve and enjoy!

---

525. Barbecue Pork Club Sandwich With Mustard

Ingredients:

2 slices of white bread
1 tbsp. softened butter
½ lb. cut pork (Get the meat cut into cubes)
1 small capsicum
¼ tbsp. red chili sauce
1 tbsp. tomato ketchup
½ cup water.
¼ tbsp. Worcestershire sauce
½ tsp. olive oil
½ flake garlic crushed
¼ cup chopped onion
¼ tsp. mustard powder
½ tbsp. sugar
A pinch of salt and black pepper to taste

Directions:

Take the slices of bread and remove the edges. Now cut the slices horizontally. Cook the ingredients for the sauce and wait till it thickens. Now, add the pork to the sauce and stir till it obtains the flavors. Roast the capsicum and peel the skin off. Cut the capsicum into slices.   Mix the ingredients together and apply it to the bread slices.   Pre-heat the Cuisinart oven for 5 minutes at 300 Fahrenheit. Open the basket of the Fryer and place the prepared Classic Sandwiches in it such that no two Classic Sandwiches are touching each other.   Now keep the fryer at 250 degrees for around 15 minutes.   Turn the Classic Sandwiches in between the cooking process to cook both slices. Serve the Classic Sandwiches with tomato ketchup or mint sauce.

---

526. Copycat Taco Bell Crunch Wraps

Servings: 6   Cooking Time: 2 Minutes

Ingredients:

6 wheat tostadas	6 12-inch wheat
2 C. sour cream	tortillas
2 C. Mexican blend	1 1/3 C. water
cheese	2 packets low-sodium
2 C. shredded lettuce	taco seasoning
12 ounces low-	2 pounds of lean
sodium nacho cheese	ground beef
3 Roma tomatoes	

Directions:

Preparing the Ingredients. Ensure your air fryer oven is preheated to 400 degrees.   Make beef according to taco seasoning packets.   Place 2/3 C. prepared beef, 4 tbsp. cheese, 1 tostada, 1/3 C. sour cream, 1/3 C. lettuce, 1/6th of tomatoes and 1/3 C. cheese on each tortilla.   Fold up tortillas edges and repeat with remaining ingredients.   Lay the folded sides of tortillas down into the air fryer oven and spray with olive oil.   Air Frying. Set temperature to 400°F, and set time to 2 minutes.   Cook 2 minutes till browned.

Nutrition Info: CALORIES: 311; FAT: 9G; PROTEIN:22G; SUGAR:2

---

527. Pomegranate Chicken With Couscous Salad

Servings: 4   Cooking Time: 20 Minutes

Ingredients:

3 tablespoons plus 2 teaspoons pomegranate molasses	1 tablespoon minced fresh parsley
½ teaspoon ground cinnamon	2 ounces (57 g) cherry tomatoes, quartered
1 teaspoon minced fresh thyme	1 scallion, white part minced, green part sliced thin on bias
Salt and ground black pepper, to taste	1 tablespoon extra-virgin olive oil
2 (12-ounce / 340-g) bone-in split chicken breasts, trimmed	1 ounce (28 g) feta cheese, crumbled
¼ cup chicken broth	Cooking spray
¼ cup water	
½ cup couscous	

Directions:

Spritz the air fryer basket with cooking spray. Combine 3 tablespoons of pomegranate molasses, cinnamon, thyme, and ⅛ teaspoon of salt in a small bowl. Stir to mix well. Set aside.   Place the chicken breasts in the basket, skin side down, and spritz with cooking spray. Sprinkle with salt and ground black pepper.   Put the air fryer basket on the baking pan and slide into Rack Position 2, select Air Fry, set temperature to 350°F (180°C) and set time to 20 minutes.   Flip the chicken and brush with pomegranate molasses mixture halfway through. Meanwhile, pour the broth and water in a pot and bring to a boil over medium-high heat. Add the couscous and sprinkle with salt. Cover and simmer for 7 minutes or until the liquid is almost absorbed. Combine the remaining ingredients, except for the cheese, with cooked couscous in a large bowl. Toss to mix well. Scatter with the feta cheese.   When cooking is complete, remove the chicken from the oven and allow to cool for 10 minutes. Serve with vegetable and couscous salad.

---

528. Pork Burger Cutlets With Fresh Coriander Leaves

Ingredients:

½ lb. pork (Make sure that you mince the pork fine)	1 green chili finely chopped
½ cup breadcrumbs	1 tsp. lemon juice
½ cup of boiled peas	1 tbsp. fresh coriander leaves.
¼ tsp. cumin powder	Chop them finely
A pinch of salt to taste	¼ tsp. red chili powder
¼ tsp. ginger finely chopped	¼ tsp. dried mango powder

Directions:

Take a container and into it pour all the masalas, onions, green chilies, peas, coriander leaves, lemon juice, and ginger and 1-2 tbsp. breadcrumbs. Add the minced pork as well. Mix all the ingredients well. Mold the mixture into round Cutlets. Press them gently. Now roll them out carefully. Pre heat the Cuisinart oven at 250 Fahrenheit for 5 minutes. Open the basket of the Fryer and arrange the Cutlets in the basket. Close it carefully. Keep the fryer at 150 degrees for around 10 or 12 minutes. In between the cooking process, turn the Cutlets over to get a uniform cook. Serve hot with mint sauce.

---

529. Spice-coated Steaks With Cucumber And Snap Pea Salad

Servings: 4   Cooking Time: 15 Minutes

Ingredients:

1 (1½-pound / 680-g) boneless top sirloin steak, trimmed and halved crosswise	⅛ teaspoon ground cinnamon
1½ teaspoons chili powder	3 tablespoons mayonnaise
1½ teaspoons ground cumin	1½ tablespoons white wine vinegar
¾ teaspoon ground coriander	1 tablespoon minced fresh dill
⅛ teaspoon cayenne	1 small garlic clove, minced
	8 ounces (227 g)

pepper
1¼ teaspoons plus ⅛ teaspoon salt, divided
½ teaspoon plus ⅛ teaspoon ground black pepper, divided
1 teaspoon plus 1½ tablespoons extra-virgin olive oil, divided

sugar snap peas, strings removed and cut in half on bias
½ English cucumber, halved lengthwise and sliced thin
2 radishes, trimmed, halved and sliced thin
2 cups baby arugula

Directions:
In a bowl, mix chili powder, cumin, coriander, cayenne pepper, cinnamon, 1¼ teaspoons salt and ½ teaspoon pepper until well combined.   Add the steaks to another bowl and pat dry with paper towels. Brush with 1 teaspoon oil and transfer to the bowl of spice mixture. Roll over to coat thoroughly. Arrange the coated steaks in the basket, spaced evenly apart.   Put the air fryer basket on the baking pan and slide into Rack Position 2, select Air Fry, set temperature to 400°F (205°C) and set time to 15 minutes.   Flip the steak halfway through to ensure even cooking.   When cooking is complete, an instant-read thermometer inserted in the thickest part of the meat should register at least 145°F (63°C).   Transfer the steaks to a clean work surface and wrap with aluminum foil. Let stand while preparing salad.   Make the salad: In a large bowl, stir together 1½ tablespoons olive oil, mayonnaise, vinegar, dill, garlic, ⅛ teaspoon salt, and ⅛ teaspoon pepper. Add snap peas, cucumber, radishes and arugula. Toss to blend well.   Slice the steaks and serve with the salad.

530.   Glazed Duck With Cherry Sauce

Servings: 12   Cooking Time: 32 Minutes
Ingredients:
1 whole duck (about 5 pounds / 2.3 kg in total), split in half, back and rib bones removed, fat trimmed
1 teaspoon olive oil
Salt and freshly ground black pepper, to taste
Cherry Sauce:
1 tablespoon butter

1 shallot, minced
½ cup sherry
1 cup chicken stock
1 teaspoon white wine vinegar
¾ cup cherry preserves
1 teaspoon fresh thyme leaves
Salt and freshly ground black pepper, to taste

Directions:
On a clean work surface, rub the duck with olive oil, then sprinkle with salt and ground black pepper to season.   Place the duck in the air fryer basket, breast side up.   Put the air fryer basket on the baking pan and slide into Rack Position 2, select Air Fry, set temperature to 400°F (205°C) and set time to 25 minutes.   Flip the ducks halfway through the cooking time.   Meanwhile, make the cherry sauce: Heat the butter in a skillet over medium-high heat or until melted.   Add the shallot and sauté for 5 minutes or until lightly browned.   Add the sherry and simmer for 6 minutes or until it reduces in half. Add the chicken stick, white wine vinegar, and

cherry preserves. Stir to combine well. Simmer for 6 more minutes or until thickened.   Fold in the thyme leaves and sprinkle with salt and ground black pepper. Stir to mix well.   When the cooking of the duck is complete, glaze the duck with a quarter of the cherry sauce, then air fry for another 4 minutes.   Flip the duck and glaze with another quarter of the cherry sauce. Air fry for an additional 3 minutes.   Transfer the duck on a large plate and serve with remaining cherry sauce.

531.   Spicy Pork Chops With Carrots And Mushrooms

Servings: 4   Cooking Time: 15 Minutes
Ingredients:
2 carrots, cut into sticks
1 cup mushrooms, sliced
2 garlic cloves, minced
2 tablespoons olive oil
1 pound (454 g) boneless pork chops

1 teaspoon dried oregano
1 teaspoon dried thyme
1 teaspoon cayenne pepper
Salt and ground black pepper, to taste
Cooking spray

Directions:
In a mixing bowl, toss together the carrots, mushrooms, garlic, olive oil and salt until well combined.   Add the pork chops to a different bowl and season with oregano, thyme, cayenne pepper, salt and black pepper.   Lower the vegetable mixture in the greased basket. Place the seasoned pork chops on top.   Put the air fryer basket on the baking pan and slide into Rack Position 2, select Air Fry, set temperature to 360°F (182°C) and set time to 15 minutes.   After 7 minutes, remove from the oven. Flip the pork and stir the vegetables. Return to the oven and continue cooking.   When cooking is complete, the pork chops should be browned and the vegetables should be tender.   Transfer the pork chops to the serving dishes and let cool for 5 minutes. Serve warm with vegetable on the side.

532.   Crispy Honey Garlic Chicken Wings

Servings: 8   Cooking Time: 25 Minutes
Ingredients:
1/8 C. water
½ tsp. salt
4 tbsp. minced garlic
¼ C. vegan butter

¼ C. raw honey
¾ C. almond flour
16 chicken wings

Directions:
Preparing the Ingredients. Rinse off and dry chicken wings well.   Spray air fryer rack/basket with olive oil.   Coat chicken wings with almond flour and add coated wings to the Cuisinart air fryer oven. Air Frying. Set temperature to 380°F, and set time to 25 minutes. Cook shaking every 5 minutes. When the timer goes off, cook 5-10 minutes at 400 degrees till skin becomes crispy and dry.   As chicken cooks, melt butter in a saucepan and add garlic. Sauté garlic 5 minutes. Add salt and honey, simmering 20 minutes. Make sure to stir every so often, so the sauce does not burn. Add a bit of water

after 15 minutes to ensure sauce does not harden. Take out chicken wings from air fryer oven and coat in sauce. Enjoy!

Nutrition Info:CALORIES: 435; FAT: 19G; PROTEIN:31G; SUGAR:6

533. Hearty Mushroom And Sausage Calzones

Servings: 4   Cooking Time: 24 Minutes

Ingredients:

2 links Italian sausages (about ½ pound / 227 g)	3 tablespoons olive oil, divided
1 pound (454 g) pizza dough, thawed	½ cup roasted mushrooms
¼ cup Marinara sauce	1 cup shredded Mozzarella cheese

Directions:

Place the sausages in the baking pan.   Slide the baking pan into Rack Position 2, select Roast, set temperature to 375°F (190°C), and set time to 12 minutes.   After 6 minutes, remove from the oven and turn over the sausages. Return to the oven and continue cooking.   While the sausages cook, divide the pizza dough into 4 equal pieces. One at a time, place a piece of dough onto a square of parchment paper 9 inches in diameter. Brush the dough on both sides with ¾ teaspoon of olive oil, then top the dough with another piece of parchment. Press the dough into a 7-inch circle. Remove the top piece of parchment and set aside. Repeat with the remaining pieces of dough.   When cooking is complete, remove from the oven. Place the sausages on a cutting board. Let them cool for several minutes, then slice into ¼-inch rounds and cut each round into 4 pieces.   One at a time, spread a tablespoon of marinara sauce over half of a dough circle, leaving a ½-inch border at the edges. Cover with a quarter of the sausage pieces and add a quarter of the mushrooms. Sprinkle with ¼ cup of cheese. Pull the other side of the dough over the filling and pinch the edges together to seal. Transfer from the parchment to the baking pan. Repeat with the other rounds of dough, sauce, sausage, mushrooms, and cheese. Brush the tops of the calzones with 1 tablespoon of olive oil.   Select Roast, set temperature to 450°F (235°C), and set time to 12 minutes.   After 6 minutes, remove from the oven. The calzones should be golden brown. Turn over the calzones and brush the tops with the remaining olive oil. Return the pan to the oven and continue cooking.   When cooking is complete, the crust should be a deep golden brown on both sides. Remove from the oven. The center should be molten; let cool for several minutes before serving.

534. Meatballs(12)

Servings: 6   Cooking Time: 25 Minutes

Ingredients:

1 lb ground turkey	1 tsp olive oil
1 egg, lightly beaten	1/2 tsp ground ginger
2 tbsp basil, chopped	1/2 tsp salt
2 tbsp coconut flour	

Directions:

Fit the Cuisinart oven with the rack in position   In a bowl, mix turkey, basil, coconut flour, olive oil, ginger, egg, and salt until well combined.   Make small balls from the meat mixture and place it into the parchment-lined baking pan.   Set to bake at 375 F for 30 minutes. After 5 minutes place the baking pan in the preheated oven.   Serve and enjoy.

Nutrition Info: Calories 185 Fat 10.5 g Carbohydrates 2.9 g Sugar 0.4 g Protein 22.3 g Cholesterol 104 mg

535. Easy Pork Bites

Servings: 4   Cooking Time: 15 Minutes

Ingredients:

1 lb pork belly, cut into 3/4-inch cubes	1 tsp soy sauce
	Pepper
1/2 tsp onion powder	Salt
1/2 tsp garlic powder	

Directions:

Fit the Cuisinart oven with the rack in position 2. In a mixing bowl, toss pork cubes with onion powder, garlic powder, soy sauce, pepper, and salt.   Place pork cubes in the air fryer basket then place an air fryer basket in the baking pan.   Place a baking pan on the oven rack. Set to air fry at 400 F for 15 minutes.   Serve and enjoy.

Nutrition Info: Calories 526 Fat 30.5 g Carbohydrates 0.6 g Sugar 0.2 g Protein 52.5 g Cholesterol 131 mg

536. Curried Beef Patties

Servings: 6   Cooking Time: 25 Minutes

Ingredients:

1 lb ground beef	1/2 onion, chopped
2 eggs, lightly beaten	1/2 tsp chili powder
2 medium zucchini, grated and squeeze out all liquid	1 tsp curry powder
	1 cup breadcrumbs
	Pepper
	Salt

Directions:

Fit the Cuisinart oven with the rack in position Add all ingredients into the large bowl and mix until well combined.   Make small patties from the meat mixture and place it into the baking pan.   Set to bake at 400 F for 30 minutes. After 5 minutes place the baking pan in the preheated oven.   Serve and enjoy.

Nutrition Info: Calories 248 Fat 7.3 g Carbohydrates 16.4 g Sugar 2.8 g Protein 28.1 g Cholesterol 122 mg

537. Cripsy Crusted Pork Chops

Servings: 4   Cooking Time: 40 Minutes

Ingredients:

4 pork chops, boneless	1 cup breadcrumbs
1 cup parmesan cheese	1/2 tsp Italian seasoning
1 tbsp olive oil	Pepper
1 tsp garlic powder	Salt

Directions:

Fit the Cuisinart oven with the rack in position   In a shallow dish, mix breadcrumbs, parmesan cheese,

Italian seasoning, garlic powder, pepper, and salt. Brush pork chops with oil and coat with breadcrumb mixture. Place coated pork chops in a baking pan. Set to bake at 350 F for 45 minutes. After 5 minutes place the baking pan in the preheated oven. Serve and enjoy.

Nutrition Info: Calories 469 Fat 29.8 g Carbohydrates 20.8 g Sugar 1.9 g Protein 28.9 g Cholesterol 85 mg

538. Air Fryer Sweet And Sour Pork

Servings: 6   Cooking Time: 12 Minutes
Ingredients:

3 tbsp. olive oil	Sweet and Sour
1/16 tsp. Chinese Five Spice	Sauce:
¼ tsp. pepper	¼ tsp. sea salt
½ tsp. sea salt	½ tsp. garlic powder
1 tsp. pure sesame oil	1 tbsp. low-sodium
2 eggs	soy sauce
1 C. almond flour	½ C. rice vinegar
2 pounds pork, sliced into chunks	5 tbsp. tomato paste
	1/8 tsp. water
	½ C. sweetener of choice

Directions:
Preparing the Ingredients. To make the dipping sauce, whisk all sauce ingredients together over medium heat, stirring 5 minutes. Simmer uncovered 5 minutes till thickened. Meanwhile, combine almond flour, five spice, pepper, and salt. In another bowl, mix eggs with sesame oil. Dredge pork in flour mixture and then in egg mixture. Shake any excess off before adding to air fryer rack/basket. Air Frying. Set temperature to 340°F, and set time to 12 minutes. Serve with sweet and sour dipping sauce!

Nutrition Info:CALORIES: 371; FAT: 17G; PROTEIN:27G; SUGAR:1G

539. Lamb Cheese Homemade Fried Sticks

Ingredients:

2 cups lamb (Cut the lamb into long strips)	1 tbsp. ginger-garlic paste
1 cup cheddar cheese	For seasoning, use
1 big lemon-juiced	salt and red chili
4 or 5 tbsp. corn flour	powder in small
1 cup of water	amounts
	½ tsp. carom
	One or two
	poppadums'

Directions:
Make a mixture of lemon juice, red chili powder, salt, ginger garlic paste and carom to use as a marinade. Let the lamb pieces marinate in the mixture for some time and then roll them in dry corn flour. Leave them aside for around 20 minutes. Take the poppadum into a pan and roast them. Once they are cooked, crush them into very small pieces. Now take another container and pour around 100 ml of water into it. Dissolve 2 tbsp. of corn flour in this water. Dip the cottage cheese pieces in this solution of corn flour and roll them on to the pieces of crushed poppadum so that the poppadum sticks to the lamb. Pre heat the Cuisinart oven for 10 minutes at 300 Fahrenheit. Then open the basket of the fryer and place the lamb pieces inside it. Close the basket properly. Let the fryer stay at 250 degrees for another 20 minutes. Halfway through, open the basket and toss the lamb around a bit to allow for uniform cooking. Once they are done, you can serve it either with ketchup or mint sauce. Another recommended side is mint sauce.

540. Sweet & Spicy Chicken Wings

Servings: 4   Cooking Time: 30 Minutes
Ingredients:

12 chicken wings	Pepper
1/2 cup hot sauce	Salt
1/2 cup honey	

Directions:
Fit the Cuisinart oven with the rack in position 2. Season chicken wings with pepper and salt. Arrange chicken wings in the air fryer basket then place an air fryer basket in the baking pan. Place a baking pan on the oven rack. Set to air fry at 400 F for 25 minutes. Meanwhile, add honey and hot sauce in a saucepan and heat over medium heat for 5 minutes. Add chicken wings in a bowl. Pour sauce over chicken wings and toss well. Serve and enjoy.

Nutrition Info: Calories 698 Fat 22.2 g Carbohydrates 35.4 g Sugar 35.2 g Protein 89.4 g Cholesterol 256 mg

541. Juicy Pork Ribs Ole

Servings: 4   Cooking Time: 25 Minutes
Ingredients:

1 rack of pork ribs	1 can tomato sauce
1/2 cup low-fat milk	1 teaspoon seasoned
1 tablespoon envelope	salt
taco seasoning mix	1 tablespoon
1/2 teaspoon ground	cornstarch
black pepper	1 teaspoon canola oil

Directions:
Preparing the Ingredients. Place all ingredients in a mixing dish; let them marinate for 1 hour. Air Frying. Cook the marinated ribs approximately 25 minutes at 390 degrees F   Work with batches. Enjoy .

542. Green Chili Chicken Noodle Casserole

Servings: 6   Cooking Time: 30 Minutes
Ingredients:

3 cups cooked chicken, shredded	1 1/3 cups milk
4 oz can green chilies	1 tsp chili powder
1/3 cup parmesan cheese, shredded	1 onion, diced
3 cups cheddar cheese, shredded	1/3 cup bell pepper, diced
10.5 oz cream of chicken soup	3 tbsp butter
	3 cups shell noodles, uncooked
	1/2 tsp salt

Directions:

Fit the Cuisinart oven with the rack in position Cook noodles according to the packet instructions and drain well. Melt butter in a pan over medium heat. Add bell pepper and onion and sauté for 5 minutes. Stir in chili powder and salt. In a large bowl, mix chicken soup, parmesan cheese, 2 cups cheddar cheese, milk, and sautéed onion bell pepper. Stir in green chilies, noodles, and chicken. Pour mixture into the greased 9*13-inch baking dish and top with remaining cheese. Set to bake at 375 F for 35 minutes. After 5 minutes place the baking dish in the preheated oven. Serve and enjoy.

Nutrition Info: Calories 560 Fat 32.6 g Carbohydrates 23.9 g Sugar 5 g Protein 42.2 g Cholesterol 156 mg

---

543.	Bell Pepper Stuffed Chicken Roll-ups

Servings: 4   Cooking Time: 12 Minutes

Ingredients:

2 (4-ounce / 113-g) boneless, skinless chicken breasts, slice in half horizontally	2 tablespoons taco seasoning
1 tablespoon olive oil	½ green bell pepper, cut into strips
Juice of ½ lime	½ red bell pepper, cut into strips
	¼ onion, sliced

Directions:

Unfold the chicken breast slices on a clean work surface. Rub with olive oil, then drizzle with lime juice and sprinkle with taco seasoning. Top the chicken slices with equal amount of bell peppers and onion. Roll them up and secure with toothpicks. Arrange the chicken roll-ups in the basket. Put the air fryer basket on the baking pan and slide into Rack Position 2, select Air Fry, set temperature to 400°F (205°C) and set time to 12 minutes. Flip the chicken roll-ups halfway through. When cooking is complete, the internal temperature of the chicken should reach at least 165°F (74°C). Remove the chicken from the oven. Discard the toothpicks and serve immediately.

544.	Crunchy Parmesan Pork Chops

Servings: 4   Cooking Time: 10 Minutes

Ingredients:

4 pork chops, boneless	1/4 tsp smoked paprika
2 tbsp olive oil	2 tbsp breadcrumbs
1/4 tsp pepper	1/4 cup parmesan cheese, grated
1/2 tsp garlic powder	
1 tsp dried parsley	

Directions:

Fit the Cuisinart oven with the rack in position In a shallow dish, mix breadcrumbs, paprika, parmesan cheese, garlic powder, parsley, and pepper. Brush pork chops with oil and coat with breadcrumb mixture. Place coated pork chops into the baking pan. Set to bake at 450 F for 15 minutes. After 5 minutes place the baking pan in the preheated oven. Serve and enjoy.

Nutrition Info: Calories 350 Fat 28.3 g Carbohydrates 3.1 g Sugar 0.3 g Protein 20.4 g Cholesterol 73 mg

---

545.	Meatballs(2)

Servings: 4   Cooking Time: 15 Minutes

Ingredients:

1 lb ground lamb	1 tbsp garlic, minced
1 tsp onion powder	1 tsp ground cumin
1 tsp ground coriander	Pepper
	Salt

Directions:

Fit the Cuisinart oven with the rack in position Add all ingredients into the mixing bowl and mix until well combined. Make small balls from the meat mixture and place them into the baking pan. Set to bake at 400 F for 20 minutes. After 5 minutes place the baking pan in the preheated oven. Serve and enjoy.

Nutrition Info: Calories 218 Fat 8.5 g Carbohydrates 1.4 g Sugar 0.2 g Protein 32.1 g Cholesterol 102 mg

---

546.	Sweet Marinaded Pork Chops

Servings: 3   Cooking Time: 15 Minutes

Ingredients:

3 pork chops, ½-inch thick	1 tbsp maple syrup
Salt and black pepper to taste to season	1 ½ tbsp minced garlic
	3 tbsp mustard

Directions:

In a bowl, add maple syrup, garlic, mustard, salt, and pepper; mix well. Add in the pork and toss to coat. Slide-out the basket and place the chops inside. Fit in the baking tray and cook in your Cuisinart at 350 F for 6 minutes on Air Fry function. Flip the chops with a spatula and cook further for 6 minutes. Once ready, remove them to a platter and serve with steamed asparagus.

547.	Air Fried Golden Wasabi Spam

Servings: 3   Cooking Time: 12 Minutes

Ingredients:

⅔ cup all-purpose flour	2 cups panko bread crumbs
2 large eggs	6 ½-inch-thick spam slices
1½ tablespoons wasabi paste	Cooking spray

Directions:

Spritz the air fryer basket with cooking spray. Pour the flour in a shallow plate. Whisk the eggs with wasabi in a large bowl. Pour the panko in a separate shallow plate. Dredge the spam slices in the flour first, then dunk in the egg mixture, and then roll the spam over the panko to coat well. Shake the excess off. Arrange the spam slices in the pan and spritz with cooking spray. Put the air fryer basket on the baking pan and slide into Rack Position 2, select Air Fry, set temperature to 400°F (205°C) and set time to 12 minutes. Flip the spam slices halfway through. When cooking is complete, the spam slices should be golden and crispy.   Serve immediately.

548.   Spicy Thai Beef Stir-fry

Servings: 4   Cooking Time: 9 Minutes

Ingredients:

1 pound sirloin steaks, thinly sliced	½ cup beef broth
2 tablespoons lime juice, divided	1½ cups broccoli florets
⅓ cup crunchy peanut butter	2 cloves garlic, sliced
1 tablespoon olive oil	1 to 2 red chile peppers, sliced

Directions:

Preparing the Ingredients. In a medium bowl, combine the steak with 1 tablespoon of the lime juice. Set aside.   Combine the peanut butter and beef broth in a small bowl and mix well. Drain the beef and add the juice from the bowl into the peanut butter mixture.   In a 6-inch metal bowl, combine the olive oil, steak, and broccoli.   Air Frying. Cook for 3 to 4 minutes or until the steak is almost cooked and the broccoli is crisp and tender, shaking the basket once during cooking time.   Add the garlic, chile peppers, and the peanut butter mixture and stir.   Cook for 3 to 5 minutes or until the sauce is bubbling and the broccoli is tender.   Serve over hot rice.

Nutrition Info:CALORIES: 387; FAT: 22G; PROTEIN:42G; FIBER:2G

549.   Chicken Thighs With Radish Slaw

Servings: 4   Cooking Time: 27 Minutes

Ingredients:

4 bone-in, skin-on chicken thighs	3 cups shredded cabbage
1½ teaspoon kosher salt, divided	½ small red onion, thinly sliced
1 tablespoon smoked paprika	4 large radishes, julienned
½ teaspoon granulated garlic	3 tablespoons red wine vinegar
½ teaspoon dried oregano	2 tablespoons olive oil
¼ teaspoon freshly ground black pepper	Cooking spray

Directions:

Salt the chicken thighs on both sides with 1 teaspoon of kosher salt. In a small bowl, combine the paprika, garlic, oregano, and black pepper. Sprinkle half this mixture over the skin sides of the thighs. Spritz the baking pan with cooking spray and place the thighs skin-side down in the pan. Sprinkle the remaining spice mixture over the other sides of the chicken pieces.   Slide the baking pan into Rack Position 2, select Roast, set temperature to 375°F (190°C), and set time to 27 minutes.   After 10 minutes, remove from the oven and turn over the chicken thighs. Return to the oven and continue cooking.   While the chicken cooks, place the cabbage, onion, and radishes in a large bowl. Sprinkle with the remaining kosher salt, vinegar, and olive oil. Toss to coat. After another 9 to 10 minutes, remove from the oven

and place the chicken thighs on a cutting board. Place the cabbage mixture in the pan and toss with the chicken fat and spices.   Spread the cabbage in an even layer on the pan and place the chicken on it, skin-side up. Return the pan to the oven and continue cooking. Roast for another 7 to 8 minutes. When cooking is complete, the cabbage is just becoming tender. Remove from the oven. Taste and adjust the seasoning if necessary. Serve.

550.   Lamb Kofta

Servings: 4   Cooking Time: 10 Minutes

Ingredients:

1 pound (454 g) ground lamb	1 teaspoon garlic powder
1 tablespoon ras el hanout (North African spice)	1 teaspoon cumin
½ teaspoon ground coriander	2 tablespoons mint, chopped
1 teaspoon onion powder	Salt and ground black pepper, to taste
	Special Equipment: 4 bamboo skewers

Directions:

Combine the ground lamb, ras el hanout, coriander, onion powder, garlic powder, cumin, mint, salt, and ground black pepper in a large bowl. Stir to mix well. Transfer the mixture into sausage molds and sit the bamboo skewers in the mixture. Refrigerate for 15 minutes.   Spritz the air fryer basket with cooking spray. Place the lamb skewers in the pan and spritz with cooking spray.   Put the air fryer basket on the baking pan and slide into Rack Position 2, select Air Fry, set temperature to 380°F (193°C) and set time to 10 minutes.   Flip the lamb skewers halfway through.   When cooking is complete, the lamb should be well browned.   Serve immediately.

551.   Chicken Schnitzel

Servings: 4   Cooking Time: 5 Minutes

Ingredients:

½ cup all-purpose flour	1 teaspoon lemon juice
1 teaspoon marjoram	1 teaspoon water
½ teaspoon thyme	1 cup bread crumbs
1 teaspoon dried parsley flakes	4 chicken tenders, pounded thin, cut in half lengthwise
½ teaspoon salt	Cooking spray
1 egg	

Directions:

Spritz the air fryer basket with cooking spray. Combine the flour, marjoram, thyme, parsley, and salt in a shallow dish. Stir to mix well.   Whisk the egg with lemon juice and water in a large bowl. Pour the bread crumbs in a separate shallow dish.   Roll the chicken halves in the flour mixture first, then in the egg mixture, and then roll over the bread crumbs to coat well. Shake the excess off.   Arrange the chicken halves in the basket and spritz with cooking spray on both sides.   Put the air fryer basket on the baking pan and slide into Rack Position 2, select Air Fry, set temperature to 390°F (199°C) and set time to 5 minutes.   Flip the halves halfway through.   When cooking is complete, the chicken halves should be golden brown and crispy.   Serve immediately.

552. Cheesy Chicken Fritters

Servings: 17 Fritters   Cooking Time: 20 Minutes

Ingredients:

Chicken Fritters:
½ tsp. salt
1/8 tsp. pepper
1 ½ tbsp. fresh dill
1 1/3 C. shredded mozzarella cheese
1/3 C. coconut flour
1/3 C. vegan mayo
2 eggs

1 ½ pounds chicken breasts
Garlic Dip:
1/8 tsp. pepper
¼ tsp. salt

½ tbsp. lemon juice
1 pressed garlic cloves
1/3 C. vegan mayo

Directions:
Preparing the Ingredients. Slice chicken breasts into 1/3" pieces and place in a bowl. Add all remaining fritter ingredients to the bowl and stir well. Cover and chill 2 hours or overnight.   Ensure your air fryer oven is preheated to 350 degrees. Spray basket with a bit of olive oil.   Air Frying. Add marinated chicken to the Cuisinart air fryer oven. Set temperature to 350°F, and set time to 20 minutes and cook 20 minutes, making sure to turn halfway through cooking process.   To make the dipping sauce, combine all the dip ingredients until smooth.
Nutrition Info: CALORIES: 467; FAT: 27G; PROTEIN:21G; SUGAR:3G

553. Turkey Burger Cutlets

Ingredients:

½ lb. minced turkey
½ cup breadcrumbs
A pinch of salt to taste
¼ tsp. ginger finely chopped
1 green chili finely chopped
1 tsp. lemon juice

1 tbsp. fresh coriander leaves. Chop them finely
¼ tsp. red chili powder
½ cup of boiled peas
¼ tsp. cumin powder
¼ tsp. dried mango powder

Directions:
Take a container and into it pour all the masalas, onions, green chilies, peas, coriander leaves, lemon juice, ginger and 1-2 tbsp. breadcrumbs. Add the minced turkey as well. Mix all the ingredients well. Mold the mixture into round Cutlets. Press them gently. Now roll them out carefully. Pre heat the Cuisinart oven at 250 Fahrenheit for 5 minutes. Open the basket of the Fryer and arrange the Cutlets in the basket. Close it carefully.   Keep the fryer at 150 degrees for around 10 or 12 minutes. In between the cooking process, turn the Cutlets over to get a uniform cook. Serve hot with mint sauce.

554. Baked Italian Lemon Chicken

Servings: 4   Cooking Time: 25 Minutes

Ingredients:

1 1/4 lbs chicken breasts, skinless and boneless
3 tbsp butter, melted
1 tsp Italian

1 tbsp fresh parsley, chopped
2 tbsp fresh lemon juice
1/4 cup water

seasoning
1 tbsp olive oil

Pepper
Salt

Directions:
Fit the Cuisinart oven with the rack in position Season chicken with Italian seasoning, pepper, and salt.   Heat oil in a pan over medium-high heat. Add chicken to the pan and cook for 3-5 minutes on each side.   Transfer chicken to a baking dish. In a small bowl, mix together butter, lemon juice, and water.   Pour butter mixture over chicken. Set to bake at 400 F for 30 minutes. After 5 minutes place the baking dish in the preheated oven. Garnish with parsley and serve.
Nutrition Info: Calories 382 Fat 23.1 g Carbohydrates 0.4 g Sugar 0.3 g Protein 41.2 g Cholesterol 150 mg

555. Honey & Garlic Chicken Thighs

Servings: 4   Cooking Time: 30 Minutes

Ingredients:

4 thighs, skin-on
3 tbsp honey
2 tbsp Dijon mustard

½ tbsp garlic powder
Salt and black pepper to taste

Directions:
In a bowl, mix honey, mustard, garlic, salt, and black pepper. Coat the thighs in the mixture and arrange them on the greased basket. Fit in the baking tray and cook for 16 minutes at 400 F on Air Fry function, turning once halfway through. Serve warm.

556. Chili Chicken Strips With Aioli

Servings: 4   Cooking Time: 20 Minutes

Ingredients:

1 lb chicken breasts, cut into strips
2 tbsp olive oil
1 cup breadcrumbs

½ tbsp garlic powder
½ tbsp chili powder
½ cup mayonnaise

Directions:
Preheat Cuisinart on AirFry function to 350 F. Mix breadcrumbs, garlic powder, and chili in a plate. Coat the strips in the breadcrumb mixture. Drizzle with olive oil.   Arrange the chicken strips on the basket and press Start. Cook for 12-14 minutes. To prepare the aioli: combine mayo with ground chili. Serve with the chicken strips.

557. Asian Pork Shoulder

Servings: 4   Cooking Time: 15 Minutes

Ingredients:

1 lb pork shoulder, boneless
1 tbsp wine
1 tbsp sugar
2 tbsp soy sauce

4 tbsp honey
1 tsp Chinese five-spice
2 tsp ginger, minced
2 tsp garlic, minced

Directions:
Fit the Cuisinart oven with the rack in position 2. Add all ingredients except pork into the large zip-lock bag and mix well.   Add pork and seal the bag and place it in the fridge overnight.   Remove pork from marinade and place in an air fryer basket then place an air fryer basket in baking pan.   Place a

baking pan on the oven rack. Set to air fry at 390 F for 15 minutes.   Serve and enjoy.
Nutrition Info: Calories 419 Fat 24.3 g Carbohydrates 22.1 g Sugar 20.5 g Protein 27.1 g Cholesterol 102 mg

558.   Beef & Veggie Spring Rolls

Servings: 10   Cooking Time: 12 Minutes
Ingredients:

2-ounce Asian rice noodles	1 cup fresh mixed vegetables
1 tablespoon sesame oil	1 teaspoon soy sauce
7-ounce ground beef	1 packet spring roll skins
1 small onion, chopped	2 tablespoons water
3 garlic cloves, crushed	Olive oil, as required

Directions:
Preparing the Ingredients. Soak the noodles in warm water till soft.   Drain and cut into small lengths. In a pan heat the oil and add the onion and garlic and sauté for about 4-5 minutes.   Add beef and cook for about 4-5 minutes.   Add vegetables and cook for about 5-7 minutes or till cooked through.   Stir in soy sauce and remove from the heat.   Immediately, stir in the noodles and keep aside till all the juices have been absorbed. Preheat the Cuisinart air fryer oven to 350 degrees F. and preheat the oven to 350 degrees F also. Place the spring rolls skin onto a smooth surface. Add a line of the filling diagonally across.   Fold the top point over the filling and then fold in both sides. On the final point, brush it with water before rolling to seal.   Brush the spring rolls with oil.   Air Frying. Arrange the rolls in batches in the Cuisinart air fryer oven and Cook for about 8 minutes. Repeat with remaining rolls.   Now, place spring rolls onto a baking sheet.   Bake for about 6 minutes per side

559.   Flavorful Sirloin Steak

Servings: 2   Cooking Time: 14 Minutes
Ingredients:

1 lb sirloin steaks	1/2 tsp onion powder
1/2 tsp garlic powder	1 tsp olive oil
1/4 tsp smoked paprika	Pepper
	Salt

Directions:
Fit the Cuisinart oven with the rack in position 2. Line the air fryer basket with parchment paper. Brush steak with olive oil and rub with garlic powder, onion powder, paprika, pepper, and salt.   Place the steak in the air fryer basket then places an air fryer basket in the baking pan.   Place a baking pan on the oven rack. Set to air fry at 400 F for 14 minutes.   Serve and enjoy.
Nutrition Info: Calories 447 Fat 16.5 g Carbohydrates 1.2 g Sugar 0.4 g Protein 69 g Cholesterol 203 mg

560.   Mexican Salsa Chicken

Servings: 6   Cooking Time: 30 Minutes
Ingredients:

4 chicken breasts, skinless & boneless	1/4 tsp garlic powder
1/4 tsp cumin	12 oz salsa
1 3/4 cups Mexican shredded cheese	1/4 tsp pepper
	1/4 tsp salt

Directions:
Fit the Cuisinart oven with the rack in position Place chicken breasts into the baking dish and season with cumin, garlic powder, pepper, and salt. Pour salsa over chicken breasts.   Sprinkle shredded cheese on top of chicken.   Set to bake at 375 F for 35 minutes. After 5 minutes place the baking dish in the preheated oven.   Serve and enjoy.
Nutrition Info: Calories 330 Fat 17.8 g Carbohydrates 6.1 g Sugar 1.8 g Protein 36.1 g Cholesterol 116 mg

561.   Pork Wellington

Servings: 6   Cooking Time: 30 Minutes
Ingredients:

1 ½ lb. pork tenderloin	1 tbsp. Dijon mustard
½ tsp salt	1 tbsp. olive oil
½ tsp pepper	1 tbsp. butter
1 tsp thyme	8 oz. mushrooms, chopped
1 sheet puff pastry	1 shallot, chopped
4 oz. prosciutto, sliced thin	1 egg, beaten

Directions:
Season tenderloin with salt, pepper, and thyme on all sides.   On parchment covered work surface, roll out pastry as long as the tenderloin and wide enough to cover it completely.   Lay the prosciutto across the pastry to cover it and spread with mustard. Melt butter and oil in a large skillet over high heat. Add mushrooms and shallot and cook 5-10 minutes, until golden brown. Remove from pan.   Add tenderloin to the skillet and brown on all sides. Spread mushrooms over mustard and add pork. Roll up to completely cover tenderloin. Use beaten egg to seal the edge.   Set oven to bake on 425°F for 35 minutes.   Line baking pan with parchment paper and place pork on it, seam side down. Brush top with remaining egg. After oven preheats 5 minutes, place pan in position 1 and cook 30 or until puffed and golden brown.   Remove from oven and let rest 5 minutes before slicing and serving.
Nutrition Info: Calories 457, Total Fat 25g, Saturated Fat 7g, Total Carbs 20g, Net Carbs 19g, Protein 38g, Sugar 1g, Fiber 1g, Sodium 627mg, Potassium 706mg, Phosphorus 409mg

562.   Cheesy Chicken Escallops

Servings: 4   Cooking Time: 10 Minutes
Ingredients:

4 skinless chicken breasts	1 ounce Parmesan cheese, grated
2 ½ oz panko breadcrumbs	6 sage leaves, chopped
1 ¼ ounces flour	2 beaten eggs

Directions:
Place the chicken breasts between a cling film, beat well using a rolling pin until a ½ inch thickness is achieved.   In a bowl, add Parmesan cheese, sage,

and breadcrumbs. Dredge the chicken into the seasoned flour and then into the eggs. Finally, coat in the breadcrumbs. Spray the chicken breasts with cooking spray and cook in your Cuisinart oven for 14-16 minutes at 350 F on Air Fry function.

---

563. Chicken Thighs In Waffles

Servings: 4   Cooking Time: 20 Minutes
Ingredients:

For the chicken:	Cooking spray
4 chicken thighs, skin on	For the waffles:
1 cup low-fat buttermilk	½ cup all-purpose flour
½ cup all-purpose flour	½ cup whole wheat pastry flour
½ teaspoon garlic powder	1 large egg, beaten
½ teaspoon mustard powder	1 cup low-fat buttermilk
1 teaspoon kosher salt	1 teaspoon baking powder
½ teaspoon freshly ground black pepper	2 tablespoons canola oil
¼ cup honey, for serving	½ teaspoon kosher salt
	1 tablespoon granulated sugar

Directions:
Combine the chicken thighs with buttermilk in a large bowl. Wrap the bowl in plastic and refrigerate to marinate for at least an hour.   Spritz the air fryer basket with cooking spray.   Combine the flour, mustard powder, garlic powder, salt, and black pepper in a shallow dish. Stir to mix well. Remove the thighs from the buttermilk and pat dry with paper towels. Sit the bowl of buttermilk aside. Dip the thighs in the flour mixture first, then into the buttermilk, and then into the flour mixture. Shake the excess off.   Arrange the thighs in the basket and spritz with cooking spray.   Put the air fryer basket on the baking pan and slide into Rack Position 2, select Air Fry, set temperature to 360°F (182°C) and set time to 20 minutes.   Flip the thighs halfway through.   When cooking is complete, an instant-read thermometer inserted in the thickest part of the chicken thighs should register at least 165°F (74°C).   Meanwhile, make the waffles: combine the ingredients for the waffles in a large bowl. Stir to mix well, then arrange the mixture in a waffle iron and cook until a golden and fragrant waffle forms.   Remove the waffles from the waffle iron and slice into 4 pieces. Remove the chicken thighs from the oven and allow to cool for 5 minutes.   Arrange each chicken thigh on each waffle piece and drizzle with 1 tablespoon of honey. Serve warm.

---

564. Ham And Eggs

Ingredients:

Bread slices (brown or white)	1 tsp sugar for every 2 slices
1 egg white for every 2 slices	½ lb. sliced ham

Directions:

Put two slices together and cut them along the diagonal. In a bowl, whisk the egg whites and add some sugar.   Dip the bread triangles into this mixture. Cook the chicken now. Pre heat the Cuisinart oven at 180° C for 4 minutes. Place the coated bread triangles in the fry basket and close it. Let them cook at the same temperature for another 20 minutes at least.   Halfway through the process, turn the triangles over so that you get a uniform cook. Top with ham and serve.

---

565. Garlic Venison With Red Chili Flakes

Ingredients:

1 lb. boneless venison cut into Oregano Fingers	2 tsp. oregano
2 cup dry breadcrumbs	2 tsp. garlic paste
	1 ½ tbsp. ginger-garlic paste
6 tbsp. corn flour	4 tbsp. lemon juice
4 eggs	2 tsp. salt
2 tsp. red chili flakes	1 tsp. red chili powder

Directions:
Mix all the ingredients for the marinade and put the venison Oregano Fingers inside and let it rest overnight.   Mix the breadcrumbs, oregano and red chili flakes well and place the marinated Oregano Fingers on this mixture. Cover it with plastic wrap and leave it till right before you serve to cook.   Pre heat the Cuisinart oven at 160 degrees Fahrenheit for 5 minutes. Place the Oregano Fingers in the fry basket and close it. Let them cook at the same temperature for another 15 minutes or so. Toss the Oregano Fingers well so that they are cooked uniformly. Drizzle the garlic paste and serve.

---

566. Meatballs(16)

Servings: 6   Cooking Time: 12 Minutes
Ingredients:

1 egg	3/4 cups almond meal
20 oz ground beef	
1/2 cup parmesan cheese, grated	2 tbsp basil, chopped
8 tbsp almond milk	2 tbsp parsley, chopped
6 garlic cloves, minced	1 tsp black pepper
	1 tsp salt

Directions:
Fit the Cuisinart oven with the rack in position Add all ingredients into the mixing bowl and mix until well combined.   Make small balls from the meat mixture and place it into the parchment-lined baking pan.   Set to bake at 350 F for 17 minutes. After 5 minutes place the baking pan in the preheated oven.   Serve and enjoy.
Nutrition Info: Calories 331 Fat 19 g Carbohydrates 5.3 g Sugar 1.3 g Protein 35.3 g Cholesterol 117 mg

---

567. Sweet Chicken Drumsticks

Servings: 2   Cooking Time: 20 Minutes + Marinating Time
Ingredients:

2 chicken drumsticks, skin removed
2 tbsp olive oil

2 tbsp honey
½ tbsp garlic, minced

Directions:
Add all the ingredients to a resealable bag; massage until well-coated. Allow the chicken to marinate for 30 minutes in the fridge. Preheat Cuisinart on Air Fry function to 390 F. Remove the chicken drumsticks from the fridge and add them to the greased basket. Fit in the baking tray and cook for 15 minutes, shaking once. Serve hot.

568. Turkey Grandma's Easy To Cook Wontons

Ingredients:

1 ½ cup all-purpose flour
½ tsp. salt
5 tbsp. water
2 cups minced turkey

2 tbsp. oil
2 tsp. ginger-garlic paste
2 tsp. soya sauce
2 tsp. vinegar

Directions:
Squeeze the dough and cover it with plastic wrap and set aside. Next, cook the ingredients for the filling and try to ensure that the turkey is covered well with the sauce. Roll the dough and place the filling in the center. Now, wrap the dough to cover the filling and pinch the edges together. Pre heat the Cuisinart oven at 200° F for 5 minutes. Place the wontons in the fry basket and close it. Let them cook at the same temperature for another 20 minutes. Recommended sides are chili sauce or ketchup.

569. Duck Poppers

Ingredients:

½ cup hung curd
1 tsp. lemon juice
1 tsp. red chili flakes
1 cup cubed duck

1 ½ tsp. garlic paste
Salt and pepper to taste
1 tsp. dry oregano
1 tsp. dry basil

Directions:
Add the ingredients into a separate bowl and mix them well to get a consistent mixture. Dip the duck pieces in the above mixture and leave them aside for some time. Pre heat the Cuisinart oven at 180° C for around 5 minutes. Place the coated duck pieces in the fry basket and close it properly. Let them cook at the same temperature for 20 more minutes. Keep turning them over in the basket so that they are cooked properly. Serve with tomato ketchup.

570. Rustic Pork Ribs

Servings: 4   Cooking Time: 15 Minutes

Ingredients:

1 rack of pork ribs
3 tablespoons dry red wine
1 tablespoon soy sauce
1/2 teaspoon dried thyme
1/2 teaspoon onion powder

1/2 teaspoon garlic powder
1/2 teaspoon ground black pepper
1 teaspoon smoke salt
1 tablespoon cornstarch
1/2 teaspoon olive oil

Directions:
Preparing the Ingredients. Begin by preheating your Cuisinart air fryer oven to 390 degrees F. Place all ingredients in a mixing bowl and let them marinate at least 1 hour. Air Frying. Cook the marinated ribs approximately 25 minutes at 390 degrees F. Serve hot.

571. Honey Bbq Lamb Chops

Servings: 6   Cooking Time: 10 Minutes

Ingredients:

Nonstick cooking spray
2 tbsp. tomato sauce
2 tbsp. honey
1 tsp garlic, crushed

1 tsp green chili, diced fine
12 lamb loin chops or cutlets

Directions:
Place baking pan in position 2 of the oven. Lightly spray the fryer basket with cooking spray. In a small bowl, whisk together tomato sauce, honey, garlic, and green chili. Heat the oven to broil on 400°F for 15 minutes. Brush both sides of lamb with sauce. Place in a single layer in the basket, you will need to cook them in batches. After the oven preheats for 5 minutes, place basket on the baking pan. Cook 6-7 minutes, turning chops over halfway through cooking time. Serve immediately.
Nutrition Info: Calories 372, Total Fat 6g, Saturated Fat 2g, Total Carbs 6g, Net Carbs 6g, Protein 17g, Sugar 6g, Fiber 0g, Sodium 91mg, Potassium 296mg, Phosphorus 161mg

572. Shrimp Paste Chicken

Servings: 2   Cooking Time: 30 Minutes

Ingredients:

6 chicken wings
½ tbsp sugar
2 tbsp cornflour
1 tbsp white wine

1 tbsp shrimp paste
1 tbsp grated ginger
½ tbsp olive oil

Directions:
In a bowl, mix shrimp paste, olive oil, ginger, white wine, and sugar. Cover the chicken wings with the prepared marinade and roll in the flour. Place the chicken in the greased baking dish and cook in your Cuisinart for 20 minutes at 350 F on Air Fry function. Serve.

573. Pork Wonton Wonderful

Servings: 3   Cooking Time: 25 Minutes

Ingredients:

8 wanton wrappers (Leasa brand works great, though any will do)
4 ounces of raw minced pork
1 medium-sized green apple
1 tablespoon of vegetable oil

1 cup of water, for wetting the wanton wrappers
½ tablespoon of oyster sauce
1 tablespoon of soy sauce
Large pinch of ground white pepper

Directions:
Preparing the Ingredients. Cover the basket of the Cuisinart air fryer oven with a lining of tin foil, leaving the edges uncovered to allow air to circulate

through the basket. Preheat the air fryer oven to 350 degrees.   In a small mixing bowl, combine the oyster sauce, soy sauce, and white pepper, then add in the minced pork and stir thoroughly. Cover and set in the fridge to marinate for at least 15 minutes.   Core the apple, and slice into small cubes – smaller than bite-sized chunks.   Add the apples to the marinating meat mixture, and combine thoroughly. Spread the wonton wrappers, and fill each with a large spoonful of the filling. Wrap the wontons into triangles, so that the wrappers fully cover the filling, and seal with a drop of the water. Coat each filled and wrapped wonton thoroughly with the vegetable oil, to help ensure a nice crispy fry. Place the wontons on the foil-lined air-fryer rack/basket. Place the Rack on the middle-shelf of the Cuisinart air fryer oven.   Air Frying. Set the Cuisinart air fryer oven timer to 25 minutes. Halfway through cooking time, shake the handle of the air fryer rack/basket vigorously to jostle the wontons and ensure even frying. After 25 minutes, when the Cuisinart air fryer oven shuts off, the wontons will be crispy golden-brown on the outside and juicy and delicious on the inside. Serve directly from the Oven rack/basket and enjoy while hot.

574.   Cheesy Bacon Chicken

Servings: 4   Cooking Time: 30 Minutes
Ingredients:

4 chicken breasts, sliced in half	8 bacon slices, cooked & chopped
1 cup cheddar cheese, shredded	Pepper
6 oz cream cheese	Salt

Directions:
Fit the Cuisinart oven with the rack in position Place season chicken with pepper and salt and place it into the greased baking dish.   Add cream cheese and bacon on top of chicken.   Sprinkle shredded cheddar cheese on top of chicken.   Set to bake at 400 F for 35 minutes. After 5 minutes place the baking dish in the preheated oven.   Serve and enjoy.
Nutrition Info: Calories 745 Fat 50.9 g Carbohydrates 2.1 g Sugar 0.2 g Protein 66.6 g Cholesterol 248 mg

575.   Garlic Chicken

Servings: 6   Cooking Time: 40 Minutes
Ingredients:

2 lbs chicken thighs, skinless and boneless	2 tbsp fresh parsley, chopped
10 garlic cloves, sliced	1 fresh lemon juice
2 tbsp olive oil	Pepper
	Salt

Directions:
Fit the Cuisinart oven with the rack in position Place chicken in baking pan and season with pepper and salt.   Sprinkle parsley and garlic over the chicken. Drizzle with oil and lemon juice.   Set to bake at 450 F for 45 minutes. After 5 minutes place the baking pan in the preheated oven.   Serve and enjoy.

Nutrition Info: Calories 337 Fat 16 g Carbohydrates 1.9 g Sugar 0.2 g Protein 44.2 g Cholesterol 135 mg

576.   Beef Meatballs With Zesty Marinara Sauce

Servings: 4   Cooking Time: 8 Minutes
Ingredients:

1 pound (454 g) lean ground sirloin beef	¼ teaspoon kosher salt
2 tablespoons seasoned bread crumbs	1 cup marinara sauce, for serving
1 large egg, beaten	Cooking spray

Directions:
Spritz the air fryer basket with cooking spray.   Mix all the ingredients, except for the marinara sauce, into a bowl until well blended. Shape the mixture into sixteen meatballs.   Arrange the meatballs in the prepared basket and mist with cooking spray. Put the air fryer basket on the baking pan and slide into Rack Position 2, select Air Fry, set temperature to 360°F (182°C) and set time to 8 minutes.   Flip the meatballs halfway through.   When cooking is complete, the meatballs should be well browned. Divide the meatballs among four plates and serve warm with the marinara sauce.

577.   Steak Seasoned Pork Chops

Servings: 4   Cooking Time: 12 Minutes
Ingredients:

1 lb pork chops, boneless	1 tsp steak seasoning blend
1 tbsp yellow mustard	2 tsp honey

Directions:
Fit the Cuisinart oven with the rack in position 2. Line the air fryer basket with parchment paper. In a small bowl, mix honey, mustard, and steak seasoning.   Brush pork chops with honey mixture and place in air fryer basket then place air fryer basket in baking pan.   Place a baking pan on the oven rack. Set to air fry at 350 F for 12 minutes. Serve and enjoy.
Nutrition Info: Calories 376 Fat 28.3 g Carbohydrates 3.1 g Sugar 2.9 g Protein 25.7 g Cholesterol 98 mg

578.   Easy Pork Chop Roast

Servings: 2   Cooking Time: 20 Minutes
Ingredients:

2 (10-ounce / 284-g) bone-in, center cut pork chops, 1-inch thick	2 teaspoons Worcestershire sauce
Cooking spray	Salt and ground black pepper, to taste

Directions:
Rub the Worcestershire sauce on both sides of pork chops.   Season with salt and pepper to taste. Spritz the air fryer basket with cooking spray and place the chops in the basket side by side.   Put the air fryer basket on the baking pan and slide into Rack Position 2, select Roast, set the temperature to 350°F (180°C) and set the time to 20 minutes. After 10 minutes, remove from the oven. Flip the

pork chops with tongs. Return to the oven and continue cooking. When cooking is complete, the pork should be well browned on both sides. Let rest for 5 minutes before serving.

579. Crispy Chicken Nuggets

Servings: 4   Cooking Time: 25 Minutes

Ingredients:

1 1/2 lbs chicken breast, boneless & cut into chunks	1/4 cup parmesan cheese, shredded
1/4 cup mayonnaise	1/2 tsp garlic powder
	1/4 tsp salt

Directions:
Fit the Cuisinart oven with the rack in position 2. In a bowl, mix mayonnaise, cheese, garlic powder, and salt. Add chicken and mix until well coated. Arrange coated chicken in the air fryer basket then place an air fryer basket in the baking pan. Place a baking pan on the oven rack. Set to air fry at 400 F for 25 minutes. Serve and enjoy.

Nutrition Info: Calories 270 Fat 10.4 g Carbohydrates 4 g Sugar 1 g Protein 38.1 g Cholesterol 117 mg

580. Gold Cutlets With Aloha Salsa

Servings: 4   Cooking Time: 7 Minutes

Ingredients:

2 eggs	Aloha Salsa:
2 tablespoons milk	1 cup fresh pineapple, chopped in small pieces
¼ cup all-purpose flour	
¼ cup panko bread crumbs	¼ cup red bell pepper, chopped
4 teaspoons sesame seeds	½ teaspoon ground cinnamon
1 pound (454 g) boneless, thin pork cutlets (½-inch thick)	1 teaspoon soy sauce
	¼ cup red onion, finely chopped
¼ cup cornstarch	
Salt and ground lemon pepper, to taste	⅛ teaspoon crushed red pepper
Cooking spray	⅛ teaspoon ground black pepper

Directions:
In a medium bowl, stir together all ingredients for salsa. Cover and refrigerate while cooking the pork. Beat together eggs and milk in a large bowl. In another bowl, mix the flour, panko, and sesame seeds. Pour the cornstarch in a shallow dish. Sprinkle pork cutlets with lemon pepper and salt. Dip pork cutlets in cornstarch, egg mixture, and then panko coating. Spritz both sides with cooking spray. Put the air fryer basket on the baking pan and slide into Rack Position 2, select Air Fry, set the temperature to 400°F (205°C) and set the time to 7 minutes. After 3 minutes, remove from the oven. Flip the cutlets with tongs. Return to the oven and continue cooking. When cooking is complete, the pork should be crispy and golden brown on both sides. Serve the fried cutlets with the Aloha salsa on the side.

581. Braised Chicken With Hot Peppers

Servings: 4   Cooking Time: 27 Minutes

Ingredients:

1½ teaspoon kosher salt, divided	4 bone-in, skin-on chicken thighs (about 1½ pounds / 680 g)
1 link sweet Italian sausage (about 4 ounces / 113 g), whole	
	1 tablespoon olive oil
8 ounces (227 g) miniature bell peppers, halved and deseeded	4 hot pickled cherry peppers, deseeded and quartered, along with 2 tablespoons pickling liquid from the jar
1 small onion, thinly sliced	
2 garlic cloves, minced	¼ cup chicken stock
	Cooking spray

Directions:
Salt the chicken thighs on both sides with 1 teaspoon of kosher salt. Spritz the baking pan with cooking spray and place the thighs skin-side down on the pan. Add the sausage. Slide the baking pan into Rack Position 2, select Roast, set temperature to 375°F (190°C), and set time to 27 minutes. While the chicken and sausage cook, place the bell peppers, onion, and garlic in a large bowl. Sprinkle with the remaining kosher salt and add the olive oil. Toss to coat. After 10 minutes, remove from the oven and flip the chicken thighs and sausage. Add the pepper mixture to the pan. Return the pan to the oven and continue cooking. After another 10 minutes, remove from the oven and add the pickled peppers, pickling liquid, and stock. Stir the pickled peppers into the peppers and onion. Return the pan to the oven and continue cooking. When cooking is complete, the peppers and onion should be soft and the chicken should read 165°F (74°C) on a meat thermometer. Remove from the oven. Slice the sausage into thin pieces and stir it into the pepper mixture. Spoon the peppers over four plates. Top with a chicken thigh.

582. Ricotta And Parsley Stuffed Turkey Breasts

Servings: 4   Cooking Time: 25 Minutes

Ingredients:

1 turkey breast, quartered	1 egg, beaten
1 cup Ricotta cheese	1 teaspoon paprika
1/4 cup fresh Italian parsley, chopped	Salt and ground black pepper, to taste
1 teaspoon garlic powder	Crushed tortilla chips
1/2 teaspoon cumin powder	1 ½ tablespoons extra-virgin olive oil

Directions:
Preparing the Ingredients. Firstly, flatten out each piece of turkey breast with a rolling pin. Prepare three mixing bowls. In a shallow bowl, combine Ricotta cheese with the parsley, garlic powder, and cumin powder. Place the Ricotta/parsley mixture in the middle of each piece. Repeat with the remaining pieces of the turkey breast and roll them up. In another shallow bowl, whisk the egg

together with paprika. In the third shallow bowl, combine the salt, pepper, and crushed tortilla chips. Dip each roll in the whisked egg, then, roll them over the tortilla chips mixture.   Transfer prepared rolls to the Oven rack/basket. Drizzle olive oil over all. Place the Rack on the middle-shelf of the Cuisinart air fryer oven.   Air Frying. Cook at 350 degrees F for 25 minutes, working in batches. Serve warm, garnished with some extra parsley, if desired.

583.   Meatballs(6)

Servings: 8   Cooking Time: 25 Minutes
Ingredients:

3 eggs	1/2 cup fresh parsley,
2 lbs ground beef	minced
2 tsp cumin	1 tsp cinnamon
5 garlic cloves,	2 tsp dried oregano
minced	1 tsp pepper
1 onion, grated	2 tsp salt
1 cup breadcrumbs	

Directions:
Fit the Cuisinart oven with the rack in position Add all ingredients into the large mixing bowl and mix until well combined.   Make small meatballs from mixture and place in baking pan.   Set to bake at 400 F for 30 minutes. After 5 minutes place the baking pan in the preheated oven.   Serve and enjoy.
Nutrition Info: Calories 302 Fat 9.7 g Carbohydrates 12.9 g Sugar 1.6 g Protein 38.8 g Cholesterol 163 mg

584.   Meatballs(10)

Servings: 6   Cooking Time: 20 Minutes
Ingredients:

2 lbs ground chicken	1 tsp Italian
1/2 cup parmesan	seasoning
cheese, grated	1 tsp garlic, minced
1 cup breadcrumbs	2 tbsp olive oil
1 egg, lightly beaten	Pepper
1 tbsp fresh parsley,	Salt
chopped	

Directions:
Fit the Cuisinart oven with the rack in position Add all ingredients into the bowl and mix until well combined.   Make small balls from meat mixture and place in baking pan.   Set to bake at 400 F for 25 minutes. After 5 minutes place the baking pan in the preheated oven.   Serve and enjoy.
Nutrition Info: Calories 436 Fat 19.4 g Carbohydrates 13.6 g Sugar 1.3 g Protein 49.5 g Cholesterol 168 mg

585.   Flavors Cheesy Chicken Breasts

Servings: 6   Cooking Time: 45 Minutes
Ingredients:

3 lbs chicken breasts,	1 tsp garlic powder
sliced in half	1 cup Greek yogurt
1/2 cup parmesan	1/2 tsp pepper
cheese, shredded	1/2 tsp salt

Directions:
Fit the Cuisinart oven with the rack in position Place chicken breasts into the greased baking dish.

Mix parmesan cheese, yogurt, garlic powder, pepper, and salt and pour over chicken.   Set to bake at 375 F for 50 minutes. After 5 minutes place the baking dish in the preheated oven.   Serve and enjoy.
Nutrition Info: Calories 482 Fat 19.1 g Carbohydrates 2.1 g Sugar 1.5 g Protein 71.5 g Cholesterol 209 mg

586.   Air Fried Crispy Venison

Servings: 4   Cooking Time: 10 Minutes
Ingredients:

2 eggs	½ teaspoon salt
¼ cup milk	1 pound (454 g)
1 cup whole wheat	venison backstrap,
flour	sliced
¼ teaspoon ground	Cooking spray
black pepper	

Directions:
Spritz the air fryer basket with cooking spray. Whisk the eggs with milk in a large bowl. Combine the flour with salt and ground black pepper in a shallow dish.   Dredge the venison in the flour first, then into the egg mixture. Shake the excess off and roll the venison back over the flour to coat well. Arrange the venison in the pan and spritz with cooking spray.   Put the air fryer basket on the baking pan and slide into Rack Position 2, select Air Fry, set temperature to 360ºF (182ºC) and set time to 10 minutes.   Flip the venison halfway through. When cooking is complete, the internal temperature of the venison should reach at least 145ºF (63ºC) for medium rare.   Serve immediately.

587.   Cheesy Chicken Casserole

Servings: 4   Cooking Time: 20 Minutes
Ingredients:

1 lb cooked chicken,	1/2 cup salsa
shredded	1/4 cup Greek yogurt
4 oz cream cheese,	1 cup cheddar cheese,
softened	shredded
4 cups cauliflower	1/8 tsp pepper
florets	1/2 tsp kosher salt

Directions:
Fit the Cuisinart oven with the rack in position Add cauliflower into the boiling water and cook until tender. Drain well.   In a mixing bowl, mix cauliflower, salsa, cream cheese, chicken, yogurt, pepper, and salt.   Pour cauliflower mixture into the greased casserole dish and top with shredded cheddar cheese.   Set to bake at 375 F for 25 minutes. After 5 minutes place the casserole dish in the preheated oven.   Serve and enjoy.
Nutrition Info: Calories 427 Fat 23.1 g Carbohydrates 9 g Sugar 4.1 g Protein 45.8 g Cholesterol 149 mg

588.   Crispy Lamb Chops

Servings: 5   Cooking Time: 15 Minutes
Ingredients:

10 lamb chop cutlets,	2 eggs
bone in & fat	¼ tsp salt
removed	¼ tsp pepper
1 cup bread crumbs	

1 tbsp. parmesan cheese, grated

Nonstick cooking spray

Directions:
In a shallow dish, combine breadcrumbs and parmesan. In a separate shallow dish, whisk eggs with salt and pepper. Place baking pan in position 2 of the oven. Lightly spray fryer basket with cooking spray. Dip chops first in egg mixture then in breadcrumbs to coat both sides. Place in single layer in the basket, these will need to be cooked in batches. Place basket on the baking pan and set oven to air fry on 350°F for 6 minutes. Cook chops turning them over halfway through cooking time. Repeat with remaining chops and serve.

Nutrition Info: Calories 233, Total Fat 9g, Saturated Fat 3g, Total Carbs 16g, Net Carbs 15g, Protein 22g, Sugar 1g, Fiber 1g, Sodium 386mg, Potassium 348mg, Phosphorus 240mg

589. Squab Cutlet

Ingredients:

2 lb. boneless squab cut into slices
1st Marinade:
3 tbsp. vinegar or lemon juice
2 or 3 tsp. paprika
1 tsp. black pepper
1 tsp. salt
3 tsp. ginger-garlic paste
2nd Marinade:
1 cup yogurt

4 tsp. tandoori masala
2 tbsp. dry fenugreek leaves
1 tsp. black salt
1 tsp. chat masala
1 tsp. garam masala powder
1 tsp. red chili powder
1 tsp. salt
3 drops of red color

Directions:
Make the first marinade and soak the cut squab in it for four hours. While this is happening, make the second marinade and soak the squab in it overnight to let the flavors blend. Pre heat the Cuisinart oven at 160 degrees Fahrenheit for 5 minutes. Place the Oregano Fingers in the fry basket and close it. Let them cook at the same temperature for another 15 minutes or so. Toss the Oregano Fingers well so that they are cooked uniformly. Serve them with mint sauce.

590. Meatloaf(1)

Servings: 4   Cooking Time: 20 Minutes
Ingredients:

1 lb ground pork
1 egg, lightly beaten
1 tbsp thyme, chopped
1/4 tsp garlic powder
4 tbsp breadcrumbs

1 onion, chopped
1/2 tsp Italian seasoning
Pepper
Salt

Directions:
Fit the Cuisinart oven with the rack in position Add all ingredients into the mixing bowl and mix until well combined. Pour meat mixture into the greased loaf pan. Set to bake at 375 F for 25 minutes. After 5 minutes place the loaf pan in the preheated oven. Serve and enjoy.

Nutrition Info: Calories 220 Fat 5.7 g Carbohydrates 8.2 g Sugar 1.8 g Protein 32.4 g Cholesterol 124 mg

591. Delicious Pork Belly

Servings: 6   Cooking Time: 55 Minutes
Ingredients:

3 lbs pork belly, cut into 2-inch cubes
3 green onions stalk, chopped
1/4 tsp pepper
1 tbsp sesame oil
2 tbsp brown sugar

1/4 cup rice vinegar
1/4 cup soy sauce
1 tsp red chili flakes
1 tsp garlic, minced
1/4 tsp salt

Directions:
Fit the Cuisinart oven with the rack in position Add all ingredients into the zip-lock bag, seal bag shake well and place in the refrigerator for 1 hour. Place marinated pork belly cubes into the parchment-lined baking pan. Set to bake at 400 F for 60 minutes. After 5 minutes place the baking pan in the preheated oven. Turn pork belly cubes after 30 minutes. Serve and enjoy.

Nutrition Info: Calories 362 Fat 32.3 g Carbohydrates 5.5 g Sugar 3.3 g Protein 10.4 g Cholesterol 51 mg

592. Mushroom In Bacon-wrapped Filets Mignons

Servings: 8   Cooking Time: 13 Minutes
Ingredients:

1 ounce (28 g) dried porcini mushrooms
½ teaspoon granulated white sugar
½ teaspoon salt
½ teaspoon ground white pepper

8 (4-ounce / 113-g) filets mignons or beef tenderloin steaks
8 thin-cut bacon strips

Directions:
Put the mushrooms, sugar, salt, and white pepper in a spice grinder and grind to combine. On a clean work surface, rub the filets mignons with the mushroom mixture, then wrap each filet with a bacon strip. Secure with toothpicks if necessary. Arrange the bacon-wrapped filets mignons in the basket, seam side down. Put the air fryer basket on the baking pan and slide into Rack Position 2, select Air Fry, set temperature to 400°F (205°C) and set time to 13 minutes. Flip the filets halfway through. When cooking is complete, the filets should be medium rare. Serve immediately.

593. Savory Pulled Pork With Cheddar & Bacon

Servings: 2   Cooking Time: 50 Minutes
Ingredients:

1 pork steak
1 tsp steak seasoning
Salt and black pepper to taste
5 thick bacon slices, chopped

1 cup grated Cheddar cheese
½ tbsp Worcestershire sauce
2 bread buns, halved

Directions:
Preheat Cuisinart on Bake function to 380 F. Place the pork steak in the baking pan and season with pepper, salt, and steak seasoning. Cook for 20-22 minutes, turning once. Remove the steak onto a

chopping board and using two forks, shred it into pieces. Return to the baking pan.   Place the bacon in a skillet over medium heat and cook for 5 minutes until crispy. Add the bacon to the pork pan and stir. Mix in Worcestershire sauce, cheddar cheese, salt, and pepper.   Place again the pan in the oven and cook for 4 minutes. Slide-out, stir with a spoon, and cook further for 1 minute. Spoon the meat into the halved buns and serve with tomato dip.

594.   Roast Duck

Servings: 6   Cooking Time: 1 Hour

Ingredients:

3 lb. duck	3 tbsp. soy sauce,
1 tsp salt	divided
3 tbsp. crushed red	3 tbsp. honey
pepper flakes	2 tbsp. rice vinegar

Directions:
Wash the duck and pat dry with paper towels. Place in an 8x11-inch baking dish.   In a small bowl, stir together salt and pepper flakes. Rub over the skin of the duck. Sprinkle 2 tablespoons soy sauce over duck. Cover and refrigerate 2 hours.   Place rack in position 1 and set oven to convection bake on 375°F for 5 minutes.   In a small bowl, whisk together honey, vinegar, and remaining soy sauce. Brush over duck.   Once the oven has preheated, place duck inside and cook 1 hour. Serve.
Nutrition Info: Calories 519, Total Fat 35g, Saturated Fat 11g, Total Carbs 11g, Net Carbs 10g, Protein 40g, Sugar 9g, Fiber 1g, Sodium 772mg, Potassium 652mg, Phosphorus 401mg

595.   Italian Veggie Chicken

Servings: 4   Cooking Time: 30 Minutes

Ingredients:

1 cup mozzarella	4 chicken breasts
cheese, shredded	1 cup cherry
6 bacon slices,	tomatoes, cut in half
cooked & chopped	1 zucchini, sliced
8 oz can artichoke	1 tbsp dried basil
hearts, sliced	1/4 tsp salt

Directions:
Fit the Cuisinart oven with the rack in position Place chicken breasts into the casserole dish and sprinkle with basil and salt.   Spread artichoke hearts, cherry tomatoes, and zucchini on top of chicken.   Sprinkle shredded cheese and bacon on top of vegetables.   Set to bake at 375 F for 35 minutes. After 5 minutes place the casserole dish in the preheated oven.   Serve and enjoy.
Nutrition Info: Calories 484 Fat 24.2 g Carbohydrates 6.9 g Sugar 2.5 g Protein 56.8 g Cholesterol 165 mg

596.   Fried Chicken Tenderloins

Servings: 4   Cooking Time: 15 Minutes

Ingredients:

8 chicken tenderloins	2 oz breadcrumbs
2 tbsp butter,	1 large egg, whisked
softened	

Directions:
Preheat Cuisinart on Air Fry function to 380 F. Combine butter and breadcrumbs in a bowl. Keep

mixing and stirring until the mixture gets crumbly. Dip the chicken in the egg, then in the crumb mix. Place in the greased basket and fit in the baking tray; cook for 10 minutes, flipping once until crispy. Set on Broil function for crispier taste. Serve.

597.   Mutton Fried Baked Pastry

Ingredients:

A small amount of	½ tsp cumin
ginger either grated	1 ½ cup all-purpose
or finely chopped	flour
1 or 2 green chilies	A pinch of salt to
that are finely	taste
chopped or mashed	Add as much water as
1 tsp coarsely crushed	required to make the
whole coriander	dough stiff and firm
1 dry red chili broken	For filling:
into pieces	2 cups minced
A small amount of	mutton
salt	¼ cup boiled peas
2 tbsp. unsalted	
butter	½ tsp dried mango
	powder
	½ tsp red chili power
	1-2 tbsp. coriander

Directions:
You will first need to make the outer covering. In a large bowl, add the flour, butter and enough water to knead it into dough that is stiff. Transfer this to a container and leave it to rest for five minutes. Place a pan on medium flame and add the oil. Roast the mustard seeds and once roasted, add the coriander seeds and the chopped dry red chilies. Add all the dry ingredients for the filling and mix the ingredients well. Add a little water and continue to stir the ingredients. Make small balls out of the dough and roll them out.   Cut the rolled-out dough into halves and apply a little water on the edges to help you fold the halves into a cone. Add the filling to the cone and close up the samosa. Pre-heat the Cuisinart oven for around 5 to 6 minutes at 300 Fahrenheit. Place all the samosas in the fry basket and close the basket properly. Keep the Cuisinart oven at 200 degrees for another 20 to 25 minutes. Around the halfway point, open the basket and turn the samosas over for uniform cooking. After this, fry at 250 degrees for around 10 minutes in order to give them the desired golden-brown color. Serve hot. Recommended sides are tamarind or mint sauce.

598.   Mustard Chicken Thighs

Servings: 4   Cooking Time: 50 Minutes

Ingredients:

1 1/2 lbs chicken	1/4 cup French
thighs, skinless and	mustard
boneless	1/4 cup maple syrup
2 tbsp Dijon mustard	1 tbsp olive oil

Directions:
Fit the Cuisinart oven with the rack in position   In a bowl, mix maple syrup, olive oil, Dijon mustard, and French mustard.   Add chicken to the bowl and coat well.   Arrange chicken in a baking dish. Set to bake at 375 F for 55 minutes. After 5 minutes

place the baking dish in the preheated oven. Serve and enjoy.

Nutrition Info: Calories 410 Fat 16.5 g Carbohydrates 13.6 g Sugar 11.8 g Protein 49.6 g Cholesterol 151 mg

---

599.   Herby Turkey Balls

Servings: 2   Cooking Time: 20 Minutes

Ingredients:

½ lb ground turkey
1 egg, beaten
1 cup breadcrumbs
1 tbsp dried thyme
½ tbsp dried parsley
Salt and black pepper to taste

Directions:

Preheat Cuisinart on AirFry function to 350 F. In a bowl, place ground turkey, thyme, parsley, salt, and pepper. Mix well and shape the mixture into balls. Dip in breadcrumbs, then in the egg, and finally in the breadcrumbs again. Place the nuggets in the basket and cook for 15 minutes.

---

600.   Caraway Crusted Beef Steaks

Servings: 4   Cooking Time: 10 Minutes

Ingredients:

2 teaspoons caraway seeds
2 teaspoons garlic powder
Sea salt and cayenne pepper, to taste
4 beef steaks
1 tablespoon melted butter
⅓ cup almond flour
2 eggs, beaten

Directions:

Add the beef steaks to a large bowl and toss with the caraway seeds, garlic powder, salt and pepper until well coated.   Stir together the melted butter and almond flour in a bowl. Whisk the eggs in a different bowl.   Dredge the seasoned steaks in the eggs, then dip in the almond and butter mixture. Arrange the coated steaks in the basket.   Put the air fryer basket on the baking pan and slide into Rack Position 2, select Air Fry, set temperature to 355°F (179°C) and set time to 10 minutes.   Flip the steaks once halfway through to ensure even cooking.   When cooking is complete, the internal temperature of the beef steaks should reach at least 145°F (63°C) on a meat thermometer.   Transfer the steaks to plates. Let cool for 5 minutes and serve hot.

---

601.   Ranch Pork Chops

Servings: 6   Cooking Time: 35 Minutes

Ingredients:

6 pork chops, boneless
1 tsp dried parsley
2 tbsp dry ranch mix
1/4 cup olive oil

Directions:

Fit the Cuisinart oven with the rack in position Place pork chops in baking dish.   Mix together remaining ingredients and pour over pork chops. Set to bake at 425 F for 40 minutes. After 5 minutes place the baking dish in the preheated oven. Serve and enjoy.

Nutrition Info: Calories 330 Fat 28.3 g Carbohydrates 0.4 g Sugar 0 g Protein 18 g Cholesterol 69 mg

---

602.   Meatballs(7)

Servings: 4   Cooking Time: 10 Minutes

Ingredients:

2 eggs
1 tsp sesame oil
1 tsp ginger, minced
1 tsp garlic, minced
1/2 cup breadcrumbs
1/3 tsp red chili pepper flakes
2 lbs ground pork
1 tbsp scallions, diced
1 tsp soy sauce
Pepper
Salt

Directions:

Fit the Cuisinart oven with the rack in position 2. Add all ingredients into the large bowl and mix until well combined.   Make small balls from meat mixture and place in the air fryer basket then place the air fryer basket in the baking pan.   Place a baking pan on the oven rack. Set to air fry at 400 F for 10 minutes.   Serve and enjoy.

Nutrition Info: Calories 423 Fat 12 g Carbohydrates 10.7 g Sugar 1.1 g Protein 64.1 g Cholesterol 247 mg

Meatless Recipes

603. Garlic Toast With Cheese

Ingredients:

2 tsp. of oregano seasoning
Some red chili flakes to sprinkle on top
Take some French bread and cut it into slices
1 tbsp. olive oil (Optional)

¾ cup grated cheese
2 tbsp. softened butter
4-5 flakes crushed garlic
A pinch of salt to taste
½ tsp. black pepper powder

Directions:

Take a clean and dry container. Place all the ingredients mentioned under the heading "Garlic Butter" into it and mix properly to obtain garlic butter. On each slice of the French bread, spread some of this garlic butter. Sprinkle some cheese on top of the layer of butter. Pour some oil if wanted. Sprinkle some chili flakes and some oregano. Pre heat the Cuisinart oven at 240 Fahrenheit for around 5 minutes. Open the fry basket and place the bread in it making sure that no two slices touch each other. Close the basket and continue to cook the bread at 160 degrees for another 10 minutes to toast the bread well.

604. Masala French Fries

Ingredients:

2 medium sized potatoes peeled and cut into thick pieces lengthwise
1 tbsp. olive oil
1 tsp. mixed herbs

1 tbsp. lemon juice
½ tsp. red chili flakes
A pinch of salt to taste

Directions:

Boil the potatoes and blanch them. Cut the potato into Oregano Fingers. Mix the ingredients for the marinade and add the potato Oregano Fingers to it making sure that they are coated well. Pre heat the Cuisinart oven for around 5 minutes at 300 Fahrenheit. Take out the basket of the fryer and place the potato Oregano Fingers in them. Close the basket. Now keep the fryer at 200 Fahrenheit for 20 or 25 minutes. In between the process, toss the fries twice or thrice so that they get cooked properly.

605. Gherkins Flat Cakes

Ingredients:

2 or 3 green chilies finely chopped
1 ½ tbsp. lemon juice
Salt and pepper to taste
2 tbsp. garam masala

2 cups sliced gherkins
3 tsp. ginger finely chopped
1-2 tbsp. fresh coriander leaves

Directions:

Mix the ingredients in a clean bowl and add water to it. Make sure that the paste is not too watery but is enough to apply on the gherkin. Pre heat the Cuisinart oven at 160 degrees Fahrenheit for 5

minutes. Place the French Cuisine Galettes in the fry basket and let them cook for another 25 minutes at the same temperature. Keep rolling them over to get a uniform cook. Serve either with mint sauce or ketchup.

606. Winter Vegetarian Frittata

Servings: 4   Cooking Time: 30 Minutes

Ingredients:

1 leek, peeled and thinly sliced into rings
2 cloves garlic, finely minced
3 medium-sized carrots, finely chopped
2 tablespoons olive oil

6 large-sized eggs
Sea salt and ground black pepper, to taste
1/2 teaspoon dried marjoram, finely minced
1/2 cup yellow cheese of choice

Directions:

Preparing the Ingredients. Sauté the leek, garlic, and carrot in hot olive oil until they are tender and fragrant; reserve. In the meantime, preheat your Cuisinart air fryer oven to 330 degrees F. In a bowl, whisk the eggs along with the salt, ground black pepper, and marjoram. Then, grease the inside of your baking dish with a nonstick cooking spray. Pour the whisked eggs into the baking dish. Stir in the sautéed carrot mixture. Top with the cheese shreds. Air Frying. Place the baking dish in the Cuisinart air fryer oven cooking basket. Cook about 30 minutes and serve warm

607. French Bean Toast

Ingredients:

1 tsp. sugar for every 2 slices
Crushed cornflakes
2 cups baked beans

Bread slices (brown or white)
1 egg white for every 2 slices

Directions:

Put two slices together and cut them along the diagonal. In a bowl, whisk the egg whites and add some sugar. Dip the bread triangles into this mixture and then coat them with the crushed cornflakes. Pre heat the Cuisinart oven at 180° C for 4 minutes. Place the coated bread triangles in the fry basket and close it. Let them cook at the same temperature for another 20 minutes at least. Halfway through the process, turn the triangles over so that you get a uniform cook. Top with baked beans and serve.

608. Cauliflower Bites

Servings: 4   Cooking Time: 18 Minutes

Ingredients:

1 Head Cauliflower, cut into small florets
Pinch of Salt and Pepper

Tsps Garlic Powder
1 Tbsp Butter, melted
1/2 Cup Chili Sauce
Olive Oil

Directions:

Preparing the Ingredients. Place cauliflower into a bowl and pour oil over florets to lightly cover. Season florets with salt, pepper, and the garlic powder and toss well. Air Frying. Place florets into the Cuisinart air fryer oven at 350 degrees for 14 minutes. Remove cauliflower from the Air fryer oven. Combine the melted butter with the chili sauce Pour over the florets so that they are well coated. Return to the Cuisinart air fryer oven and cook for additional 3 to 4 minutes Serve as a side or with ranch or cheese dip as a snack.

609. Potato Spicy Lemon Kebab

Ingredients:

2 tsp. coriander powder	1-2 tbsp. mint (finely chopped)
1 ½ tbsp. chopped coriander	2 cups sliced potato
½ tsp. dried mango powder	1-2 green chilies chopped finely
1 cup dry breadcrumbs	¼ tsp. red chili powder
¼ tsp. black salt	A pinch of salt to taste
1-2 tbsp. all-purpose flour for coating purposes	½ tsp. roasted cumin powder
Half inch ginger grated or one and a half tsp. of ginger-garlic paste	1 onion that has been finely chopped
	½ cup milk

Directions:
Take the potato slices and add the grated ginger and the cut green chilies. Grind this mixture until it becomes a thick paste. Keep adding water as and when required. Now add the onions, mint, the breadcrumbs and all the various masalas required. Mix this well until you get a soft dough. Now take small balls of this mixture (about the size of a lemon) and mold them into the shape of flat and round kebabs. Here is where the milk comes into play. Pour a very small amount of milk onto each kebab to wet it. Now roll the kebab in the dry breadcrumbs. Pre heat the Cuisinart oven for 5 minutes at 300 Fahrenheit. Take out the basket. Arrange the kebabs in the basket leaving gaps between them so that no two kebabs are touching each other. Keep the fryer at 340 Fahrenheit for around half an hour. Half way through the cooking process, turn the kebabs over so that they can be cooked properly. Recommended sides for this dish are mint sauce, tomato ketchup or yoghurt sauce.

610. Simple Ricotta & Spinach Balls

Servings: 4   Cooking Time: 20 Minutes

Ingredients:

14 oz store-bought crescent dough	1 cup steamed spinach
1 cup crumbled ricotta cheese	¼ tsp garlic powder
	1 tsp chopped oregano
	¼ tsp salt

Directions:

Preheat Cuisinart on Air Fry function to 350 F. Roll the dough onto a lightly floured flat surface. Combine the ricotta cheese, spinach, oregano, salt, and garlic powder together in a bowl. Cut the dough into 4 equal pieces. Divide the spinach/feta mixture between the dough pieces. Make sure to place the filling in the center. Fold the dough and secure with a fork. Place onto a lined baking dish and then in your Cuisinart oven. Cook for 12 minutes until lightly browned. Serve.

611. Mushrooms Stuffed With Tempeh & Cheddar

Servings: 4   Cooking Time: 20 Minutes
Ingredients:

14 small button mushrooms	4 slices tempeh, chopped
1 garlic clove, minced	¼ cup cheddar cheese, grated
Salt and black pepper to taste	
1 tbsp olive oil	1 tbsp fresh parsley, chopped

Directions:
Preheat on AirFry function to 390 F. In a bowl, mix the oil, tempeh, cheddar cheese, parsley, salt, pepper, and garlic. Cut the mushroom stalks off and fill them with the tempeh mixture. Place the stuffed mushrooms in the basket and press Start. Cook at 390 F for 8 minutes. Once golden and crispy, plate them and serve with a green salad.

612. Veggie Delight

Servings: 2   Cooking Time: 30 Minutes
Ingredients:

1 parsnip, sliced in a 2-inch thickness	1 cup celery, chopped
1 cup chopped butternut squash	1 tbsp fresh thyme, chopped
2 small red onions, cut in wedges	Salt and black pepper to taste
	2 tsp olive oil

Directions:
Preheat Cuisinart on AirFry function to 350 F. In a bowl, add turnip, squash, red onions, celery, thyme, pepper, salt, and olive oil and mix well. Add the veggies to the frying basket and press Start. Cook for 16 minutes, tossing once halfway through. Serve warm.

613. Cabbage Fritters(1)

Ingredients:

1-2 tbsp. fresh coriander leaves	2 tbsp. garam masala
2 or 3 green chilies finely chopped	2 cups cabbage
1 ½ tbsp. lemon juice	1 ½ cup coarsely crushed peanuts
Salt and pepper to taste	3 tsp. ginger finely chopped

Directions:
Mix the ingredients in a clean bowl. Mold this mixture into round and flat fritters. Wet the fritters slightly with water. Coat each fritter with the crushed peanuts. Pre heat the Cuisinart oven at 160 degrees Fahrenheit for 5 minutes. Place the fritters in the fry basket and let them cook for another 25 minutes at the same temperature. Keep

rolling them over to get a uniform cook. Serve either with mint sauce or ketchup.

614. Fenugreek French Cuisine Galette

Ingredients:

2 or 3 green chilies finely chopped	2 medium potatoes boiled and mashed
1 ½ tbsp. lemon juice	3 tsp. ginger finely chopped
Salt and pepper to taste	1-2 tbsp. fresh coriander leaves
2 cups fenugreek	

Directions:
Mix the ingredients in a clean bowl. Mold this mixture into round and flat French Cuisine Galettes. Wet the French Cuisine Galettes slightly with water. Pre heat the Cuisinart oven at 160 degrees Fahrenheit for 5 minutes. Place the French Cuisine Galettes in the fry basket and let them cook for another 25 minutes at the same temperature. Keep rolling them over to get a uniform cook. Serve either with mint sauce or ketchup.

615. Stuffed Eggplant Baskets

Ingredients:

1 tsp. cumin powder	½ tsp. pepper powder
Salt and pepper to taste	1 green chili finely chopped
3 tbsp. grated cheese	
1 tsp. red chili flakes	1 ½ tbsp. chopped coriander leaves
½ tsp. oregano	
6 eggplants	1 tsp. fenugreek
½ tsp. salt	1 tsp. dried mango powder
1 medium onion finely chopped	
	½ tsp. basil
	½ tsp. parsley

Directions:
Take all the ingredients under the heading "Filling" and mix them together in a bowl. Remove the stem of the eggplant. Cut off the caps. Remove a little of the flesh as well. Sprinkle some salt and pepper on the inside of the capsicums. Leave them aside for some time. Now fill the eggplant with the filling prepared but leave a small space at the top. Sprinkle grated cheese and also add the seasoning. Pre heat the Cuisinart oven at 140 degrees Fahrenheit for 5 minutes. Put the capsicums in the fry basket and close it. Let them cook at the same temperature for another 20 minutes. Turn them over in between to prevent over cooking.

616. Roasted Vegetable Mélange With Herbs

Servings: 4   Cooking Time: 16 Minutes

Ingredients:

1 (8-ounce / 227-g) package sliced mushrooms	1 tablespoon olive oil
	½ teaspoon dried basil
1 yellow summer squash, sliced	½ teaspoon dried thyme
1 red bell pepper, sliced	
3 cloves garlic, sliced	½ teaspoon dried tarragon

Directions:
Toss the mushrooms, squash, and bell pepper with the garlic and olive oil in a large bowl until well coated. Mix in the basil, thyme, and tarragon and toss again. Spread the vegetables evenly in the air fryer basket. Put the air fryer basket on the baking pan and slide into Rack Position 2, select Roast, set temperature to 350°F (180°C), and set time to 16 minutes. When cooking is complete, the vegetables should be fork-tender. Remove from the oven and cool for 5 minutes before serving.

617. Veggie Gratin

Servings: 4   Cooking Time: 30 Minutes

Ingredients:

1 cup eggplants, cubed	4 pimiento-stuffed olives, sliced
¼ cup red peppers, chopped	1 tsp capers
¼ cup green peppers, chopped	¼ tsp dried basil
¼ cup onions, chopped	¼ tsp dried marjoram
⅓ cup tomatoes, chopped	Salt and black pepper to taste
1 garlic clove, minced	¼ cup mozzarella cheese, grated
	1 tbsp breadcrumbs

Directions:
In a bowl, add eggplants, green and red peppers, onions, tomatoes, olives, garlic, basil, marjoram, capers, salt, and black pepper. Lightly grease the tray with cooking spray. Ladle the eggplant mixture into the baking tray and level it using the vessel. Sprinkle mozzarella cheese on top and cover with breadcrumbs. Place the dish in the Cuisinart oven and press Start. Cook for 20 minutes on Bake function at 320 F. Serve.

618. Chickpea Fritters

Servings: 4   Cooking Time: 10 Minutes

Ingredients:

Nonstick cooking spray	¼ tsp salt
1 cup chickpeas, cooked	¼ tsp pepper
	¼ tsp turmeric
1 onion, chopped	¼ tsp coriander

Directions:
Place the baking pan in position 2. Lightly spray the fryer basket with cooking spray. Add the onion to a food processor and pulse until finely diced. Add remaining ingredients and pulse until combined but not pureed. Form the mixture into 8 patties and place them in the fryer basket, these may need to be cooked in two batches. Place the basket in the oven and set to air fry on 350°F for 10 minutes. Cook fritters until golden brown and crispy, turning over halfway through cooking time. Serve with your favorite dipping sauce.
Nutrition Info: Calories 101, Total Fat 1g, Saturated Fat 0g, Total Carbs 14g, Net Carbs 10g,

Protein 4g, Sugar 3g, Fiber 4g, Sodium 149mg, Potassium 159mg, Phosphorus 77mg

619. Garlicky Vermouth Mushrooms

Servings: 4   Cooking Time: 20 Minutes

Ingredients:

2 lb portobello mushrooms, sliced	1 tbsp olive oil
2 tbsp vermouth	2 tsp herbs
½ tsp garlic powder	1 tbsp duck fat, softened

Directions:
In a bowl, mix the duck fat, garlic powder, and herbs. Rub the mushrooms with the mixture and place them in a baking tray. Drizzle with vermouth and cook in your Cuisinart for 15 minutes on Bake function at 350 F. Serve.

620. Sago French Cuisine Galette

Ingredients:

2 or 3 green chilies finely chopped	1 ½ cup coarsely crushed peanuts
1 ½ tbsp. lemon juice	3 tsp. ginger finely chopped
Salt and pepper to taste	1-2 tbsp. fresh coriander leaves
2 cup sago soaked	

Directions:
Wash the soaked sago and mix it with the rest of the ingredients in a clean bowl.   Mold this mixture into round and flat French Cuisine Galettes.   Wet the French Cuisine Galettes slightly with water. Coat each French Cuisine Galette with the crushed peanuts.   Pre heat the Cuisinart oven at 160 degrees Fahrenheit for 5 minutes. Place the French Cuisine Galettes in the fry basket and let them cook for another 25 minutes at the same temperature. Keep rolling them over to get a uniform cook. Serve either with mint sauce or ketchup.

621. Cheese Stuffed Green Peppers With Tomato Sauce

Servings: 4   Cooking Time: 35 Minutes

Ingredients:

2 cans green chili peppers	2 tbsp all-purpose flour
1 cup cheddar cheese, shredded	2 large eggs, beaten
1 cup Monterey Jack cheese, shredded	½ cup milk
	1 can tomato sauce

Directions:
Preheat Cuisinart on AirFry function to 380 F. Spray a baking dish with cooking spray. Take half of the chilies and arrange them in the baking dish. Top with half of the cheese and cover with the remaining chilies. In a medium bowl, combine eggs, milk, and flour and pour over the chilies.   Press Start and cook for 20 minutes. Remove the chilies and pour the tomato sauce over them; cook for 15 more minutes. Top with the remaining cheese and serve.

622. Cauliflower French Cuisine Galette

Ingredients:

3 tsp. ginger finely chopped	Salt and pepper to taste
1-2 tbsp. fresh coriander leaves	2 tbsp. garam masala
2 or 3 green chilies finely chopped	2 cups cauliflower
1 ½ tbsp. lemon juice	1 ½ cup coarsely crushed peanuts

Directions:
Mix the ingredients in a clean bowl.   Mold this mixture into round and flat French Cuisine Galettes. Wet the French Cuisine Galettes slightly with water. Coat each French Cuisine Galette with the crushed peanuts.   Pre heat the Cuisinart oven at 160 degrees Fahrenheit for 5 minutes. Place the French Cuisine Galettes in the fry basket and let them cook for another 25 minutes at the same temperature. Keep rolling them over to get a uniform cook. Serve either with mint sauce or ketchup.

623. Cheese With Spinach Enchiladas

Servings: 4   Cooking Time: 20 Minutes

Ingredients:

8 corn tortillas, warm	1 garlic clove, minced
2 cups mozzarella cheese, shredded	½ cup sliced onions
1 cup ricotta cheese	½ cup sour cream
1 cup spinach, torn	1 tbsp butter
	1 can enchilada sauce

Directions:
Warm olive oil In a saucepan over medium heat and sauté garlic and onion for 3 minutes until soft. Stir in the spinach and cook for 5 more minutes until wilted. Remove from the heat and stir in the ricotta cheese, sour cream, and half of the mozzarella cheese.   Spoon ¼ cup of the spinach mixture in the middle of each tortilla. Roll up and place seam side down in a baking dish. Pour the enchilada sauce over the tortillas and sprinkle with the remaining cheese. Cook in your Cuisinart for 15 minutes at 380 F on Air Fry function.

624. Banana Best Homemade Croquette

Ingredients:

2 tsp. garam masala	3 onions chopped
4 tbsp. chopped coriander	5 green chilies-roughly chopped
3 tbsp. cream	
3 tbsp. chopped capsicum	1 ½ tbsp. ginger paste
3 eggs	1 ½ tsp. garlic paste
2 ½ tbsp. white sesame seeds	1 ½ tsp. salt
2 cups sliced banana	3 tsp. lemon juice

Directions:
Grind the ingredients except for the egg and form a smooth paste. Coat the banana in the paste. Now, beat the eggs and add a little salt to it.   Dip the coated bananas in the egg mixture and then transfer to the sesame seeds and coat the vegetables well. Place the vegetables on a stick.   Pre heat the Cuisinart oven at 160 degrees Fahrenheit for around 5 minutes. Place the sticks in the basket and let them

cook for another 25 minutes at the same temperature. Turn the sticks over in between the cooking process to get a uniform cook.

625.   Classic Baked Potatoes

Servings: 4   Cooking Time: 30 Minutes

Ingredients:

2 garlic cloves, minced	1 lb potatoes
Salt and black pepper to taste	1 tsp rosemary
	1 tsp butter, melted

Directions:

Preheat Cuisinart oven to 360 F on AirFry function. Prick the potatoes with a fork. Place into frying basket and press Start. Cook for 25 minutes. Cut the potatoes in half and top with butter and rosemary. Season with salt and pepper and serve.

626.   Coconut Vegan Fries

Servings: 2   Cooking Time: 20 Minutes

Ingredients:

2 potatoes, spiralized	Salt and black pepper to taste
1 tbsp tomato ketchup	2 tbsp coconut oil
2 tbsp olive oil	

Directions:

In a bowl, mix olive oil, coconut oil, salt, and pepper. Add in the potatoes and toss to coat. Place them in the basket and fit in the baking tray; cook for 15 minutes on Air Fry function at 360 F. Serve with ketchup and enjoy!

627.   Baked Macaroni Pasta

Ingredients:

	For tossing pasta:
½ tsp. basil	
2 tbsp. olive oil	1 ½ tbsp. olive oil
2 tbsp. all-purpose flour	½ cup carrot small pieces
2 cups of milk	Salt and pepper to taste
1 tsp. dried oregano	
1 cup pasta	½ tsp. oregano
7 cups of boiling water	½ tsp. dried basil
1 ½ tbsp. olive oil	½ tsp. dried parsley
A pinch of salt	Salt and pepper to taste

Directions:

Boil the pasta and sieve it when done. You will need to toss the pasta in the ingredients mentioned above and set aside.   For the sauce, add the ingredients to a pan and bring the ingredients to a boil. Stir the sauce and continue to simmer to make a thicker sauce. Add the pasta to the sauce and transfer this into a glass bowl garnished with cheese.   Pre heat the Cuisinart oven at 160 degrees for 5 minutes. Place the bowl in the basket and close it. Let it continue to cook at the same temperature for 10 minutes more. Keep stirring the pasta in between.

628.   Crispy Eggplant Slices With Parsley

Servings: 4   Cooking Time: 12 Minutes

Ingredients:

1 cup flour	2 eggplants, sliced
4 eggs	2 garlic cloves, sliced
Salt, to taste	2 tablespoons chopped parsley
2 cups bread crumbs	Cooking spray
1 teaspoon Italian seasoning	

Directions:

Spritz the air fryer basket with cooking spray. Set aside.   On a plate, place the flour. In a shallow bowl, whisk the eggs with salt. In another shallow bowl, combine the bread crumbs and Italian seasoning.   Dredge the eggplant slices, one at a time, in the flour, then in the whisked eggs, finally in the bread crumb mixture to coat well.   Lay the coated eggplant slices in the basket.   Put the air fryer basket on the baking pan and slide into Rack Position 2, select Air Fry, set temperature to 390°F (199°C), and set time to 12 minutes.   Flip the eggplant slices halfway through the cooking time. When cooking is complete, the eggplant slices should be golden brown and crispy. Transfer the eggplant slices to a plate and sprinkle the garlic and parsley on top before serving.

629.   Honey-glazed Baby Carrots

Servings: 4   Cooking Time: 12 Minutes

Ingredients:

1 pound (454 g) baby carrots	1 tablespoon honey
2 tablespoons olive oil	1 teaspoon dried dill
	Salt and black pepper, to taste

Directions:

Place the carrots in a large bowl. Add the olive oil, honey, dill, salt, and pepper and toss to coat well. Transfer the carrots to the air fryer basket.   Put the air fryer basket on the baking pan and slide into Rack Position 2, select Roast, set temperature to 350°F (180°C), and set time to 12 minutes.   Stir the carrots once during cooking.   When cooking is complete, the carrots should be crisp-tender. Remove from the oven and serve warm.

630.   Buffalo Cauliflower

Servings: 2   Cooking Time: 15 Minutes

Ingredients:

Cauliflower:	Buffalo Coating:
1 C. panko breadcrumbs	¼ C. Vegan Buffalo sauce
1 tsp. salt	¼ C. melted vegan butter
4 C. cauliflower florets	

Directions:

Preparing the Ingredients. Melt butter in microwave and whisk in buffalo sauce.   Dip each cauliflower floret into buffalo mixture, ensuring it gets coated well. Hold over a bowl till floret is done dripping. Mix breadcrumbs with salt.   Air Frying. Dredge dipped florets into breadcrumbs and place into the air fryer oven. Set the temperature to 350°F, and set time to 15 minutes.   When slightly browned, they are ready to eat!   Serve with your favorite keto dipping sauce!

Nutrition Info:CALORIES: 194; FAT: 17G; PROTEIN:10G; SUGAR:

631. Veggie & Garlic Bake

Servings: 4   Cooking Time: 20 Minutes

Ingredients:

1 large red onion, cut into rings	1 lb turnips, sliced
1 large zucchini, sliced	2 cloves garlic, crushed
Salt and black pepper to taste	1 bay leaf, cut in 6 pieces
	1 tbsp olive oil

Directions:

Place turnips, onion, and zucchini in a bowl. Toss with olive oil and season with salt and pepper. Preheat Cuisinart on AirFry function to 330 F. Place the veggies into a baking pan.   Slip the bay leaves in the different parts of the slices and tuck the garlic cloves in between the slices. Press Start and cook for 15 minutes. Serve warm with as a side to a meat dish or salad.

632. Cheesy Rice And Olives Stuffed Peppers

Servings: 4   Cooking Time: 16 To 17 Minutes

Ingredients:

4 red bell peppers, tops sliced off	¾ cup tomato sauce
2 cups cooked rice	1 tablespoon Greek seasoning
1 cup crumbled feta cheese	Salt and black pepper, to taste
1 onion, chopped	2 tablespoons chopped fresh dill, for serving
¼ cup sliced kalamata olives	

Directions:

Microwave the red bell peppers for 1 to 2 minutes until tender.   When ready, transfer the red bell peppers to a plate to cool.   Mix the cooked rice, feta cheese, onion, kalamata olives, tomato sauce, Greek seasoning, salt, and pepper in a medium bowl and stir until well combined.   Divide the rice mixture among the red bell peppers and transfer to a greased baking pan.   Slide the baking pan into Rack Position 1, select Convection Bake, set temperature to 360°F (182°C) and set time to 15 minutes.   When cooking is complete, the rice should be heated through and the vegetables should be soft.   Remove from the oven and serve with the dill sprinkled on top.

633. Rosemary Butternut Squash Roast

Servings: 2   Cooking Time: 30 Minutes

Ingredients:

1 butternut squash	2 tbsp maple syrup
1 tbsp dried rosemary	Salt to taste

Directions:

Place the squash on a cutting board and peel. Cut in half and remove the seeds and pulp. Slice into wedges and season with salt. Preheat Cuisinart on Air Fry function to 350 F. Spray the wedges with cooking spray and sprinkle with rosemary. Place the wedges in the basket without overlapping and fit in the baking tray. Cook for 20 minutes, flipping once halfway through. Serve with maple syrup and goat cheese.

634. Cabbage Flat Cakes

Ingredients:

2 or 3 green chilies finely chopped	2 cups halved cabbage leaves
1 ½ tbsp. lemon juice	3 tsp. ginger finely chopped
Salt and pepper to taste	1-2 tbsp. fresh coriander leaves
2 tbsp. garam masala	

Directions:

Mix the ingredients in a clean bowl and add water to it. Make sure that the paste is not too watery but is enough to apply on the cabbage.   Pre heat the Cuisinart oven at 160 degrees Fahrenheit for 5 minutes. Place the French Cuisine Galettes in the fry basket and let them cook for another 25 minutes at the same temperature. Keep rolling them over to get a uniform cook. Serve either with mint sauce or ketchup.

635. Roasted Asparagus With Eggs And Tomatoes

Servings: 4   Cooking Time: 12 Minutes

Ingredients:

2 pounds (907 g) asparagus, trimmed	3 tablespoons extra-virgin olive oil, divided
1 teaspoon kosher salt, divided	4 large eggs
1 pint cherry tomatoes	¼ teaspoon freshly ground black pepper

Directions:

Put the asparagus in the baking pan and drizzle with 2 tablespoons of olive oil, tossing to coat. Season with ½ teaspoon of kosher salt.   Slide the baking pan into Rack Position 2, select Roast, set temperature to 375°F (190°C), and set time to 12 minutes.   Meanwhile, toss the cherry tomatoes with the remaining 1 tablespoon of olive oil in a medium bowl until well coated.   After 6 minutes, remove the pan and toss the asparagus. Evenly spread the asparagus in the middle of the pan. Add the tomatoes around the perimeter of the pan. Return the pan to the oven and continue cooking. After 2 minutes, remove from the oven.   Carefully crack the eggs, one at a time, over the asparagus, spacing them out. Season with the remaining ½ teaspoon of kosher salt and the pepper. Return the pan to the oven and continue cooking. Cook for an additional 3 to 7 minutes, or until the eggs are cooked to your desired doneness.   When done, divide the asparagus and eggs among four plates. Top each plate evenly with the tomatoes and serve.

636. Garlicky Veggie Bake

Servings: 3   Cooking Time: 25 Minutes

Ingredients:

1 large red onion, cut into rings	3 turnips, sliced
1 large zucchini, sliced	2 cloves garlic, crushed
Salt and black pepper to taste	1 bay leaf, cut in 6 pieces
	1 tbsp olive oil

Directions:

Place the turnips, onion, and zucchini in a bowl. Toss with olive oil, salt, and pepper. Preheat Cuisinart on Air Fry function to 380 F. Place the veggies into a baking pan. Slip the bay leaves in the different parts of the slices and tuck the garlic cloves in between the slices. Cook for 15 minutes. Serve warm with as a side to a meat dish or salad.

637. Roasted Vegetables With Rice

Servings: 4   Cooking Time: 12 Minutes

Ingredients:

2 teaspoons melted butter
1 cup chopped mushrooms
1 cup cooked rice
1 cup peas
1 carrot, chopped
1 red onion, chopped
1 garlic clove, minced
Salt and black pepper, to taste
2 hard-boiled eggs, grated
1 tablespoon soy sauce

Directions:

Coat the baking pan with melted butter. Stir together the mushrooms, cooked rice, peas, carrot, onion, garlic, salt, and pepper in a large bowl until well mixed. Pour the mixture into the prepared baking pan. Slide the baking pan into Rack Position 2, select Roast, set temperature to 380°F (193°C), and set time to 12 minutes. When cooking is complete, remove from the oven. Divide the mixture among four plates. Serve warm with a sprinkle of grated eggs and a drizzle of soy sauce.

638. Cashew Cauliflower With Yogurt Sauce

Servings: 2   Cooking Time: 12 Minutes

Ingredients:

4 cups cauliflower florets (about half a large head)
1 tablespoon olive oil
1 teaspoon curry powder
Salt, to taste
½ cup toasted, chopped cashews, for garnish
Yogurt Sauce:
¼ cup plain yogurt
2 tablespoons sour cream
1 teaspoon honey
1 teaspoon lemon juice
Pinch cayenne pepper
Salt, to taste
1 tablespoon chopped fresh cilantro, plus leaves for garnish

Directions:

In a large mixing bowl, toss the cauliflower florets with the olive oil, curry powder, and salt. Place the cauliflower florets in the air fryer basket. Put the air fryer basket on the baking pan and slide into Rack Position 2, select Air Fry, set temperature to 400°F (205°C) and set time to 12 minutes. Stir the cauliflower florets twice during cooking. When cooking is complete, the cauliflower should be golden brown. Meanwhile, mix all the ingredients for the yogurt sauce in a small bowl and whisk to combine. Remove the cauliflower from the oven and drizzle with the yogurt sauce. Scatter the toasted cashews and cilantro on top and serve immediately.

639. Butter Burgers

Servings: 4   Cooking Time: 30 Minutes

Ingredients:

Nonstick cooking spray
½ cup black beans, rinsed & drained
12 oz. mushrooms, sliced
1 ½ cup brown rice, cooked
½ cup oats
1 tsp salt
½ tsp pepper
1 tsp garlic powder
1 tsp onion powder
¼ tsp red pepper flakes
¼ cup Vegan butter
2 cups onions, sliced

Directions:

Place baking pan in position 2 in the oven. Lightly spray fryer basket with cooking spray. Pat the beans with paper towel to get them as dry as possible. Heat a medium skillet over med-high heat. Add mushrooms and cook, stirring frequently, until almost no moisture remains. Add mushrooms, beans, rice, oats, and seasonings to a food processor. Pulse to chop and combine ingredients. Do not over blend. Let mixture rest 20 minutes. Melt butter in a large skillet over medium heat. Add onions and cook until browned and tender. Form mushroom mixture into 4 patties and place in the fryer basket. Place in oven and set to air fry on 350°F for 10 minutes. Cook burgers 8-10 minutes, until nicely browned, turning over halfway through cooking time. Serve on toasted buns topped with cooked onions.

Nutrition Info: Calories 351, Total Fat 15g, Saturated Fat 8g, Total Carbs 44g, Net Carbs 37g, Protein 10g, Sugar 4g, Fiber 7g, Sodium 704mg, Potassium 604mg, Phosphorus 286mg

640. Cottage Cheese Patties

Ingredients:

1 tbsp. fresh coriander leaves
¼ tsp. red chili powder
¼ tsp. cumin powder
1 cup grated cottage cheese
A pinch of salt to taste
¼ tsp. ginger finely chopped
1 green chili finely chopped
1 tsp. lemon juice

Directions:

Mix the ingredients together and ensure that the flavors are right. You will now make round patties with the mixture and roll them out well. Pre heat the Cuisinart oven at 250 Fahrenheit for 5 minutes. Open the basket of the Fryer and arrange the patties in the basket. Close it carefully. Keep the fryer at 150 degrees for around 10 or 12 minutes. In between the cooking process, turn the patties over to get a uniform cook. Serve hot with mint sauce.

641. Cayenne Tahini Kale

Servings: 2 To 4   Cooking Time: 15 Minutes

Ingredients:

Dressing:
¼ cup fresh lemon juice
2 tablespoons olive oil
1 teaspoon sesame seeds
½ teaspoon garlic
¼ cup tahini
Kale:
4 cups packed torn kale leaves (stems and ribs removed and leaves torn into palm-size pieces)

powder
¼ teaspoon cayenne pepper

Kosher salt and freshly ground black pepper, to taste

Directions:
Make the dressing: Whisk together the tahini, lemon juice, olive oil, sesame seeds, garlic powder, and cayenne pepper in a large bowl until well mixed. Add the kale and massage the dressing thoroughly all over the leaves. Sprinkle the salt and pepper to season. Place the kale in the air fryer basket in a single layer. Put the air fryer basket on the baking pan and slide into Rack Position 2, select Air Fry, set temperature to 350ºF (180ºC), and set time to 15 minutes. When cooking is complete, the leaves should be slightly wilted and crispy. Remove from the oven and serve on a plate.

642. Gorgonzola Cheese & Pumpkin Salad

Servings: 2   Cooking Time: 30 Minutes + Chilling Time

Ingredients:

½ lb pumpkin
2 oz gorgonzola cheese, crumbled
2 tbsp pine nuts, toasted
1 tbsp olive oil
½ cup baby spinach

1 spring onion, sliced
2 radishes, thinly sliced
1 tsp apple cider vinegar

Directions:
Preheat Cuisinart on Bake function to 360 F. Peel the pumpkin and chop it into small pieces. Place in a greased baking dish and bake for 20 minutes. Let cool. Add baby spinach, radishes, and spring onion in a serving bowl and toss with olive oil and vinegar. Top with the pumpkin and gorgonzola cheese and sprinkle with the pine nuts to serve.

643. Ratatouille

Servings: 6   Cooking Time: 12 Minutes

Ingredients:

1 medium zucchini, sliced ½-inch thick
1 small eggplant, peeled and sliced ½-inch thick
2 teaspoons kosher salt, divided
4 tablespoons extra-virgin olive oil, divided
1 small red bell pepper, cut into ½-inch chunks
1 small green bell pepper, cut into ½-inch chunks

3 garlic cloves, minced
1 small onion, chopped
½ teaspoon dried oregano
¼ teaspoon freshly ground black pepper
1 pint cherry tomatoes
2 tablespoons minced fresh basil
1 cup panko bread crumbs
½ cup grated Parmesan cheese (optional)

Directions:
Season one side of the zucchini and eggplant slices with ¾ teaspoon of salt. Put the slices, salted side down, on a rack set over a baking sheet. Sprinkle the other sides with ¾ teaspoon of salt. Allow to sit for 10 minutes, or until the slices begin to exude water. When ready, rinse and dry them. Cut the zucchini slices into quarters and the eggplant slices into eighths. Pour the zucchini and eggplant into a large bowl, along with 2 tablespoons of olive oil, garlic, onion, bell peppers, oregano, and black pepper. Toss to coat well. Arrange the vegetables in the air fryer basket. Put the air fryer basket on the baking pan and slide into Rack Position 2, select Roast, set temperature to 375ºF (190ºC), and set time to 12 minutes. Meanwhile, add the tomatoes and basil to the large bowl. Sprinkle with the remaining ½ teaspoon of salt and 1 tablespoon of olive oil. Toss well and set aside. Stir together the remaining 1 tablespoon of olive oil, panko, and Parmesan cheese (if desired) in a small bowl. After 6 minutes, remove from the oven and add the tomato mixture and stir to mix well. Scatter the panko mixture on top. Return to the oven and continue cooking for 6 minutes, or until the vegetables are softened and the topping is golden brown. Cool for 5 minutes before serving.

644. Spinach Enchiladas With Mozzarella

Servings: 4   Cooking Time: 20 Minutes

Ingredients:

8 corn tortillas, warm
2 cups mozzarella cheese, shredded
1 cup ricotta cheese, crumbled
½ cup sliced onions

1 package frozen spinach
1 garlic clove, minced
½ cup sour cream
1 tbsp butter
1 can enchilada sauce

Directions:
In a saucepan, heat oil and sauté garlic and onion for 3 minutes. Stir in the spinach and cook for 5 more minutes. Remove and stir in the ricotta cheese, sour cream and some mozzarella. Spoon ¼ cup of spinach mixture in the middle of a tortilla. Roll up and place seam side down in the basket. Repeat the process with the remaining tortillas. Pour the enchilada sauce all over and sprinkle with the remaining mozzarella. Cook for 15 minutes at 380 F on AirFry function.

645. Cauliflower Spicy Lemon Kebab

Ingredients:

3 tsp. lemon juice
2 tsp. garam masala
3 eggs
2 ½ tbsp. white sesame seeds
2 cups cauliflower florets
3 onions chopped

5 green chilies-roughly chopped
1 ½ tbsp. ginger paste
1 ½ tsp. garlic paste
1 ½ tsp. salt

Directions:
Grind the ingredients except for the egg and form a smooth paste. Coat the florets in the paste. Now, beat the eggs and add a little salt to it. Dip the coated florets in the egg mixture and then transfer to the sesame seeds and coat the florets well. Place the vegetables on a stick. Pre heat the Cuisinart oven at 160 degrees Fahrenheit for around 5

minutes. Place the sticks in the basket and let them cook for another 25 minutes at the same temperature. Turn the sticks over in between the cooking process to get a uniform cook.

646. Mushroom Pops

Ingredients:

1 tsp. dry basil
1 tsp. lemon juice
1 tsp. red chili flakes
1 cup whole mushrooms
1 ½ tsp. garlic paste
Salt and pepper to taste
1 tsp. dry oregano

Directions:
Add the ingredients into a separate bowl and mix them well to get a consistent mixture. Dip the mushrooms in the above mixture and leave them aside for some time. Pre heat the Cuisinart oven at 180° C for around 5 minutes. Place the coated cottage cheese pieces in the fry basket and close it properly. Let them cook at the same temperature for 20 more minutes. Keep turning them over in the basket so that they are cooked properly. Serve with tomato ketchup.

647. Cottage Cheese French Cuisine Galette

Ingredients:

1-2 tbsp. fresh coriander leaves
2 or 3 green chilies finely chopped
1 ½ tbsp. lemon juice
Salt and pepper to taste
2 tbsp. garam masala
2 cups grated cottage cheese
1 ½ cup coarsely crushed peanuts
3 tsp. ginger finely chopped

Directions:
Mix the ingredients in a clean bowl. Mold this mixture into round and flat French Cuisine Galettes. Wet the French Cuisine Galettes slightly with water. Coat each French Cuisine Galette with the crushed peanuts. Pre heat the Cuisinart oven at 160 degrees Fahrenheit for 5 minutes. Place the French Cuisine Galettes in the fry basket and let them cook for another 25 minutes at the same temperature. Keep rolling them over to get a uniform cook. Serve either with mint sauce or ketchup.

648. Pineapple Spicy Lemon Kebab

Ingredients:

4 tbsp. chopped coriander
3 tbsp. cream
3 tbsp. chopped capsicum
3 eggs
2 ½ tbsp. white sesame seeds
2 cups cubed pineapples
3 onions chopped
5 green chilies- roughly chopped
1 ½ tbsp. ginger paste
1 ½ tsp. garlic paste
1 ½ tsp. salt
3 tsp. lemon juice
2 tsp. garam masala

Directions:
Grind the ingredients except for the egg and form a smooth paste. Coat the pineapples in the paste. Now, beat the eggs and add a little salt to it. Dip the coated vegetables in the egg mixture and then transfer to the sesame seeds and coat the pineapples well. Place the vegetables on a stick. Pre heat the Cuisinart oven at 160 degrees Fahrenheit for around 5 minutes. Place the sticks in the basket and let them cook for another 25 minutes at the same temperature. Turn the sticks over in between the cooking process to get a uniform cook.

649. Crispy Fried Okra With Chili

Servings: 4   Cooking Time: 10 Minutes
Ingredients:

3 tablespoons sour cream
2 tablespoons semolina
½ teaspoon red chili powder
2 tablespoons flour
Salt and black pepper, to taste
1 pound (454 g) okra, halved
Cooking spray

Directions:
Spray the air fryer basket with cooking spray. Set aside. In a shallow bowl, place the sour cream. In another shallow bowl, thoroughly combine the flour, semolina, red chili powder, salt, and pepper. Dredge the okra in the sour cream, then roll in the flour mixture until evenly coated. Transfer the okra to the air fryer basket. Put the air fryer basket on the baking pan and slide into Rack Position 2, select Air Fry, set temperature to 400°F (205°C), and set time to 10 minutes. Flip the okra halfway through the cooking time. When cooking is complete, the okra should be golden brown and crispy. Remove from the oven and cool for 5 minutes before serving.

650. Mushroom Marinade Cutlet

Ingredients:

2 cup fresh green coriander
½ cup mint leaves
4 tsp. fennel
2 tbsp. ginger-garlic paste
1 small onion
6-7 flakes garlic (optional)
Salt to taste
2 cups sliced mushrooms
1 big capsicum (Cut this capsicum into big cubes)
1 onion (Cut it into quarters. Now separate the layers carefully.)
5 tbsp. gram flour
A pinch of salt to taste
3 tbsp. lemon juice

Directions:
Take a clean and dry container. Put into it the coriander, mint, fennel, and ginger, onion/garlic, salt and lemon juice. Mix them. Pour the mixture into a grinder and blend until you get a thick paste. Slit the mushroom almost till the end and leave them aside. Now stuff all the pieces with the paste and set aside. Take the sauce and add to it the gram flour and some salt. Mix them together properly. Rub this mixture all over the stuffed mushroom. Now, to the leftover sauce, add the capsicum and onions. Apply the sauce generously on each of the pieces of capsicum and onion. Now take satay sticks and arrange the cottage cheese pieces and vegetables on separate sticks. Pre heat the Cuisinart oven at 290 Fahrenheit for around 5 minutes. Open the basket. Arrange the satay sticks properly. Close the basket. Keep the sticks with the mushroom at 180 degrees for around half an hour

while the sticks with the vegetables are to be kept at the same temperature for only 7 minutes. Turn the sticks in between so that one side does not get burnt and also to provide a uniform cook.

651. Onion French Cuisine Galette

Ingredients:

2 or 3 green chilies finely chopped	2 tbsp. garam masala
1 ½ tbsp. lemon juice	1 ½ cup coarsely crushed peanuts
Salt and pepper to taste	3 tsp. ginger finely chopped
2 medium onions (Cut long)	1-2 tbsp. fresh coriander leaves

Directions:
Mix the ingredients in a clean bowl. Mold this mixture into round and flat French Cuisine Galettes. Wet the French Cuisine Galettes slightly with water. Coat each French Cuisine Galette with the crushed peanuts. Pre heat the Cuisinart oven at 160 degrees Fahrenheit for 5 minutes. Place the French Cuisine Galettes in the fry basket and let them cook for another 25 minutes at the same temperature. Keep rolling them over to get a uniform cook. Serve either with mint sauce or ketchup.

652. Cabbage Fritters(2)

Ingredients:

1 ½ tsp. salt	3 onions chopped
3 tsp. lemon juice	5 green chilies- roughly chopped
2 tsp. garam masala	
3 eggs	1 ½ tbsp. ginger paste
2 ½ tbsp. white sesame seeds	
10 leaves cabbage	1 ½ tsp. garlic paste

Directions:
Grind the ingredients except for the egg and form a smooth paste. Coat the leaves in the paste. Now, beat the eggs and add a little salt to it. Dip the coated leaves in the egg mixture and then transfer to the sesame seeds and coat the florets well. Place the vegetables on a stick. Pre heat the Cuisinart oven at 160 degrees Fahrenheit for around 5 minutes. Place the sticks in the basket and let them cook for another 25 minutes at the same temperature. Turn the sticks over in between the cooking process to get a uniform cook.

653. Cabbage Steaks With Fennel Seeds

Servings: 3   Cooking Time: 25 Minutes

Ingredients:

1 cabbage head	1 tbsp garlic paste
Salt and black pepper to taste	2 tbsp olive oil
	2 tsp fennel seeds

Directions:
Preheat Cuisinart on AirFry function to 350 F. Slice the cabbage into 1 ½-inch slice. In a small bowl, combine all the other ingredients; brush cabbage with the mixture. Arrange the steaks on a greased baking dish and press Start. Cook for 15 minutes.

654. Nutmeg Broccoli With Eggs & Cheddar Cheese

Servings: 4   Cooking Time: 15 Minutes

Ingredients:

1 lb broccoli, cut into florets	4 eggs
	1 cup heavy cream
1 cup cheddar cheese, shredded	1 pinch of nutmeg
	1 tsp ginger powder

Directions:
In boiling water, steam the broccoli for 5 minutes. Drain and place in a bowl. Add in 1 egg, heavy cream, nutmeg, and ginger. Divide the mixture between greased ramekins and sprinkle the cheddar cheese on top. Cook for 10 minutes at 280 F on AirFry function.

655. Parmesan Breaded Zucchini Chips

Servings: 5   Cooking Time: 20 Minutes

Ingredients:

For the zucchini chips:	For the lemon aioli:
2 medium zucchini	½ cup mayonnaise
2 eggs	½ tablespoon olive oil
⅓ cup bread crumbs	
⅓ cup grated Parmesan cheese	Juice of ½ lemon
Salt	1 teaspoon minced garlic
Pepper	Salt
Cooking oil	Pepper

Directions:
Preparing the Ingredients. To make the zucchini chips: Slice the zucchini into thin chips (about ⅛ inch thick) using a knife or mandoline. In a small bowl, beat the eggs. In another small bowl, combine the bread crumbs, Parmesan cheese, and salt and pepper to taste. Spray the Oven rack/basket with cooking oil. Dip the zucchini slices one at a time in the eggs and then the bread crumb mixture. You can also sprinkle the bread crumbs onto the zucchini slices with a spoon. Place the zucchini chips in the Oven rack/basket, but do not stack. Place the Rack on the middle-shelf of the Cuisinart air fryer oven. Air Frying. Cook in batches. Spray the chips with cooking oil from a distance (otherwise, the breading may fly off). Cook for 10 minutes. Remove the cooked zucchini chips from the air fryer oven, then repeat step 5 with the remaining zucchini. To make the lemon aioli: While the zucchini is cooking, combine the mayonnaise, olive oil, lemon juice, and garlic in a small bowl, adding salt and pepper to taste. Mix well until fully combined. Cool the zucchini and serve alongside the aioli.
Nutrition Info:CALORIES: 192; FAT: 13G; PROTEIN: 6

656. Mozzarella Eggplant Patties

Servings: 1   Cooking Time: 10 Minutes

Ingredients:

1 hamburger bun	1 eggplant, sliced
1 mozzarella slice, chopped	1 lettuce leaf
	½ tbsp tomato sauce
	1 pickle, sliced

1 red onion cut into 3
rings

Directions:
Preheat Cuisinart on Bake function to 330 F. Place the eggplant slices in a greased baking tray and cook for 6 minutes. Take out the tray and top the eggplant with mozzarella cheese and cook for 30 more seconds. Spread tomato sauce on one half of the bun. Place the lettuce leaf on top of the sauce. Place the cheesy eggplant on top of the lettuce. Top with onion rings and pickles and then with the other bun half to serve.

657. Vegetable Pie

Ingredients:

2 cups roasted vegetables	1 tbsp. unsalted butter
2 tbsp. sugar	4tsp. powdered sugar
½ tsp. cinnamon	2 cups cold milk
2 tsp. lemon juice	½ cup roasted nuts
1 cup plain flour	

Directions:
In a large bowl, mix the flour, butter and sugar with your Oregano Fingers. The mixture should resemble breadcrumbs. Squeeze the dough using the cold milk and wrap it and leave it to cool for ten minutes. Now, roll the dough out and cut into two circles. Press the dough into the pie tins and prick on all sides using a fork. Cook the ingredients for the filling on a low flame and pour into the tin. Cover the pie tin with the second round. Preheat the fryer to 300 Fahrenheit for five minutes. You will need to place the tin in the basket and cover it. When the pastry has turned golden brown, you will need to remove the tin and let it cool. Cut into slices and serve with a dollop of cream.

658. Black Gram French Cuisine Galette

Ingredients:

2 or 3 green chilies finely chopped	2 cup black gram
1 ½ tbsp. lemon juice	1 ½ cup coarsely crushed peanuts
Salt and pepper to taste	3 tsp. ginger finely chopped
2 medium potatoes boiled and mashed	1-2 tbsp. fresh coriander leaves

Directions:
Mix the ingredients in a clean bowl. Mold this mixture into round and flat French Cuisine Galettes. Wet the French Cuisine Galettes slightly with water. Pre heat the Cuisinart oven at 160 degrees Fahrenheit for 5 minutes. Place the French Cuisine Galettes in the fry basket and let them cook for another 25 minutes at the same temperature. Keep rolling them over to get a uniform cook. Serve either with mint sauce or ketchup.

659. Classic Ratatouille

Servings: 2   Cooking Time: 30 Minutes

Ingredients:

3 roma tomatoes, thinly sliced	1 tbsp olive oil
2 garlic cloves,	1 tbsp red wine vinegar

minced
1 zucchini, thinly
sliced
2 yellow bell peppers,
sliced

2 tbsp herbs de
Provence
Salt and black pepper
to taste

Directions:
Preheat Cuisinart on Air Fry function to 390 F. In a bowl, mix together olive oil, garlic, vinegar, herbs, salt, and pepper. Add in tomatoes, zucchini, and bell peppers and toss to coat. Arrange the vegetables in a baking dish and cook for 15 minutes, shaking occasionally. Let sit for 5 more minutes after the timer goes off. Serve.

660. Mixed Vegetable Pancakes

Ingredients:

2 cups shredded vegetables	1 ½ cups almond flour
Salt and Pepper to taste	3 eggs
3 tbsp. Butter	2 tsp. dried basil
	2 tsp. dried parsley

Directions:
Preheat the air fryer to 250 Fahrenheit. In a small bowl, mix the ingredients together. Ensure that the mixture is smooth and well balanced. Take a pancake mold and grease it with butter. Add the batter to the mold and place it in the air fryer basket. Cook till both the sides of the pancake have browned on both sides and serve with maple syrup.

661. Roasted Carrots

Servings: 4   Cooking Time: 15 Minutes

Ingredients:

20 oz carrots, julienned	1 tsp cumin seeds
1 tbsp olive oil	2 tbsp fresh cilantro, chopped

Directions:
In a bowl, mix olive oil, carrots, and cumin seeds; stir to coat. Place the carrots in a baking tray and cook in your Cuisinart on Bake function at 300 F for 10 minutes. Scatter fresh coriander over the carrots and serve.

662. Balsamic Eggplant Caviar

Servings: 4   Cooking Time: 20 Minutes

Ingredients:

½ red onion, chopped and blended	3 medium eggplants
2 tbsp balsamic vinegar	1 tbsp olive oil
	Salt to taste

Directions:
Arrange the eggplants on the basket and cook them in the Cuisinart oven for 15 minutes at 380 F on Bake function. Let cool. Cut the eggplants in half, lengthwise and empty their insides. Pulse the onion the inside of the eggplants in a blender. Add in vinegar, olive oil, and salt, then blend again. Serve cool with bread and tomato sauce or ketchup.

663. Eggplant Patties With Mozzarella

Servings: 1   Cooking Time: 10 Minutes

Ingredients:

2-inch eggplant slices, cut along the round axis
1 mozzarella cheese slice

1 hamburger bun
3 red onion rings
1 lettuce leaf
½ tbsp tomato sauce
1 pickle, sliced

Directions:
Preheat Cuisinart on Bake function to 330 F. Cook in the eggplant slices to roast for 6 minutes. Place the mozzarella slice on top of the eggplant and cook for 30 more seconds. Spread tomato sauce on one half of the bun. Place the lettuce leaf on top of the sauce. Place the cheesy eggplant on top of the lettuce. Top with onion rings and pickles, and then with the other bun half and enjoy.

664. Vegetable And Cheese Stuffed Tomatoes

Servings: 4   Cooking Time: 18 Minutes
Ingredients:

4 medium beefsteak tomatoes, rinsed
½ cup grated carrot
1 medium onion, chopped
1 garlic clove, minced
2 teaspoons olive oil

2 cups fresh baby spinach
¼ cup crumbled low-sodium feta cheese
½ teaspoon dried basil

Directions:
On your cutting board, cut a thin slice off the top of each tomato. Scoop out a ¼- to ½-inch-thick tomato pulp and place the tomatoes upside down on paper towels to drain. Set aside. Stir together the carrot, onion, garlic, and olive oil in the baking pan. Slide the baking pan into Rack Position 1, select Convection Bake, set temperature to 350°F (180°C) and set time to 5 minutes. Stir the vegetables halfway through. When cooking is complete, the carrot should be crisp-tender. Remove from the oven and stir in the spinach, feta cheese, and basil. Spoon ¼ of the vegetable mixture into each tomato and transfer the stuffed tomatoes to the oven. Set time to 13 minutes. When cooking is complete, the filling should be hot and the tomatoes should be lightly caramelized. Let the tomatoes cool for 5 minutes and serve.

665. Amazing Macadamia Delight

Servings: 6   Cooking Time: 20 Minutes
Ingredients:

3 cups macadamia nuts
3 tbsp liquid smoke

Salt to taste
2 tbsp molasses

Directions:
Preheat Cuisinart on Bake function to 360 F. In a bowl, add salt, liquid, molasses, and cashews and toss to coat. Place the cashews ina baking tray and press Start. Cook for 10 minutes, shaking the basket every 5 minutes. Serve.

666. Masala Vegetable Skewers

Servings: 4   Cooking Time: 20 Minutes
Ingredients:

2 tbsp cornflour
1 cup canned white beans, drained

½ tsp garam masala powder

⅓ cup carrots, grated
2 potatoes, boiled and mashed
¼ cup fresh mint leaves, chopped

½ cup paneer
1 green chili
1-inch piece of fresh ginger
3 garlic cloves
Salt to taste

Directions:
Preheat Cuisinart on AirFry function to 390 F. Place the beans, carrots, garlic, ginger, chili, paneer, and mint in a food processor and blend until smooth. Transfer to a bowl. Add in the mashed potatoes, cornflour, salt, and garam masala powder and mix until fully incorporated. Divide the mixture into 12 equal pieces. Thread each of the pieces onto a skewer. Press Start and cook skewers for 10 minutes. Serve.

667. Caucasia Gnocchi's

Servings: Cooking Time:
Ingredients:

2 cups minced colas Asia
2 tbsp. oil
2 tsp. ginger-garlic paste
2 tsp. soya sauce

2 tsp. vinegar
1 ½ cup all-purpose flour
½ tsp. salt
5 tbsp. water

Directions:
Squeeze the dough and cover it with plastic wrap and set aside. Next, cook the ingredients for the filling and try to ensure that the colas Asia is covered well with the sauce. Roll the dough and place the filling in the center. Now, wrap the dough to cover the filling and pinch the edges together. Pre heat the Cuisinart oven at 200° F for 5 minutes. Place the gnocchi's in the fry basket and close it. Let them cook at the same temperature for another 20 minutes. Recommended sides are chili sauce or ketchup.

668. Jalapeño Cheese Balls

Servings: 12   Cooking Time: 8 Minutes
Ingredients:

4 ounces cream cheese
⅓ cup shredded mozzarella cheese
⅓ cup shredded Cheddar cheese
2 jalapeños, finely chopped

½ cup bread crumbs
2 eggs
½ cup all-purpose flour
Salt
Pepper
Cooking oil

Directions:
Preparing the Ingredients. In a medium bowl, combine the cream cheese, mozzarella, Cheddar, and jalapeños. Mix well. Form the cheese mixture into balls about an inch thick. Using a small ice cream scoop works well. Arrange the cheese balls on a sheet pan and place in the freezer for 15 minutes. This will help the cheese balls maintain their shape while frying. Spray the Oven rack/basket with cooking oil. Place the bread crumbs in a small bowl. In another small bowl, beat the eggs. In a third small bowl, combine the flour with salt and pepper to taste, and mix well. Remove the cheese balls from the freezer. Dip the cheese balls in the flour, then the eggs, and then the bread crumbs. Air Frying. Place the cheese balls in the Oven

rack/basket. Spray with cooking oil. Place the Rack on the middle-shelf of the Cuisinart air fryer oven. Cook for 8 minutes. Open the air fryer oven and flip the cheese balls. I recommend flipping them instead of shaking, so the balls maintain their form. Cook an additional 4 minutes. Cool before serving.
Nutrition Info:CALORIES: 96; FAT: 6G; PROTEIN:4G; SUGAR:

669. Cheese French Fries

Ingredients:

2 medium sized potatoes peeled and cut into thick pieces lengthwise	1 tbsp. lemon juice
1 tsp. mixed herbs	1 cup melted cheddar cheese (You could put this into a piping bag and
½ tsp. red chili flakes	
A pinch of salt to taste	1 tbsp. olive oil create a pattern of it on the fries.)

Directions:
Take all the ingredients mentioned under the heading "For the marinade" and mix them well. Now pour into a container 3 cups of water. Add a pinch of salt into this water. Bring it to the boil. Now blanch the pieces of potato for around 5 minutes. Drain the water using a sieve. Dry the potato pieces on a towel and then place them on another dry towel. Coat these potato Oregano Fingers with the marinade made in the previous step. Pre heat the Cuisinart oven for around 5 minutes at 300 Fahrenheit. Take out the basket of the fryer and place the potato Oregano Fingers in them. Close the basket. Now keep the fryer at 220 Fahrenheit for 20 or 25 minutes. In between the process, toss the fries twice or thrice so that they get cooked properly. Towards the end of the cooking process (the last 2 minutes or so), sprinkle the cut coriander leaves on the fries. Add the melted cheddar cheese over the fries and serve hot.

670. Roasted Brussels Sprouts With Parmesan

Servings: 4   Cooking Time: 20 Minutes
Ingredients:

1 pound (454 g) fresh Brussels sprouts, trimmed	½ teaspoon salt
1 tablespoon olive oil	⅛ teaspoon pepper
	¼ cup grated Parmesan cheese

Directions:
In a large bowl, combine the Brussels sprouts with olive oil, salt, and pepper and toss until evenly coated. Spread the Brussels sprouts evenly in the air fryer basket. Put the air fryer basket on the baking pan and slide into Rack Position 2, select Air Fry, set temperature to 330°F (166°C), and set time to 20 minutes. Stir the Brussels sprouts twice during cooking. When cooking is complete, the Brussels sprouts should be golden brown and crisp. Sprinkle the grated Parmesan cheese on top and serve warm.

671. Cheddar & Tempeh Stuffed Mushrooms

Servings: 3 To 4   Cooking Time: 20 Minutes
Ingredients:

1 clove garlic, minced	14 mushroom caps
Salt and pepper to taste	¼ cup grated Cheddar cheese
4 slices tempeh, chopped	1 tbsp olive oil
	1 tbsp chopped parsley

Directions:
Preheat on Air Fry function to 390 F. In a bowl, add olive oil, tempeh, cheddar cheese, parsley, salt, pepper, and garlic. Mix well with a spoon. Fill the mushroom caps with the tempeh mixture. Place the stuffed mushrooms in the basket and fit in the baking tray; cook for 8 minutes. Once golden and crispy, plate them and serve with green salad.

672. Air Fried Kale Chips

Servings: 6   Cooking Time: 10 Minutes
Ingredients:

¼ tsp. Himalayan salt	Avocado oil
3 tbsp. yeast	1 bunch of kale

Directions:
Preparing the Ingredients. Rinse kale and with paper towels, dry well. Tear kale leaves into large pieces. Remember they will shrink as they cook so good sized pieces are necessary. Place kale pieces in a bowl and spritz with avocado oil till shiny. Sprinkle with salt and yeast. With your hands, toss kale leaves well to combine. Air Frying. Pour half of the kale mixture into the Cuisinart air fryer oven, set temperature to 350°F, and set time to 5 minutes. Remove and repeat with another half of kale.
Nutrition Info:CALORIES: 55; FAT: 10G; PROTEIN: 1G; SUGAR:0G

673. Garlic Stuffed Mushrooms

Servings: 2   Cooking Time: 12 Minutes
Ingredients:

18 medium-sized white mushrooms	2 teaspoons cumin powder
1 small onion, peeled and chopped	A pinch ground allspice
4 garlic cloves, peeled and minced	Fine sea salt and freshly ground black pepper, to taste
2 tablespoons olive oil	

Directions:
On a clean work surface, remove the mushroom stems. Using a spoon, scoop out the mushroom gills and discard. Thoroughly combine the onion, garlic, olive oil, cumin powder, allspice, salt, and pepper in a mixing bowl. Stuff the mushrooms evenly with the mixture. Place the stuffed mushrooms in the air fryer basket. Put the air fryer basket on the baking pan and slide into Rack Position 2, select Roast, set temperature to 345°F (174°C) and set time to 12 minutes. When

cooking is complete, the mushroom should be browned. Cool for 5 minutes before serving.

674. Garlicky Sesame Carrots

Servings: 4 To 6   Cooking Time: 16 Minutes
Ingredients:

1 pound (454 g) baby carrots	Freshly ground black pepper, to taste
1 tablespoon sesame oil	6 cloves garlic, peeled
½ teaspoon dried dill	3 tablespoons sesame seeds
Pinch salt	

Directions:
In a medium bowl, drizzle the baby carrots with the sesame oil. Sprinkle with the dill, salt, and pepper and toss to coat well. Place the baby carrots in the air fryer basket. Put the air fryer basket on the baking pan and slide into Rack Position 2, select Roast, set temperature to 380°F (193°C), and set time to 16 minutes. After 8 minutes, remove from the oven and stir in the garlic. Return the pan to the oven and continue roasting for 8 minutes more. When cooking is complete, the carrots should be lightly browned. Remove from the oven and serve sprinkled with the sesame seeds.

675. Awesome Sweet Potato Fries

Servings: 4   Cooking Time: 30 Minutes
Ingredients:

½ tsp salt	3 tbsp olive oil
½ tsp garlic powder	3 sweet potatoes, cut into thick strips
½ tsp chili powder	
¼ tsp cumin	

Directions:
In a bowl, mix salt, garlic powder, chili, and cumin, and olive oil. Coat the strips well in this mixture and arrange them in the basket without overcrowding. Fit in the baking tray and cook for 20 minutes at 380 F on Air Fry function or until crispy. Serve.

676. Dill Baby Carrots With Honey

Servings: 4   Cooking Time: 20 Minutes
Ingredients:

1 lb baby carrots	1 tbsp honey
1 tsp dried dill	Salt and black pepper to taste
1 tbsp olive oil	

Directions:
Preheat Cuisinart Oven to 360 F on AirFry function. In a bowl, mix oil, carrots, and honey; stir to coat. Season with dill, pepper, and salt. Place the carrots in the basket and cook for 15 minutes.

677. Crispy Potato Lentil Nuggets

Servings: 4   Cooking Time: 10 Minutes
Ingredients:

Nonstick cooking spray	1 cup potato, grated
1 cup red lentils	½ cup flour
1 tbsp. olive oil	½ tsp salt
1 cup onion, grated	½ tsp garlic powder
1 cup carrot, grated	¾ tsp paprika
	¼ tsp pepper

Directions:
Place baking pan in position 2. Lightly spray fryer basket with cooking spray. Soak lentils in just enough water to cover them for 25 minutes. Heat oil in a large skillet over medium heat. Add onion, carrot, and potato. Cook, stirring frequently until vegetables are tender, 12-15 minutes. Drain the lentils and place them in a food processor. Add flour and spices and pulse to combine, leave some texture to the mixture. Add cooked veggies to the food processor and pulse just until combined. Mixture will be sticky, so oil your hands. Form mixture into nugget shapes and add to the fryer basket in a single layer. Place basket in the oven and set air fry on 350°F for 10 minutes. Turn nuggets over halfway through cooking time. Repeat with remaining mixture. Serve with your favorite dipping sauce.
Nutrition Info: Calories 317, Total Fat 5g, Saturated Fat 1g, Total Carbs 54g, Net Carbs 46g, Protein 14g, Sugar 3g, Fiber 8g, Sodium 317mg, Potassium 625mg, Phosphorus 197mg

678. Parsley Feta Triangles

Servings: 4   Cooking Time: 20 Minutes
Ingredients:

4 oz feta cheese	1 scallion, finely chopped
2 sheets filo pastry	
1 egg yolk	2 tbsp olive oil
2 tbsp parsley, finely chopped	salt and black pepper

Directions:
In a bowl, beat the yolk and mix with feta cheese, parsley, scallion, salt, and black pepper. Cut each filo sheet in three parts or strips. Put a teaspoon of the feta mixture on the bottom. Roll the strip in a spinning spiral way until the filling of the inside mixture is wrapped in a triangle. Preheat Cuisinart on Bake function to 360 F. Brush the surface of filo with olive oil. Arrange the triangles on a greased baking tray and cook for 5 minutes. Lower the temperature to 330 F and cook for 3 more minutes or until golden brown. Serve chilled.

679. Teriyaki Tofu

Servings: 3   Cooking Time: 15 Minutes
Ingredients:

Nonstick cooking spray	½ tsp salt
14 oz. firm or extra firm tofu, pressed & cut in 1-inch cubes	½ tsp ginger
	½ tsp white pepper
¼ cup cornstarch	3 tbsp. olive oil
	12 oz. bottle vegan teriyaki sauce

Directions:
Lightly spray baking pan with cooking spray. In a shallow dish, combine cornstarch, salt, ginger, and pepper. Heat oil in a large skillet over med-high heat. Toss tofu cubes in cornstarch mixture then add to skillet. Cook 5 minutes, turning over halfway through, until tofu is nicely seared. Transfer the tofu to the prepared baking pan. Set oven to convection bake on 350°F for 15 minutes. Pour all but ½ cup teriyaki sauce over tofu and stir to coat. After oven has preheated for 5 minutes, place the

baking pan in position 2 and bake tofu 10 minutes. Turn tofu over, spoon the sauce in the pan over it and bake another 10 minutes. Serve with reserved sauce for dipping.

Nutrition Info: Calories 469, Total Fat 25g, Saturated Fat 4g, Total Carbs 33g, Net Carbs 30g, Protein 28g, Sugar 16g, Fiber 3g, Sodium 2424mg, Potassium 571mg, Phosphorus 428mg

---

680.   Cheese And Garlic French Fries

Ingredients:

1 cup molten cheese	1 tbsp. lemon juice
2 tsp. garlic powder	1 tbsp. olive oil
2 medium sized potatoes peeled and cut into thick pieces lengthwise ingredients for the marinade:	1 tsp. mixed herbs
	½ tsp. red chili flakes
	A pinch of salt to taste

Directions:
Boil the potatoes and blanch them. Cut the potato into Oregano Fingers. Mix the ingredients for the marinade and add the potato Oregano Fingers to it making sure that they are coated well.   Pre heat the Cuisinart oven for around 5 minutes at 300 Fahrenheit. Take out the basket of the fryer and place the potato Oregano Fingers in them. Close the basket.   Now keep the fryer at 200 Fahrenheit for 20 or 25 minutes. In between the process, toss the fries twice or thrice so that they get cooked properly.

---

681.   Cottage Cheese Fingers

Ingredients:

2 tsp. salt	4 eggs
1 tsp. pepper powder	2 cup dry breadcrumbs
1 tsp. red chili powder	
6 tbsp. corn flour	2 tsp. oregano
2 cups cottage cheese Oregano Fingers	1 ½ tbsp. ginger-garlic paste
	4 tbsp. lemon juice

Directions:
Mix all the ingredients for the marinade and put the chicken Oregano Fingers inside and let it rest overnight.   Mix the breadcrumbs, oregano and red chili flakes well and place the marinated Oregano Fingers on this mixture. Cover it with plastic wrap and leave it till right before you serve to cook.   Pre heat the Cuisinart oven at 160 degrees Fahrenheit for 5 minutes. Place the Oregano Fingers in the fry basket and close it. Let them cook at the same temperature for another 15 minutes or so. Toss the Oregano Fingers well so that they are cooked uniformly.

---

682.   Bottle Gourd Flat Cakes

Ingredients:

2 or 3 green chilies finely chopped	2 cups sliced bottle gourd
1 ½ tbsp. lemon juice	3 tsp. ginger finely chopped
Salt and pepper to taste	
2 tbsp. garam masala	1-2 tbsp. fresh coriander leaves

Directions:

Mix the ingredients in a clean bowl and add water to it. Make sure that the paste is not too watery but is enough to apply on the bottle gourd slices. Pre heat the Cuisinart oven at 160 degrees Fahrenheit for 5 minutes.   Place the French Cuisine Galettes in the fry basket and let them cook for another 25 minutes at the same temperature. Keep rolling them over to get a uniform cook. Serve either with mint sauce or ketchup.

---

683.   Cottage Cheese Homemade Fried Sticks

Ingredients:

One or two poppadums'	1 big lemon-juiced
4 or 5 tbsp. corn flour	For seasoning, use salt and red chili powder in small amounts
1 cup of water	
2 cups cottage cheese	
1 tbsp. ginger-garlic paste	½ tsp. carom

Directions:
Take the cottage cheese. Cut it into long pieces. Now, make a mixture of lemon juice, red chili powder, salt, ginger garlic paste and carom to use as a marinade. Let the cottage cheese pieces marinate in the mixture for some time and then roll them in dry corn flour. Leave them aside for around 20 minutes. Take the poppadum into a pan and roast them. Once they are cooked, crush them into very small pieces. Now take another container and pour around 100 ml of water into it. Dissolve 2 tbsp. of corn flour in this water. Dip the cottage cheese pieces in this solution of corn flour and roll them on to the pieces of crushed poppadum so that the poppadum sticks to the cottage cheese   . Pre heat the Cuisinart oven for 10 minutes at 290 Fahrenheit. Then open the basket of the fryer and place the cottage cheese pieces inside it. Close the basket properly. Let the fryer stay at 160 degrees for another 20 minutes. Halfway through, open the basket and toss the cottage cheese around a bit to allow for uniform cooking. Once they are done, you can serve it either with ketchup or mint sauce. Another recommended side is mint sauce.

---

684.   Hearty Roasted Veggie Salad

Servings: 2   Cooking Time: 20 Minutes

Ingredients:

1 potato, chopped	¼ teaspoon sea salt
1 carrot, sliced diagonally	A handful of arugula
1 cup cherry tomatoes	A handful of baby spinach
½ small beetroot, sliced	Juice of 1 lemon
¼ onion, sliced	3 tablespoons canned chickpeas, for serving
½ teaspoon turmeric	
½ teaspoon cumin	Parmesan shavings, for serving
2 tablespoons olive oil, divided	

Directions:
Combine the potato, carrot, cherry tomatoes, beetroot, onion, turmeric, cumin, salt, and 1 tablespoon of olive oil in a large bowl and toss until well coated.   Arrange the veggies in the air fryer

basket. Put the air fryer basket on the baking pan and slide into Rack Position 2, select Roast, set temperature to 370°F (188°C) and set time to 20 minutes. Stir the vegetables halfway through. When cooking is complete, the potatoes should be golden brown. Let the veggies cool for 5 to 10 minutes in the oven. Put the arugula, baby spinach, lemon juice, and remaining 1 tablespoon of olive oil in a salad bowl and stir to combine. Mix in the roasted veggies and toss well. Scatter the chickpeas and Parmesan shavings on top and serve immediately.

685. Radish Flat Cakes

Ingredients:

1-2 tbsp. fresh coriander leaves	1 ½ tbsp. lemon juice
2 or 3 green chilies finely chopped	2 tbsp. garam masala
Salt and pepper to taste	2 cups sliced radish
	3 tsp. ginger finely chopped

Directions:

Mix the ingredients in a clean bowl and add water to it. Make sure that the paste is not too watery but is enough to apply on the radish. Pre heat the Cuisinart oven at 160 degrees Fahrenheit for 5 minutes. Place the French Cuisine Galettes in the fry basket and let them cook for another 25 minutes at the same temperature. Keep rolling them over to get a uniform cook. Serve either with mint sauce or ketchup.

686. Gourd French Cuisine Galette

Ingredients:

2 or 3 green chilies finely chopped	1 ½ cup coarsely crushed peanuts
1 ½ tbsp. lemon juice	3 tsp. ginger finely chopped
Salt and pepper to taste	1-2 tbsp. fresh coriander leaves
2 tbsp. garam masala	
2 cups sliced gourd	

Directions:

Mix the ingredients in a clean bowl. Mold this mixture into round and flat French Cuisine Galettes. Wet the French Cuisine Galettes slightly with water. Coat each French Cuisine Galette with the crushed peanuts. Pre heat the Cuisinart oven at 160 degrees Fahrenheit for 5 minutes. Place the French Cuisine Galettes in the fry basket and let them cook for another 25 minutes at the same temperature. Keep rolling them over to get a uniform cook. Serve either with mint sauce or ketchup

687. Zucchini Parmesan Crisps

Servings: 4   Cooking Time: 25 Minutes

Ingredients:

4 small zucchini, cut lengthwise	¼ cup chopped parsley
½ cup Parmesan cheese, grated	4 garlic cloves, minced
½ cup breadcrumbs	Salt and black pepper to taste
¼ cup melted butter	

Directions:

Preheat Cuisinart on Air Fry function to 350 F. In a bowl, mix breadcrumbs, Parmesan cheese, garlic, parsley, salt, and pepper. Stir in butter. Place the zucchinis cut-side up in a baking tray. Spread the cheese mixture onto the zucchini evenly. Cook for 13 minutes. Increase the temperature to 370 F and cook for 3 more minutes for extra crunchiness. Serve hot.

688. Cornflakes French Toast

Ingredients:

1 tsp. sugar for every 2 slices	Crushed cornflakes
Bread slices (brown or white)	1 egg white for every 2 slices

Directions:

Put two slices together and cut them along the diagonal. In a bowl, whisk the egg whites and add some sugar. Dip the bread triangles into this mixture and then coat them with the crushed cornflakes. Pre heat the Cuisinart oven at 180° C for 4 minutes. Place the coated bread triangles in the fry basket and close it. Let them cook at the same temperature for another 20 minutes at least. Halfway through the process, turn the triangles over so that you get a uniform cook. Serve these slices with chocolate sauce.

689. Carrot & Chickpea Oat Balls With Cashews

Servings: 4   Cooking Time: 30 Minutes

Ingredients:

2 tbsp olive oil	½ cup cashews, toasted
2 tbsp soy sauce	
1 tbsp flax meal	Juice of 1 lemon
2 cups canned chickpeas, drained	½ tsp turmeric
½ cup sweet onions, diced	1 tsp cumin
½ cup carrots, grated	1 tsp garlic powder
	1 cup rolled oats

Directions:

Preheat Cuisinart on AirFry function to 380 F. Heat olive oil in a skillet and sauté onions and carrots for 5 minutes. Ground the oats and cashews in a food processor. Transfer to a bowl. Place the chickpeas, lemon juice, and soy sauce in the food processor and process until smooth. Add them to the bowl as well. Mix in the onions and carrots. Stir in the remaining ingredients until fully incorporated. Make balls out of the mixture. Place them in the frying basket and press Start. Cook for 12 minutes. Serve warm.

690. Carrots & Shallots With Yogurt

Servings: 4   Cooking Time: 25 Minutes

Ingredients:

2 tsp olive oil	2 garlic cloves, minced
2 shallots, chopped	
3 carrots, sliced	3 tbsp parsley, chopped
Salt to taste	
¼ cup yogurt	

Directions:

In a bowl, mix sliced carrots, salt, garlic, shallots, parsley, and yogurt. Sprinkle with oil. Place the veggies in the basket and press Start. Cook for 15 minutes on AirFry function at 370 F. Serve with basil and garlic mayo.

691. Simple Ratatouille

Servings: 2   Cooking Time: 16 Minutes

Ingredients:

2 Roma tomatoes, thinly sliced	2 tablespoons olive oil
1 zucchini, thinly sliced	2 tablespoons herbes de Provence
2 yellow bell peppers, sliced	1 tablespoon vinegar
2 garlic cloves, minced	Salt and black pepper, to taste

Directions:

Place the tomatoes, zucchini, bell peppers, garlic, olive oil, herbes de Provence, and vinegar in a large bowl and toss until the vegetables are evenly coated. Sprinkle with salt and pepper and toss again. Pour the vegetable mixture into the baking pan.   Slide the baking pan into Rack Position 2, select Roast, set temperature to 390°F (199°C) and set time to 16 minutes.   Stir the vegetables halfway through. When cooking is complete, the vegetables should be tender.   Let the vegetable mixture stand for 5 minutes in the oven before removing and serving.

692. Teriyaki Cauliflower

Servings: 4   Cooking Time: 14 Minutes

Ingredients:

½ cup soy sauce	1 teaspoon cornstarch
⅓ cup water	½ teaspoon chili powder
1 tablespoon brown sugar	1 big cauliflower head, cut into florets
1 teaspoon sesame oil	
2 cloves garlic, chopped	

Directions:

Make the teriyaki sauce: In a small bowl, whisk together the soy sauce, water, brown sugar, sesame oil, cornstarch, garlic, and chili powder until well combined.   Place the cauliflower florets in a large bowl and drizzle the top with the prepared teriyaki sauce and toss to coat well.   Put the cauliflower florets in the air fryer basket.   Put the air fryer basket on the baking pan and slide into Rack Position 2, select Air Fry, set temperature to 340°F (171°C) and set time to 14 minutes.   Stir the cauliflower halfway through.   When cooking is complete, the cauliflower should be crisp-tender. Let the cauliflower cool for 5 minutes before serving.

693. Mexican Burritos

Ingredients:

1 medium onion finely sliced	1 tbsp. Olive oil
3 flakes garlic crushed	½ cup mushrooms thinly sliced
1 tsp. freshly ground peppercorns	½ cup shredded cabbage
½ cup pickled	1 tbsp. coriander,

jalapenos (Chop them up finely)
2 carrots (Cut in to long thin slices)
1-2 lettuce leaves shredded.
1 or 2 spring onions chopped finely. Also cut the greens.
Take one tomato. Remove the seeds and chop it into small pieces.
½ cup French beans (Slice them lengthwise into thin and long slices)
1 cup cottage cheese cut in too long and slightly thick Oregano Fingers

chopped
1 tbsp. vinegar
1 tsp. white wine
½ cup red kidney beans (soaked overnight)
½ small onion chopped
1 tbsp. olive oil
2 tbsp. tomato puree
¼ tsp. red chili powder
1 tsp. of salt to taste
4-5 flour tortillas
A pinch of salt to taste
½ tsp. red chili flakes
1 green chili chopped.
1 cup of cheddar cheese grated.

Directions:

Cook the beans along with the onion and garlic and mash them finely. Now, make the sauce you will need for the burrito. Ensure that you create a slightly thick sauce.   For the filling, you will need to cook the ingredients well in a pan and ensure that the vegetables have browned on the outside.   To make the salad, toss the ingredients together.

694. Honey Chili Potatoes

Ingredients:

1 capsicum, cut into thin and long pieces (lengthwise).	2 ½ tsp. ginger-garlic paste
2 tbsp. olive oil	¼ tsp. salt
2 onions. Cut them into halves.	1 tsp. red chili sauce
1 ½ tbsp. sweet chili sauce	¼ tsp. red chili powder/black pepper
1 ½ tsp. ginger garlic paste	A few drops of edible orange food coloring
½ tbsp. red chili sauce.	2 tsp. soya sauce
2 tbsp. tomato ketchup	2 tsp. vinegar
3 big potatoes (Cut into strips or cubes)	A pinch of black pepper powder
	1-2 tsp. red chili flakes

Directions:

Create the mix for the potato Oregano Fingers and coat the chicken well with it.   Pre heat the Cuisinart oven at 250 Fahrenheit for 5 minutes or so. Open the basket of the Fryer. Place the Oregano Fingers inside the basket. Now let the fryer stay at 290 Fahrenheit for another 20 minutes. Keep tossing the Oregano Fingers periodically through the cook to get a uniform cook.   Add the ingredients to the sauce and cook it with the vegetables till it thickens. Add the Oregano Fingers to the sauce and cook till the flavors have blended.

695. Potato Flat Cakes

Ingredients:

2 or 3 green chilies finely chopped
1 ½ tbsp. lemon juice
Salt and pepper to taste
2 tbsp. garam masala

2 cups sliced potato
3 tsp. ginger finely chopped
1-2 tbsp. fresh coriander leaves

Directions:
Mix the ingredients in a clean bowl and add water to it. Make sure that the paste is not too watery but is enough to apply on the potato slices.   Pre heat the Cuisinart oven at 160 degrees Fahrenheit for 5 minutes. Place the French Cuisine Galettes in the fry basket and let them cook for another 25 minutes at the same temperature. Keep rolling them over to get a uniform cook. Serve either with mint sauce or ketchup.

---

696.   Chili Sweet Potato Fries

Servings: 4   Cooking Time: 30 Minutes
Ingredients:
½ tsp salt
½ tsp garlic powder
½ tsp chili powder
¼ tsp ground cumin

3 tbsp olive oil
3 sweet potatoes, cut into thick strips

Directions:
In a bowl, mix salt, garlic powder, chili powder, and cumin, and whisk in oil. Coat in the potato strips and arrange them on the basket, without overcrowding. Press Start and cook for 20-25 minutes at 380 F on AirFry function or until crispy. Serve hot.

---

697.   Vegetable Fried Mix Chips

Servings: 4   Cooking Time: 45 Minutes
Ingredients:
1 large eggplant
4 potatoes
3 zucchinis

½ cup cornstarch
½ cup olive oil
Salt to season

Directions:
Preheat Cuisinart on Air Fry function to 390 F. Cut the eggplant and zucchini in long 3-inch strips. Peel and cut the potatoes into 3-inch strips; set aside. In a bowl, stir in cornstarch, ½ cup of water, salt, pepper, oil, eggplant, zucchini, and potatoes. Place one-third of the veggie strips in the basket and fit in the baking tray; cook for 12 minutes, shaking once. Once ready, transfer them to a serving platter. Repeat the cooking process for the remaining veggie strips. Serve warm.

---

698.   Korean Tempeh Steak With Broccoli

Servings: 4   Cooking Time: 15 Minutes + Marinating Time
Ingredients:
16 oz tempeh, cut into 1 cm thick pieces
1 pound broccoli, cut into florets
⅓ cup fermented soy sauce
2 tbsp sesame oil

⅓ cup sherry
1 tsp soy sauce
1 tsp white sugar
1 tsp cornstarch
1 tbsp olive oil
1 garlic clove, minced

Directions:

In a bowl, mix cornstarch, sherry, fermented soy sauce, sesame oil, soy sauce, sugar, and tempeh pieces. Marinate for 45 minutes.   Then, add in garlic, olive oil, and ginger. Place in the basket and fit in the baking tray; cook for 10 minutes at 390 F on Air Fry function, turning once halfway through. Serve.

---

699.   Yam Spicy Lemon Kebab

Ingredients:
2 tsp. garam masala
4 tbsp. chopped coriander
3 tbsp. cream
3 tbsp. chopped capsicum
3 eggs
2 ½ tbsp. white sesame seeds
2 cups sliced yam

3 onions chopped
5 green chilies- roughly chopped
1 ½ tbsp. ginger paste
1 ½ tsp. garlic paste
1 ½ tsp. salt
3 tsp. lemon juice

Directions:
Grind the ingredients except for the egg and form a smooth paste. Coat the yam in the paste. Now, beat the eggs and add a little salt to it.   Dip the coated vegetables in the egg mixture and then transfer to the sesame seeds and coat the yam well. Place the vegetables on a stick.   Pre heat the Cuisinart oven at 160 degrees Fahrenheit for around 5 minutes. Place the sticks in the basket and let them cook for another 25 minutes at the same temperature. Turn the sticks over in between the cooking process to get a uniform cook.

---

700.   Macaroni Fried Baked Pastry

Ingredients:
2 carrot sliced
2 cabbage sliced
2 tbsp. soya sauce
2 tsp. vinegar
Some salt and pepper to taste
2 tbsp. olive oil
1 cup all-purpose flour
2 tbsp. unsalted butter
Take the amount of water sufficient enough to make a stiff dough

½ tsp. axiomata
A pinch of salt to taste
3 cups boiled macaroni
2 onion sliced
2 capsicum sliced
2 tbsp. ginger finely chopped
2 tbsp. garlic finely chopped
2 tbsp. green chilies finely chopped
2 tbsp. ginger-garlic paste

Directions:
Mix the dough for the outer covering and make it stiff and smooth. Leave it to rest in a container while making the filling. Cook the ingredients in a pan and stir them well to make a thick paste. Roll the paste out.   Roll the dough into balls and flatten them. Cut them in halves and add the filling. Use water to help you fold the edges to create the shape of a cone. Pre-heat the Cuisinart oven for around 5 to 6 minutes at 300 Fahrenheit. Place all the samosas in the fry basket and close the basket properly. Keep

the Cuisinart oven at 200 degrees for another 20 to 25 minutes. Around the halfway point, open the basket and turn the samosas over for uniform cooking. After this, fry at 250 degrees for around 10 minutes in order to give them the desired golden-brown color. Serve hot. Recommended sides are tamarind or mint sauce.

701. Tomato & Feta Bites With Pine Nuts

Servings: 2   Cooking Time: 25 Minutes

Ingredients:

1 heirloom tomato, sliced	1 clove garlic
1 (4- oz) block Feta cheese, sliced	1 ½ tbsp toasted pine nuts
1 small red onion, thinly sliced	¼ cup fresh parsley, chopped
2 tsp + ¼ cup olive oil	¼ cup grated Parmesan cheese
	¼ cup chopped basil

Directions:

Add basil, pine nuts, garlic, and salt to a food processor. Process while slowly adding ¼ cup of olive oil. Once finished, pour basil pesto into a bowl and refrigerate for 30 minutes. Preheat Cuisinart oven on AirFry function to 390 F. Spread some pesto on each slice of tomato. Top with feta cheese and onion and drizzle with the remaining olive oil. Place in the frying basket and press Start. Cook for 12 minutes. Top with the remaining pesto and serve.

702. Spicy Kung Pao Tofu

Servings: 4   Cooking Time: 10 Minutes

Ingredients:

1 teaspoon cornstarch	⅓ cup Asian-Style sauce
½ teaspoon red pepper flakes, or more to taste	1 small green bell pepper, cut into bite-size pieces
1 pound (454 g) firm or extra-firm tofu, cut into 1-inch cubes	3 scallions, sliced, whites and green parts separated
1 small carrot, peeled and cut into ¼-inch-thick coins	3 tablespoons roasted unsalted peanuts

Directions:

In a large bowl, whisk together the sauce, cornstarch, and red pepper flakes. Fold in the tofu, carrot, pepper, and the white parts of the scallions and toss to coat. Spread the mixture evenly in the baking pan. Slide the baking pan into Rack Position 2, select Roast, set temperature to 375ºF (190ºC), and set time to 10 minutes. Stir the ingredients once halfway through the cooking time. When done, remove from the oven. Serve sprinkled with the peanuts and scallion greens.

703. Cottage Cheese And Mushroom Mexican Burritos

Ingredients:

½ cup mushrooms thinly sliced	¼ tsp. red chili powder
1 cup cottage cheese cut in too long and slightly thick Oregano Fingers	1 tsp. of salt to taste
	4-5 flour tortillas
A pinch of salt to taste	1 or 2 spring onions chopped finely. Also cut the greens.
½ tsp. red chili flakes	Take one tomato. Remove the seeds and chop it into small pieces.
1 tsp. freshly ground peppercorns	
½ cup pickled jalapenos	1 green chili chopped.
1-2 lettuce leaves shredded.	1 cup of cheddar cheese grated.
½ cup red kidney beans (soaked overnight)	1 cup boiled rice (not necessary).
½ small onion chopped	A few flour tortillas to put the filing in.
1 tbsp. olive oil	
2 tbsp. tomato puree	

Directions:

Cook the beans along with the onion and garlic and mash them finely. Now, make the sauce you will need for the burrito. Ensure that you create a slightly thick sauce. For the filling, you will need to cook the ingredients well in a pan and ensure that the vegetables have browned on the outside. To make the salad, toss the ingredients together. Place the tortilla and add a layer of sauce, followed by the beans and the filling at the center. Before you roll it, you will need to place the salad on top of the filling. Pre-heat the Cuisinart oven for around 5 minutes at 200 Fahrenheit. Open the fry basket and keep the burritos inside. Close the basket properly. Let the Air Fryer remain at 200 Fahrenheit for another 15 minutes or so. Halfway through, remove the basket and turn all the burritos over in order to get a uniform cook.

704. Cheese & Vegetable Pizza

Servings: 1   Cooking Time: 15 Minutes

Ingredients:

1 tbsp tomato paste	4 red onion rings
¼ cup mozzarella cheese, grated	½ green bell pepper, chopped
1 tbsp sweet corn, cooked	3 cherry tomatoes, quartered
4 zucchini slices	1 tortilla
4 eggplant slices	¼ tsp oregano

Directions:

Preheat Cuisinart on Pizza function to 350 F. Spread the tomato paste on the tortilla. Top with zucchini and eggplant slices first, then green peppers, and onion rings. Arrange the cherry tomatoes on top and scatter the corn. Sprinkle with oregano and top with mozzarella cheeses. Press Start and cook for 10-12 minutes. Serve warm.

---

705. Cottage Cheese Spicy Lemon Kebab

Ingredients:

3 tsp. lemon juice

2 tbsp. coriander powder

3 tbsp. chopped capsicum

2 tbsp. peanut flour

2 cups cubed cottage

5 green chilies-roughly chopped

1 ½ tbsp. ginger paste

1 ½ tsp. garlic paste

1 ½ tsp. salt

3 eggs

cheese

3 onions chopped

Directions:

Coat the cottage cheese cubes with the corn flour and mix the other ingredients in a bowl. Make the mixture into a smooth paste and coat the cheese cubes with the mixture. Beat the eggs in a bowl and add a little salt to them. Dip the cubes in the egg mixture and coat them with sesame seeds and leave them in the refrigerator for an hour. Pre heat the Cuisinart oven at 290 Fahrenheit for around 5 minutes. Place the kebabs in the basket and let them cook for another 25 minutes at the same temperature. Turn the kebabs over in between the cooking process to get a uniform cook. Serve the kebabs with mint sauce.

Snacks And Desserts Recipes

706. Apple Fritters

Servings: 6   Cooking Time: 7 Minutes
Ingredients:

1 cup chopped, peeled Granny Smith apple	1 teaspoon baking powder
½ cup granulated sugar	1 teaspoon salt
1 teaspoon ground cinnamon	2 tablespoons milk
1 cup all-purpose flour	2 tablespoons butter, melted
	1 large egg, beaten
	Cooking spray

Directions:
¼ cup confectioners' sugar (optional)   Mix together the apple, granulated sugar, and cinnamon in a small bowl. Allow to sit for 30 minutes. Combine the flour, baking powder, and salt in a medium bowl. Add the milk, butter, and egg and stir to incorporate.   Pour the apple mixture into the bowl of flour mixture and stir with a spatula until a dough forms.   Make the fritters: On a clean work surface, divide the dough into 12 equal portions and shape into 1-inch balls. Flatten them into patties with your hands.   Line the baking pan with parchment paper and spray it with cooking spray. Transfer the apple fritters onto the parchment paper, evenly spaced but not too close together. Spray the fritters with cooking spray.   Slide the baking pan into Rack Position 1, select Convection Bake, set temperature to 350°F (180°C), and set time to 7 minutes.   Flip the fritters halfway through the cooking time.   When cooking is complete, the fritters should be lightly browned.   Remove from the oven to a plate and serve with the confectioners' sugar sprinkled on top, if desired.

707. Baked Peaches And Blueberries

Servings: 6   Cooking Time: 10 Minutes
Ingredients:

3 peaches, peeled, halved, and pitted	¼ teaspoon ground cinnamon
2 tablespoons packed brown sugar	1 teaspoon pure vanilla extract
1 cup plain Greek yogurt	1 cup fresh blueberries

Directions:
Place the peaches in the baking pan, cut-side up. Top with a generous sprinkle of brown sugar.   Slide the baking pan into Rack Position 1, select Convection Bake, set temperature to 380°F (193°C), and set time to 10 minutes.   Meanwhile, whisk together the yogurt, cinnamon, and vanilla in a small bowl until smooth.   When cooking is complete, the peaches should be lightly browned and caramelized.   Remove the peaches from the oven to a plate. Serve topped with the yogurt mixture and fresh blueberries.

708. Chocolate Coffee Cake

Servings: 8   Cooking Time: 15 Minutes

Ingredients:

1 ½ cups almond flour	1 egg
1/2 cup coconut meal	Topping:
2/3 cup swerve	1/4 cup coconut flour
1 teaspoon baking powder	1/2 cup confectioner's swerve
1/4 teaspoon salt	1/2 teaspoon ground cardamom
1 stick butter, melted	1 teaspoon ground cinnamon
1/2 cup hot strongly brewed coffee	3 tablespoons coconut oil
1/2 teaspoon vanilla	

Directions:
Mix all dry ingredients for your cake; then, mix in the wet ingredients. Mix until everything is well incorporated.   Spritz a baking pan with cooking spray. Scrape the batter into the baking pan. Then, make the topping by mixing all ingredients. Place on top of the cake. Smooth the top with a spatula.   Bake at 330 degrees F for 30 minutes or until the top of the cake springs back when gently pressed with your fingers. Serve with your favorite hot beverage.
Nutrition Info: 285 Calories; 21g Fat; 6g Carbs; 8g Protein; 3g Sugars; 1g Fiber

709. Tofu Steaks

Servings: 4   Cooking Time: 35 Minutes
Ingredients:

1 package tofu, press and remove excess liquid	1/4 cup olive oil
	1/4 tsp dried thyme
2 tbsp lemon zest	1/4 cup lemon juice
3 garlic cloves, minced	Pepper
	Salt

Directions:
Fit the Cuisinart oven with the rack in position 2. Cut tofu into eight pieces.   In a bowl, mix together olive oil, thyme, lemon juice, lemon zest, garlic, pepper, and salt.   Add tofu into the bowl and coat well and place it in the refrigerator overnight. Place marinated tofu in an air fryer basket then places an air fryer basket in the baking pan.   Place a baking pan on the oven rack. Set to air fry at 350 F for 35 minutes.   Serve and enjoy.
Nutrition Info: Calories 139 Fat 14.1 g Carbohydrates 2.3 g Sugar 0.7 g Protein 2.9 g Cholesterol 0 mg

710. Easy Egg Custard

Servings: 6   Cooking Time: 40 Minutes
Ingredients:

2 egg yolks	1/2 cup erythritol
1 tsp nutmeg	3 eggs
2 cups heavy whipping cream	1/2 tsp vanilla

Directions:
Fit the Cuisinart oven with the rack in position Add all ingredients into the large mixing bowl and beat until just well combined.   Pour custard mixture into the greased pie dish.   Set to bake at

350 F for 40 minutes. After 5 minutes place the pie dish in the preheated oven.   Serve.
Nutrition Info: Calories 190 Fat 18.6 g Carbohydrates 1.7 g Sugar 0.4 g Protein 4.5 g Cholesterol 207 mg

711. Broccoli Nuggets

Servings: 4   Cooking Time: 15 Minutes
Ingredients:

2 cups broccoli florets, cooked & mashed	1 cup mozzarella cheese, shredded
1/4 cup almond flour	2 egg whites
	1/8 tsp salt

Directions:
Fit the Cuisinart oven with the rack in position 2. Add all ingredients to the bowl and mix well to combine.   Make nuggets from broccoli mixture and place in the air fryer basket then place an air fryer basket in the baking pan.   Place a baking pan on the oven rack. Set to air fry at 325 F for 15 minutes. Serve and enjoy.
Nutrition Info: Calories 165 Fat 9.9 g Carbohydrates 8.4 g Sugar 1.5 g Protein 11 g Cholesterol 30 mg

712. Cinnamon & Honey Apples With Hazelnuts

Servings: 2   Cooking Time: 15 Minutes
Ingredients:

4 apples	Zest of 1 orange
1 oz butter	2 oz mixed seeds
2 oz breadcrumbs	1 tsp cinnamon
2 tbsp chopped hazelnuts	2 tbsp honey

Directions:
Preheat Cuisinart on Bake function to 350 F. Core the apples. Make sure to also score their skin to prevent from splitting.   Combine the remaining ingredients in a bowl; stuff the apples with the mixture and press Start. Bake for 10 minutes. Serve topped with chopped hazelnuts.

713. Banana Clafouti

Ingredients:

1 tsp vanilla extract	2 tsp fresh lemon juice
2 Tbsp butter, melted	1 cup whole milk
1/4 tsp salt	1/4 cup whipping cream
1/2 cup all-purpose flour	3 eggs
2 bananas, peeled and thinly sliced	1/2 cup granulated sugar

Directions:
Preheat the oven to 350°F.   Whisk together milk, cream, eggs, sugar, extract, butter and salt.   Add the flour and whisk gently until incorporated. Place sliced bananas in a bowl with lemon juice. Lightly grease Cuisinart oven and heat in oven for 5 minutes. Remove and pour in batter.   Scatter bananas over batter and bake until golden and puffed, about 35 minutes.

714.   Corn And Black Bean Salsa

Servings: 4   Cooking Time: 10 Minutes
Ingredients:

1/2 (15-ounce / 425-g) can corn, drained and rinsed	1/4 cup shredded reduced-fat Cheddar cheese
1/2 (15-ounce / 425-g) can black beans, drained and rinsed	1/2 teaspoon paprika
1/4 cup chunky salsa	1/2 teaspoon ground cumin
2 ounces (57 g) reduced-fat cream cheese, softened	Salt and freshly ground black pepper, to taste

Directions:
Combine the corn, black beans, salsa, cream cheese, Cheddar cheese, paprika, and cumin in a medium bowl. Sprinkle with salt and pepper and stir until well blended.   Pour the mixture into the baking pan.   Slide the baking pan into Rack Position 2, select Air Fry, set temperature to 325°F (163°C), and set time to 10 minutes.   When cooking is complete, the mixture should be heated through. Rest for 5 minutes and serve warm.

715. Flavors Pumpkin Custard

Servings: 6   Cooking Time: 40 Minutes
Ingredients:

4 egg yolks	3/4 cup coconut cream
1/2 tsp cinnamon	
1 tsp liquid stevia	1/8 tsp cloves
15 oz pumpkin puree	1/8 tsp ginger

Directions:
Fit the Cuisinart oven with the rack in position   In a large bowl, mix together pumpkin puree, cloves, ginger, cinnamon, and swerve.   Add egg yolks and beat until well combined.   Add coconut cream and stir well.   Pour mixture into the six ramekins. Set to bake at 350 F for 45 minutes. After 5 minutes place ramekins in the preheated oven.   Serve chilled and enjoy.
Nutrition Info: Calories 130 Fat 10.4 g Carbohydrates 8 g Sugar 3.4 g Protein 3.3 g Cholesterol 140 mg

716.   Lemon-raspberry Muffins

Servings: 6   Cooking Time: 15 Minutes
Ingredients:

2 cups almond flour	1/2 teaspoon grated lemon zest
3/4 cup Swerve	
1 1/4 teaspoons baking powder	1/4 teaspoon salt
1/3 teaspoon ground allspice	2 eggs
	1 cup sour cream
1/3 teaspoon ground anise star	1/2 cup coconut oil
	1/2 cup raspberries

Directions:
Line a muffin pan with 6 paper liners.   In a mixing bowl, mix the almond flour, Swerve, baking powder, allspice, anise, lemon zest, and salt.   In another mixing bowl, beat the eggs, sour cream, and coconut oil until well mixed. Add the egg mixture to the flour mixture and stir to combine. Mix in the raspberries.

Scrape the batter into the prepared muffin cups, filling each about three-quarters full. Put the muffin pan into Rack Position 1, select Convection Bake, set temperature to 345°F (174°C), and set time to 15 minutes. When cooking is complete, the tops should be golden and a toothpick inserted in the middle should come out clean. Allow the muffins to cool for 10 minutes in the muffin pan before removing and serving.

717. Almond Peanut Butter Bars

Servings: 8   Cooking Time: 30 Minutes
Ingredients:

2 eggs	1/2 cup peanut butter
1/2 cup erythritol	1 tbsp coconut flour
1/2 cup butter softened	1/2 cup almond flour

Directions:
Fit the Cuisinart oven with the rack in position   In a bowl, beat together butter, eggs, and peanut butter until well combined.   Add dry ingredients and mix until a smooth batter is formed.   Spread batter evenly in greased baking pan.   Set to bake at 350 F for 35 minutes. After 5 minutes place the baking pan in the preheated oven.   Slice and serve.
Nutrition Info: Calories 168 Fat 12.5 g Carbohydrates 9.7 g Sugar 1.8 g Protein 6.5 g Cholesterol 41 mg

718. Air Fried Chicken Wings

Servings: 4   Cooking Time: 18 Minutes
Ingredients:

2 pounds (907 g) chicken wings	Cooking spray

Directions:
Marinade: cup buttermilk   ½ teaspoon salt   ½ teaspoon black pepper   Coating: cup flour   cup panko bread crumbs   tablespoons poultry seasoning   teaspoons salt   Whisk together all the ingredients for the marinade in a large bowl. Add the chicken wings to the marinade and toss well. Transfer to the refrigerator to marinate for at least an hour.   Spritz the air fryer basket with cooking spray. Set aside.   Thoroughly combine all the ingredients for the coating in a shallow bowl. Remove the chicken wings from the marinade and shake off any excess. Roll them in the coating mixture.   Place the chicken wings in the basket in a single layer. Mist the wings with cooking spray. Put the air fryer basket on the baking pan and slide into Rack Position 2, select Air Fry, set temperature to 360°F (182°C), and set time to 18 minutes. Flip the wings halfway through the cooking time. When cooking is complete, the wings should be crisp and golden brown on the outside. Remove from the oven to a plate and serve hot.

719. Baked Cream

Ingredients:

1 cup fresh blueberries	2 cups condensed milk
1 cup blackberries	2 cups fresh cream
Handful of mint	1 cup fresh
leaves	strawberries
3 tsp. sugar	4 tsp. water

Directions:
Blend the cream and add the milk to it. Whisk the ingredients well together and transfer this mixture into small baking bowls ensuring you do not overfill the bowls.   Preheat the fryer to 300 Fahrenheit for five minutes. You will need to place the bowls in the basket and cover it. Cook it for fifteen minutes. When you shake the bowls, the mixture should just shake but not break. Leave it in the refrigerator to set and then arrange the fruits, garnish and serve.

720. Lemon Ricotta Cake

Servings: 6   Cooking Time: 25 Minutes
Ingredients:

17.5 ounces (496 g) ricotta cheese	3 tablespoons flour
5.4 ounces (153 g) sugar	1 lemon, juiced and zested
3 eggs, beaten	2 teaspoons vanilla extract

Directions:
In a large mixing bowl, stir together all the ingredients until the mixture reaches a creamy consistency.   Pour the mixture into the baking pan.   Slide the baking pan into Rack Position 1, select Convection Bake, set temperature to 320°F (160°C), and set time to 25 minutes.   When cooking is complete, a toothpick inserted in the center should come out clean.   Allow to cool for 10 minutes on a wire rack before serving.

721. Parmesan Green Beans

Servings: 4   Cooking Time: 15 Minutes
Ingredients:

1 lb green beans	2 tbsp olive oil
4 tbsp parmesan cheese	Pinch of salt

Directions:
Fit the Cuisinart oven with the rack in position   Add green beans in a large bowl.   Add remaining ingredients on top of green beans and toss to coat.   Spread green beans in baking pan.   Set to bake at 400 F for 20 minutes. After 5 minutes place the baking pan in the preheated oven.   Serve and enjoy.
Nutrition Info: Calories 114 Fat 8.4 g Carbohydrates 8.3 g Sugar 1.6 g Protein 4 g Cholesterol 4 mg

722. Orange Citrus Blend

Ingredients:

3 tbsp. powdered sugar	2 persimmons (sliced)
3 tbsp. unsalted butter	2 cups milk
2 oranges (sliced)	2 cups almond flour
	2 tbsp. custard powder

Directions:
Boil the milk and the sugar in a pan and add the custard powder followed by the almond flour and stir till you get a thick mixture. Add the sliced fruits to the mixture.   Preheat the fryer to 300 Fahrenheit for five minutes. Place the dish in the

basket and reduce the temperature to 250 Fahrenheit. Cook for ten minutes and set aside to cool.

723. Delicious Banana Cake

Servings: 8   Cooking Time: 40 Minutes
Ingredients:

2 large eggs, beaten	1 cup milk
1 tsp baking powder	2 cups all-purpose
1 1/2 cup sugar,	flour
granulated	2 bananas, mashed
1 tsp vanilla extract	1 tsp baking soda
1/2 cup butter	

Directions:
Fit the Cuisinart oven with the rack in position   In a mixing bowl, beat together sugar and butter until creamy. Add beaten eggs and mix well.   Add milk, vanilla extract, baking soda, baking powder, flour, and mashed bananas into the mixture and beat for 2 minutes. Mix well.   Pour batter into the greased baking dish.   Set to bake at 350 F for 45 minutes. After 5 minutes place the baking dish in the preheated oven.   Slices and serve.
Nutrition Info: Calories 418 Fat 13.8 g Carbohydrates 80 g Sugar 42.7 g Protein 6.2 g Cholesterol 80 mg

724. Chocolate Donuts

Servings: 8-10   Cooking Time: 20 Minutes
Ingredients:

(8-ounce) can jumbo biscuits	Chocolate sauce, such as Hershey's
Cooking oil	

Directions:
Preparing the Ingredients. Separate the biscuit dough into 8 biscuits and place them on a flat work surface. Use a small circle cookie cutter or a biscuit cutter to cut a hole in the center of each biscuit. You can also cut the holes using a knife.   Spray the Oven rack/basket with cooking oil. Place the Rack on the middle-shelf of the Cuisinart air fryer oven. Air Frying. Place 4 donuts in the air fryer oven. Do not stack. Spray with cooking oil. Cook for 4 minutes. Open the air fryer oven and flip the donuts. Cook for an additional 4 minutes.   Remove the cooked donuts from the air fryer, then repeat steps 3 and 4 for the remaining 4 donuts.   Drizzle chocolate sauce over the donuts and enjoy while warm.
Nutrition Info:CALORIES: 181; FAT:98G; PROTEIN:3G; FIBER:1G

725. Sweet Cinnamon Peaches

Servings: 4   Cooking Time: 10 Minutes
Ingredients:

2 tablespoons sugar	4 peaches, cut into
¼ teaspoon ground cinnamon	wedges
	Cooking spray

Directions:
Spritz the air fryer basket with cooking spray.   In a large bowl, stir together the sugar and cinnamon. Add the peaches to the bowl and toss to coat evenly. Spread the coated peaches in a single layer on the basket.   Put the air fryer basket on the baking pan and slide into Rack Position 2, select Air Fry, set

temperature to 350°F (180°C) and set time to 10 minutes.   After 5 minutes, remove from the oven. Turn the peaches over. Lightly mist them with cooking spray. Return to the oven to continue cooking.   When cooking is complete, the peaches will be lightly browned and caramelized. Remove from the oven and let rest for 5 minutes before serving.

726. Air Fryer Cinnamon Rolls

Servings: 8   Cooking Time: 5 Minutes
Ingredients:

1 ½ tbsp. cinnamon	½ tsp. vanilla
¾ C. brown sugar	
¼ C. melted coconut oil	1 ¼ C. powdered erythritol
1 pound frozen bread dough, thawed	2 tbsp. softened ghee
Glaze:	3 ounces softened cream cheese

Directions:
Preparing the Ingredients. Lay out bread dough and roll out into a rectangle. Brush melted ghee over dough and leave a 1-inch border along edges.   Mix cinnamon and sweetener together and then sprinkle over the dough.   Roll dough tightly and slice into 8 pieces. Let sit 1-2 hours to rise.   To make the glaze, simply mix ingredients together till smooth. Air Frying. Once rolls rise, place into the Cuisinart air fryer oven and cook 5 minutes at 350 degrees. Serve rolls drizzled in cream cheese glaze. Enjoy!
Nutrition Info:CALORIES: 390; FAT:8G; PROTEIN:1G; SUGAR:7G

727. Cheddar Dip

Servings: 6   Cooking Time: 15 Minutes
Ingredients:

8 oz. cheddar cheese; grated	12 oz. coconut cream
	2 tsp. hot sauce

Directions:
In ramekin, mix the cream with hot sauce and cheese and whisk.   Put the ramekin in the fryer and cook at 390°F for 12 minutes. Whisk, divide into bowls and serve as a dip
Nutrition Info: Calories: 170; Fat: 9g; Fiber: 2g; Carbs: 4g; Protein: 12g

728. Lemon Butter Cake

Servings: 10   Cooking Time: 55 Minutes
Ingredients:

4 eggs	2 tbsp lemon zest
1/2 cup butter softened	1/2 cup fresh lemon juice
2 tsp baking powder	1/4 cup erythritol
1/4 cup coconut flour	1 tbsp vanilla
2 cups almond flour	

Directions:
Fit the Cuisinart oven with the rack in position   In a large bowl, whisk all ingredients until a smooth batter is formed.   Pour batter into the loaf pan. Set to bake at 300 F for 60 minutes. After 5 minutes place the loaf pan in the preheated oven.   Slice and serve.

Nutrition Info: Calories 85 Fat 5.7 g
Carbohydrates 5 g Sugar 0.9 g Protein 3.8 g
Cholesterol 65 mg

729.	**Cheesy Baked Potatoes**

Servings: 6   Cooking Time: 20 Minutes
Ingredients:

1 teaspoon kosher salt, divided	12 small red potatoes
1 tablespoon extra-virgin olive oil	¼ cup sour cream
¼ cup grated sharp Cheddar cheese	2 tablespoons chopped chives
	2 tablespoons grated Parmesan cheese

Directions:
Add the potatoes to a large bowl. Sprinkle with the ½ teaspoon of the salt and drizzle with the olive oil. Toss to coat. Place the potatoes in the baking pan. Slide the baking pan into Rack Position 2, select Roast, set temperature to 375ºF (190ºC) and set time to 15 minutes.   When cooking is complete, remove the pan and let the potatoes rest for 5 minutes. Halve the potatoes lengthwise. Using a spoon, scoop the flesh into a bowl, leaving a thin shell of skin. Arrange the potato halves in the pan. Mash the potato flesh until smooth. Stir in the remaining ½ teaspoon of the salt, Cheddar cheese, sour cream and chives. Transfer the filling into a pastry bag with one corner snipped off. Pipe the filling into the potato shells, mounding up slightly. Sprinkle with the Parmesan cheese.   Select Roast, set temperature to 375ºF (190ºC) and set time to 5 minutes.   When cooking is complete, the tops should be browning slightly. Remove from the oven and let the potatoes cool slightly before serving.

730.	**Salsa Cheese Dip**

Servings: 10   Cooking Time: 30 Minutes
Ingredients:

16 oz cream cheese, softened	3 cups cheddar cheese, shredded
1 cup sour cream	1/2 cup hot salsa

Directions:
Fit the Cuisinart oven with the rack in position   In a bowl, mix all ingredients until just combined and pour into the baking dish.   Set to bake at 350 F for 35 minutes. After 5 minutes place the baking dish in the preheated oven.   Serve and enjoy.
Nutrition Info: Calories 348 Fat 31.9 g
Carbohydrates 3.4 g Sugar 0.7 g Protein 12.8 g
Cholesterol 96 mg

731.	**Baked Almonds**

Servings: 6   Cooking Time: 20 Minutes
Ingredients:

1 1/2 cups raw almonds	1/2 tsp garlic powder
1/2 tsp cayenne	1/2 tsp cumin
1/4 tsp onion powder	1 1/2 tsp chili powder
1/4 tsp dried basil	1/2 tsp sea salt
2 tbsp butter, melted	

Directions:
Fit the Cuisinart oven with the rack in position   Add almonds and remaining ingredients into the mixing bowl and toss well.   Spread almonds in

baking pan.   Set to bake at 350 F for 25 minutes. After 5 minutes place the baking pan in the preheated oven.   Serve and enjoy.
Nutrition Info: Calories 176 Fat 15.9 g
Carbohydrates 5.9 g Sugar 1.2 g Protein 5.2 g
Cholesterol 10 mg

732.	**Tomato Bites**

Servings: 6   Cooking Time: 15 Minutes
Ingredients:

6 tomatoes; halved	3 tsp. sugar-free apricot jam
2 oz. watercress	2 tsp. oregano; dried
3 oz. cheddar cheese; grated	A pinch of salt and black pepper
1 tbsp. olive oil	

Directions:
Spread the jam on each tomato half, sprinkle oregano, salt and pepper and drizzle the oil all over them   Introduce them in the fryer's basket, sprinkle the cheese on top and cook at 360ºF for 20 minutes   Arrange the tomatoes on a platter, top each half with some watercress and serve as an appetizer.
Nutrition Info: Calories: 131; Fat: 7g; Fiber: 2g; Carbs: 4g; Protein: 7g

733.	**Avocado Chips**

Servings: 4   Cooking Time: 10 Minutes
Ingredients:

1 egg	¾ cup panko bread crumbs
1 tablespoon lime juice	¼ cup cornmeal
⅛ teaspoon hot sauce	¼ teaspoon salt
2 tablespoons flour	

Directions:
1 large avocado, pitted, peeled, and cut into ½-inch slices   Cooking spray   Whisk together the egg, lime juice, and hot sauce in a small bowl.   On a sheet of wax paper, place the flour. In a separate sheet of wax paper, combine the bread crumbs, cornmeal, and salt.   Dredge the avocado slices one at a time in the flour, then in the egg mixture, finally roll them in the bread crumb mixture to coat well. Place the breaded avocado slices in the air fryer basket and mist them with cooking spray.   Put the air fryer basket on the baking pan and slide into Rack Position 2, select Air Fry, set temperature to 390ºF (199ºC), and set time to 10 minutes.   When cooking is complete, the slices should be nicely browned and crispy. Transfer the avocado slices to a plate and serve.

734.	**Bbq Pulled Mushrooms**

Servings: 2   Cooking Time: 15 Minutes
Ingredients:

4 large portobello mushrooms	1 tbsp. salted butter; melted.
½ cup low-carb, sugar-free barbecue sauce	¼ tsp. onion powder.
1 tsp. paprika	¼ tsp. ground black pepper
	1 tsp. chili powder

Directions:

Remove stem and scoop out the underside of each mushroom. Brush the caps with butter and sprinkle with pepper, chili powder, paprika and onion powder. Place mushrooms into the air fryer basket. Adjust the temperature to 400 Degrees F and set the timer for 8 minutes. When the timer beeps, remove mushrooms from the basket and place on a cutting board or work surface. Using two forks, gently pull the mushrooms apart, creating strands. Place mushroom strands into a 4-cup round baking dish with barbecue sauce. Place dish into the air fryer basket. Adjust the temperature to 350 Degrees F and set the timer for 4 minutes. Stir halfway through the cooking time. Serve warm.
Nutrition Info: Calories: 108; Protein: 3.3g; Fiber: 2.7g; Fat: 5.9g; Carbs: 10.9g

735. Tuna Melts With Scallions

Servings: 6   Cooking Time: 6 Minutes
Ingredients:

2 (5- to 6-ounce / 142- to 170-g) cans oil-packed tuna, drained	1 tablespoon capers, drained
1 large scallion, chopped	¼ teaspoon celery salt
1 small stalk celery, chopped	12 slices cocktail rye bread
⅓ cup mayonnaise	2 tablespoons butter, melted
1 tablespoon chopped fresh dill	6 slices sharp Cheddar cheese

Directions:
In a medium bowl, stir together the tuna, scallion, celery, mayonnaise, dill, capers and celery salt. Brush one side of the bread slices with the butter. Arrange the bread slices in the baking pan, buttered-side down. Scoop a heaping tablespoon of the tuna mixture on each slice of bread, spreading it out evenly to the edges. Cut the cheese slices to fit the dimensions of the bread and place a cheese slice on each piece. Slide the baking pan into Rack Position 2, select Roast, set temperature to 375°F (190°C) and set time to 6 minutes. After 4 minutes, remove from the oven and check the tuna melts. The tuna melts are done when the cheese has melted and the tuna is heated through. If needed, continue cooking. When cooking is complete, remove from the oven. Use a spatula to transfer the tuna melts to a clean work surface and slice each one in half diagonally. Serve warm.

736. Roasted Mixed Nuts

Servings: 6   Cooking Time: 20 Minutes
Ingredients:

2 cups mixed nuts (walnuts, pecans, and almonds)	2 tablespoons sugar
2 tablespoons egg white	1 teaspoon paprika
	1 teaspoon ground cinnamon
	Cooking spray

Directions:
Line the air fryer basket with parchment paper and spray with cooking spray. Stir together the mixed nuts, egg white, sugar, paprika, and cinnamon in a small bowl until the nuts are fully coated. Place the nuts in the basket. Put the air fryer basket on the baking pan and slide into Rack Position 2, select Roast, set temperature to 300°F (150°C), and set time to 20 minutes. Stir the nuts halfway through the cooking time. When cooking is complete, remove from the oven. Transfer the nuts to a bowl and serve warm.

737. Beefy Mini Pies

Ingredients:

1 cup shredded Colby cheese	½ teaspoon dried dill weed
2 eggs	½ pound ground beef
½ cup half-and-half	
1 (10-ounce) package refrigerated flaky dinner rolls	1 small onion, chopped
	2 cloves garlic, minced

Directions:
Preheat oven to 350°F. Remove rolls from package and divide each roll into 3 rounds. Place each round into a 3-inch muffin cup; press firmly onto bottom and up sides. In a heavy skillet, cook ground beef with onion and garlic until beef is done. Drain well. Place 1 tablespoon beef mixture into each dough-lined muffin cup. Sprinkle cheese over beef mixture. In a small bowl, beat together eggs, half-and-half, and dill weed. Spoon this mixture over beef in muffin cups, making sure not to overfill cups. Bake at 350°F for 10 to 13 minutes or until filling is puffed and set. Flash freeze in single layer on baking sheet. When frozen solid, wrap, label, and freeze. To thaw and reheat: Thaw pies in single layer in refrigerator overnight. Bake at 350°F for 7 to 9 minutes or until hot.

738. Authentic Raisin Apple Treat

Servings: 4   Cooking Time: 15 Minutes
Ingredients:

4 apples, cored	¾ oz raisins
1 ½ oz almonds	2 tbsp sugar

Directions:
Preheat Cuisinart on Bake function to 360 F. In a bowl, mix sugar, almonds, and raisins. Blend the mixture using a hand mixer. Fill cored apples with the almond mixture. Place the apples in a baking tray and cook for 10 minutes. Serve with a sprinkle of powdered sugar.

739. Muffins And Jam

Ingredients:

1 tbsp. unsalted butter	1 ½ cups + 2 tbsp. all-purpose flour
2 cups buttermilk	1 tsp. baking powder
Parchment paper	½ tsp. baking soda
1 cup + 2 tbsp. powdered sugar	2 tbsp. jam

Directions:
In a bowl, add the flour and the buttermilk. Fold the mixture using a spatula. Add the jam and whisk the ingredients to ensure that the jam has thinned. Add the remaining ingredients to the bowl and continue to mix the ingredients. Do not mix too much. Grease the muffin cups and line them with the

parchment paper. Transfer the mixture into the cups and set them aside. Preheat the fryer to 300 Fahrenheit for five minutes. Place the muffin cups in the basket and reduce the temperature to 250 Fahrenheit. Cool in the basket and serve warm.

740. Breaded Bananas With Chocolate Sauce

Servings: 6   Cooking Time: 7 Minutes

Ingredients:
- ¼ cup cornstarch
- ¼ cup plain bread crumbs
- 3 bananas, halved crosswise
- 1 large egg, beaten
- Cooking spray
- Chocolate sauce, for serving

Directions:
Place the cornstarch, bread crumbs, and egg in three separate bowls.   Roll the bananas in the cornstarch, then in the beaten egg, and finally in the bread crumbs to coat well.   Spritz the air fryer basket with cooking spray.   Arrange the banana halves in the basket and mist them with cooking spray.   Put the air fryer basket on the baking pan and slide into Rack Position 2, select Air Fry, set temperature to 350°F (180°C), and set time to 7 minutes.   After about 5 minutes, flip the bananas and continue to air fry for another 2 minutes. When cooking is complete, remove the bananas from the oven to a serving plate. Serve with the chocolate sauce drizzled over the top.

741. Yummy Scalloped Pineapple

Servings: 6   Cooking Time: 35 Minutes

Ingredients:
- 3 eggs, lightly beaten
- 8 oz can crushed pineapple, un-drained
- 2 cups of sugar
- 4 cups of bread cubes
- 1/4 cup milk
- 1/2 cup butter, melted

Directions:
Fit the Cuisinart oven with the rack in position   In a mixing bowl, whisk eggs with milk, butter, crushed pineapple, and sugar.   Add bread cubes and stir well to coat.   Transfer mixture to the greased baking dish.   Set to bake at 350 F for 40 minutes. After 5 minutes place the baking dish in the preheated oven.   Serve and enjoy.
Nutrition Info: Calories 510 Fat 17 g Carbohydrates 85 g Sugar 71 g Protein 3.4 g Cholesterol 123 mg

742. Cherry Apple Risotto

Servings: 4   Cooking Time: 12 Minutes

Ingredients:
- 1 tablespoon of butter
- ¼ cup of brown sugar
- ½ cup of apple juice
- 1½ cups of milk
- ¾ cup of Arborio rice, boiled
- 1 apple, diced
- 2 pinches salt
- ¾ teaspoon of cinnamon powder
- ¼ cup of dried cherries
- 1½ tablespoons of almonds, roasted and sliced

- ¼ cup of whipped cream

Directions:
Set the Instant Vortex on Air fryer to 375 degrees F for 12 minutes. Combine rice with butter, sugar, apple juice, milk, apple, salt, and cinnamon in a bowl. Pour the rice mixture into the cooking tray. Insert the cooking tray in the Vortex when it displays "Add Food". Toss the food when it displays "Turn Food". Remove from the oven when cooking time is complete. Top with the dried cherries, almonds, and whipped cream to serve.
Nutrition Info: Calories: 317 Cal Total Fat: 8.5 g Saturated Fat: 0 g   Cholesterol: 0 mg   Sodium: 0 mg   Total Carbs: 54.8 g   Fiber: 0 g   Sugar: 0 g Protein: 6.2 g

743. Ultimate Chocolate And Coconut Pudding

Servings: 10   Cooking Time: 15 Minutes

Ingredients:
- 1 stick butter
- 1 ¼ cups bakers' chocolate, unsweetened
- 1 teaspoon liquid stevia
- 2 tablespoons full fat coconut milk
- 2 eggs, beaten
- 1/3 cup coconut, shredded

Directions:
Begin by preheating your Air Fryer to 330 degrees F. In a microwave-safe bowl, melt the butter, chocolate, andstevia. Allow it to cool to room temperature. Add the remaining ingredients to the chocolate mixture; stir to combine well. Scrape the batter into a lightly greased baking pan.   Bake in the preheated Air Fryer for 15 minutes or until a toothpick comes out dry and clean. Enjoy!
Nutrition Info:229 Calories; 23g Fat; 4g Carbs; 4g Protein; 5g Sugars; 3g Fiber

744. Peach-blueberry Tart

Servings: 6 To 8   Cooking Time: 30 Minutes

Ingredients:
- 4 peaches, pitted and sliced
- 1 cup fresh blueberries
- 2 tablespoons cornstarch
- 1 tablespoon freshly squeezed lemon juice
- 3 tablespoons sugar
- Cooking spray
- 1 sheet frozen puff pastry, thawed
- 1 tablespoon nonfat or low-fat milk
- Confectioners' sugar, for dusting

Directions:
Add the peaches, blueberries, cornstarch, sugar, and lemon juice to a large bowl and toss to coat.   Spritz a round baking pan with cooking spray.   Unfold the pastry and put in the prepared baking pan. Lay the peach slices on the pan, slightly overlapping them.   Scatter the blueberries over the peach. Drape the pastry over the outside of the fruit and press pleats firmly together.   Brush the milk over the pastry.   Slide the baking pan into Rack Position 1, select Convection Bake, set temperature to 400°F (205°C), and set time to 30 minutes.   Bake until the crust is golden brown and the fruit is bubbling.

When cooking is complete, remove from the oven and allow to cool for 10 minutes. Serve the tart with the confectioners' sugar sprinkled on top.

745. Carrot, Raisin & Walnut Bread

Servings: 8   Cooking Time: 35 Minutes

Ingredients:

2 cups all-purpose flour	½ cup applesauce
1½ teaspoons ground cinnamon	¼ cup honey
2 teaspoons baking soda	¼ cup plain yogurt
½ teaspoon salt	2 teaspoons vanilla essence
3 eggs	2½ cups carrots, peeled and shredded
½ cup sunflower oil	½ cup raisins
	½ cup walnuts

Directions:
Line the bottom of a greased baking pan with parchment paper.   In a medium bowl, sift together the flour, baking soda, cinnamon and salt. In a large bowl, add the eggs, oil, applesauce, honey and yogurt and with a hand-held mixer, mix on medium speed until well combined.   Add the eggs, one at a time and whisk well.   Add the vanilla and mix well.   Add the flour mixture and mix until just combined.   Fold in the carrots, raisins and walnuts.   Place the mixture into a lightly greased baking pan.   With a piece of foil, cover the pan loosely.   Press "Power Button" of Air Fry Oven and turn the dial to select the "Air Crisp" mode. Press the Time button and again turn the dial to set the cooking time to 30 minutes.   Now push the Temp button and rotate the dial to set the temperature at 347 degrees F.   Press "Start/Pause" button to start.   When the unit beeps to show that it is preheated, open the lid.   Arrange the pan in "Air Fry Basket" and insert in the oven.   After 25 minutes of cooking, remove the foil.   Place the pan onto a wire rack to cool for about 10 minutes. Carefully, invert the bread onto wire rack to cool completely before slicing.   Cut the bread into desired-sized slices and serve.
Nutrition Info: Calories 441 Total Fat 20.3 g Saturated Fat 2.2 g Cholesterol 62mg Sodium 592 mg Total Carbs 57.6 g Fiber 5.7 g Sugar 23.7 g Protein 9.2 g

746. Apricot Crumble With Blackberries

Servings: 4   Cooking Time: 30 Minutes

Ingredients:

2 ½ cups fresh apricots, de-stoned and cubed	½ cup sugar
1 cup fresh blackberries	2 tbsp lemon Juice
	1 cup flour
	5 tbsp butter

Directions:
Preheat Cuisinart on Bake function to 360 F. Add the apricot cubes to a bowl and mix with lemon juice, 2 tbsp sugar, and blackberries. Scoop the mixture into a greased dish and spread it evenly.   In another bowl, mix flour and remaining sugar. Add 1 tbsp of cold water and butter and keep mixing until you have a crumbly mixture. Pour over the fruit mixture and cook for 20 minutes.

747. Tomatoes Dip

Servings: 6   Cooking Time: 15 Minutes

Ingredients:

12 oz. cream cheese, soft	1 pint grape tomatoes; halved
8 oz. mozzarella cheese; grated	2 tbsp. thyme; chopped.
¼ cup basil; chopped.	½ tbsp. oregano; chopped.
¼ cup parmesan; grated	1 tsp. olive oil
4 garlic cloves; minced	A pinch of salt and black pepper

Directions:
Put the tomatoes in your air fryer's basket and cook them at 400°F for 15 minutes.   In a blender, combine the fried tomatoes with the rest of the ingredients and pulse well   Transfer this to a ramekin, place it in the air fryer and cook at 400°F for 5 - 6 minutes more. Serve as a snack
Nutrition Info: Calories: 184; Fat: 8g; Fiber: 3g; Carbs: 4g; Protein: 8g

748. Jalapeno Spinach Dip

Servings: 6   Cooking Time: 30 Minutes

Ingredients:

10 oz frozen spinach, thawed and drained	1/2 cup onion, diced
2 tsp jalapeno pepper, minced	2 tsp garlic, minced
	1/2 cup mozzarella cheese, shredded
1/2 cup cheddar cheese, shredded	1/2 cup Monterey jack cheese, shredded
8 oz cream cheese	1/2 tsp salt

Directions:
Fit the Cuisinart oven with the rack in position Add all ingredients into the mixing bowl and mix until well combined.   Pour mixture into the 1-quart casserole dish.   Set to bake at 350 F for 35 minutes. After 5 minutes place the casserole dish in the preheated oven.   Serve and enjoy.
Nutrition Info: Calories 228 Fat 19.8 g Carbohydrates 4.2 g Sugar 0.8 g Protein 9.7 g Cholesterol 61 mg

749. Berry Crumble With Lemon

Servings: 6   Cooking Time: 30 Minutes

Ingredients:

12 oz fresh strawberries	5 tbsp cold butter
7 oz fresh raspberries	2 tbsp lemon juice
5 oz fresh blueberries	1 cup flour
	½ cup sugar
	1 tbsp water
	A pinch of salt

Directions:
Preheat Cuisinart on Bake function to 360 F. Gently mash the berries, but make sure there are chunks left. Mix with the lemon juice and 2 tbsp of sugar. Place the berry mixture at the bottom of a greased

cake pan. Combine the flour with salt and sugar in a bowl. Mix well. Add the water and rub the butter with your fingers until the mixture becomes crumbled. Pour the batter over the berries. Press Start and cook for 20 minutes. Serve chilled.

750. Easy Blackberry Cobbler

Servings: 6   Cooking Time: 20 To 25 Minutes

Ingredients:

3 cups fresh or frozen blackberries	8 tablespoons (1 stick) butter, melted
1¾ cups sugar, divided	1 cup self-rising flour
1 teaspoon vanilla extract	Cooking spray

Directions:

Spritz the baking pan with cooking spray. Mix the blackberries, 1 cup of sugar, and vanilla in a medium bowl and stir to combine. Stir together the melted butter, remaining sugar, and flour in a separate medium bowl. Spread the blackberry mixture evenly in the prepared pan and top with the butter mixture. Slide the baking pan into Rack Position 1, select Convection Bake, set temperature to 350°F (180°C), and set time to 25 minutes. After about 20 minutes, check if the cobbler has a golden crust and you can't see any batter bubbling while it cooks. If needed, bake for another 5 minutes. Remove from the oven and place on a wire rack to cool to room temperature. Serve immediately.

751. Caramelized Peaches

Servings: 4   Cooking Time: 10 To 13 Minutes

Ingredients:

2 tablespoons sugar	4 peaches, cut into wedges
¼ teaspoon ground cinnamon	Cooking spray

Directions:

Toss the peaches with the sugar and cinnamon in a medium bowl until evenly coated. Lightly spray the air fryer basket with cooking spray. Place the peaches in the basket in a single layer. Lightly mist the peaches with cooking spray. Put the air fryer basket on the baking pan and slide into Rack Position 2, select Air Fry, set temperature to 350°F (180°C), and set time to 10 minutes. After 5 minutes, remove from the oven and flip the peaches. Return to the oven and continue cooking for 5 minutes. When cooking is complete, the peaches should be caramelized. If necessary, continue cooking for 3 minutes. Remove from the oven. Let the peaches cool for 5 minutes and serve warm.

752. Mini Crab Cakes

Ingredients:

½ cup dried bread crumbs	½ cup mayonnaise
¼ cup minced green onions	1 cup fresh cilantro leaves
3 tablespoons olive oil	½ cup chopped walnuts
1-pound canned lump crabmeat	½ cup grated Romano cheese

2 tablespoons olive oil	

Directions:

Drain crabmeat well and pick over to remove any cartilage. Set aside in large bowl. In food processor or blender, combine cilantro, walnuts, cheese, and 2 tablespoons olive oil (6 tablespoons for triple batch). Process or blend until mixture forms a paste. Stir into crabmeat. Add bread crumbs, mayonnaise, and green onions to crab mixture. Stir to combine. Form into 2- inch patties about ½-inch thick. Flash freeze on baking sheet. When frozen solid, pack crab cakes in rigid containers, with waxed paper between the layers. Label crab cakes and freeze. Reserve remaining olive oil in pantry. To thaw and reheat: Thaw crab cakes in refrigerator overnight. Heat 3 tablespoons olive oil (9 for triple batch) in large, heavy skillet over medium heat. Fry crab cakes until golden and hot, turning once, about 3 to 5 minutes on each side.

753. Cinnamon Apple Wedges

Servings: 4   Cooking Time: 12 Minutes

Ingredients:

2 medium apples, cored and sliced into ¼-inch wedges	1 teaspoon canola oil
2 teaspoons peeled and grated fresh ginger	½ teaspoon ground cinnamon
	½ cup low-fat Greek vanilla yogurt, for serving

Directions:

In a large bowl, toss the apple wedges with the canola oil, ginger, and cinnamon until evenly coated. Put the apple wedges in the air fryer basket. Put the air fryer basket on the baking pan and slide into Rack Position 2, select Air Fry, set temperature to 360°F (182°C), and set time to 12 minutes. When cooking is complete, the apple wedges should be crisp-tender. Remove the apple wedges from the oven and serve drizzled with the yogurt.

754. Flavorful Coconut Cake

Servings: 8   Cooking Time: 20 Minutes

Ingredients:

5 eggs, separated	1/2 tsp vanilla
1/2 cup erythritol	1/2 cup butter softened
1/4 cup coconut milk	Pinch of salt
1/2 cup coconut flour	
1/2 tsp baking powder	

Directions:

Fit the Cuisinart oven with the rack in position Grease cake pan with butter and set aside. In a bowl, beat sweetener and butter until combined. Add egg yolks, coconut milk, and vanilla and mix well. Add baking powder, coconut flour, and salt and stir well. In another bowl, beat egg whites until stiff peak forms. Gently fold egg whites into the cake mixture. Pour batter in a prepared cake pan. Set to bake at 400 F for 25 minutes. After 5 minutes place the cake pan in the preheated oven. Slice and serve.

Nutrition Info: Calories 84 Fat 5.9 g Carbohydrates 4.2 g Sugar 0.6 g Protein 4 g Cholesterol 102 mg

755. Lemon Cookies

Servings: 12   Cooking Time: 15 Minutes

Ingredients:

- ¼ cup cashew butter, soft
- 1 egg, whisked
- ¾ cup swerve
- 1 cup coconut cream
- Juice of 1 lemon
- 1 tsp. baking powder
- 1 tsp. lemon peel, grated

Directions:

In a bowl, combine all the ingredients gradually and stir well.   Spoon balls this on a cookie sheet lined with parchment paper and flatten them.   Put the cookie sheet in the fryer and cook at 350°F for 20 minutes. Serve the cookies cold

Nutrition Info: Calories: 121; Fat: 5g; Fiber: 1g; Carbs: 4g; Protein: 2g

756. Yogurt Cake(1)

Servings: 12   Cooking Time: 15 Minutes

Ingredients:

- 6 eggs, whisked
- 8 oz. Greek yogurt
- 9 oz. coconut flour
- 4 tbsp. stevia
- 1 tsp. vanilla extract
- 1 tsp. baking powder

Directions:

Take a bowl and mix all the ingredients and whisk well.   Pour this into a cake pan that fits the air fryer lined with parchment paper.   Put the pan in the air fryer and cook at 330°F for 30 minutes

Nutrition Info: Calories: 181; Fat: 13g; Fiber: 2g; Carbs: 4g; Protein: 5g

757. Oats Muffins

Ingredients:

- 1 cup sugar
- 3 tsp. vinegar
- 1 cup oats
- ½ tsp. vanilla essence
- Muffin cups or butter paper cups.
- 2 cups All-purpose flour
- 1 ½ cup milk
- ½ tsp. baking powder
- ½ tsp. baking soda
- 2 tbsp. butter

Directions:

Mix the ingredients together and use your Oregano Fingers to get a crumbly mixture. You will need to divide the milk into two parts and add one part to the baking soda and the other to the vinegar. Now, mix both the milk mixtures together and wait till the milk begins to foam. Add this to the crumbly mixture and begin to whisk the ingredients very fast. Once you have obtained a smooth batter, you will need to transfer the mixture into a muffin cup and set aside. Preheat the fryer to 300 Fahrenheit for five minutes. You will need to place the muffin cups in the basket and cover it. Cook the muffins for fifteen minutes and check whether or not the muffins are cooked using a toothpick. Remove the cups and serve hot.

758. Olive Tarts With Mushrooms

Ingredients:

- ½ cup sliced black olives
- ½ cup sliced green olives
- ½ teaspoon dried thyme leaves
- 2 sheets frozen puff pastry, thawed
- 1 onion, chopped
- 1 cup shredded Gouda cheese
- 2 cloves garlic, minced
- ½ cup chopped mushrooms
- 1 tablespoon olive oil

Directions:

Preheat oven to 400°F. In heavy skillet, sauté onion, garlic, and mushrooms in olive oil until tender. Remove from heat and add olives and thyme. Gently roll puff pastry dough with rolling pin until ¼-inch thick. Using a 3-inch cookie cutter, cut 24 circles from pastry. Line muffin cups with dough. Place a spoonful of filling in each pastry-lined cup. Bake at 400°F for 10 to 12 minutes or until crust is golden brown and filling is set.   Remove from muffin cups and cool on wire rack. Flash freeze; when frozen solid, pack tarts into zipper-lock bags. Attach zipper-lock bag filled with shredded cheese; label and freeze.   To thaw and reheat: Thaw tarts in single layer overnight in refrigerator. Top each tart with cheese and bake at 400°F for 5 to 6 minutes or until hot and cheese is melted.

759. Apple Hand Pies

Servings: 6   Cooking Time: 8 Minutes

Ingredients:

- 15-ounces no-sugar-added apple pie filling
- 1 store-bought crust

Directions:

Preparing the Ingredients. Lay out pie crust and slice into equal-sized squares.   Place 2 tbsp. filling into each square and seal crust with a fork.   Air Frying. Place into the Cuisinart air fryer oven. Cook 8 minutes at 390 degrees until golden in color.

Nutrition Info: CALORIES: 278; FAT:10G; PROTEIN:5G; SUGAR:4G

760. Margherita Pizza

Servings: 4   Cooking Time: 18 Minutes

Ingredients:

- 1 whole-wheat pizza crust
- 1/2 cup mozzarella cheese, grated
- 1/2 cup can tomatoes
- 2 tbsp olive oil
- 3 Roma tomatoes, sliced
- 10 basil leaves

Directions:

Fit the Cuisinart oven with the rack in position Roll out whole wheat pizza crust using a rolling pin. Make sure the crust is ½-inch thick.   Sprinkle olive oil on top of pizza crust.   Spread can tomatoes over pizza crust.   Arrange sliced tomatoes and basil on pizza crust. Sprinkle grated cheese on top.   Place pizza on top of the oven rack and set to bake at 425 F for 23 minutes.   Slice and serve.

Nutrition Info: Calories 126 Fat 7.9 g Carbohydrates 11.3 g Sugar 4.2 g Protein 3.6 g Cholesterol 2 mg

761. Healthy Carrot Fries

Servings: 4   Cooking Time: 25 Minutes
Ingredients:

4 medium carrots, peel and cut into fries shape	1/2 tbsp paprika
	1 1/2 tbsp olive oil
	1/2 tsp salt

Directions:
Fit the Cuisinart oven with the rack in position Add carrots, paprika, oil, and salt into the mixing bowl and toss well.   Transfer carrot fries in baking pan.   Set to bake at 450 F for 30 minutes. After 5 minutes place the baking pan in the preheated oven. Serve and enjoy.
Nutrition Info: Calories 73 Fat 5.4 g Carbohydrates 6.5 g Sugar 3.1 g Protein 0.6 g Cholesterol 0 mg

762. Gluten-free Fried Bananas

Servings: 8   Cooking Time: 15 Minutes
Ingredients:

8 bananas	1 egg white
3 tbsp vegetable oil	¾ cup breadcrumbs
3 tbsp cornflour	

Directions:
Preheat Cuisinart on Toast function to 350 F. Combine the oil and breadcrumbs in a small bowl. Coat the bananas with the corn flour first, brush them with egg white, and dip them in the breadcrumb mixture. Arrange on a lined baking sheet and cook for 8-12 minutes. Serve.

763. Oatmeal Cake

Servings: 8   Cooking Time: 40 Minutes
Ingredients:

2 eggs, beaten	1 3/4 cups flour
1 tbsp cocoa powder	1 cup quick oats
1/2 tsp salt	3/4 cup mix nuts, chopped
1 tsp baking soda	
1/2 cup butter, softened	2 cups chocolate chips
1 cup granulated sugar	1 3/4 cup boiling water
1 cup brown sugar	

Directions:
Fit the Cuisinart oven with the rack in position Combine together boiling water and oats in a large bowl.   Add butter and sugar stir until butter melted.   Add flour, baking soda, salt, cocoa powder, 1 cup chocolate chips, half chopped nuts, and egg. Mix until combine.   Pour batter into the greased cake pan and sprinkle remaining nuts and chocolate chips over the top of cake batter.   Set to bake at 350 F for 45 minutes. After 5 minutes place the baking dish in the preheated oven.   Slice and serve.
Nutrition Info: Calories 699 Fat 30.6 g Carbohydrates 97.9 g Sugar 4.1 g Protein 64.8 g Cholesterol 81 mg

764. Blueberry Apple Crumble

Servings: 6   Cooking Time: 15 Minutes
Ingredients:

1 medium apple, finely diced	2 tablespoons of sugar
1/2 cup of frozen blueberries strawberries	1/2 teaspoon of ground cinnamon
2/3 cup of rice flour	2 tablespoons of nondairy butter

Directions:
Set the Instant Vortex on Air fryer to 350 degrees F for 15 minutes. Combine apple with blueberries in a bowl. Mingle butter with flour, cinnamon, and sugar in another bowl. Pour the butter mixture into the apple mixture. Transfer this mixture on the cooking tray. Insert the cooking tray in the Vortex when it displays "Add Food". Flip the sides when it displays "Turn Food". Remove from the oven when cooking time is complete. Serve warm.
Nutrition Info: Calories: 379 Cal Total Fat: 29.7 g Saturated Fat: 0 g   Cholesterol: 0 mg   Sodium: 0 mg   Total Carbs: 23.7 g   Fiber: 0 g   Sugar: 0 g   Protein: 5.2 g

765. Sausage And Onion Rolls

Servings: 12   Cooking Time: 15 Minutes
Ingredients:

1 pound (454 g) bulk breakfast sausage	½ teaspoon dried sage
½ cup finely chopped onion	1 large egg, beaten
½ cup fresh bread crumbs	1 garlic clove, minced
½ teaspoon dried mustard	2 sheets (1 package) frozen puff pastry, thawed
¼ teaspoon cayenne pepper	All-purpose flour, for dusting

Directions:
In a medium bowl, break up the sausage. Stir in the onion, bread crumbs, mustard, sage, cayenne pepper, egg and garlic. Divide the sausage mixture in half and tightly wrap each half in plastic wrap. Refrigerate for 5 to 10 minutes.   Lay the pastry sheets on a lightly floured work surface. Using a rolling pin, lightly roll out the pastry to smooth out the dough. Take out one of the sausage packages and form the sausage into a long roll. Remove the plastic wrap and place the sausage on top of the puff pastry about 1 inch from one of the long edges. Roll the pastry around the sausage and pinch the edges of the dough together to seal. Repeat with the other pastry sheet and sausage.   Slice the logs into lengths about 1½ inches long. Place the sausage rolls in the baking pan, cut-side down.   Slide the baking pan into Rack Position 2, select Roast, set temperature to 350°F (180°C) and set time to 15 minutes. When cooking is complete, the rolls will be golden brown and sizzling. Remove from the oven and let cool for 5 minutes.

766. Tiny Filled Puffs

Ingredients:

3 eggs	1 cup water
½ cup grated Parmesan cheese	½ cup butter
1 tablespoon dried chives	½ teaspoon salt
	1 cup flour

Directions:
Preheat oven to 375°F. Line baking sheet with parchment paper and set aside. In heavy saucepan,

combine water and butter. Bring to a rolling boil that cannot be stirred down. Add salt and flour all at once. Cook and stir over medium heat until dough forms a ball and cleans sides of pan. Remove from heat and beat in eggs, one at a time, until well combined. Stir in cheese and chives. Drop dough by teaspoons onto prepared baking sheet. Bake at 375°F for 18 to 22 minutes or until dough is puffed, golden brown, and firm. Remove from baking sheet and cool on wire rack. Flash freeze puffs in single layer on baking sheet. Then carefully pack into rigid containers. Label puffs and freeze. To reheat: Place frozen puffs on baking sheet. Bake in preheated 400°F oven for 5 to 8 minutes, until hot. Let cool slightly, then cut puffs in half and fill with desired filling.

767. Old Bay Chicken Wings

Servings: 4   Cooking Time: 13 Minutes

Ingredients:

2 tablespoons Old Bay seasoning	2 pounds (907 g) chicken wings, patted dry
2 teaspoons baking powder	
2 teaspoons salt	Cooking spray

Directions:

Combine the Old Bay seasoning, baking powder, and salt in a large zip-top plastic bag. Add the chicken wings, seal, and shake until the wings are thoroughly coated in the seasoning mixture. Lightly spray the air fryer basket with cooking spray. Lay the chicken wings in the basket in a single layer and lightly mist them with cooking spray. Put the air fryer basket on the baking pan and slide into Rack Position 2, select Air Fry, set temperature to 400°F (205°C), and set time to 13 minutes. Flip the wings halfway through the cooking time. When cooking is complete, the wings should reach an internal temperature of 165°F (74°C) on a meat thermometer. Remove from the oven to a plate and serve hot.

768. Cranberry Scones

Servings: 4   Cooking Time: 10 Minutes

Ingredients:

1 cup of fresh cranberries	2 cups of flour
⅓ Cup of sugar	¼ teaspoon of salt
1 tablespoon of orange zest	¼ cup of butter, chilled and diced
¾ cup of half and half cream	¼ cup of brown sugar
¼ teaspoon of ground nutmeg	1 tablespoon of baking powder
	1 egg

Directions:

Set the Instant Vortex on Air fryer to 365 degrees F for 10 minutes. Strain nutmeg, flour, baking powder, salt, and sugar in a bowl. Blend in the cream and egg. Fold in the orange zest and cranberries to form a smooth dough. Roll the dough and cut into scones. Place the scones on the cooking tray. Insert the cooking tray in the Vortex when it displays "Add Food". Flip the sides when it displays "Turn Food".

Remove from the oven when cooking time is complete. Serve warm.

Nutrition Info: Calories: 219 Cal Total Fat: 19.7 g Saturated Fat: 0 g   Cholesterol: 0 mg   Sodium: 0 mg   Total Carbs: 23.7 g   Fiber: 0 g   Sugar: 0 g Protein: 5.2 g

769. Paprika Potato Chips

Servings: 3   Cooking Time: 22 Minutes

Ingredients:

2 medium potatoes, preferably Yukon Gold, scrubbed	¼ teaspoon paprika
Cooking spray	¼ teaspoon plus ⅛ teaspoon sea salt
2 teaspoons olive oil	¼ teaspoon freshly ground black pepper
½ teaspoon garlic granules	Ketchup or hot sauce, for serving

Directions:

Spritz the air fryer basket with cooking spray. On a flat work surface, cut the potatoes into ¼-inch-thick slices. Transfer the potato slices to a medium bowl, along with the olive oil, garlic granules, paprika, salt, and pepper and toss to coat well. Transfer the potato slices to the basket. Put the air fryer basket on the baking pan and slide into Rack Position 2, select Air Fry, set temperature to 392°F (200°C), and set time to 22 minutes. Stir the potato slices twice during the cooking process. When cooking is complete, the potato chips should be tender and nicely browned. Remove from the oven and serve alongside the ketchup for dipping.

770. Kale Chips With Sesame

Servings: 5   Cooking Time: 8 Minutes

Ingredients:

1½ tablespoons olive oil	8 cups deribbed kale leaves, torn into 2-inch pieces
¾ teaspoon chili powder	½ teaspoon paprika
¼ teaspoon garlic powder	2 teaspoons sesame seeds

Directions:

In a large bowl, toss the kale with the olive oil, chili powder, garlic powder, paprika, and sesame seeds until well coated. Transfer the kale to the air fryer basket. Put the air fryer basket on the baking pan and slide into Rack Position 2, select Air Fry, set temperature to 350°F (180°C), and set time to 8 minutes. Flip the kale twice during cooking. When cooking is complete, the kale should be crispy. Remove from the oven and serve warm.

771. Strawberry Shortcake Quickie

Servings: 4   Cooking Time: 25 Minutes

Ingredients:

Almond flour, 2/3 cup	Halved strawberries, 1 cup
Eggs, 3	Vanilla extract, 1 tsp.
Liquid stevia, ¼ tsp.	Erythritol, 1/3 cup
Salt, ¼ tsp.	
Butter, ½ cup	

Baking powder, ½ tsp.

Directions:
Preheat the air fryer for 5 minutes. Mix all ingredients in a bowl with the exception of the strawberries. Use a hand mixer to mix everything. Pour into greased mugs. Top with sliced strawberries Place the mugs in the fryer basket. Bake for 25 minutes at 350F. Chill in the refrigerator before serving.
Nutrition Info: Calories: 265 Carbs: 3.7g Protein: 2.5 g Fat: 26.7g

---

772. Easy Spanish Churros

Servings: 4   Cooking Time: 15 Minutes
Ingredients:

3/4 cup water	1/4 teaspoon ground
1 tablespoon swerve	cloves
1/4 teaspoon sea salt	6 tablespoons butter
1/4 teaspoon grated	3/4 cup almond flour
nutmeg	2 eggs

Directions:
To make the dough, boil the water in a pan over medium-high heat; now, add the swerve, salt, nutmeg, and cloves; cook until dissolved. Add the butter and turn the heat to low. Gradually stir in the almond flour, whisking continuously, until the mixture forms a ball. Remove from the heat; fold in the eggs one at a time, stirring to combine well. Pour the mixture into a piping bag with a large star tip. Squeeze 4-inch strips of dough into the greased Air Fryer pan. Cook at 410 degrees F for 6 minutes, working in batches.
Nutrition Info:321 Calories; 31g Fat; 4g Carbs; 4g Protein; 1g Sugars; 3g Fiber

---

773. Garlic Cauliflower Florets

Servings: 4   Cooking Time: 20 Minutes
Ingredients:

5 cups cauliflower	4 tablespoons olive
florets	oil
6 garlic cloves,	1/2 tsp cumin powder
chopped	1/2 tsp salt

Directions:
Fit the Cuisinart oven with the rack in position 2. Add all ingredients into the large bowl and toss well. Add cauliflower florets in air fryer basket then place air fryer basket in baking pan. Place a baking pan on the oven rack. Set to air fry at 400 F for 20 minutes. Serve and enjoy.
Nutrition Info: Calories 159 Fat 14.2 g Carbohydrates 8.2 g Sugar 3.1 g Protein 2.8 g Cholesterol 0 mg

---

774. Mozzarella Sticks

Servings: 12 Sticks   Cooking Time: 15 Minutes
Ingredients:

6 (1-oz.mozzarella	2 large eggs.
string cheese sticks	½ cup grated
½ oz. pork rinds,	Parmesan cheese.
finely ground	1 tsp. dried parsley.

Directions:
Place mozzarella sticks on a cutting board and cut in half. Freeze 45 minutes or until firm. If freezing overnight, remove frozen sticks after 1 hour and place into airtight zip-top storage bag and place back in freezer for future use. Take a large bowl, mix Parmesan, ground pork rinds and parsley Take a medium bowl, whisk eggs Dip a frozen mozzarella stick into beaten eggs and then into Parmesan mixture to coat. Repeat with remaining sticks. Place mozzarella sticks into the air fryer basket. Adjust the temperature to 400 Degrees F and set the timer for 10 minutes or until golden. Serve warm.
Nutrition Info: Calories: 236; Protein: 12g; Fiber: 0g; Fat: 18g; Carbs: 7g

---

775. Cuban Sandwiches

Servings: 4 Sandwiches   Cooking Time: 8 Minutes
Ingredients:

8 slices ciabatta bread, about ¼-inch thick	Toppings:
	4 ounces (113 g) thinly sliced deli turkey
Cooking spray	
1 tablespoon brown mustard	⅓ cup bread and butter pickle slices
6 to 8 ounces (170 to 227 g) thinly sliced leftover roast pork	2 to 3 ounces (57 to 85 g) Pepper Jack cheese slices

Directions:
On a clean work surface, spray one side of each slice of bread with cooking spray. Spread the other side of each slice of bread evenly with brown mustard. Top 4 of the bread slices with the roast pork, turkey, pickle slices, cheese, and finish with remaining bread slices. Transfer to the air fryer basket. Put the air fryer basket on the baking pan and slide into Rack Position 2, select Air Fry, set temperature to 390°F (199°C), and set time to 8 minutes. When cooking is complete, remove from the oven. Cool for 5 minutes and serve warm.

---

776. Autumn Walnut Crisp

Servings: 8   Cooking Time: 15 Minutes
Ingredients:

1 cup walnuts	½ cup swerve
1/2 cup swerve	
Topping:	½ teaspoon ground
1 ½ cups almond flour	cardamom
1/2 cup coconut flour	A pinch of salt
1 teaspoon crystallized ginger	1 stick butter, cut into pieces

Directions:
Place walnuts and 1/2 cup of swerve in a baking pan lightly greased with nonstick cooking spray. In a mixing dish, thoroughly combine all the topping ingredients. Sprinkle the topping ingredients over the walnut layer. Bake in the preheated Air Fryer at 330 degrees F for 35 minutes.
Nutrition Info:288 Calories; 25g Fat; 2g Carbs; 6g Protein; 3g Sugars; 4g Fiber

---

777.Preparation Time: 35 Minutes

Servings: 3   Cooking Time: 15 Minutes
Ingredients:

158

1/2 cup coconut flour
1 teaspoon baking powder
1/4 teaspoon salt
2 tablespoons erythritol
1/2 teaspoon cinnamon
1 teaspoon red paste food color
1 egg
1/2 cup milk
1 teaspoon vanilla
Topping:
2 ounces cream cheese, softened
2 tablespoons butter, softened
3/4 cup powdered swerve

Directions:
Mix the coconut flour, baking powder, salt, erythritol, cinnamon, red paste food color in a large bowl. Gradually add the egg and milk, whisking continuously, until well combined. Let it stand for 20 minutes. Spritz the Air Fryer baking pan with cooking spray. Pour the batter into the pan using a measuring cup. Cook at 230 degrees F for 4 to 5 minutes or until golden brown. Repeat with the remaining batter. Meanwhile, make your topping by mixing the ingredients until creamy and fluffy. Decorate your pancakes with topping.
Nutrition Info:315 Calories; 33g Fat; 3g Carbs; 5g Protein; 3g Sugars; 1g Fiber

778.   Healthy Broccoli Tots

Servings: 4   Cooking Time: 12 Minutes
Ingredients:
1 lb broccoli, cooked & chopped
1/2 tsp garlic powder
1/2 cup almond flour
1/4 cup ground flaxseed
1 tsp salt

Directions:
Fit the Cuisinart oven with the rack in position 2. Add broccoli into the food processor and process until it looks like rice. Transfer broccoli to a large mixing bowl. Add remaining ingredients into the bowl and mix until well combined. Make tots from broccoli mixture and place in the air fryer basket then place an air fryer basket in the baking pan. Place a baking pan on the oven rack. Set to air fry at 375 F for 12 minutes. Serve and enjoy.
Nutrition Info: Calories 97 Fat 4.3 g Carbohydrates 10.5 g Sugar 2.3 g Protein 5.3 g Cholesterol 0 mg

779.   Garlic Cheese Dip

Servings: 10   Cooking Time: 15 Minutes
Ingredients:
1 lb. mozzarella; shredded
6 garlic cloves; minced
1 tbsp. thyme; chopped.
3 tbsp. olive oil
1 tsp. rosemary; chopped.
A pinch of salt and black pepper

Directions:
In a pan that fits your air fryer, mix all the ingredients, whisk really well, introduce in the air fryer and cook at 370°F for 10 minutes. Divide into bowls and serve right away.
Nutrition Info: Calories: 184; Fat: 11g; Fiber: 3g; Carbs: 5g; Protein: 7g

780.   Strawberry And Rhubarb Crumble

Servings: 6   Cooking Time: 12 To 17 Minutes
Ingredients:
1½ cups sliced fresh strawberries
⅓ cup sugar
¾ cup sliced rhubarb
⅔ cup quick-cooking oatmeal
¼ cup packed brown sugar
½ cup whole-wheat pastry flour
½ teaspoon ground cinnamon
3 tablespoons unsalted butter, melted

Directions:
Place the strawberries, sugar, and rhubarb in the baking pan and toss to coat. Combine the oatmeal, brown sugar, pastry flour, and cinnamon in a medium bowl. Add the melted butter to the oatmeal mixture and stir until crumbly. Sprinkle this generously on top of the strawberries and rhubarb. Slide the baking pan into Rack Position 1, select Convection Bake, set temperature to 370°F (188°C), and set the time to 12 minutes. Bake until the fruit is bubbly and the topping is golden brown. Continue cooking for an additional 2 to 5 minutes if needed. When cooking is complete, remove from the oven and serve warm.

781.   Cookie Custards

Ingredients:
2 tbsp. margarine
A pinch of baking soda and baking powder
1 cup all-purpose flour
½ cup icing sugar
½ cup custard powder

Directions:
Cream the margarine and sugar together. Add the remaining ingredients and fold them together. Prepare a baking tray by greasing it with butter. Make balls out of the dough, coat them with flour and place them in the tray. Preheat the fryer to 300 Fahrenheit for five minutes. You will need to place the baking tray in the basket and cover it. Cook till you find that the balls have turned golden brown. Remove the tray and leave it to cool outside for half an hour. Store in an airtight container.

782.   Fried Pickles

Servings: 6   Cooking Time: 3 Minutes
Ingredients:
Cold dill pickle slices, 36.
Chopped fresh dill, 2 tbsps.
Salt, 1 tsp.
Divided cornstarch, 1 cup
Ranch dressing
Cayenne, ¼ tsp.
Black pepper, 2 tsps.
Almond meal, ½ cup
Large egg, 1.
Almond milk, ¾ cup
Paprika, 2 tsps.
Canola oil

Directions:
Whisk together cayenne, milk, and egg. Spread half-cup cornstarch in a shallow dish. Mix the remaining ½-cup cornstarch with almond meal, salt,

pepper, dill, and paprika. Dredge the pickle slices first through the cornstarch then dip them in an egg wash. Coat them with almond meal mixture and shake off the excess. Place them in the fryer basket and spray them with oil. Return the basket to the fryer and air fry the pickles for 3 minutes at 370 F working in batches as to not crowd the basket. Serve warm.
Nutrition Info: Calories: 138   Fat: 12.2 g   Carbs: 5.8 g   Protein: 4 g

783.   Healthy Baked Pecans

Servings: 8   Cooking Time: 15 Minutes
Ingredients:

4 cups pecans	1/4 cup olive oil
1/4 tsp onion powder	2 tsp lemon zest
1/4 tsp garlic powder	1/4 tsp paprika
4 tbsp fresh rosemary, chopped	2 tsp Himalayan salt

Directions:
Fit the Cuisinart oven with the rack in position Add all ingredients except lemon zest into the large bowl and toss well. Transfer pecans in baking pan. Set to bake at 350 F for 20 minutes. After 5 minutes place the baking pan in the preheated oven. Add lemon zest on top of roasted pecans and stir well. Serve and enjoy.
Nutrition Info: Calories 269 Fat 28 g Carbohydrates 5.6 g Sugar 1.2 g Protein 3.3 g Cholesterol 0 mg

784.   Bread Pudding

Ingredients:

2 tbsp. custard powder	3 tbsp. unsalted butter
3 tbsp. powdered sugar	6 slices bread
	2 cups milk

Directions:
Spread butter and jam on the slices of bread and cut them into the shapes you would like. Place them in a greased dish. Boil the milk and the sugar in a pan and add the custard powder and stir till you get a thick mixture. Preheat the fryer to 300 Fahrenheit for five minutes. Place the dish in the basket and reduce the temperature to 250 Fahrenheit. Cook for ten minutes and set aside to cool.

785.   Fudgy Chocolate Brownies

Servings: 8   Cooking Time: 21 Minutes
Ingredients:

1 stick butter, melted	1 teaspoon baking powder
1 cup Swerve	
2 eggs	1 teaspoon vanilla essence
1 cup coconut flour	
1/2 cup unsweetened cocoa powder	A pinch of salt
	A pinch of ground cardamom
2 tablespoons flaxseed meal	Cooking spray

Directions:
Spray the baking pan with cooking spray. Beat together the melted butter and Swerve in a large mixing dish until fluffy. Whisk in the eggs. Add the coconut flour, cocoa powder, flaxseed meal, baking powder, vanilla essence, salt, and cardamom and stir with a spatula until well incorporated. Spread the mixture evenly into the prepared baking pan. Slide the baking pan into Rack Position 1, select Convection Bake, set temperature to 350°F (180°C), and set time to 21 minutes. When cooking is complete, a toothpick inserted in the center should come out clean. Remove from the oven and place on a wire rack to cool completely. Cut into squares and serve immediately.

786.   Strawberry Cobbler

Servings: 6   Cooking Time: 45 Minutes
Ingredients:

2 cups strawberries, diced	1 1/4 cup sugar
	1 tsp vanilla
1 cup milk	1/2 cup butter, melted
1 cup self-rising flour	

Directions:
Fit the Cuisinart oven with the rack in position In a bowl, mix together flour and 1 cup sugar. Add milk and whisk until smooth. Add vanilla and butter and mix well. Pour mixture into the greased baking dish and sprinkle with strawberries and top with remaining sugar. Set to bake at 350 F for 50 minutes. After 5 minutes place the baking dish in the preheated oven. Serve and enjoy.
Nutrition Info: Calories 405 Fat 16.5 g Carbohydrates 63.4 g Sugar 46 g Protein 4 g Cholesterol 44 mg

787.   Italian Pork Skewers

Ingredients:

1/4 cup finely minced onion	2 pounds pork tenderloin
1 teaspoon dried Italian seasoning	1/4 cup balsamic vinegar
1/2 teaspoon salt	
teaspoon pepper	1/4 cup olive oil

Directions:
Trim excess fat from tenderloin. Cut pork, on a slant, into 1/4-inch-thick slices, each about 4 inches long. In large bowl, combine remaining ingredients and mix well with wire whisk. Add tenderloin slices and mix gently to coat. Cover and refrigerate for 2 to 3 hours. Meanwhile, soak 8-inch wooden skewers in cold water. Remove pork from marinade and thread onto soaked skewers. Flash freeze on baking sheet in single layer. When frozen solid, pack skewers in rigid containers, with layers separated by waxed paper. Label skewers and freeze. To thaw and reheat: Thaw overnight in refrigerator. Cook skewers 4 to 6 inches from medium coals on grill, or broil 4 to 6 inches from heat source, for about 4 to 6 minutes or until cooked (160°F on an instant-read thermometer), turning once.

788.   Egg Rolls

Ingredients:

1 cup shredded Napa cabbage	1 package egg roll wrappers
2 tablespoons soy sauce	1/2 pound ground pork
1 tablespoon oyster	

sauce
2 tablespoons cornstarch 1 tablespoon water
3 cups peanut oil

½ pound ground shrimp
1 carrot, shredded
2 cloves garlic, minced
1 bunch green onions, finely chopped

Directions:
In a large skillet, brown ground pork until almost done. Add ground shrimp, carrot, and garlic; cook and stir for 4 to 6 minutes or until pork is cooked. Remove from heat, drain well, and add green onions, cabbage, soy sauce, and oyster sauce. Combine cornstarch and water in a small bowl and blend well. To form egg rolls, place one wrapper, point-side down, on work surface. Place 1 tablespoon filling 1 inch from corner. Brush all edges of the egg roll wrapper with cornstarch mixture. Fold point over filling, then fold in sides and roll up egg roll, using cornstarch mixture to seal as necessary. At this point, egg rolls may be flash frozen, or you can flash freeze them after frying. Once frozen, pack, label, and freeze in rigid containers. To reheat untried egg rolls: Fry the frozen rolls in peanut oil heated to 375°F for 2 to 3 minutes, turning once, or until deep golden brown. To reheat fried egg rolls: Place frozen egg rolls on baking sheet. Bake at 375°F for 8 to 10 minutes or until crisp and hot.

789.	Bebinca

Ingredients:

2 tbsp. custard powder
3 tbsp. powdered sugar
1 cup coconut milk

3 tbsp. unsalted butter
1 cup almond flour
2 cups milk

Directions:
Boil the milk and the sugar in a pan and add the custard powder followed by the flour and coconut milk and stir till you get a thick mixture. Preheat the fryer to 300 Fahrenheit for five minutes. Place the dish in the basket and reduce the temperature to 250 Fahrenheit. Cook for ten minutes and set aside to cool.

790.	Pistachio Pudding

Ingredients:

3 tbsp. powdered sugar
3 tbsp. unsalted butter
2 cups milk

2 cups almond flour
2 tbsp. custard powder
2 cups finely chopped pistachio

Directions:
Boil the milk and the sugar in a pan and add the custard powder followed by the almond flour and stir till you get a thick mixture. Add the pistachio nuts to the mixture. Preheat the fryer to 300 Fahrenheit for five minutes. Place the dish in the basket and reduce the temperature to 250 Fahrenheit. Cook for ten minutes and set aside to cool.

791.	Buttermilk Biscuits

Ingredients:

4 tsp baking powder
¼ tsp baking soda
4 Tbsp softened butter
1 cup all-purpose flour

¼ tsp salt
1 cup whole wheat flour
2 Tbsp sugar
1¼ cups cold buttermilk

Directions:
Preheat oven to 400°F. In a bowl, combine flours, sugar, baking powder, baking soda and salt. Add softened butter and use your Oregano Fingers to work the butter into the flour until the mixture resembles coarse crumbs. Stir in the buttermilk, forming a soft dough. Turn the dough onto a floured surface and pat into a ¾ inch thick circle. With a 2-inch biscuit cutter, cut out biscuits, gathering dough as needed to shape more biscuits. Arrange biscuits in Cuisinart oven and bake until golden brown, about 12 minutes.

792.	Blackberry Chocolate Cake

Servings: 8   Cooking Time: 22 Minutes
Ingredients:

½ cup butter, at room temperature
2 ounces (57 g) Swerve
4 eggs
1 cup almond flour
1 teaspoon baking soda

⅓ teaspoon baking powder
½ cup cocoa powder
1 teaspoon orange zest
⅓ cup fresh blackberries

Directions:
With an electric mixer or hand mixer, beat the butter and Swerve until creamy. One at a time, mix in the eggs and beat again until fluffy. Add the almond flour, baking soda, baking powder, cocoa powder, orange zest and mix well. Add the butter mixture to the almond flour mixture and stir until well blended. Fold in the blackberries. Scrape the batter into the baking pan. Slide the baking pan into Rack Position 1, select Convection Bake, set temperature to 335°F (168°C), and set time to 22 minutes. When cooking is complete, a toothpick inserted into the center of the cake should come out clean. Allow the cake cool on a wire rack to room temperature. Serve immediately.

793.	Cinnamon Plums

Servings: 4   Cooking Time: 20 Minutes
Ingredients:

2 teaspoons cinnamon powder
4 plums, halved

4 tablespoons butter, melted
3 tablespoons swerve

Directions:
In a pan that fits your air fryer, mix the plums with the rest of the ingredients, toss, put the pan in the air fryer and cook at 300 degrees F for 20 minutes. Divide into cups and serve cold.
Nutrition Info:calories 162, fat 3, fiber 2, carbs 4, protein 5

794.	Apple-peach Crisp With Oatmeal

Servings: 4   Cooking Time: 10 To 12 Minutes

Ingredients:

2 peaches, peeled, pitted, and chopped	3 tablespoons packed brown sugar
1 apple, peeled and chopped	½ cup quick-cooking oatmeal
2 tablespoons honey	⅓ cup whole-wheat pastry flour
2 tablespoons unsalted butter, at room temperature	½ teaspoon ground cinnamon

Directions:
Place the peaches, apple, and honey in the baking pan and toss until thoroughly combined. Mix together the brown sugar, butter, oatmeal, pastry flour, and cinnamon in a medium bowl and stir until crumbly. Sprinkle this mixture generously on top of the peaches and apples. Slide the baking pan into Rack Position 1, select Convection Bake, set temperature to 380°F (193°C), and set the time to 10 minutes. Bake until the fruit is bubbling and the topping is golden brown. Once cooking is complete, remove from the oven and allow to cool for 5 minutes before serving.

---

795. Honey Hazelnut Apples

Servings: 4   Cooking Time: 13 Minutes

Ingredients:

4 apples	Zest of 1 orange
1 oz butter	2 oz mixed seeds
2 oz breadcrumbs	1 tsp cinnamon
2 tbsp chopped hazelnuts	2 tbsp honey

Directions:
Preheat Cuisinart on Bake function to 350 F. Core the apples. Make sure to also score their skin to prevent from splitting. Combine the remaining ingredients in a bowl; stuff the apples with the mixture and cook for 10 minutes. Serve topped with chopped hazelnuts.

---

796. Choco-peanut Mug Cake

Servings: 1   Cooking Time: 20 Minutes

Ingredients:

Softened butter, 1 tsp.	Egg, 1.
Peanut butter, 1 tbsp.	Erythritol, 2 tbsps.
Vanilla extract, ½ tsp.	Unsweetened cocoa powder, 2 tbsps.
	Baking powder, ¼ tsp.
	Heavy cream, 1 tbsp.

Directions:
Preheat the air fryer for 5 minutes. Combine all ingredients in a mixing bowl. Pour into a greased mug. Set in the air fryer basket and cook for 20 minutes at 400F

Nutrition Info: Calories: 293   Protein: 12.4g
Fat: 23.3g   Carbs: 8.5g

---

797. Chocolate Soufflé

Servings: 2   Cooking Time: 16 Minutes

Ingredients:

3 oz. semi-sweet chocolate, chopped	3 tablespoons sugar
	2 tablespoons all-

purpose flour
1 teaspoon powdered sugar plus extra for dusting

¼ cup butter
2 eggs, yolks and whites separated
½ teaspoon pure vanilla extract

Directions:
In a microwave-safe bowl, place the butter, and chocolate. Microwave on high heat for about 2 minutes or until melted completely, stirring after every 30 seconds. Remove from microwave and stir the mixture until smooth. In another bowl, add the egg yolks and whisk well. Add the sugar, and vanilla extract and whisk well. Add the chocolate mixture and mix until well combined. Add the flour and mix well. In a clean glass bowl, add the egg whites and whisk until soft peaks form. Fold the whipped egg whites in 3 portions into the chocolate mixture. Grease 2 ramekins and sprinkle each with a pinch of sugar. Place mixture into the prepared ramekins and with the back of a spoon, smooth the top surface. Press "Power Button" of Air Fry Oven and turn the dial to select the "Air Fry" mode. Press the Time button and again turn the dial to set the cooking time to 14 minutes. Now push the Temp button and rotate the dial to set the temperature at 330 degrees F. Press "Start/Pause" button to start. When the unit beeps to show that it is preheated, open the lid. Arrange the ramekins in "Air Fry Basket" and insert in the oven. Place the ramekins onto a wire rack to cool slightly. Sprinkle with the powdered sugar and serve warm.

Nutrition Info: Calories 591 Total Fat 38.7 g Saturated Fat 23 g Cholesterol 225 mg Sodium 225 mg Total Carbs 52.6 g Fiber 0.2 g Sugar 41.1 g Protein 9.4 g

---

798. Apple Wedges With Apricots

Servings: 4   Cooking Time: 15 To 18 Minutes

Ingredients:

2 tablespoons olive oil	4 large apples, peeled and sliced into 8 wedges
½ cup dried apricots, chopped	½ teaspoon ground cinnamon
1 to 2 tablespoons sugar	

Directions:
Toss the apple wedges with the olive oil in a mixing bowl until well coated. Place the apple wedges in the air fryer basket. Put the air fryer basket on the baking pan and slide into Rack Position 2, select Air Fry, set temperature to 350°F (180°C), and set time to 15 minutes. After about 12 minutes, remove from the oven. Sprinkle with the dried apricots and air fry for another 3 minutes. Meanwhile, thoroughly combine the sugar and cinnamon in a small bowl. Remove the apple wedges from the oven to a plate. Serve sprinkled with the sugar mixture.

---

799. Classic Pound Cake

Servings: 8   Cooking Time: 30 Minutes

Ingredients:

1 stick butter, at room temperature
1 cup Swerve
4 eggs
1½ cups coconut flour
½ teaspoon baking soda
½ teaspoon baking powder
½ cup buttermilk
¼ teaspoon salt
1 teaspoon vanilla essence
A pinch of ground star anise
A pinch of freshly grated nutmeg
Cooking spray

Directions:
Spray the baking pan with cooking spray. With an electric mixer or hand mixer, beat the butter and Swerve until creamy. One at a time, mix in the eggs and whisk until fluffy. Add the remaining ingredients and stir to combine. Transfer the batter to the prepared baking pan. Slide the baking pan into Rack Position 1, select Convection Bake, set temperature to 320ºF (160ºC), and set time to 30 minutes. When cooking is complete, the center of the cake should be springy. Allow the cake to cool in the pan for 10 minutes before removing and serving.

800.	Banana Pudding

Ingredients:
3 tbsp. unsalted butter
3 tbsp. chopped mixed nuts
1 cup banana juice
2 cups milk
2 tbsp. custard powder
3 tbsp. powdered sugar

Directions:
Boil the milk and the sugar in a pan and add the custard powder followed by the banana juice and stir till you get a thick mixture. Preheat the fryer to 300 Fahrenheit for five minutes. Place the dish in the basket and reduce the temperature to 250 Fahrenheit. Cook for ten minutes and set aside to cool. Garnish with nuts.

CPSIA information can be obtained
at www.ICGtesting.com
Printed in the USA
LVHW021529050121
675633LV00014B/390

9 781801 242592